WHAT A BODY CAN DO

In *What a Body Can Do*, Ben Spatz develops, for the first time, a rigorous theory of embodied technique as knowledge. He argues that understanding technique as both training and research has much to offer current discussions around the role of practice in the university, including the debates around "practice as research."

Drawing on critical perspectives from the sociology of knowledge, phenomenology, dance studies, enactive cognition, and other areas, Spatz argues that technique is a major area of historical and ongoing research in physical culture, performing arts, and everyday life.

Ben Spatz is Lecturer in Drama, Theatre and Performance at the University of Huddersfield. He holds a PhD in Theatre from The Graduate Center, CUNY, and has been a member of the Performance as Research working groups of both IFTR and ASTR. Ben is founder and artistic director of Urban Research Theater since 2004.

Praise for *What a Body Can Do*:

What is taking place when bodies make their way in the world? In this book, Ben Spatz answers this question by providing an atlas of bodily techniques which generates new and vibrant epistemic impulses each chiming with the other. The result is both intense and intensely satisfying.

Nigel Thrift, Vice-Chancellor
University of Warwick

This book is an important contribution to the interdisciplinary field of body studies. It is both deeply personal in its commitments, and deeply academic in its scope and quality. Chasing the performance of philosophy and the materiality of epistemology through its various limbs and organs, Spatz's provocations continue to demonstrate that the body is "good to think with" as a means for the discovery of new practices.

Dr Chris Shilling, Professor of Sociology, Director
of Postgraduate Studies (Research)
University of Kent

In many cultures, especially in the Western world, body and mind are characteristically held separate as ways of understanding the world. Here, Ben Spatz combats this way of thinking, seeking to show that "embodied practice is epistemic". Carefully weaving among the thickets, Spatz embraces concepts as wide as research, embodiment, performance, language, agency, the public sphere, gender, identity and everyday life ... This is a brave story, adroitly told and offers a most valuable addition to the field.

Ronald Barnett, Emeritus Professor of Higher Education
Institute of Education, London

A significant and innovative contribution.

Rick Kemp, Head of Acting and Directing
Indiana University of Pennsylvania

The breadth of Spatz's reading and application is impressive. *What a Body Can Do* is a useful contribution to the field.

Rhonda Blair, Professor Meadows School of the Arts, SMU

WHAT A BODY CAN DO

Technique as Knowledge, Practice as Research

UniversityCampus Oldham

A partnership between
the University of Huddersfield & Oldham College

Library & Computing Centre: 0161 344 8888
UCO Main Reception: 0161 344 8800
Cromwell Street, Oldham, OL1 1BB

Text renewals: text `renew' and your UCO ID number to 07950 081389.

This book is to be returned by the date on the self-service receipt.
Your library account can be accessed online at:
http://www.uco.oldham.ac.uk/library/catalogue.aspx
Follow UCO Library on Twitter: www.twitter.com/ucolcc

First published 2015
by Routledge
2 Park Square, Milton Park, Abingdon, Oxon OX14 4RN

and by Routledge
711 Third Avenue, New York, NY 10017

Routledge is an imprint of the Taylor & Francis Group, an informa business

© 2015 Ben Spatz

The right of Ben Spatz to be identified as author of this work has
been asserted by him in accordance with sections 77 and 78 of the Copyright,
Designs and Patents Act 1988.

British Library Cataloguing in Publication Data
A catalogue record for this book is available from the British Library

Library of Congress Cataloging in Publication Data
Spatz, Ben.
What a body can do : technique as knowledge, practice as research /
by Ben Spatz.
pages cm
Includes bibliographical references and index.
1. Performing arts Technique. 2. Movement (Acting) I. Title.
PN1590.T43S63 2015
792.028--dc23
2014035938

ISBN: 978-1-138-85409-3 (hbk)
ISBN: 978-1-138-85410-9 (pbk)
ISBN: 978-1-315-72234-4 (ebk)

Typeset in Sabon
by Taylor & Francis Books

FOR CALEB REZA

CONTENTS

FOREWORD

To Benjamin Spatz, as to others who have worked carefully and thoughtfully in the studio as well as the study, live performance is not an ephemeral art. In *What a Body Can Do: Technique as Knowledge, Practice as Research*, he points out a fundamental truth: that the highly evolved practices of physical culture (as in sport or martial arts) and performing arts (as in theater or music-voice) "are products of sustained research in embodied technique." Embodied techniques live on in the communicable practices of master teachers and their students, who transmit them not only across town, like viruses, but across time, like genes. Spatz's objective is to understand those transmittable (and hence researchable) techniques in the broad spectrum of "social epistemologies." He does so with full awareness of how powerfully embodied techniques in the arts may reflect and influence the practices of everyday life in gender roles and other roles. Appositely, he begins his book with Spinoza's very practical philosophical question: "What can a body do?" Through five chapters, he suggests many answers, of which my personal favorite remains, "A body can mind."

Ben Spatz isn't working unopposed. As the most chicken-brained idea of Western metaphysics, "the separation of mind and body" still rules the roost. Mind–body dualism underlies the distinction between mental and manual labor, for instance, which grounds the current world order of economic injustice in gross income inequality. Less egregiously but still exasperatingly, mind–body dualism also still constrains meaningful conversations across the hall between studio and study, even in institutions that should have left it behind long ago. Acting students are still told—I have heard it recently from teachers who ought to know better and almost certainly do—that actors need first of all "to get out of their heads," as if decapitation is a viable option as prerequisite to a course of study. Dance teachers are still told—I have heard it recently from administrators who don't know any better and probably never will—that students can't possibly be learning anything academically rigorous if they're on their feet and moving.

To cut through this philosophical and pragmatic Gordian knot, a new pedagogy needs a sharper knife. To sever ties to a false instrumentalist valuation of the arts, teachers and students alike deserve more muscular theory and more thoughtful practice. *What a Body Can Do* whets one version of this useful blade. Generationally inflected by the work of Jerzy Grotowski and his legatees, Spatz well knows that "technique" is not merely technical. Healthily skeptical of the British Practice as Research (PaR) movement, he also well knows that practice without documentable outcomes cannot be valued as research. Disposed to storytelling as well as principled abstraction (like all good acting teachers), he well knows that generality and specificity are partners. As a sometimes close reader of the historical literature on the actor's art, he also knows that acting has always had the potential to be understood as a science. If this has a familiar ring, that is because to write a proper Foreword one needs to look backwards. Thirty-five years ago, having earned tenure as an acting teacher and director before giving my first paper at an academic conference, I was thinking similar but (mostly) unwritten thoughts. Ben Spatz's book now embodies some of the most important of them and others besides, and perhaps now their time has come.

Joseph Roach
Sterling Professor of Theater
Yale University

ACKNOWLEDGEMENTS

The area of contemporary thought in which this book intervenes is very lively at the moment. If I were writing it now I would certainly engage with recent works like Michael Schwab's *Experimental Systems: Future Knowledge in Artistic Research* (2013); John Matthews's *Anatomy of Training* (2014); Philip A. Mellor and Chris Shilling's *Sociology of the Sacred: Religion, Embodiment and Social Change* (2014); and Robin Bauer's *Queer BDSM Intimacies: Critical Consent and Pushing Boundaries* (2014). I will be grateful if this book is received as a contribution alongside such gifts as these. Thanks to the editors of the *Journal of Dramatic Theory and Criticism* for permission to include material on Stanislavski's method of physical actions (Chapter 3), a version of which first appeared in that journal. Thanks as well to the Schatz Ornstein Studio (<www.howardschatz.com>), which has provided the cover image for this book: not a line drawing in fact but a black-and-white photograph of a body with paint poured over it. In those lines of dripping paint, I see a metaphorical depiction of the fractally branching pathways that I argue characterize the epistemic territory of embodied technique.

This book is the result of countless conversations, debates, and discussions, as well as untold hours of embodied practice, performance, and training. While I cannot thank everyone whose voices influenced its development, I would like to mention some of those whose impact was most significant. These are first of all the individuals with whom I wrestled intellectually in the development of these ideas, beginning with Maurya Wickstrom, whose guidance, care, and critique substantially defined my experience of doctoral education at the Graduate Center of the City University of New York, where this project was initiated. Likewise Professors Judith Milhous, Jean Graham-Jones, David Savran, James Wilson, Deborah Kapchan, and others influenced my formation as a scholar. I am grateful to Paul Allain, Bruce Barton, Sally Ann Ness,

Vincent Crapanzano, and others who read my essays and articles and took the time to give me productive and challenging feedback. Especially valuable have been my extended conversations with Daniel Mroz, Joy Brooke Fairfield, and Stefanie Jones. At the same time, I hope it will be clear that my critical engagement, herein, with recent works by Phillip Zarrilli, Robin Nelson, and Kris Salata, indicates the high degree of respect and admiration I hold for each of them. Of course, all mistakes are my own.

I want to thank very deeply those who have journeyed with me along a path of artistic discovery and embodied research: especially Massimiliano Balduzzi and Michele Farbman, as well as Beata Zalewska, Iza Młynarz, Małgosia Szkandera, and Margot Bassett. I thank the participants of two "What a Body Can Do" events: at the 19th Performance Studies International conference (Stanford University, 2013) and in Maurya Wickstrom's New Performance class (College of Staten Island, 2013); the students at Long Island University who dared to enroll in a new course, Training the Body: Perspectives in Movement, which I saw as a first step towards shaping a possible new field; and Laura Tesman, for giving me extraordinary teaching opportunities at Brooklyn College. I am grateful to Movement Research, Ximena Garnica and Shige Moriya of Leimay/Cave, and Peter Sciscioli for supporting my artistic work in New York City over the past decade. I also owe a profound debt of gratitude to the many teachers and artists in both dance and theatre whose work has profoundly affected my practice and my life. During two years in Poland (2003–2005), I was transformed by my encounters with Włodzimierz Staniewski and the actors of the Gardzienice Theatre Association, with Rena Mirecka, and with the Workcenter of Jerzy Grotowski and Thomas Richards, as well as others who passed through the Grotowski Institute in Wrocław. Many thanks to Grzegorz Ziołkowski and Jarosław Fret for hosting me there. Although I never met him, I must thank Jerzy Grotowski for affecting so many lives that have so deeply affected mine. I want also to mention Pedro Alejandro, Cheryl Cutler, and Hope Weissman, my undergraduate mentors at Wesleyan University; and Gerry Speca, whose theatre classes at the Cambridge Rindge and Latin School gave me my first taste of physically dynamic, formally experimental, ensemble-based theatre.

My current teaching, practice, and research is supported by the University of Huddersfield and by my extraordinary colleagues, especially the Centre for Psychophysical Performance Research led by Franc Chamberlain and Deb Middleton. The development of this book was made possible by the editorial guidance of Talia Rogers, Harriet Affleck, and Ben Piggott. Thanks to James Thomas and Jennifer Parkin for proofreading. I am grateful to Joe Roach for agreeing to write the Foreword even after reading my critique of the final pages of *The Player's Passion,* a book that has long inspired me with its mixture of historical rigor and critical verve. My deepest thanks go to my parents, Morris Rabinowitz and Elaine Spatz-Rabinowitz, and to my sister, Rebecca Rabinowitz. Their love and wisdom formed me as a person and continue to shape me today. Ben Blum-Smith I count as a brother in all but blood, with whom I talked for years about these questions before I knew their names. Finally I thank Michelle Mina Goldsmith for being my partner in life throughout these varied years. We have long been each other's keepers and now together are responsible for the formation of a new being, Caleb Reza Goldsmith-Spatz, to whom this book is dedicated.

Ben Spatz
Lecturer in Drama, Theatre and Performance
University of Huddersfield

[A] mode is said to have affections by virtue of a certain capacity of being affected. A horse, a fish, a man, or even two men compared one with the other, do not have the same capacity to be affected: they are not affected by the same things, or not affected by the same things in the same way. A mode ceases to exist when it can no longer maintain between its parts the relation that characterizes it; and it ceases to exist when "it is rendered completely incapable of being affected in many ways." In short, relations are inseparable from the capacity to be affected. So that Spinoza can consider two fundamental questions as equivalent: *What is the structure* (fabrica) *of a body?* And: **What can a body do?** A body's structure is the composition of its relation. What a body can do corresponds to the nature and limits of its capacity to be affected.

(Deleuze 1990: 217–18)

Everything that can be said about spiritual things can be translated into the language of master techniques.

(Grotowski 1990)[1]

INTRODUCTION
What Can a Body Do?

A body can ...

"What can a body do?"

Gilles Deleuze borrows this question from seventeenth-century philosopher Baruch Spinoza. Yet equating the structure of a body with its capacities aptly crystallizes a series of much more recent movements in philosophy: from rational thought to unconscious intersubjectivity, from systemic coherence to irreducible difference, and from the abstraction of mind to the materiality of bodies. How then is this question to be answered? With what kinds of bodies, and what kinds of doings, should we be concerned? In this book, I take the Deleuzo-Spinozan question as the starting point for a theory of embodied knowledge, or what I call an *epistemology of practice*. In developing this theory, I wrestle with divergent ideas about knowledge, practice, and embodiment, examining them in relation to each other and applying them to a series of historical and contemporary case studies. My examples are drawn from three major areas: physical culture, performing arts, and everyday life. Together these are part of a larger domain, *embodied practice*. I argue that embodied practice is structured by knowledge in the form of technique, which is made up of countless specific answers to the question: *What can a body do?* The technique of dance, acting, martial arts, yoga, and even everyday life will here be understood as a contiguous field of substantive answers to this question. The central argument of this book can be summarized as follows: *Technique is knowledge that structures practice.*

By surveying technique across the domains of physical culture, performing arts, and everyday life—linking theatre, dance, and performance studies to other strands of social and cultural thought—I attempt to develop an epistemologically rigorous concept of technique as

1

knowledge. This concept, I argue, allows us to conceive of the field of embodied practice as fundamentally epistemic—structured by knowledge—which in turn leads to new and provocative ideas about the relationship between specialized and everyday practices. What are the real possibilities of bodies, alone and together, in motion and in stillness, immediately and in the long term? What are the limits of embodiment in practice? If embodied knowledge is both substantive and diverse, then what kind of research produces it, and how does it move from one body or cultural context to another? On what common grounds can physical disciplines like martial arts or postural yoga, performing arts like dance and theatre, and embodied identities such as those of gender, race, and class be said to intersect? From what epistemological perspective could such practices be viewed as contiguous and hence mutually transformative in ways that go beyond mediation, representation, and conscious thought? To answer these questions, I draw on theories of embodiment and epistemology from theatre, dance, and performance studies, as well as from cultural studies, religious studies, anthropology, sociology, and philosophy. Although theatre and performance studies is my home discipline, I understand this project as part of a growing, interdisciplinary interest in embodied practice—part of what has been called the "practice turn" in theory and philosophy (Schatzki *et al.* 2001).

Philosophical answers to the Deleuzo-Spinozan question come from many sources. However, the question of what bodies can do is not one that can be answered through discursive means alone. Rather, as Deleuze asserts, we must "concretely try to become active" (1990: 226). To concretize my desire for a more substantive vision of embodied practice—as distinct but related to theatre and performance—in the past year I organized two small events under the title "What a Body Can Do." Both events took place under the auspices of theatre and performance: one at the 19th Performance Studies International conference held at Stanford University (Mahmoud 2014), and another as a guest workshop for an undergraduate course on New Performance at the College of Staten Island in New York City. Before each event, I issued a call for embodied presentations from the participants. Instead of short performances, I requested "demonstrations" or "enactments" that responded to the question: *What can a body do?* Each contributor had to provide a title, in the form: "A body can _____." The contributions presented ranged across many axes: from skilled to unskilled, verbal to athletic, technological to naked, abstract to specific, solitary to interactive, and more. The titles, which can scarcely do justice to the enactments they name, included the following:

2

A body can do the Charleston

A body can undo

A body can bend your perspective

A body can resonate

A body can mind

A body can invite you to listen

A body can respond to questions

A body can manipulate sound

A body can become perfect through imperfection

A body can imagine itself a rock

A body can time travel

A body can pulse

A body can interpret

A body can warm up

A body can stagnate

A body can conform

A body can tell a story

A body can be labeled

A body can think

A body can expand

A body can alliterate

A body can overcome

A body can jump a hundred times

A body can sing an old Jewish folk song

My background includes substantial physical and vocal training as a theatre artist. However, at each "What a Body Can Do" event, I tried to create a space in which people could come together and share embodied practices without any pressure to perform in a virtuosic way. I wanted to create the opposite of a talent show, the opposite of popular television programs like *American Idol* and *So You Think You Can Dance*. Such shows draw attention to the embodied technique of song and dance, but they do so under the assumption that *we already know what bodies can do*. The question posed by such shows is: *Who can do it best?* The competitive format demands that all performances be ranked as winners and losers, best and worst and runners-up. This approach puts individual ability at the center, rather than transmissible knowledge. In contrast, I want to advocate the fostering and support of "research culture" in diverse areas of physical culture, performing arts, and everyday life. The notion of research, further elaborated below, demands that the question remain open: *We do not yet know what a body can do*. From this perspective, individual ability is less important than the continuous creation and transmission of knowledge. Hence, this book contains numerous examples of what I will call *research in embodied technique*. As I will show, such research is distinct from but analogous to scholarly research, which may analyze or study embodied technique to better understand it. The kind of research on which I focus here aims to generate not new facts or information, but rather *new technique*.

Melissa Gregg and Gregory J. Seigworth have recently noted that Spinoza's fundamental assertion—"No one has yet determined what the body can do"—is "still very much with us more than 330 years after Spinoza composed his *Ethics*" (2010: 3). Indeed, they affirm, "No one will ever finally exclaim: 'So, there it is: now, we know all that a body can do! Let's call it a day.'" Brian Massumi concurs: "The short answer to the question 'Do you know what a body can do?' is simply: 'No!'" (in Böhler *et al.* 2014: 23). Much as I agree with this sentiment, I do not find the question of bodies and doings to be adequately answered—or even adequately posed—by the critical affect theory that Gregg, Seigworth, and Massumi champion. There is a lack of concreteness in the concept of affect that fails to recognize the detailed and effortful labor of those who search in tangible ways for answers to the question: *What can a body do?* On the other hand, the "cognitive turn" in theatre studies— discussed further below—goes too far in the other direction, assuming that science holds the key to understanding what bodies can do. Moreover, I fear that there are many who do think we have answered the question and who are ready to call it a day when it comes to embodied technique. Sociologists recognize "a widespread consensus today that contemporary Western societies are in one sense or another ruled by knowledge and expertise" (Cetina 1999: 5). But this knowledge and expertise is commonly assumed to be about the manufacture and usage of advanced technologies. There can be no doubt as to the urgency of technological questions, but what about knowledge of embodiment?

What about the possibilities afforded to us as bodily beings? It may seem as though, after hundreds of thousands of years of embodied existence, humans have thoroughly explored all the possibilities of embodiment—that we now know all there is to know about what bodies can do. This book argues the contrary, namely that embodied technique remains a vital area of ongoing exploration, in which the potential for valuable new discoveries has in no way been exhausted.

Five stories

In 2006, I came across a newspaper article about Will Lawton, a man who started training in martial arts when he was in his thirties and eventually opened his own training studio in Bronx, NY. According to this article, Lawton had been hanging around several martial arts studios for some time without taking his practice seriously. Then, one day,

> a friend took him to the concrete basement—a subterranean room on Morris Avenue where eight men were practicing jujitsu. "I saw these guys throwing each other and said, 'That's what I want, right there,'" he recalls. The next day he showed up with a uniform. That was 17 years ago.
>
> (Murphy 2006)

The story is striking because it tells of a room where something of great intensity and meaning is taking place: a practice, an exploration, a way of life. What was so special about this room? Why is it that Lawton had never taken the study of martial arts seriously until he came to that particular place? The image of "guys throwing each other" invokes athleticism, masculinity, and artistry—all topics of concern in the chapters that follow. But what stands out from this story is the sense of recognition and clarity Lawton experiences when he witnesses their practice. "That's what I want, right there," he says to himself, and begins a process of physical, mental, and vocational transformation that will extend for decades.

Lawton's story resonated with me in 2006 because I had recently spent time in a very different kind of "concrete basement." In 2003, I moved to Poland, where I lived for two years, working with a number of theatre artists influenced by sustained contact with Jerzy Grotowski. For eight months I was an apprentice performer with the Gardzienice theatre company, where I performed in touring versions of *Elektra* and *Metamorfozy* under the direction of Włodzimierz Staniewski. The following year, I had a Fulbright Fellowship at the Grotowski Institute in

Wrocław. Numerous experiences during those two years profoundly affected my understanding of art, knowledge, and practice, but one memory will do for now: It was late summer in Gardzienice and a group of young actors and apprentices had been rehearsing for several days in the lead-up to an important premiere. Finally, three of the older actors arrived to join us: Tomasz Rodowicz, Elżbieta Rojek, and Dorota Porowska. The force of their deeply embodied singing transformed the atmosphere in an instant, almost taking my breath away. Where did such power come from? At that moment, I felt like Lawton in the concrete basement: "That's what I want, right there." I felt the same thing a year later when I worked with Rena Mirecka, one of the founding members of Jerzy Grotowski's Theatre Laboratory, and again the next summer when I spent three weeks in Moscow with the Workcenter of Jerzy Grotowski and Thomas Richards from Pontedera, Italy. Although I did not continue to work directly with any of these practitioners, my encounters with them began a substantial journey in embodied technique, of which the present volume is one product.[2]

What knowledge is contained and transferred in the studios, rehearsal rooms, and concrete basements of embodied practice? In their introduction to *Martial Arts as Embodied Knowledge*, D. S. Farrer and John Whalen-Bridge remind us that the "arts" in question are not reducible to their martial application. "Supposedly people go to martial arts studios to fend off attackers in the street, but practitioners know that this is an inadequate explanation of the phenomena" (2011: 6). The point is easily transferable to the performing arts: *Supposedly people join theatre and dance companies to perform in front of paying audiences, but practitioners know that this is an inadequate explanation of the phenomena.* For me, as for Lawton, the desire to join a particular community of practice was at once more immediate and less spectacular than touring a show or becoming a professional actor. What is it that makes a person latch onto a certain kind of embodied technique and dive into it, devoting years or decades to a particular practice? Why are we drawn to develop certain embodied capacities—whether physical or vocal, therapeutic or presentational, affective or athletic—and not others? What kind of recognition takes place when a particular area of technique strikes us to the core?

Three more stories to go ...

While writing this book, I taught introductory acting to students at multiple schools in the City University of New York. These classes brought together individuals with diverse backgrounds and interests, many of whom had never studied or practiced theatre and were unlikely to do so in the future. I soon realized that it made no sense to think of such classes as leading towards possible acting careers. Instead, I began to ask myself how I would teach Acting 1 as a basic unit of general education, like English composition or algebra. The assumption is that introductory courses in writing and mathematics impart knowledge that will be useful to students in all careers and all walks of life. What if the same assumption were made about performance technique? Acting classes are often justified in terms of building confidence and creativity, or of helping students become more comfortable in their bodies. These are fine justifications, but I want to affirm that transformations like these take place through the *transmission of knowledge* in the form of technique. Students become confident, creative, and comfortable because they learn how to maintain eye contact and stillness; how to read the body language and rhythmic patterns of others; how to activate emotional and physiological energies in their own bodies; how to develop, practice, and repeat a score. Acting class is not something other than the transmission of knowledge. It is, or it can be, an introduction to embodied technique as an epistemic field.

With this in mind, I once proposed—during a graduate course on Global Political Theatre and Performance—that we consider the politics of embodied practice as distinct from those of representation and spectacle. I asked: What if some of the most effective political theatre unfolds, like yoga classes, away from the public eye? What if the politics of actor training are not limited to how we prepare young actors for the stage, but intersect directly with other kinds of embodied pedagogies by revealing and foreclosing possible avenues of everyday practice? Could this not suggest a very different understanding of how theatre embodies politics? A fellow student objected to my suggestion: "But no one would see it." *No one would see it.* As if seeing were the only way to be transformed by technique. As if the enactment of technique in one's own body could not be just as transformative as seeing it practiced by someone else—or even more so. As if politics were only a matter of representation. My peer's assumption reflects a bias in theatre and performance studies that privileges the phenomena of (public) spectatorship as a site for social intervention. But there are many dimensions of theatrical practice, from experimental actor training to applied theatre and drama therapy, that do not rely upon public spectacle to find their meaning. We cannot afford to assume that the politics of practice are the same as those of representation. Another language is needed.

Two more stories …

In his seventies, my father began taking lessons in *taijiquan*. He told me that sometimes, when he is waiting in New York City's Penn Station— that infamously stressful train station—he goes into a corner and makes some of the movements from his *taiji* class. "It's not really *taiji*," he said, "just some of the warm-ups." He is not trying to attract attention. There is no sense of display in his actions. They are for him. They work to separate him from the bother and bustle of the station, giving him mental clarity, focus, and relaxation. Another thing my father does is recite poetry in his mind. This is less visible, less physical, but still a kind of embodied technique. Both the *taiji* and the poetry have specific cultural and historical lineages. Having studied English poetry of the seventeenth century, my father knows many poems from that era by heart. The *taiji* is newer for him. I don't know the lineage of his teachers and, at such a basic level, it hardly matters. In fact, it does not matter whether what he is doing is "really" *taiji*. Nor does the cultural or representational value of these forms explain how they serve him in that moment, when he is waiting in the station for his track to be announced. In that context, technique functions not as cultural sign but as the structure of embodied repetition. It serves him and, in another sense, he serves it—the poetry no less than the *taiji*.

Finally …

A story from Jewish lore: A wise person instructed that the words of a song of praise should be "written on the heart." Someone asked: "Why is it written 'on' the heart and not 'in' the heart?" The wise person answered: We do not have the power to write it in our hearts. All we can do is to write it *on* our hearts, and then, after some time, it may sink in. Maybe, the tenth time we sing that song, it glows for us. But maybe, the eleventh time, that glow is gone. We cannot control what is inside the heart, only what we inscribe upon it. My sister told me this story. When she sings in temple, she says, sometimes it has a golden quality, sometimes not. But when the quality is there, she says, "It has something to do with the fact that I know I'll be there again the next week." Practice. Repetition. In the inscription written "on" the heart, I see Konstantin Stanislavski's caution to the actor, which Grotowski repeated: We cannot control our emotions. What we *do*—that we can control (Richards 1995: 103). But the inscription written on the heart is also Foucault's inscription: the body inscribed by instruments of power, referred to by Judith Butler as "a site where regimes of discourse and power inscribe themselves, a nodal point or nexus for relations of juridical and productive power" (Butler 1989: 601). How might we reconcile these different notions of bodily inscription? How can we understand the depths at which technique changes us through practice, over time and sometimes radically? What is the relationship between knowledge and power, in the practice of embodied technique? Do we sing the song, or does the song sing us?

These stories concern experiences of embodiment: my own as well as those of my friends and family, teachers and colleagues. However, I am not mainly interested here in "experience." Instead, what concerns me is transmissible knowledge. In these stories, people are learning *what bodies can do*: Lawton training *jujitsu* in his thirties; my encounter with embodied song in Gardzienice; my students learning basic acting at the City University of New York; my father starting *taiji* practice in his seventies; my sister singing Jewish songs at Hillel. *What can a body do?* It is a practical question, a question of doing. It provokes not one answer but hundreds, thousands, millions of answers—answers that take the form of technique.

From performance to practice

As these stories show, training in the craft of performance is at the heart of my project. But the questions at hand also extend beyond the performing arts, requiring us to map the much larger territory of embodied practice. As a result, the approach taken here is distinct from one that would examine "Theatre among the Other Arts," as in the title of a recent session of the Mellon School of Theater and Performance Research at Harvard University (2014). My topic instead is *acting among other embodied practices*. I am not concerned here with "art" in its contemporary sense, except in the specific chapter that addresses the performing arts. After all, as philosopher Jacques Rancière reminds us, "art in the singular has only existed for two centuries" (2004: 52). Here, I prefer to suspend that singular notion of "art" in favor of an older understanding of "arts" as fields of craft, technique, and knowledge. This theoretical move suggests a recontextualization of the performing arts alongside healing, martial, and ritual arts, all of which are defined by the embodied encounter of bodies rather than by the spectator's encounter with an art object that may or may not be "live."[3] By pulling theatre away from its common associations with film, literature, and painting, and examining it instead as a site for embodied practice, I hope to escape the apparent dependence of theatre upon an allegedly "public" sphere in which spectacles are presented to a general audience. The result is a book in which acting serves as a central example, but which is not ultimately about acting or theatre.

In this book, I critique two dominant trends in performance studies: one that romanticizes performance as exceptionally ephemeral and unavailable to discourse, verging on the magical; and another that sees everyday performances (or "performativity") as thoroughly socially constructed, thereby replacing freedom with habit and choice with the unconscious reproduction of social norms. The concept of technique, as I understand it, resolves this dilemma by conceiving of both specialized and everyday practices in terms of their knowledge content. Recent discussions of acting, like Phillip Zarrilli's *Psychophysical Acting* (2009) and John Lutterbie's *Toward a General Theory of Acting* (2011), draw upon a wide range of critical and philosophical theories, including many that I also consider here. I find much to praise in these, as well as in Simon Shepherd's reframing of theatre as "an art of bodily possibility" and "a place which exhibits what a human body is, what it does, what it is capable of" (2006: 10, 1). However, rather than proposing a theory of acting or of theatre, this book offers a theory of embodied practice within which acting might be recontextualized. In spirit, my project is closer to John Matthews's *Training for Performance: A Meta-disciplinary Account* (2011), which examines actor training alongside physical therapy and monastic discipline; Richard Sennett's history of artisan expertise in *The Craftsman* (2009); Carrie Noland's analysis of gesture in *Agency and Embodiment* (2009); and even Peter Sloterdijk's *You Must Change Your Life* (2013), which calls for a return to "the practicing life" in the context of a sweeping history of "anthropotechnics" from antiquity to the present. There is much overlap of concern in these works, although none proposes an epistemology of practice in the sense developed here.

Some months after returning from Poland, I found myself alone in the studio, called there by a need to encounter myself through what I would now call the embodied technique of *song-action*. In the studio, I learned the value of articulating my desires in technical terms: making that crucial translation from a deep and inchoate impulse to a task that could be directly attempted. Soon I felt called to answer the question, posed by myself and others: What is happening in this room? What is taking place? How is this similar or different to what has taken place in Gardzienice, or in Grotowski's Theatre Laboratory, or in Lawton's concrete basement, or in an urban yoga studio? Is this theatre or therapy, spirituality or research? In struggling to articulate my practice, a crucial point emerged for me when "technique" and the "technical" crossed over from my studio practice into my scholarly writing. At that point I began to think about acting and other practices in terms of the technique that structures them, and I have never stopped doing so. I hope my conclusion and central thesis—that embodied practice is structured by technique at every level—may suggest to the reader some new ways of thinking about structure and agency, discipline and creativity, vocation and identity.

Embodiment and sustainability

The practices that concern me here are *embodied*. But a clarification is in order: In this context, "embodiment" absolutely does not refer to a distinction between mind and body. As Chapter 1 of this book demonstrates, even scientists no longer believe that the mind can be separated from the body, while in the humanities and social sciences the mind/body dualism of Descartes has long been discredited. My assumption here is that mind and body are holistically intertwined—or rather, following current trends in cognitive studies, that mind is an emergent property of body, just as body is the material basis for mind. Thought and language are fully embodied processes. Therefore, when I refer to "embodiment" and "embodied practice" throughout this book, I mean to include all of the following: thought, mind, brain, intellect, rationality, speech, and language. While "body" or "bodily" could be taken to mean only that which is *physical*, such as movement and gesture, I use "embodied" to indicate a wider territory: everything that bodies can do. In addition to the physical, this space of possibility includes much that we might categorize as mental, emotional, spiritual, vocal, somatic, interpersonal, expressive, and more. The important distinction here is then not between mind and body, but rather between *embodiment*—inclusive of mind— and the world-changing, epoch-defining, but historically very recent advances in technology that characterize our present global situation.

In basing my argument on a distinction between *technique* and *technology*, I realize that I am swimming against the tide with respect to some current theoretical trends that understand bodies and technologies as so thoroughly enmeshed as to be inextricable or even indistinguishable. Elizabeth Grosz, for example, has written:

> Anything that comes into contact with the surface of the body and remains there long enough will be incorporated into the body image—clothing, jewelry, other bodies, objects ... External objects, implements, and instruments with which the subject continuously interacts become, while they are being used, intimate, vital, even libidinally cathected parts of the body image.
>
> (Grosz 1994: 80)

Grosz is not alone in suggesting that the human body is inextricably bound up with its tools and technologies. Today it seems obvious that, from genetic engineering to the ways in which our homes and vehicles shape our physical bodies, no clean or sharp line can be drawn between embodiment and technology. As Jennifer Parker-Starbuck observes in

Cyborg Theatre: "Our daily operations are surrounded by, immersed in, and/or intersect with technology" (2011: 4). How then can I hope, even theoretically, to set aside technology—from clothing and jewelry to more complex "objects, implements, and instruments"—in order to focus on embodied technique? Has not each of us long since become a cyborg, a "hybrid of machine and organism" (Haraway 2004: 7)? Are not recent critical turns—like those hinging on affect, practice, or "somatechnics" (Sullivan and Murray 2009)—intended precisely to highlight the inherent fusion of human and tool, society and machine?

There are at least two ways to develop a theoretical distinction between embodied technique and technology. The first is to see the prioritization of embodiment as part of the phenomenological attitude, or "reduction," defined as a set of "cognitive and pragmatic techniques" that work continually to return us to the primacy of lived experience as the basis of all knowledge and understanding (Depraz *et al.* 2003: 184). This attitude does not imply a final rejection of technology or scientific knowledge; it is rather a question of *where to begin*. In the words of Maurice Merleau-Ponty: "The world is not what I think, but what I live through. I am open to the world, I have no doubt that I am in communication with it, but I do not possess it; it is inexhaustible" (2002: xviii–xix). The phenomenological move distinguishes between the direct, embodied experience of life and the mentally constructed world in which we assume we live. To place embodiment before technology is then to remind ourselves that machines, no matter how powerful their effects, involve us only to the extent that they make contact with our experience through the necessary medium of embodiment. From the common chair to the most complex industrial machines, the meaning of any technology can be defined as its effect upon embodied technique. Perhaps more than any other philosophical tradition, phenomenology offers an approach to reality that begins from embodiment. For this reason, it has been taken up by many theorists of theatre, dance, and performance, as well as thinkers of everyday life.[4] In the present context, however, I also want to consider a more specifically contemporary and urgent rationale for distinguishing between technique and technology.

In the first part of the twenty-first century, exponential advances in technology, and the population increases they enable, pose specific dangers to the ecological balance that sustains our and other species on earth. In this sense, an engagement with embodied technique can be seen as an ecopolitical rather than purely philosophical move. As important as it is, Grosz's point about the incorporation of objects into the body "image" leaves out crucial material differences in the (re)production processes that give rise to bodies and technologies, allowing what is essentially the consumer's ignorance of production under capitalism to go unchallenged. For it is only by ignoring the temporal trajectories of bodies and objects, and their ecologies of production, that one can imagine a total loss of boundaries between the embodied and the technological. In fact, while there is ample precedent for the human species living in ecological balance with its natural environment, there is no such precedent for the sustainability of energy-intensive, high-tech, "developed" societies like those we see today. This does not mean that technology is bad or even suspect. It simply means that our "cyborg" nature does not (yet) entitle us to dissolve the conceptual differences between biology, ecology, and technology. Only from a position of historically unprecedented wealth and privilege—much of which may not be sustainable in the long run—can the integration of bodies and technologies appear as a foregone conclusion rather than a simultaneously exhilarating and terrifying proposition.

Today, more than ever, the distinction between what bodies can *do* and what bodies can *make* or *build* demands close and urgent attention. No essentialism or primitivism is therefore needed in order to place special value on embodiment and embodied practice—only a historical sense of just how recent our technologies are in comparison with the ecology of bodies. We do not need to "return" to the body so much as to locate it, to sort it apart from its recent material products, and to maintain a critical awareness of where our objects come from. I would very much support an investigation of technology that addressed its continual impact on human and other life forms, starting with the embodied labor that produces it. Such an analysis would avoid the fetishization of technology that allows us to ignore the role of embodied technique in the production process, or which renders technology transparent by romanticizing its interaction with bodies in technologically advanced societies (see Note 4 above). If anything, the increasing technologization of the world calls for a renewed focus on embodied technique. Far from being unrelated to technology, specialized embodied practices like martial arts, dance, sport, and live performance play an increasingly important role in technological societies and may perhaps be understood as part of a general reaction to the increasing presence of advanced technologies in every aspect of life. Such practices may be seen as calling for a less technological world, but perhaps what they really call for is a more sustainable world in which technology figures differently.

It would of course be naïve simply to equate embodied practices with sustainable ones. As Allison Hui points out, an apparently sustainable and ecologically "green" practice like Ashtanga yoga—discussed at length in Chapter 2 of this book—can be negatively offset by carbon-intensive practices, like international air travel, to which it may be linked. In this respect, the "mass migration of yoga students contrasts sharply with the low levels of travel and resource consumption that are needed for everyday yoga practice" (in Shove and Spurling 2013: 182). While the practice of yoga may itself be low-tech and virtually carbon-neutral, it becomes carbon-intensive and drastically unsustainable when combined with regular trips to the global centers of yoga training. Karl Georg Høyer makes a similar point about the unintentional ironies of what he calls the "travelling circus of climate change," in which well-intentioned academics generate much higher than average levels of energy consumption and carbon emissions as they jet from country to country to attend conferences dedicated to slowing climate change (in Bhaskar et al. 2010: 227). We cannot therefore look to embodied practice—whether physical or discursive—to save us in any simple way from the social and material crisis of climate change. On the other hand, it seems reasonable to investigate possible alliances between embodied and sustainable practice, insofar as the former re-centers effort around the capacities of bodies and in this sense may be fundamentally aligned and allied with the goal of sustainability.

Placing embodied technique in this context gives new meaning to what Peter Brook called "the empty space" (1968) of theatrical play. It has been noted in response that there is no such thing as an empty space. An empty room still has a floor. A naked actor still has to eat. Moreover, as Ngũgĩ wa Thiong'o observes, "the performance space is never empty ... It is always the site of physical, social, and psychic forces in society" (1997: 13). Yet for those of us engaged in practices that foreground the possibilities of embodiment—whether in the performing arts or in other contexts—the contemporary turn to embodiment remains ethically and politically salient. This is at least in part because the empty spaces of theatre, dance, yoga, and martial arts studios across the globe are not neutral with respect to sociopolitical concerns, nor are they generically "empty." Rather, these spaces have been actively *emptied*. The numerous and varied items—books, furniture, computers, etc.—that fill so many of our rooms today have been conscientiously removed. Such intentionally "emptied spaces" are zones in which technology has been cleared away, in order to bring forth and make space for embodied technique.

Methodology and chapters

This book is intended as a work of performance philosophy and the philosophy of practice.[5] Its methodology is perhaps closest to Deleuze and Guattari's understanding of philosophy as "the creation of concepts." According to Massumi, Deleuze's

> image for a concept is not a brick, but a "tool box." He calls his kind of philosophy "pragmatics" because its goal is the invention of concepts that do not add up to a system of belief or an architecture of propositions that you either enter or you don't, but instead pack a potential in the way a crowbar in a willing hand envelops an energy of prying … The question is not: is it true? But: does it work?
>
> (Deleuze and Guattari 1987: xv)

With this in mind, I have tried to develop concepts with which something productive can be done. Ideally, the reader will come away with a sense of new projects in the offing, or new ways to articulate current projects that may result in a shift of direction or emphasis. Above all, I hope that the ideas contained here will be of use to those who wish to articulate the complexity and importance of embodied knowledge and practice in the world today.

As with any project, there are doubtless gaps and failures. One notable absence is the lack of an explicit discussion of spirituality. I don't think I have left questions of spirit out of this book, although I do not address them directly. I intend for the reader to be able to engage with my arguments without making assumptions about the relevance of spirituality to the practices discussed. Peter Sloterdijk has recently declared that "religion does not exist"; there are only "variously misinterpreted anthropotechnic practice systems" (2013: 84). We do not have to follow Sloterdijk that far in order to recognize the importance of embodied technique in all religions and spiritualities, to the extent that these are defined not only by orthodoxy—right belief—but also by "orthopraxy"—right action (Bell 2009: 191). In a sense, this book can be read as an attempt to explicate the spiritual in technical terms, or at least to provide some foundations for such a project. In this I follow Grotowski, who provides one of the introduction's epigraphs: *Everything that can be said about spiritual things can be translated into the language of master techniques* (Grotowski 1990). As Jean Graham-Jones pointed out to me, Grotowski does not suggest that spirituality itself is synonymous with technique. Rather, it is the desire to render spirituality in words that brings us to the language of technique. Steeped in a lifetime of embodied research (see Chapter 3), Grotowski's assertion may be an appropriate counterpoint to Deleuze's philosophic inquiry. Each chapter that follows is likewise preceded by one or two epigraphs highlighting a key point or central tension in what follows.

Another possible complaint regards the density of scholarly references and language, which may be off-putting to some readers—particularly those whose expertise lies in embodied technique rather than scholarly discourse. I have tried to state my arguments clearly, and to keep tangential comments within footnotes, but in a book intended to influence scholarly thought and practice, a certain degree of terminological intricacy or even difficulty is necessary. While I have kept a general reader in mind at all times, I have also wanted to be thorough in laying out a robust theoretical framework that I hope will prove firm enough to support future work—both my own and that of others. It may be worth noting that, as abstract as my argument may sometimes appear, I wrote each of these chapters for myself and for my colleagues and fellow practitioners, to solve concrete practical questions and to provide a stronger theoretical basis for articulating and framing embodied practice. Each substantive chapter in this book has at its root a very personal goal: to pinpoint a powerful contemporary tension between athletics and somatics (Chapter 2); to reframe the legacies of Stanislavski and Grotowski so that practitioners of my generation can locate ourselves in relation to them (Chapter 3); to better understand the everyday practice of gender as it functions in my life and that of my newborn child, who arrived during the writing of this book (Chapter 4); and finally to make a case for the importance and validity of embodied knowledge and research in academia (Chapter 5). A brief outline of these chapters is all that remains by way of introduction.

Chapter 1 lays out a theoretical framework based on the relationship between technique and practice. Following a brief introduction to social epistemology, the chapter undertakes a selective genealogy of the concept of technique, from Aristotle's *techne* through the writings of Marcel Mauss and Michel Foucault and into the more recent work of sociologist Nick Crossley and dance theorist Randy Martin. Technique, I argue, differs from related concepts like performativity and habitus in that it emphasizes the *epistemic* dimension of practice. Embodied technique then refers to transmissible and repeatable knowledge of relatively reliable possibilities afforded by human embodiment. Unlike those other terms, technique emphasizes conscious as well as unconscious repetition and provides a model for how these relate to each other through the sedimentation and circulation of agency. Chapter 1 concludes with a discussion of how new embodied technique is generated through a process of iterative discovery that warrants the name "research." Drawing on the sociology of knowledge, I consider the epistemic nature of such research, asking what it might look like and how we should expect to recognize it. The epistemology of practice proposed in this chapter is the basis for everything that follows. However, some readers may find the discussion here particularly dense or abstract. The reader with more "practical" interests is invited to skip ahead to later chapters, referring back to Chapter 1 as needed, in order to clarify the intended meaning of key terms—especially *technique, practice, knowledge*, and *research*.

Chapter 2 analyzes the development and subsequent global spread of postural yoga during the twentieth century, treating this as a particularly clear example of both the invention and the dissemination of embodied technique. In addition to its evident commercial success, postural yoga is a tidy example with which to begin because of its (relatively recent) emphasis on the possibilities of the physical body. I examine the genesis of modern postural yoga in Mysore, India, during the first part of the twentieth century, and look at how successive generations of the students of Tirumalai Krishnamacharya continually adapted the practice of yoga as they transmitted it across time and space. After showing how the global spread and growth of postural yoga may be illuminated by an epistemological understanding of technique, my discussion expands to address the larger territory of physical culture, including a diversity of practices ranging across a spectrum from the athletic to the somatic. I argue that yoga has achieved its present success in part due to its achievement of a particularly gendered balance between the poles of athletics and somatics. The example of yoga further shows how research in embodied technique can play an important role in the politics of nationality and gender. Chapter 2 concludes with some speculative reflections on physical education, including how this official curriculum of embodied technique could be transformed by the recognition that physical culture is as much a field of ongoing research as an existing discipline for training.

Chapter 3 considers another area of specialized technique, that of actor training. As in the previous chapter, I trace the development, spread, and transformation of technique from one time and place to another. Unlike modern postural yoga, the technique developed by Konstantin Stanislavski (1863–1938) and Jerzy Grotowski (1933–99) is not primarily physical. It can therefore help expand our definition of embodied technique to include other areas, such as those linked to vocalization, memory, and imagination. I argue that the concept of "actor training," which has been crucial in highlighting certain embodied practices that are not directly related to public spectacle, is limiting insofar as it fails to account for the significance of research as a necessary counterbalance to training in this field. After showing how an epistemological shift towards the mutual constitution of training and research can shed light on the legacies of both Stanislavski and Grotowski, I go on to ask what it could mean to develop a more explicit "research culture" in acting today. I end with a brief survey of some of the most important and engaging problems for current research in acting as a field of embodied technique, including the intersections of that field with physical culture, as discussed in Chapter 2, and cultural identity, as discussed in Chapter 4.

Chapters 2 and 3 focus on rereading canonical examples through the lens of technique. Rather than introduce the reader to new case studies, I have sought to test my theory of embodied knowledge against the most well-established and recognizable practices—the logic being that, if the theory works in these contexts, it can then be applied to any number of lesser known examples. As a result, I am sorely aware that these chapters propagate a historical bias towards individual men as creators and pioneers. Although I mention numerous women through-out, my three central examples are male: Krishnamacharya, Stanislavski, and Grotowski. I hope this will be understood as a strategic use of the canon aimed at opening up new lines for future research.[6] In fact, I have in general tried to err somewhat towards the conservative in methodology and style—especially in the first three chapters—in order to make my central thesis compelling to the widest possible range of readers. These chapters operate within a narrower frame in order to develop a durable theory of embodied knowledge that can then be applied more broadly. While Chapters 2 and 3 examine canonical examples of physical culture and actor training, developed by well-known (male) practitioners, Chapter 4 moves into quite different territory by applying the same epistemology to the practice of gender in everyday life.

Chapter 4 begins with a proposal for "research in everyday life," which I offer as an alternative to the Situationist call for an immediate and total "revolution of everyday life" (Vaneigem 2001 [1967]). Every-day practice is by definition not bound to a particular timeframe or location, such as the rehearsal period or theatre studio. Moreover, such research is explicitly engaged not just with what individual bodies can do, but with what bodies can do in aggregate, as communities and populations. The specific example addressed in this chapter is that of gender, understood as an area of embodied practice and technique. In the wake of Judith Butler's *Gender Trouble* (1990) and *Bodies That Matter* (1993a), theorists of gender and sexuality—especially those representing feminist, queer, and transgender perspectives—have come to see gender as substantially constructed by what Butler has called the "stylized repetition of acts" (1988: 519). According to this analysis, a person's gender is a practice as much as an identity. It should therefore be possible to analyze gender, I argue, as an area of embodied technique. Among other implications, this suggests that the current proliferation of gender(s) may be as much a result of embodied research as are the examples studied in the previous two chapters. By analogy with research in physical culture and performing arts, it becomes possible to see gender technique as an epistemic field, constituted by the mutually sustaining interaction of training and research. This chapter again concludes with a survey of current research, rereading alternative gender and sexuality practices as fundamentally epistemic projects.

Although its subject matter may be unexpected as the third term in a series that begins with postural yoga and acting technique, Chapter 4 follows the same two-phase process as the previous two: first, I show how gender practice and identity are structured by knowledge in the form of technique; then, I offer examples of current and ongoing research in the technique of gender, research that leads not to facts or theories but to the development of new gender technique. In this sense, Chapter 4 simply continues the arguments launched in Chapters 2 and 3, which discuss the development of new technique in physical culture and performing arts respectively. One significant difference is that Chapter 4 brings into sharper focus the issue of physiological differences between bodies. While such differences are already part of my discussions of yoga and acting, they are more urgent and more complex in the context of everyday embodied identities. I argue in Chapter 4 that the bodily variations we have come to call "sexual difference" are best understood as the material substrate of the embodied technique of gender. This means that the categorization of bodies into (two) sexes is as much a result of embodied research as of either nature or choice.

My intervention in current debates over gender is undertaken within the frame of my larger project to analyze the epistemological basis of embodied practice. In extending my argument to the practice of gender, I am trying to reconcile the insights and contributions of gender theory with those made by practitioners of physical culture and performing arts. The difficulties of doing so are immediately evident if we contrast, for example, the emphasis of contemporary actor training on "staying in the here and now" (Zarrilli 2009: 31) with José Esteban Muñoz's explicit rejection of the present in favor of a "then and there" of queer futurity (2009: 1); or if we observe that Virginie Magnat, who writes about women who are master teachers and elders from a perspective that values feminist and Indigenous insights, nevertheless confesses that it "seems impossible" to "argue against biological determinism while simultaneously being engaged in forms of practice-based research that foreground embodied experience" (2014: 31). At present, the languages and conceptual frameworks of physical culture and performing arts are very different from those of gender theory, even though both are centrally concerned with embodiment and practice. My stance with regard to gender politics is intended to be radically inclusive, deconstructing binary gender and taking queer and transgender experience as the basis for understanding how all gender functions, including the most apparently normative. However, this is a delicate matter, as the constituencies involved have sometimes radically different ideas about "what bodies can do." I ask the reader to read carefully, and to receive my discussion of gender in the context of the foregoing discussion of embodied technique. At the same time, I hope that the explicitly political engagements of Chapter 4 will help to reveal how the practices discussed in Chapters 2 and 3 might also turn out to be political in previously untheorized ways.

After this expansive trajectory, from physical culture through performing arts to the practice of gender in everyday life, Chapter 5 condenses back down to a consideration of the role of embodied practice and research within the specific context of the university. Here I ask how an epistemology of practice might fit into current debates over the role of academia in contemporary society and the relationship between academia, the state, and capitalist economies. I argue for the inclusion of embodied research within academia and point to some of the benefits this could have, both for the academy itself and for society at large. I also offer a critique of the concept of "Practice as Research" (PaR), an emerging trend in which artistic, creative, and embodied practices are framed as academic research. While I am sympathetic to the goals of PaR, I am also wary of some of the ways it has been theorized thus far, and of its general lack of disciplinary and methodological rigor. Having made what I hope is a convincing case for embodied technique as a field of ongoing research, I argue here for a more fully historicized and rigorously theorized engagement between academia and embodied practice. The ideas in this chapter have developed over the course of five years of engagement with the Performance as Research Working Groups of the American Society for Theatre Research (2009–13) and the International Federation for Theatre Research (2013–present). I hope they will have relevance for anyone interested in the role of embodied, creative, or artistic practice in the university. Taking courage from Ronald Barnett's invitation to boldly imagine a range of possible futures for the university (2012), I ask how and to what extent the established purposes and principles of academia might lead it to support research projects in the areas and fields I have defined as embodied technique. I conclude with concrete proposals for the design of such projects, and with a call to expand rather than contract the fundamentally epistemic mission and vision of academia as a social institution.

Notes

1 In Polish: "Wszystko to co o duchowych rzeczach da sie powiedzieć da się przetłumaczyć na język techniki mastierstwa." This text was provided to me by Kris Salata, who translates it in his doctoral dissertation (2007: 30). The translation used in the epigraph is my own. The Russian word "mastierstwa" may have been used because Grotowski was speaking to a group of Russians. See Brown (2013) on the related concept of *masterskaya*.

2 The theory offered here is already an example of "practice as research" (see Chapter 5) insofar as it could never have become thinkable without many hours and years spent in the studio, alone and with others. However, my artistic work (see Urban Research Theater 2014) is not an explicit focus of this book.

3 The debate over "liveness" (Auslander 1999) only has meaning if theatrical performances are seen alongside other art objects that are not live. If theatre is viewed as a site of embodied practice—alongside, for example, martial arts, social dance, religious ritual, and expressive arts therapies—then the question of liveness never arises.

4 In dance studies, for example, "phenomenology has replaced aesthetics as the philosophical discourse of choice" (Albright 2011: 8). In theatre, Phillip Zarrilli and others draws heavily on phenomenology (e.g., 2009: 45). Especially relevant to my argument is Sara Ahmed's phenomenological analysis of how the transparency of objects renders invisible "the 'work' of the body" (2006: 42; and 56–63).

5 A recent turn in theatre and performance studies, led by Laura Cull among others, suggests a new wave of interest in the intersections of theatre, performance, and philosophy (Performance Philosophy 2014). It remains to be seen what the concept of "performance," as distinct from "practice," can still accomplish. Here I prioritize the latter, while recognizing that many of my ideas about practice derive from experiences with highly specialized forms of theatrical performance.

6 For information about some of the women who worked alongside and after these famous men, see Sharon Marie Carnicke on Maria Knebel (in Hodge 2010) and Virginie Magnat on women in the Grotowski diaspora (2013).

Technique has a bad name; it can seem soulless. That's not how people whose hands become highly trained view technique.

(Sennett 2009: 149)

Consider, for a creature with hands there are **ways of having access to things**—ways of picking them up—that are not available to a different kind of creature. And so with money and language. Money and language expand and enhance **the repertoire of what we can do**. And so they widen and transform the range of what is available to us. **Skills, know-how, knowledge, and understanding—these are the ground of our access to what there is;** these mark out the extent of consciousness.

(Noë 2012: 32)

1

AN EPISTEMOLOGY OF PRACTICE

Which epistemology?

This book is about embodied knowledge. The word "epistemology" comes up with some frequency, referring to the study of knowledge. I also use the term "epistemic" to describe the direct engagement with or production of knowledge. By these definitions, the assertion that mathematics and ballet are both epistemic practices would be an example of an epistemological argument. Making such an argument would then depend on how one chooses to answer the question: *What is knowledge?* Knowledge can be approached from many angles. I want to clarify at the outset which epistemological traditions I will be drawing on and why.

My discussion of *technique as knowledge* is intended both to support and to challenge a recent trend in performance studies towards theorizing performance and embodied practice in terms of (embodied) knowledge. In this regard, scholars of performance have sometimes invoked the idea of "embodied knowledge" without offering a convincing epistemological account of how such knowledge relates to embodiment, materiality, and practice. For example, Diana Taylor writes that performances "function as vital acts of transfer, transmitting social knowledge." Embodied practice, according to Taylor, "offers a way of knowing" (2003: 2–3). Yvonne Daniel describes Haitian, Cuban, and Bahian practitioners as possessing "embodied knowledge—that is, knowledge found within the body, within the dancing and drumming body" (2005: 4); and Sharon Māhealani Rowe writes: "The bodies of hula dancers hold a body of knowledge, a complete philosophy with its own epistemology" (2008: 37). Elsewhere, Deidre Sklar describes "kinetic vitality as an overlooked aspect of embodied knowledge" (in Noland and Ness 2008: 85). I consider myself deeply allied with these attempts to articulate embodied knowledge. Yet my concern is that, without a more robust epistemology behind it, the concept of embodied knowledge may not be as effective as it deserves to be in transforming assumptions about knowledge both within and beyond academia. To develop an epistemological framework for analyzing embodied practice, we must do more than simply declare that particular performers or performance traditions possess embodied knowledge. If the goal is to radically change the way we think about knowledge, then theorists of practice and performance must ask and be ready to answer fundamental questions about the embodiment of knowledge.

Traditional (analytic) epistemology assumes a singular knowing subject. It asks, for example, how knowledge differs from belief, or how it relates to reason and rationality. As a subfield of philosophy, epistemology has undergone major revisions over the past few decades, as emphasis on rational thought and explicit knowledge has made way for a more complex account of knowledge as "situated" (Haraway 1988) and largely "tacit" (Polanyi 2009), along with a concomitant analysis of thought and cognition as "embodied" (Lakoff and Johnson 1999), "enactive" (Varela *et al.* 1991), and dependent upon—rather than distinct from—emotion (Damasio 1994). In recent years, scholars of theatre and performance have increasingly drawn on these thinkers. Most prominently, Bruce McConachie has declared a "cognitive turn" in theatre studies, based on the idea that cognitive studies—an interdisciplinary field involving psychology, linguistics, neuroscience, and more—can provide superior "epistemological justification" for the study of such phenomena as "theatricality, audience reception, meaning making, identity formation, the construction of culture, and processes of historical change" (McConachie and Hart 2006: ix–x). A number of recent monographs take up this argument and apply cognitive theories to various dimensions of theatre and performance (Blair 2008; Lutterbie 2011; Kemp 2012; Zarrilli *et al.* 2013). The theory of technique developed here shares with these works a basic concern for the embodiment of knowledge. However, the tenets that underpin this book are drawn less from cognitive studies than from a different epistemological tradition: that of social epistemology and the sociology of knowledge.[1]

Social epistemology differs from traditional epistemology in several respects. Most importantly, it studies the ways in which knowledge is produced and circulated within and between societies and communities.[2] A subset of this field, the sociology of scientific knowledge (abbreviated SSK), examines the complex factors involved in the production of scientific truth. While there has been much debate over the status of scientific facts and other established truths, the position taken here is that social factors are constitutive but not determining of knowledge. Some strands of SSK do reduce knowledge to culture, claiming that the former is socially determined and defining it as "any and every set of ideas and acts accepted by one or another social group or society of people" (McCarthy 1996: 24). However, more nuanced versions of SSK—such as those represented by Andrew Pickering and Karin Knorr Cetina—actively wrestle with the problem of realism and theorize the emergent interactivity of society and materiality in the production of knowledge. Here, I draw on social epistemology to highlight the knowledge-derived and knowledge-producing dimensions of practices that are not normally seen as epistemic. This is hardly reading against the grain, since one of the successes of SSK has been to show how science is similar to other practices, rather than being a distinct category of thought with a unique type of access to truth. It is therefore not difficult to apply many of the key ideas of SSK to embodied practices like those examined here. These include, for example, the concepts of incommensurability (Pickering 1995: 186–92); research (Cetina in Schatzki *et al.* 2001); epistemic culture (Cetina 1999); and the laboratory (Cetina 1981; Latour 1983).

The centrality of "practice" in SSK links the sociology of knowledge to other social theories of practice. As Theodore Schatzki explains, the difference between a "philosophy" of science (which attempts to explain how and why science achieves its special access to truth) and a sociology or social theory of science (which explains how scientific knowledge arises from social processes) lies in a "transformed conception of knowledge" as essentially inhering in practices rather than facts or even states of mind. According to this line of thinking,

> knowledge (and truth) are no longer automatically self-transparent possessions of minds. Rather, knowledge and truth, including the scientific versions, are mediated both by interactions between people and by arrangements in the world. Often, consequently, knowledge is no longer even the property of individuals, but instead a feature of groups, together with their material setups. Scientific and other knowledges also no longer amount to stockpiled representations. Not only do practical understandings, ways of proceeding, and even setups of the material environment represent forms of knowledge—propositional knowledge presupposes and depends on them.
>
> (Schatzki *et al.* 2001: 12)

This is what Schatzki calls the "practice turn" in contemporary social theory. In showing how knowledge inheres in practices—and how, by the same token, practices may be profoundly epistemic—this approach provides us with the beginnings of what I will call an *epistemology of practice*. My goal here is to apply this epistemology—which has thus far been developed primarily in reference to the "hard" sciences—to embodied practices that are not typically thought of in such terms.

To restate my argument: *Embodied practice is epistemic*. It is structured by and productive of knowledge. Accordingly, an epistemological account of embodied practice is one according to which such practice actively encounters and *comes to know* reality through technique, rather than simply producing or constructing it. Social epistemologies allow us to analyze the development and circulation of embodied knowledge—in the form of technique—through processes that are both socially enabled and materially engaged. These processes take place at the social rather than the individual level, although individuals and small groups play important roles as researchers, teachers, and students. Such processes include those of disciplinarity and interdisciplinarity, specialization and dissemination, transmission and pedagogy, research and training. These terms, which are commonly applied to scientific and academic fields, will in the present context be applied to fields and areas of embodied technique, thereby suggesting a substantially new way to ask "what bodies can do"—as well as a new way to grasp the importance of embodied practice as a site for the ceaseless posing and answering of that question. In order to understand the implications of this idea, we need to more fully develop two central and mutually defining concepts: "technique" and "practice."

A selective genealogy of technique

Technique is a fundamental dimension of embodiment and of our lives as embodied creatures.[3] It structures our actions and practices by offering a range of relatively reliable pathways through any given situation. Most artists and athletes acknowledge that technique plays a necessary if not sufficient role in what they do. In territories as diverse as human existence, practice is structured by knowledge of the capacities of embodiment—of what a body can do—of *technique*. Yet for every positive reference to technique, there is a skeptical or cautionary warning against it. Enough has been written about technique, in a variety of fields, to provide some groundwork for a discussion of its meaning and importance. However, technique has not yet emerged as a keyword for critical thought in the current era. Its epistemological and ontological status has yet to be thoroughly explored. Nor is there any consensus about how technique differs from related concepts like method, skill, and practice. The theory of embodied knowledge presented here is based on a retheorization of technique. Although I cannot offer a comprehensive history of the English word "technique"—let alone its equivalent in French or any other language—I want to begin with a selective genealogy that traces the meaning of the term through six roughly chronological points in the writings of Aristotle, Samuel Taylor Coleridge, Marcel Mauss, Michel Foucault, Nick Crossley, and Randy Martin. These six stopping points in the genealogy of technique have been chosen for the specific contributions they can make to an epistemology of practice. From each, I will extract one or more specific points of particular value to my argument. Taken together, the renewed concept of technique that emerges from this trajectory will serve as the foundation for the rest of this book.

Technique comes from the Greek word *techne,* which appears in Book VI of Aristotle's *Nichomachean Ethics* alongside four other "states in which the soul grasps the truth": *episteme, phronesis, sophia,* and *nous.* Terence Irwin translates these five modes of grasping as "craft" (*techne*), "scientific knowledge" (*episteme*), "prudence" (*phronesis*), "wisdom" (*sophia*), and "understanding" (*nous*)—but these translations are open to dispute (Aristotle 1999: 1139b15). Elsewhere, the same terms have been translated as different types of knowledge: "theoretical" (*episteme*), "productive" (*techne*), and "practical" (*phronesis*) (Haney 1999: 32).[4] It is not possible to finally determine the relations between these concepts, not least because there was considerable variation in their definition and use even among the ancient Greeks. Furthermore, as Richard Parry writes in the *Stanford Encyclopedia of Philosophy*, contemporary translations of *techne* and *episteme* "may inappropriately harbor some of our contemporary assumptions about the relation between theory (the domain of 'knowledge') and practice (the concern of 'craft' or 'art')" (Parry 2007). Surveying the appearance of these terms from the Socratic works of Xenophon and Plato through Aristotle to the Stoics and beyond, Parry offers a "mixed picture" of their relationship as one continually in flux. In some contexts, there is "no distinction between *epistêmê* as theoretical knowledge and *technê* as mere craft or skill." Nevertheless, much has been made in modern philosophical thought of these ancient distinctions.

Techne has most frequently been contrasted with *episteme* (e.g., Rawlins 1950), on the grounds that the latter involves unvarying knowledge about the world, whereas the former is context-dependent. However, Parry suggests that *techne* in Aristotle is more than just practical knowledge or context-dependent ability: "[T]he master craftsman (*technitês*) is wiser than the person of experience because he knows the cause, the reasons that things are to be done. The mere artisan (*cheir-otechnês*) acts without this knowledge" (2007). Other readers of Aristotle contrast *techne* with *phronesis*, treating the former as coldly rational and linking the latter to ethical judgment or what Irwin calls "prudence." In this vein, Joseph Dunne draws a distinction "between technical and practical reason," associating *techne* with rationalism and the objectification of knowledge (Dunne 1992: 9). In a sense, then, *techne* is located somewhere between *episteme* and *phronesis*, theory and practice, knowledge and judgment. When contrasted with *episteme*—theoretical or scientific knowledge—*techne* appears eminently practical, because it is more concerned with making and production than with abstract thought. On the other hand, when compared with *phronesis*—prudence or ethical judgment—*techne* may suggest a coldly rational or mechanistic type of knowing. We can take from these ambiguities a recognition of the slipperiness of knowledge categories in general, and also a certain double-edged significance pertaining specifically to *techne* as that which is simultaneously rational and practical, transmissible and context-dependent. The ambiguous connotations of *techne* haunt the concept of technique right up to the present day and are part of what makes it such a useful concept for rethinking the bodily grounds of knowledge.

"Technique" entered the English language in 1817, via the poetic criticism of Samuel Taylor Coleridge, who imported it from French in a biographical sketch of Wordsworth (George 2007: 195–96; and see *OED Online* 2013, s.v. "technique"). Already in this first English usage, the word was employed in a "dismissive" manner, with Coleridge intending it to name not the skillful craft of a poet but rather that which must be transcended in order for true genius to appear. Laura George traces the development of technique from this point onward, noting that, for Coleridge, a great poet arrives to greatness "by outgrowing the defects of *technique*: the poetry of genius is what is left once *technique* has been transcended by processes of natural growth and spontaneous healing" (2007: 196). This connotation, attached to technique from the moment of its first English usage, defines a negative lineage of technique that still has power today, despite the fact that technique is also used colloquially to mean "any skill requiring particular steps or knowledge" (198). According to George, much twentieth-century literary criticism assumes that "while skilled attention to technique characterizes the professional critic, real poetry occurs at the moments when mere technique is transcended" (198). The value of poetry, then, is "not in technique but in the residuum that lies beyond technique" (200). This fundamentally romantic notion remains widespread today, as in the commonplace assertion that—as Oscar Wilde asserted—"true art cannot be taught" (199). Ironically, "art" itself was formerly a synonym for craft and knowledge—the Latin *artes* translated the Greek *technai* (Parry 2007). Yet art, since Coleridge and the Romantics, has consistently been elevated above technique, while technique has been downgraded to the status of the merely mechanical.

By 1828, the words "mere" and "mechanical" were consistently linked with technique, not only in literary criticism but also in discussions of painting, dance, and other modern "arts," where the concept of technique "is simultaneously persistent and persistently dismissed" (George 2007: 198, 201). Similarly, in "modern usage, one finds repeated warnings not to mistake the *technique* and the thing itself" (200). The negative valence of technique can be followed into the twentieth century through works like Lewis Mumford's *Art and Technics* (1952) and Martin Heidegger's *The Question concerning Technology* (1977 [1954]). By the second half of the twentieth century, technique is often described as a kind of temptation: a "myth" (Barba 1972), a "lure" (Dunne 1992), an "illusion" (Barrett 1978). These authors fear the encroachment of a reductive worldview in which genuine knowledge and understanding are reduced to mere recipe and procedural routine. For Barrett, the failure of mathematical logic to provide a firm grounding for philosophy suggests "the limits of technique generally" (1978: xix). He warns of a future in which humanity has become so "enclosed" in "technical thinking" that it is unable to think in other ways (223; and see Boisvert 2008). In this line of thinking, while "mechanical reproduction" (Benjamin 1999 [1936]) becomes increasingly omnipresent, "art" is increasingly invoked as a site in which the unique is valued over the reproducible. Repetition, as in mass production, is increasingly seen as a danger rather than an achievement in "arts" that are now distinguished from mere "crafts" (Sennett 2009).

The negative view of technique informs the writings of many of the practitioners studied in this book. However, no such prejudice is found in the writings of French sociologist and anthropologist Marcel Mauss (1872–1950), who gives us the first modern theory of technique. Mauss saw technique as the greatest achievement of humankind: "It is technique which, through the development of societies, has brought about the development of reason, sensibility and will. It is technique that makes of modern humans the most perfect of animals" (2006: 47). Mauss's notion of technique is insufficient for our purposes. He defined technique as "an ensemble of movements or actions, in general and for the most part manual, which are organised and traditional, and which work together towards the achievement of a goal known to be physical or chemical or organic" (149). This is at once too vague and too narrow. The concept of technique cannot be limited to that which is manual, as it may involve the whole body—not just its physiology but its emotional and mental life as well. The terms "organized" and "traditional" require unpacking and do not apply to all that may be termed technique. Nor are the "known" goals of technique—known to whom?—necessarily restricted to the physical, chemical, and organic. Nevertheless, a flexible and rigorous theory of technique has much to gain from Mauss's work. It is worth pausing here to elaborate four basic insights about technique, all of which can be found in the writings of Mauss.

First, technique is knowledge. As Nathan Schlanger affirms, "Mauss stressed the part of knowledge and of consciousness deployed and acquired by those engaged in technical activities. To weave a fabric, to navigate a canoe, to construct a spear, to set a trap—all are actions which suppose and at the same time generate knowledge" (in Mauss 2006: 20). A corollary of this point is that technique is learned; it is not innate but acquired. This does not mean, however, that it is easy to unlearn or change one's technique, especially when it was acquired over a long period of time or during childhood. Mauss recalls:

> [O]ur generation has witnessed a complete change in [swimming] technique: we have seen the breaststroke with the head out of the water replaced by the different sorts of crawl. Moreover, the habit of swallowing water and spitting it out has gone. In my day swimmers thought of themselves as a kind of steamboat. It was stupid, but in fact I still do this: I cannot get rid of my technique.
> (Mauss 2006: 79)

In pointing out the difficulty of unlearning technique once it has been absorbed to the point of unconscious reflex, Mauss raises another issue: the relationship between knowledge and agency. If technique is knowledge, then how can it become involuntary? At the time of Mauss's writing, it might have been possible to imagine a coherent inner self or subject that makes instrumental use of the body to accomplish its goals. More recent work—such as Pierre Bourdieu's theory of habitus, Judith Butler's theory of performativity, and the enactive or actionist theory of consciousness—suggests a different and more complex understanding of agency, as will be elaborated below.

Second, technique is transmissible; it moves across time and space. Mauss's interest in "the phenomenon of borrowing and the spread of techniques" (2006: 47) from one society to another grew out of his reaction to an emerging, virulent nationalism that upheld the organic unity and evolutionary destiny of the nation. To fight this rising tide, Mauss sought to demonstrate that techniques are not tied to particular societies, but rather can be shown to move continuously across national and cultural borders. This suggests that the identity of every nation is essentially hybrid or composite and points towards a view of humanity as united by shared knowledge resources rather than divided by nation or culture. Mauss saw the history of civilization as a "history of the circulation between societies of the various goods and achievements of each," with techniques—from horse riding to agriculture and industry— being chief among these (44). The contemporary critique of imperialism makes it impossible for us to be as glib as Mauss was about the circulation of technique. We know that technique does not circulate under conditions of freedom or justice. Technique can be stolen; it can be banned. Technique can be enforced by mandatory law. It can be violent. Wars are fought over technique. It is a gross understatement to point out that the "human benefits" of technique do not accrue to all people equally. Still, Mauss's basic insight holds: Technique does not belong to any one nation or people. The power dynamics that attach to its movement are complex and deserving of more substantial analysis.

Third, technique can be understood as a "compromise between nature and humanity" (Mauss 2006: 52). By this, Mauss means to highlight the engagement of technique with the material reality of the world. Although the terms "nature" and "humanity" may now seem dated, Mauss's suggestion of a compromise between them in no way suggests a stark binary division. Rather, in the blurring of organic and material categories, Mauss's writing foreshadows much more recent work on situated and embodied knowledge. He writes:

> In practical arts, human beings make their limits recede. They advance in nature, at the same time above their proper nature, because they adjust it to nature. The human actor identifies himself with the mechanical, physical and chemical order of things. He creates and at the same time he creates himself; he creates at once his means of living, things purely human, and his thought inscribed in these things. Here is true practical reason being elaborated.
>
> (53)

Technique, here, involves a detailed and context-dependent negotiation between socially defined or symbolic meaning and the concrete possibilities offered by the material world. In this thick relationality, humanity attunes itself to its world. Technique for Mauss is not the domination or instrumental usage of the world but rather, in Deleuze's terms, a kind of *becoming-world*. What Mauss calls "nature," I will refer to as the *relative reliability* of the world, the material substrate with which technique grapples. Although technique acquires representational and symbolic meaning according to its context, Mauss's writing emphasizes the material side of technique and the way in which this provides the foundation for other kinds of meaning.

Fourth, some technique is specifically *bodily*—in my terms, embodied. As noted in the introduction, the concept of embodiment does not exclude language or thought; it rather distinguishes technique from technology in the sense of manufactured objects. While fields like economics and medicine rely on embodied technique—as must all human activity—they also rely on a massive infrastructure of technology, from books and computers to buildings and airplanes. Mauss was perhaps the first writer to explicitly recognize the importance of technique that works not through tools but through embodiment itself. To be sure, Mauss believed that most techniques are "characterised by the presence of an instrument," and he catalogued them accordingly: techniques of fire, basketry, pottery, weaponry, cooking, hunting, agriculture, building, etc. (2006: 100). But he also devoted an entire essay, now canonical, to *les techniques du corps*: "techniques of the body," sometimes translated as "body techniques" or "bodily techniques." These are techniques that take the human body itself as the "first and most natural instrument" (83), a notion that returns us to the fundamental question of what *bodies* can do.

Mauss developed his notion of *les techniques du corps* after noticing that a particular way of walking, which he first observed in New York, had traveled to Paris via the cinema (2006: 80). He then realized that human bodies differ not only in their physiological makeup but also in their technique: how they walk, swim, dig, etc. This technique is acquired through training. In later chapters, we will see how training in embodied technique takes place in specialized fields like acting—for example, in the creation of a character or role—as well as in everyday life. At this point, we can already see that there are at least two reasons why it might be difficult to transform the technique of an individual or group, two senses in which materiality resists easy control and demands compromise: first, variation in human physiology across the species; and second, prior training, which shapes one's present and future possibilities. To summarize, we can draw from the writings of Mauss four basic characteristics of technique: (1) Technique is knowledge; it is acquired and not easy to unlearn. (2) Technique is transmissible; it travels across time and space and is always hybrid and mixed. (3) Technique is a compromise between "nature" and "humanity." (4) Technique can be embodied in the sense that it may work with and through the materiality of bodies as distinct from technologies. All of these important insights are present in Mauss's work on technique, which predates by decades the work of Pierre Bourdieu, Michel Foucault, Judith Butler, and others who have theorized the intersection of social construction and material forces in practice.

The writings of Foucault in particular offer additional insights for a retheorization of technique, of which I will mention three. In the first instance, as a historian, Foucault directly addresses the evolution and transformation of technique over time. While Mauss's writing emphasizes the geographical and cultural diversity of technique, Foucault analyzes changes in technique from one time period to another. For example, in *Discipline and Punish: The Birth of the Prison* (1995), Foucault tracks the shift in Europe from an explicitly violent technique of state retribution, enacted directly upon the body of the prisoner, to a newer technique of punishing isolation and imprisonment. Foucault does not offer a definition of technique or distinguish it significantly from technology. Rather, he employs technique alongside other terms— such as instrument, procedure, method, science, and discipline—to illustrate the ubiquity and multiplicity of discursive production and regimes of power. However, the fact that technique changes over time suggests an important question that will be addressed at length below: Where does new technique come from? What is the source of innovation in (embodied) technique?

A second insight we can take from Foucault is that technique—as knowledge—is always thoroughly interwoven with the dynamics of power. "We should admit," he declares, "that power produces knowledge; … that power and knowledge directly imply one another; that there is no power relation without the correlative constitution of a field of knowledge, nor any knowledge that does not presuppose and continue at the same time power relations" (1995: 27). Foucault does not suggest that power has final control over knowledge or that knowledge is merely power in disguise. Rather, it is the hybrid interaction of "power-knowledge" that "determines the forms and possible domains of knowledge" (28). In this sense, Foucault's "power-knowledge" can be read as a more historically grounded and politically astute revision of Mauss's "compromise between humanity and nature." The hyphen linking power and knowledge represents the eternal mismatch, the ceaselessly productive and destructive tensions, between human power struggles and the limits of material reality; or, to put this another way, between what is and what could be. Knowledge, as Eve Kosofsky

Sedgwick writes, "is the magnetic field of power," the terrain within which power necessarily operates (1994: 23). If technique is knowledge, then its discovery and transmission unfold within channels determined by unequal power dynamics. Yet by the same token, technique is not reducible to social power struggles, because it also involves an epistemic project that extends beyond the human in its interaction with material reality.

Thirdly, Foucault reminds us that technique may sometimes be directed not towards an exterior product, person, or goal, but towards the self. Finding that he had "insisted too much on the technology of domination," Foucault was drawn in his later work to "the history of how an individual acts upon himself, in the technology of self" (Foucault 1988: 19). This interest led him away from the study of prisons and asylums and towards that of sexuality and the ethical practices of ancient Greek and Christian asceticism (see Hadot 1995; McGushin 2007). In the Greek notion of *askesis* (the etymological root of "ascetic"), Foucault found a radically different understanding of how the self is constructed: not through the operation of power upon a docile body but through the "care of the self," the development of one's being through repeated actions and the long-term cultivation of habits and behaviors. Moreover, Foucault's return to *techne* suggests that knowledge is above all practically applicable. Foucault's techniques and technologies, whether of domination or of the self, are always conceived of as actions to be taken rather than mere facts or information. In insisting on the synthesis of "power-knowledge," Foucault underscores the material effects of the latter. Whether burned at the stake, imprisoned, sexualized, or cared for, lived and living bodies are the site of technique. Even the most disembodied technologies, like the chart or table, are designed to observe, catalogue, and control human beings through their presence as bodies. The discipline and punishment of a person takes place through that person's body, as does the care of the self.

When Mauss's idea of bodily technique is inflected by Foucault's analysis of power, we may begin to grasp how the training we each receive reflects not only a variable knowledge of technique but also the social hierarchies that determine how this knowledge is distributed. Foucault's later work opens the door to the possibility that embodied practices might serve as ethical practices of the self rather than simple reinscriptions of power. This is a tempting idea that seems to offer new hope for the validation of such practices, prompting some theorists to analyze practices of dance or yoga by asking whether they function as oppression or resistance, discipline or liberation (e.g., Lea 2009). However, we should not assume that any given technique can be exclusively classified as either oppressive or liberatory. Rather, we should take from Foucault a critical awareness of how knowledge is interwoven with power, as well as the recognition that technique changes over time. Technical knowledge cannot be reduced to power relations. On the contrary, Foucault's work reminds us that the same technique can be deployed under different circumstances to radically different effect. Furthermore, as Wendy Brown notes (2013), Foucault does not engage directly with the issue of democracy, and his notion of power is difficult to mobilize in the name of concrete political goals.[5]

The tensions and ambiguities of technique as defined by Aristotle, Coleridge, Mauss, and Foucault are alive and well in current scholarship. In addition to these well-established sources, I want to borrow insights from two contemporary thinkers, sociologist Nick Crossley and dance theorist Randy Martin. Crossley's significance in the present context is that he shows how the category of embodied technique may extend beyond physical movement into other dimensions of human embodiment. In doing so, he provides a particularly subtle illustration of the "compromise between nature and humanity." Citing Maurice Merleau-Ponty's description of an attempt to help himself fall asleep by lying down in a sleep-like posture, Crossley points out that falling asleep is not a directly voluntary action like waving one's arm or going for a walk. Sleep is not directly subject to conscious will. Instead, the would-be sleeper must act "by indirect means" upon his embodied self—in this case, by lying down and closing his eyes (2004: 42). This is a significant point for theorizing embodied technique. Unlike previous examples, such as those offered by Mauss, the technique of putting oneself to sleep involves a complex interaction between conscious and unconscious aspects of a single self. Crossley further extends this argument by describing the use of embodied technique to "invoke" or "fend off" particular emotional states in a variety of contexts (43). For example, protesters at a rally may "use their songs, chants, and gestures to put themselves, affectively, into protest situations, to whip up the mood or atmosphere, individual and collective, necessary to an expression of dissent" (47). Like sleep, feelings of anger and sorrow may not be directly available to protesters. Instead, they must be activated indirectly, through singing or marching. The "compromise" between agency and nature here takes a specifically "reflexive" form, since both are part of the same being.

Crossley's expansion of *les techniques du corps* is essential if we are to get beyond a merely physical notion of technique.[6] To summon sleep, to arouse anger, or to stimulate joy are not actions to be taken directly, but they are certainly within the realm of embodied technique. Hans

Joas makes a similar point in his critique of "activistic" theories, which privilege "continuous activity, the permanent generation of individual acts," and which he considers both ethnocentric and patriarchal (1996: 167–68). Rather than privilege direct, consciously intentional actions, Joas prefers "a concept of action that also encompasses passivity, sensitivity, receptivity and imperturbability." Crossley's examples of falling asleep and arousing or quelling emotion involve just this kind of interplay between action and receptivity, and it will be important to keep this in mind as we develop our understanding of embodiment technique. The trajectory of this book follows an arc from the evidently physical to aspects of human embodiment that we may not be accustomed to conceiving in technical terms. In Chapter 2, a similar issue appears in the form of a juxtaposition between athletic and somatic tendencies in the practice of yoga; while Chapter 3 returns to Crossley's notion of "indirect" technique as a way of understanding the innovations in acting technique proposed by Konstantin Stanislavski.

The final station in this selective genealogy is found in the writings of dance theorist Randy Martin, who places the "movement" of dance on the same plane as that of social and cultural movements, thereby paving the way to an idea of technique that overflows the boundaries between performing arts, physical culture, and cultural identity. Although Martin does not offer what I call an epistemological perspective on technique, he compellingly describes the interaction of multiple kinds of technique within the "composite body" of the dancer (1998: 139). Significantly, Martin extends his argument beyond the dance studio and into everyday life, asking the reader to consider the similarity between how dancers embody "disparate technical sensibilities" and how all bodies are "multiply composed." Martin draws a connection between different kinds of dance technique and the "multiplicity of techniques, dancerly and otherwise," that overlap in a dancer's body (167). Martin calls this phenomenon the "intertextuality" of technique and describes how one technique may appear as "residue" in the midst of another. This happens, for example, when jazz or ballet technique appears unexpectedly in the midst of a modern dance combination. But it also happens when the training one has received as a child—to sit, stand, or speak in a particular way—manifests as an embodied technical residue in the performance of dance. This notion of technical "residue" explains why, when we train in a new area of embodied technique, we simultaneously confront our own gendered, classed, raced, cultured identities. By viewing both sociocultural identities and professional identities as essentially structured by technique, Martin offers a key to the integration of sociocultural perspectives with those drawn from the study of performing arts. This insight is a crucial starting point for my arguments in Chapters 3 and 4.

These six reference points have been selected because of their specific relevance to the project of developing an epistemology of practice. There are of course many other references to technique in contemporary theatre, dance, and performance studies. Scholars of theatre often invoke technique in a casual sense, but the term has rarely been theorized in a specifically theatrical context. One exception is Crease and Lutterbie's chapter on technique in *Staging Philosophy: Intersections of Theatre, Performance, and Philosophy* (2006), a precursor to Lutterbie's more sustained examination of technique in *Toward a General Theory of Acting* (2011: 131–59). Technique is more often an explicit focus in the study of dance, where Wendell Beavers has observed a "revolution in technique" and an ensuing "reinvestment in technique" (in Bales and Nettl-Fiol 2008: 128–29). In *Dancing Communities: Performance, Difference and Connection in the Global City*, Judith Hamera defines technique as "relational infrastructure." She writes, with Foucauldian overtones: "Technique is both the animating aesthetic principle and the core ambivalence housed in every day studio and manipulated by every teacher, every choreographer, every performer. It is both taskmaster and mastered, both warden and liberator" (2007: 19, 4). In *The Body, Dance and Cultural Theory*, Helen Thomas compares the technique of ballet and contact improvisation, contrasting their radically different approaches to the senses of vision and touch (2003: 95–113). Thomas acknowledges that both dance technique and dancers' bodies change over time, offering a thick description of what happens when, as Mauss observed, technical forms "become ossified" in the body (110). The movement of embodied technique across time and space has also been studied under the related concepts of choreography (Foster 1995) and gesture (Noland and Ness 2008; Noland 2009).

Despite this rich etymological and genealogical history, many contemporary theorists prefer to avoid the concept of technique, with its persistent connotations of mechanicity and repetition. Perhaps for this reason, a recent trend in contemporary scholarship refers to the deeply sedimented understanding and expertise of highly trained actors and dancers as embodied or bodily "technology" (Watson 2013; Lima 2013; Mroz 2011: 17–18; and see Golding 1997). Yet as Mick Wallis notes, the "elision of difference between *technē* and technological apparatus or product arguably threatens to shield the human activity of knowledge production 'properly' designated by *technē* from view" (2005: 1). In other words, these uses of "technology" render invisible the knowledge called *technique* at a time when the latter is particularly in need of recognition. While the original sense of technology could have been as broad as "theories of good making" (Hodgkin 1990: 209), today its common usage unequivocally invokes the material products of knowledge rather than knowledge itself. In turning our back on technique, we inadvertently privilege the literally mechanical over its source in embodied knowledge. At a time when our inability to obtain critical distance on the exponentially increasing omnipresence of technology—in the vernacular sense of machines and other engineered objects—threatens the human ecosystem, it seems drastically unwise to appropriate "technology" as the name for knowledge that is specifically embodied. While the association with technology may appear to lend legitimacy to embodied knowledge, it does so by rendering invisible the distinction according to which such knowledge has special import today.

Other contemporary thinkers prefer to invent new terms, as in Sullivan and Murray's "somatechnics" (2009: 3), or to refashion old ones, as in Peter Sloterdijk's "anthropotechnics" (2013: 398). Technique itself, it seems, is everywhere and nowhere in this ambiguous field of cognates and coinages. Here, I have traced a selective genealogy that conceives of technique as vital, dynamic, and complex. In this conception, technique is a kind of knowledge (Aristotle) that moves across time and space (Mauss) in ways deeply influenced but not entirely determined by social power relations (Foucault). It structures every aspect of human embodiment and works by indirect as well as direct means (Crossley). Furthermore, embodied technique of all kinds, from the mundane to the highly specialized, interacts in and through specific bodies and moments of practice (Martin). These points together provide something like a working definition of technique. Before putting this definition to work, we need to examine more closely those "moments of practice" that I have claimed are structured by technique.

The structure of practice

Unlike technique, practice has been an explicit focus and key term of a substantial body of scholarship in multiple fields since at least the 1970s. In *The Practice Turn in Contemporary Theory*, Theodore Schatzki observes that where theorists "once spoke of 'structures,' 'systems,' 'meaning,' 'life world,' 'events,' and 'actions' when naming the primary generic social thing," many today "would accord 'practices' a comparable honor" (Schatzki *et al.* 2001: 1).[7] Elsewhere, Nigel Thrift offers a stirring description of practice as the focus of what he calls "non-representational theory," an approach that looks past the play of signs and symbols in order to concentrate instead on *practices*, understood as material bodies of work or styles that have gained enough stability over time, through, for example, the establishment of corporeal routines and specialized devices, to reproduce themselves ... These material bodies are continually being rewritten as unusual circumstances arise, and new bodies are continually making an entrance but, if we are looking for something that approximates to a stable feature of a world that is continually in meltdown, that is continually bringing forth new hybrids, then I take the practice to be it. Practices are productive concatenations that have been constructed out of all manner of resources and which provide the basic intelligibility of the world.

(Thrift 2008: 8)

Thrift's definition of "practices" sounds much like what I have called technique. Why then do we need both terms? Could we not simply track the movement of practices across time and space and analyze the composition of bodies in terms of the practices they enact?

There is a fundamental problem with practice theory, acknowledged by Schatzki and others, which I hope to resolve through the retheorization of technique. In *The Practice Turn*, Schatzki characterizes the predicament as follows: "A practice is, first, a *set of actions*. For instance, farming practices comprise such actions as building fences, harvesting grain, herding sheep, judging weather, and paying for supplies ... What more is there, however, to a practice than activity?" For "practices cannot be composed of patterns alone" (Schatzki *et al.* 2001: 48–49). Elsewhere in the same volume, Stephen Turner argues that practice theory "gets into trouble" over the idea of "sharing" and "shared practices" (120). The problem for Schatzki, Turner, and others is that "practice" has two distinct meanings: first, it refers to concrete instances of action; and second, to the patterns that link such instances together. What does it mean to "share" a practice across time, space, and bodies? What is it that links together different instances of farming or cooking? Clearly, if two people are cooking the same meal in different places, they are not literally cooking the *same* meal. For that matter, when I cook the same meal on several days, it is also not literally the same meal. What then does it mean to suggest that various groups or individuals, in different times and places, are or were doing the same thing? What kind of "thing" were they doing and in what sense can it be the same?

Schatzki has attempted to solve this problem by distinguishing between what he calls "practice-as-entity" and "practice-as-performance" (Schatzki

1996: 89–90). Other theorists have since taken up this distinction and used it to ground their own analyses of how a given "practice-as-entity" may be incarnated or enacted in different instances of "practice-as-performance."[8] But what actually constitutes the abstract "entity" of a practice? What, to take one of Mauss's examples, is the "entity" of swimming? If swimming in general is an "entity," and my swimming on a particular day is a "performance," then what about intermediate categories, such as all the times I have been swimming in my life, or all the swimming in North America during the twentieth century? Is the "entity" of swimming something other than the set of all performances of swimming? Does this "entity" include both my casual swimming and the Olympic sport of swimming? Does it include ritual baths and swimming for one's life after a shipwreck? In short, it is extremely difficult to define the boundaries of any practice in its general form as "entity," not to mention drawing a line between this and actual performances. The relationship of "entity" and "performance" is not subtle enough to capture the actual variety of practice, and using "practice" for both of these concepts tells us nothing about the relationship between them. The latter also leads to a confused phrasing in which the same word refers to both the doing and the thing that is done: When I practice, what I am practicing is a practice.

Schatzki refers to cooking, child-rearing, politics, farming, negotiation, banking, and recreation as "practices" (2001: 48). But are these "practices" in the sense of specific doings, historical instances that we can study in detail and specificity? Or do these words refer instead to patterns or principles that link such concrete instances together across time and space? As soon as something like cooking is understood as a practice in the abstract, it loses the specificity and detail of a specific instance of cooking. On the other hand, if we try to define practice as concrete moments of doing, we are then faced with the problem of how that moment is linked to other moments. The tendency in practice theory is to characterize a practice like swimming or cooking as "an amalgam of elements," as "complexes" or "bundles" of meanings, competences, and material objects (Shove *et al.* 2012: 40, 81). In contrast, I propose to do away with "practice-as-entity"—a phrase with no comprehensible meaning, since it is neither abstract nor specific—and recognize instead that concrete moments of practice are structured by knowledge in the form of technique. This immediately allows us to distinguish between a given *practice* of swimming, bounded in time and space, and the *technique* of swimming, which is not merely a repeated pattern or set of rules but an area of practical and technical knowledge. Conceiving of the relationship between technique and practice in this way solves several problems in practice theory. It also opens the door to an epistemological understanding of practice that can inform our thinking about power, agency, society, and material reality.

Henceforth, I will use "practice" only to refer to concrete examples of actions, moments of doing, historical instances of materialized activity. I will rigorously avoid referring to abstract "practices" of walking, cooking, or swimming. Such references confuse the issue, since what counts as each of these may differ from one context to another. Even something as simple as walking should not be reified as an ahistorical phenomenon, as this would prevent us from analyzing similarities and differences in walking across time and space and between individuals and cultures. On the other hand, if we understand walking, cooking, and swimming as *areas of technique,* then we can dispense with the idea of practices as floating, abstract things. From this point on, I will not refer to walking, dancing, or swimming as "practices" unless I am ready to specify *who* is enacting them, *when,* and *where.* Similarly, cooking, child-rearing, politics, farming, negotiation, banking, and recreation are not "practices" unless we are referring to specific examples that can be located in time and space, in bodies and communities. Instead, each of these can be seen as an area of technique, or as the *knowledge content* of specific practices. In other words, the relationship between technique and practice is epistemic. This finally allows us to understand what may connect my practice of swimming or dancing with that of people living thousands of miles away or hundreds of years ago. If we are doing the "same thing," that is precisely and only because we are making use of the same technique, the same *knowledge of what is reliably possible* given the similarities we find in our bodies and environments.

Practice, in this sense, is not repeatable. Every moment of practice is unique, no matter how small or large: my swimming on a given day, my swimming in a given year, and the swimming in North America during the twentieth century are all examples of practice that can be studied in their specificity. None can be repeated. As knowledge, on the other hand, technique is precisely repeatable and moreover is not bound to a particular moment, place, or person. Technique is not ahistorical but transhistorical: It travels across time and space, "spreading" from society to society, as Mauss observed, and linking diverse practices to one another, whether or not its practitioners are aware of this connection. The question for theorists of practice is then not what does or does not count as an example of a given practice, but rather the extent to which different practices are structured by the same technique. This enables us to track the movement of technique across history, while at the same time retaining a highly specific and localized notion of practice.

It allows us to shift from a language of static, transferable objects to one that highlights the epistemic processes of knowledge production and dissemination. If practice is structured by knowledge in the form of technique, then what Shove and Spurling call the "coalescence," "hybridization," and "bifurcation" of practices (2013: 33) might instead be analyzed as epistemic processes of disciplinarity, interdisciplinarity, and specialization. Thinking of practice in terms of knowledge sheds a very different light on the "dynamics of social practice," from the circulation and reproduction of technique to its innovation.

Although technique is repeatable, its repetition may be habitual or innovative, conscious or unconscious, freely chosen or coerced. When I cook the same meal as you, or swim the same stroke, or walk with the same gait, there is some repetition at the level of technique. We can then ask why this repetition takes place: Did I learn the technique from you? Did we discover the same possibilities independently? Am I forced to practice this technique? Are we aware of what we have in common? In a later section, I consider the role and limits of agency in practice. First, I want to more closely examine how it is exactly that technique structures practice. It does so, I argue, through an epistemic engagement with the relative reliability of material reality. Technique consists of discoveries about specific material possibilities that can be repeated with some degree of reliability, so that what works in one context may also work in another. It is crucial to remember that this reliability is never more than relative. Often we are wrong in our expectations about the reliability of technique. Changes in the environment, or in our own embodiment, or the passage of technique from one context to another, can produce unexpected results. Yet we are able to work together and to communicate with each other because of the degree to which the material world—including our own embodiment—does respond in relatively reliable ways to actions taken. This is another way to conceive of what Mauss called the "compromise" between humanity and nature, reconceived here as a technical negotiation with the relative reliability of materiality itself.[9]

As embodied creatures, we dwell not among facts and objects but amidst what James Gibson calls "affordances": material possibilities that a given environment offers, provides, or furnishes to an animal dwelling within it (Gibson 1986: 127). As Alva Noë points out, affordances are not secondary effects of representation. That is, we do not first classify objects in our environment and then analyze them for their possible affordances. Rather, we perceive affordances directly, as opportunities for action (Noë 2012: 120; and see Gibson 1986: 134). For this reason, Mauss's assertion that technique works according to "physical or chemical or organic" principles is insufficient. Physics, chemistry, and biology are secondary explanations for why some technique works with greater or lesser reliability. They do not and are not intended to account for the effectiveness of all possible technique. We do not first "know" the world and then develop technique. Rather, we come to know the world through different kinds of technique, of which the sciences are one very important variety. The shift from "body techniques" to "embodied technique" reminds us that, although medical and scientific approaches to embodiment are extremely valuable, they do not finally pin down all its affordances—nor, for the most part, do they claim to do so. Dissection and magnetic resonance imaging can tell us a great deal about the body's organs and systems, but they do not tell us all there is to know about what we can do with our bodies. Like other mappings, they are good for certain things. They reveal certain affordances and hide others. To prioritize embodied technique is to remember that all mappings of the body are provisional. It is to reject a structuralist notion of the body—such as one that would treat the anatomical body map, with its organs, limbs, and systems, as the foundation for all embodied technique—and instead to recognize that structural mappings of the body are contingent upon particular kinds of technique. The concept of technique presumes no universal or ideal body. Instead, it approaches embodiment as a field of variation, between individuals and also within the lifetime of an individual being. This field of relative reliability and variation is what affords embodied technique as an area of knowledge.

From ballet to soccer, from martial arts to meditation, from tango to prayer, from fighting to lovemaking, the development of new embodied technique continually demands new mappings and understandings of the body. Every area of technique has its basis in the materiality of human embodiment, including our capacities for rhythm, vocalization, movement, empathy, imaginative play, and vastly more. In each case, technique structures embodied practice not absolutely but provisionally, through an engagement with the affordances of embodiment. Differences between bodies will require adjustments in technique—which may be slight or substantial—as would swimming in a liquid other than water. Nevertheless, because of the relative similarities between bodies, and because the properties of water are relatively constant, knowledge of swimming can be shared between people—and even, as Mauss showed, between cultures. New discoveries about or within the technique of swimming can be made to fulfill a variety of purposes. Swimming for speed will differ from swimming for aesthetic display, for fitness, for work, for relaxation, or for religious purposes. Two different societies may come up with very different approaches to swimming, or they may independently arrive at similar technique. As knowledge about the affordances of embodiment and materiality, swimming technique structures every concrete example of swimming practice.

Branches and pathways

We might choose any number of metaphors with which to visualize the relation of technique to practice. The one I will elaborate here is that of *technique as a network of fractally branching pathways that vein the substance of practice.* There are ample precedents for such a view, beginning with the old idea that knowledge can be "divided into branches" that traverse different "territories," "fields," and "frontiers" (Shumway and Messer-Davidow 1991: 202, 208).[10] Shove *et al.* point to the routes and pathways along which "social practices" travel in the course of a day or lifetime (2012: 69–79; and see Pred 1981). Andrew Pickering writes of scientific inquiry in terms of routes, trajectories, and vectors, referring also to the present as "branching endlessly into the future" through the emergent interaction of social and material forces (1995: 212). Thomas Kuhn's famous idea of paradigm shifts—an early landmark in social epistemology—can be diagramed in precisely this way (Wray 2011: 125). I take it that the metaphor of branching pathways can be concretely applied to specific areas of technique in at least two ways: first, as the development and sedimentation of repeatable pathways of action within an individual practitioner; and second, as a lineage or "family tree" of related practices undertaken by different groups or individuals. John Lutterbie elaborates on the former by comparing the development of neural pathways in acting and dance technique to the creation of a "rail system" in which trains "follow set patterns, and different trains use the same tracks before they branch off in different directions" (2011: 158). He borrows from a psychological study of memory to suggest that neural patterning functions like "veins in a leaf" (202). On a larger historical scale, Jonathan Pitches visualizes the "Stanislavsky tradition" in acting as a tree-like network of branches (2006: frontispiece; and see Pitches 2007). What these diverse images have in common is a *nonspatial, multiplicitous linearity*, in which each path represents a distinct and repeatable potentiality afforded by the material world.

The metaphor of branching pathways reveals two important features of the relationship between technique and practice: First, technique is not flat; it has depth. Second, technique is not singular; it is complex, even fractal, in the sense of an iterative pattern of unlimited branching that permeates the substance of practice without filling it.[11] The relationship between technique and practice is not binary or dualistic in the sense of a division of reality into two categories. Rather, the same phenomena are addressed in terms of both practice and technique. If we look at chunks of human life bounded in time and space, we are looking at practices. If we look instead at the transmissible knowledge that links such chunks together across time and space, we are looking at technique. Every instance of practice is saturated by technique along dimensions that we can metaphorically refer to as *epistemic depth and breadth*. The epistemic pathways of technique have depth in the sense that comprehension of some knowledge affords new possibilities for additional understanding not otherwise accessible. For this reason, specialized knowledge in any field is not directly accessible from the surface of everyday, commonplace knowledge. One has to find one's way into it, proceeding step by step along its paths. On the other hand, knowledge also has breadth in that different branches lead to different epistemic territories. The path to understanding advanced mathematics is entirely different from the path to understanding how to play the game of basketball or how to track an animal in the woods. Even the initial steps are different, while later steps are irrevocably separated, as if in different worlds.

In the sociology of knowledge, the distances separating divergent epistemic worlds are attributed to the phenomenon of "incommensurability" (Pickering 1995: 186; and see Wray 2011: 65–77). This refers to a basic feature of disciplinarity that derives from the branching structure of knowledge: No science or discipline can fully account for another. While two disciplines may find points of interdisciplinary contact, there is no extradisciplinary standpoint from which to construct an overall hierarchy of disciplines. In this sense, the efforts of sociology to reveal the "disunity" of science (Galison and Stump 1996) apply equally well to nonscientific disciplines and even to the epistemic dimensions of everyday life. Alva Noë has theorized incommensurability from a cognitive perspective by observing that "differences in the ways we go about achieving access to what there is" account for substantial "*variations* in the way the world shows up for us," which he calls "the varieties of presence" (2012: 33). Sara Ahmed examines the same phenomenon from a cultural and phenomenological perspective:

> When we follow specific lines, some things become reachable and others remain or even become out of reach. Such exclusions—the constitution of a field of unreachable objects—are the indirect consequences of following lines that are before us: we do not have to consciously exclude those things that are not

"on line." The direction we take excludes things for us, before we even get there.

(Ahmed 2006: 14–15)

In the present context, the incommensurability of knowledge means that following a particular line or pathway of embodied technique opens up a particular range of new possibilities while foreclosing others. This notion of epistemic incommensurability should not be confused with an uncritical relativism that would render all perspectives and opinions equal. Rather, what is at stake is a critical interdisciplinarity that recognizes the diverse ways in which epistemic practices variously achieve their "grip" upon the world (see Dreyfus and Dreyfus in Weiss and Haber 1999: 103). For our purposes, an important addition to the work of Ahmed and Noë is Pickering's recognition that, although epistemic pathways are unlimited in number, they are not for that reason trivial to discover. Although there are infinitely many possible "grips on the world," the experimental or empirical researcher finds that most attempts to proceed along a new pathway simply "do not work" (Pickering 1995: 190, x). Sustained inquiry—that is, research—is needed to extend the pathways of knowledge in particular directions.

In a sense, all skilled practices involve this kind of attentive engagement with the materiality of the world. As Tim Ingold writes, practical skill "rhythmically couples action and perception along paths of movement" by "bringing together the resistances of materials, bodily gestures and the flows of sensory experience" (2011: 16). What Ingold calls the "resistances of materials" are precisely those relative reliabilities that make possible every kind of craft. For example, in a metal like lead, its "ductility, heaviness, low melting point, resistance to electrical current, impenetrability to X-rays, and toxicity" (29). Such resistances or reliabilities provide the material basis for technique of every kind. Manuel De Landa's extraordinary history of war offers a similar account of the "tracking" of material "singularities" in the development of destructive technologies (De Landa 1991: 26). Like Ingold, De Landa reveals not only the instrumental utility of such discoveries but also the depth and variety of technical knowledge. The artisan, De Landa writes, must "follow the accidents and local vagaries of a given piece of material," letting it "have its say in the final form produced" and taking part in a "sensual interplay with metals" or other materials (30). In the present context, we are concerned with exactly this kind of skillful, experimental practice as it pertains to the materiality of embodiment. I aim to show that specialized practitioners like dancers and athletes track singularities in the materiality of embodiment with exactly the same artisan care as the woodworkers and metalsmiths described by Ingold and De Landa.[12]

In this sense, embodied technique is the very stuff of life, the fabric of practical knowledge, the network or "meshwork" (Ingold 2011: 63) of epistemic threads along which life is lived and experienced. Technique is everywhere (which is not to say that everything is technique). Its ubiquity becomes apparent if we scan any text for the word "way." More often than not, this common and inconspicuous noun is used to describe the *how* of an action, the specific path-ways along which a body moves or through which an action develops. When we replace "way" or "ways" with "technique," we begin to see just how omnipresent this kind of knowledge is. Technique structures the "way" we think, move, and understand ourselves. Its pathways are "ways of life," as in what anthropologists call *folkways* (Lomax 1968) or *foodways* (Sutton 2014). Technique is found in "the *ways* in which from society to society men know how to use their bodies" (Mauss 2006: 78, italics added in all citations); transmitted as "a *durable way* of standing, speaking, walking, and thereby of feeling and thinking" (Bourdieu 1990: 70); and explored through artistic practice as "*ways of doing and making* that intervene in the general distribution of *ways of doing and making*" (Rancière 2004: 13). Performance is an inclusive term for how "humans represent themselves in *embodied ways*" (Zarrilli *et al.* 2010: xx). Schools enforce norms "by demanding that students perform themselves and their physical relationships to their environment in *particular ways*" (Sandahl and Auslander 2005: 215). Environments "depend upon pre-discursive *ways of proceeding* which both produce and allow changes in bodily state" (Thrift 2008: 236). Technique is "the *ways* in which bodies inhabit different sexes and genders" (Salamon 2010: 71); it enables the enactment of a gesture "in an idiosyncratic and potentially subversive *way*" (Noland 2009: 214); it is the territory in which we find new "*ways* of being queer" (Warner 1993: xiii); and the basis of capitalism as a search for "new *ways* ... in which the human body can be put to use as the bearer of the capacity to labor" (Harvey 2000: 104). The embodiment of Zen Buddhism through martial and artistic technique is studied in Trevor Leggett's *Zen and the Ways* (1987); the art of improvisation in David Sudnow's *Ways of the Hand* (2001). These are just a few selections from among thousands that suggest how an epistemology of practice might be read back into key texts of philosophy and cultural studies. Even Heidegger's "ways of being" can be read either as "ways of *being*" or as "*ways* of being" (1982: xix). Of course, the point here is not to quibble over words but to suggest the extent of epistemic engagement that living entails.

Technique, then, is not a type of practice but a veritable ocean that underlies all practices. For that reason, I employ "technique" in this book as a continuous rather than a discrete noun. References to "a" technique suggest the finality of a coherent recipe or algorithm, whereas technique is actually structured in limitless detail at all levels of scale. As I argue in subsequent chapters, the notion of techniques (or "Techniques" with a capital "T") as coherent objects or systems usually has more to do with competitive marketing strategies than with a desire to accurately describe how practices are structured. While many teachers and practitioners describe their technique as if it were a stable and coherent entity—some even going so far as to trademark their particular brand—I will studiously avoid doing so here. Instead, I propose, technique behaves grammatically as a continuous noun, like mathematics or history, water or hope.[13] We can talk about elements or details of technique, or about specific technical pathways, but the enumeration of such elements is not equivalent to knowledge. Rather, knowledge involves a vast collection of such elements in aggregate, as well as countless relationships among them and contexts in which they might be applied. In contrast, I do refer to individual practices, as these are always bounded in time and space and attached to particular bodies and contexts.

Linguistic peninsulas

The theoretical shift towards embodiment and practice that undergirds this project comes on the heels of an earlier "linguistic" turn that emphasized the role of language and discourse in structuring individual consciousness and society. Because of the influence of that turn, it is important to clarify at this point that technique is not reducible to language, discourse, or signification. Rather, language—in the present model—is a particular kind of technique. To grasp this idea, we can borrow an idea from anthropologist Roy Rappaport, who asks why

> humans, who have a range of codes and markers to choose from, employ precise, subtle, energetically and materially inexpensive speech for the transmission of some messages and comparatively crude, expensive and sometimes painful physical acts for the transmission of others.
>
> (Rappaport 1999: 112; and see Strathern and Stewart 1998)

While the awkwardness of reducing physical acts to "messages" reveals the limitations of a semiotic approach, Rappaport's point about the relative energetic costs of different kinds of technique allows us to define language as a particular kind of embodied technique: that in which there is a relatively low ratio between effort and articulation. In speech, the orchestration of lips, tongue, and vocal cords allow for tremendous variation in detail with a relatively tiny expenditure of physical effort. This makes vocal production an excellent bodily site for language. The existence of gestural languages (e.g., sign language) shows that the hands and arms can also be used in this way. Both speech and gesture take place in "peninsulas" of the body: relatively small regions in which minimal effort can produce an extraordinarily wide range of articulated forms. The vast range of energetically inexpensive articulation available in these peninsulas produces what are called "signs": embodied actions that acquire virtually all their meaning through their relations with other signs, rather than through the bodily efforts required to produce them.[14]

The relative physical ease with which language is produced can sometimes allow its grounding in bodily and material production to go unremarked or unacknowledged. This makes language incredibly powerful—and the technology of writing, which has grown exponentially less energetically expensive with time, increases that power enormously, to the point where it can seem as if language determines our whole lives. Still, we should not exaggerate the independence of language from bodies. Language is just one aspect of the embodied technique that shapes and structures our lives from birth. Judith Hamera writes, "technique, like language, reaches out to meet us as we are birthed into dance" (2007: 4). Leaving out the qualification "into dance" gives us a broader perspective: Technique, like language, reaches out to meet us, to envelop us, to structure our lives and relationships, and indeed to make life possible, from the moment we are born. This is not because technique is a kind of language. Rather, language is one aspect of the technique that reaches out to us. Like other embodied technique, language is grounded in the relatively reliable possibilities of embodiment: Whatever sounds or gestures comprise a given language must be material possibilities, physical pathways through human embodiment. While tongues and hands are ideally suited to produce language, because of the ease with which they can produce a wide range of identifiably different signifiers, there is no limit in principle to what can be linguistic in this sense. Language is simply technique in which symbolic meaning takes precedence over the meaning of effortful embodied production.

The distinction between energetically "expensive" and "inexpensive" technique is of course not politically innocent. When hundreds of bodies are used to spell out words on the field of a sports match or parade, the physical effort made by those bodies is overshadowed by the symbolic meaning of the forms they take on. The same can be said for mass gymnastic displays that discipline and formalize the movement of large numbers of bodies to political ends (Roubal 2003). In such contexts, the whole body—rather than just vocal production—becomes the material basis for discursive production and linguistic technique. For this reason, it is important to avoid taking language as metaphor for embodied practice, as theorists of dance have sometimes done (Foster 1986; Hamera 2007). Even when the semiotic content of a practice seems paramount, we should not ignore or discount the embodied effort that makes it possible. Dance is linguistic only to the extent that we fail to recognize the physical work it entails: not just the effort involved in a single performance, but the long-term effort of training and rehearsal. It is only by ignoring this work that we can "read" dance as a text composed of signs. And this point applies not only to dance, but to all kinds of embodied technique, including that of everyday life. When we "read" embodied practice in terms of signification alone, we ignore much of its meaning, which is located not in the relationship between signs but in the quantity and quality of embodied effort that goes into the enactment of technique. Signification, in this sense, is a surface phenomenon. It is an important dimension of the meaning and effectiveness of embodied technique, but by no means the only one.

Sedimented agency

I stated above that the practice of technique may be habitual or innovative, conscious or unconscious, freely chosen or coerced. Yet how can technique be knowledge, if it is not always available to conscious thought? How can practice be epistemic, if it may not be freely chosen? In this section, I clarify the nature of technique by suggesting that agency can be sedimented in and as embodiment, even when we are not consciously aware of it. We know from theorists of the "practice turn" that knowledge is not fully available to consciousness. For any explicit concept or principle to function in practice, there must be what Charles Taylor calls an "unarticulated background" to support it (in Shusterman 1999: 31; see also Casey 1987; Connerton 1989). Cognitively oriented philosophers like Alva Noë see this phenomenon in a positive light, pointing to how the "solid embedding" of skills makes possible apparently simple tasks like reading (Noë 2012: 10). But the same "solid embedding" also reproduces social divisions and hierarchies. Modern societies dedicate a great deal of energy to ensuring that the technique of reading is internalized during childhood by as many people as possible, thereby turning what was once a highly specialized skill into everyday technique. Although this training is socially imposed and eventually becomes involuntary (think of how difficult it is to look at a word you know well and *not* read it), it is usually seen as empowering rather than coercive. Yet many societies today make participation difficult for those who cannot read—not to mention exclusions via implicit hierarchies of language, dialect, and style. We therefore need to ask how the technique of reading is implemented at various levels. Reading may at once be a proud achievement for a specific child; a political act for a disempowered community; an apparatus of social control for the government; a defining element of cultural identity; and more. Each of these is made possible by the fact that reading is, most fundamentally, an area of technique.

Michel Foucault's "discipline," Pierre Bourdieu's "habitus," and Judith Butler's "performativity" are all ways of understanding the limits of agency and consciousness in the face of social norms and ideologies.[15] In strikingly parallel passages, both Bourdieu and Butler sharply distinguish between the embodied practices that reproduce society and the conscious will or agency of individuals. For Bourdieu, *habitus* is "embodied history, internalized as a second nature and so forgotten as history" (1990: 56). Entirely distinct from personal agency, mastery of habitus "is only possible for someone who is completely mastered by it, who possesses it, but so much so that he is totally possessed by it, in other words depossessed" (14). Such mastery is then illusory, since no real agency is involved. According to Bourdieu, habitus is learned through a "practical mimesis" that "implies an overall relation of identification" rather than any conscious effort (73). This suggests two entirely different kinds of training: While conscious imitation may be an act of individual agency, the unconscious mimesis that reproduces habitus is "opposed to both memory and knowledge" because it takes place "below the level of consciousness." Bourdieu concludes: "What is 'learned by body' is not something that one has, like knowledge that can be brandished, but something that one is." Here I will appropriate this useful formulation in order to claim just the opposite: namely, that epistemic practice involves a continuous and mutually constituting transformation, back and forth, between the two categories of conscious and unconscious knowledge, or what one *has* (knowledge) and what one *is* (identity).

Bourdieu's distinction between conscious knowledge and unconscious habitus is repeated in one of Butler's best-known passages, where she separates performance from *performativity*. According to Butler, "performance as bounded 'act' is distinguished from performativity insofar as the latter consists in a reiteration of norms which precede, constrain, and exceed the performer and in that sense cannot be taken as the fabrication of the performer's 'will' or 'choice'" (1993a: 234). Since the time of that writing, Butler and others have struggled to disentangle the concepts of performance and performativity.[16] For my purposes here, the important point is that technique spans both categories: It is at once the conscious knowledge that structures performance and the "relational infrastructure" (Hamera 2007: 19) of performativity. Performativity is the power of technique to create the context for its own reproduction: It demands that we master and be mastered by certain kinds of technique (and not others), absorbing it into our bodies as habitus. Processes of socialization and enculturation induct us into an epistemic world that preexists us, and much of what we learn involves how to reproduce society in its current form. However, technique is more than a structure that one unwittingly enters and reproduces. As Carrie Noland reminds us: "Normative behavior may be coercively imposed (as in Foucault's account) or actively sought, imitated during infancy or gained incrementally throughout one's entire life" (Noland 2009: 3). Nor can we easily classify specific areas or branches of technique as either oppressive or liberatory, since the same technique can function very differently depending on context. The situation is complex.

Habitus and performativity emphasize the power of unconscious over conscious technique. These ideas serve as an important counterweight to a long history of European philosophy that imagined the knowing subject as master and possessor of "his" own conscious and explicitly rational knowledge (as in Descartes). Whereas rationalist epistemology was grounded in the ideal of a fully conscious agency, constructionist theories like those of Bourdieu and Butler tend to understate the importance of both consciousness and agency. A very different picture emerges if we begin by more closely examining Alva Noë's "solid embedding," or what John Matthews calls "automaticity": a form of deeply sedimented agency that is the hallmark of advanced training in any field (Matthews 2011: 186). One has only to look at a rigorously trained musician, dancer, or athlete to see that agency cannot be identified with consciousness. As Ruth Leys observes, "skilled pianists are not consciously aware of the innumerable movements their fingers must make during a performance, but this does not make those movements unintentional or negate the fact that the pianists intended to play the music" (2011: 455; and see Ingold 2011: 59–61). If agency were the same as consciousness, we would have to say that advanced performers and athletes give up their agency when they train to the point of automaticity. Yet such training is clearly intended to increase rather than decrease the practitioner's sense of agency by expanding their capacities.

In Bourdieu's terms, the sharp distinction between what one "has" and what one "is" fails to account for the fact that the latter develops directly out of the former. Long-term education and training result in the sedimentation of conscious into unconscious knowledge. In the initial moment of learning, one "has" or possesses knowledge. Later on, one comes to "be" it. Whether this moment of *automatization* is regarded as oppressive or liberating depends upon the specific relationship between a practitioner and an epistemic field. Nor is it simply the case that specialized practitioners, like musicians and dancers, strive to achieve empowered automaticity, while training in everyday life uses automaticity to reproduce oppressive social norms. On the contrary, highly specialized technique leading to the most extraordinary performances may be imposed coercively upon its practitioners, while the everyday practice of what is traditional or conventional may be full of empowerment and agency. The former point has been made by Jon McKenzie, who critiques the "liminal norm" of performance studies: the assumption that moments of performance are necessarily transgressive with respect to social norms (1998). On the other hand, the assumption that traditional, everyday practices are necessarily enacted under conditions of non-agency has been roundly critiqued by Saba Mahmood in her ethnographic work on the daily religious practices of women in the Muslim piety movement in Egypt.

Mahmood calls for a more nuanced examination of how the embodied technique of daily religious practice is learned in both childhood and adulthood (2005: 138, 162). Against the prevailing assumption that agency is "the capacity to realize one's own interests against the weight of custom, tradition, transcendental will, or other obstacles," Mahmood illustrates how agency can also work through precisely those channels of embodied technique that are most traditional and quotidian (8). The women Mahmood describes practice "the cultivation of those bodily aptitudes, virtues, habits, and desires that serve to ground Islamic principles within the practices of everyday living," treating the mosque itself as a site for "training in the requisite strategies and skills to enable such a manner of conduct" (45). In this context, embodied technique is intended as much to shape the subject from within as to affect her external environment. Thus, the desire to pray may be not merely the cause of prayer but also its result: In praying, we actively cultivate both the ability to pray and the pious self who prays. This point recalls Nick Crossley's account of the indirect and reflexive use of technique to bring about sleep or arouse particular emotions. It also underscores the need to disentangle the extent to which technique is traditional or socially mandated from its effects upon a given practitioner.

Like Leys, Mahmood invokes the example of a skilled pianist who "submits herself to the often painful regime of disciplinary practice, as well as to the hierarchical structures of apprenticeship, in order to acquire the ability—the requisite agency—to play the instrument with mastery." In some cases, then, a subject's agency may actually be

> predicated upon her ability to be taught, a condition classically referred to as "docility." Although we have come to associate docility with the abandonment of agency, the term literally implies the malleability required of someone in order for her to be instructed in a particular skill or knowledge—a meaning that carries less a sense of passivity than one of struggle, effort, exertion, and achievement.
>
> (Mahmood 2005: 29)

By drawing an explicit link between the highly trained musician and the practitioner of traditional religious identity, Mahmood reveals the limitations of theoretical perspectives that associate submission, discipline, and hierarchy with disempowerment and the loss of agency. It is not that Mahmood argues on behalf of such dynamics as inherently liberating. Rather, she suggests that we need a more complex account of agency: one that does not assume that traditional technique is always coercive, or that transgressive technique is necessarily empowering or freeing, but instead pays closer attention to the specific and contextual relationship between practitioner and practice.

There may be substantial similarities between the child who learns, through processes of socialization, to practice the embodied technique of a particular social class, gender, or religion, and the adult who learns a specialized skill, such as playing the piano. In fact, if we more closely examine these categories, we find that the assumption of a difference in age between the two types of trainees does not hold up. It is not as if only mature adults undertake specialized athletic and artistic training, while training in culture and social identity is imposed upon helpless infants. There are plenty of contexts in which children undergo intensive athletic or artistic training from a very young age, dedicating much of their waking life to a particular area of specialized technique. There are also contexts in which adults work to acquire the embodied technique of a social class, gender, or religion that is different from that into which they were born. We cannot then assume any particular causal link between consciousness and agency. Instead, we must expand our idea of agency so that it extends beyond the conscious mind. This does not mean that all technique involves agency. The point is rather that we cannot determine the relationship between technique and agency, in any given case, by discovering the contents of a practitioner's conscious mind. Deeply trained, sedimented, automatic technique may nevertheless be a manifestation of profound agency. On the other hand, technique may be enacted with full consciousness but without freedom of choice. Technique that is freely chosen at one time may later become a cage, while that which one learns under duress may later be experienced as part of one's truest self. Moreover, technique is continually moving back and forth between conscious and unconscious domains, as Richard Wilk has diagramed (in Shove *et al.* 2009: 149–51).

We must conclude that agency is substantially greater than consciousness. Agency is larger because it can be located at all levels of embodiment, from the most deeply ingrained and profoundly unconscious technique all the way up to what Nigel Thrift calls the "thin band of consciousness." The latter, on the other hand, is quite small. Thrift describes it as "a very poor thing indeed, a window of time—fifteen seconds at most—in which just a few things (normally no more than six or seven) can be addressed, which is opaque to introspection and which is easily distracted" (2008: 236, 6). We can now analyze, in more nuanced terms, Mauss's frustration at the difficulty of unlearning his childhood swimming technique: It is the swimmer's own labor of learning how to swim, as a child, that frustrates him. Back then, perhaps, social performativity demanded that he absorb a particular kind of technique. Now that he wants to change it, he must confront that technique, not as an external force but as knowledge embedded and automatized within his own body. This is not then simply a confrontation between individual agency and social norms (although there is no doubt a social history to the change in technique). Rather, it is a case of split agency, in which the divergence of two approaches to swimming in French society is incarnated as a conflict between two aspects of the same embodied self: the swimmer's deeply sedimented and now largely unconscious knowledge of how to swim and his newly conscious knowledge that there is a better way. Both are technique, but they are sedimented at different levels and to different degrees of embodiment. For this reason, one cannot simply replace the other.

Finally, it is important to note that the sedimentation of technique in and as embodiment is not just a question of learned patterns or muscle memory. Technique can also transform the material structure and physiology of the body in more obvious and measurable ways. Sally Ann Ness calls this the "inward migration" of gestural symbols, observing how in three different types of classical dance—ballet, Bharata Natyam, and Balinese—long-term embodied practice can actually alter the bone structure and anatomy of the human body (in Noland and Ness 2008: 25). Tara McAllister-Viel makes a similar point with regard to how Korean *pansori* singing changes the physiology of the vocal cords (2007). In these examples, the physical body itself is transformed by the practice of technique over time, so that the range of what a given body can do is substantially altered. Nor is such physical inscription limited to the specialized practices of professional dancers, musicians, and athletes. Tim Ingold's comparative analysis of walking (Ingold 2011: 33–50) suggests that different kinds of everyday walking technique can lead to radical differences in ability and even morphology—as when the feet are physically compressed by the wearing of shoes over time. It is therefore no exaggeration to say that different kinds of technique produce different bodies in a literal as well as metaphorical sense. The plasticity of embodiment—the degree to which it can be shaped by technique—is not unlimited. But to whatever extent the anatomy of the body is shaped through technique, physiology itself can be understood as a form of sedimented agency. This adds another dimension to the difficulties one encounters in unlearning or retraining deeply ingrained technique. It also suggests a stronger and more literal sense in which *what we know* becomes *who we are*.

The trope of excess

In the wake of Foucault, Bourdieu, and Butler, some theorists have attempted to define "performance" as inherently or even ontologically resistant to capture and control by the forces of social ideology. One of the ways this is done is through a return to the anti-technique rhetoric that was noted above in the writings of Coleridge, Heidegger, Mumford, Barrett, and Dunne. This perspective holds that the value of poetry— and by extension other creative practices—lies not in technique but in a "residuum" that is "left over once technique has been subtracted" (George 2007: 196). Coleridge called this residuum "genius." Today it may appear under other guises, for example in the commonplace assertion that a given practice or knowledge is "more than" mere technique. I call this essentially romantic gesture the *trope of excess*. It consists in identifying a particular practice as "more than" the enactment of technique and, by implication, dismissing other practices as merely technical.

Teachers and thinkers who make use of the trope of excess are correct in thinking that performance exceeds technique—but they are wrong to consider this a special case. Practice is never reducible to technique. As the image of fractally branching pathways suggests, technique is only ever a network of filaments that gives structure to practice. There is no such thing as a pure enactment of technique. Rather, the assessment of a practice as "merely" technical derives from a refusal to engage with at least some of the technique that structures it, usually because this technique is judged as improper or unworthy. The trope of excess is used in this way to rank practices according to how "technical" they are. One of the problems faced by contemporary performance studies—and, similarly, by critical affect studies—is that it has chosen to define its object of study as a kind of residuum that is "more than" discourse or structure and which inherently resists critical analysis. This makes any attempt to study performance inherently "paradoxical" (Kershaw 2007: 23). In contrast, the theory proposed here acknowledges that practice always exceeds technique, but it does not valorize or romanticize this excess.

Practice exceeds technique because knowledge is limited. All the countless layers of sedimented technique that structure an instance of practice nevertheless fail to determine it. Every chunk of practice exceeds the technique that structures it. There is, then, little to be gained by attempting to name the residuum that is left over when technique is subtracted from practice. Even if we could find an example of a practice entirely unstructured by technique, there is no reason to think that it would be particularly valuable, ethical, or free. The escape of practice from technique only seems like freedom if we treat technique as a constraint. But technique, as we have seen, is more than habitus or performativity. It structures all levels of practice, from the conscious to the unconscious, and is complexly interwoven with agency throughout. There is no way to escape technique, nor any reason to search for such an escape. Rather than attempting to distinguish between practices based on the extent to which they are technical, we would do better to ask what kinds of technique structure a given practice and how different practices may be similar or different at the level of technique. By the same token, rather than searching for a practice that transcends technique, we should search for the pathways and areas of technical exploration that are most necessary to our lives and communities.

We must therefore reject the trend in performance studies that romanticizes the ephemerality of performance. While I have argued that technique is transmissible and repeatable, performance theory has for some time now tended to emphasize the uniqueness and unrepeatability of the live event. What McKenzie has criticized as the "liminal norm" in performance studies (1998) is an example of the trope of excess: It romanticizes and reifies the allegedly excessive qualities of embodied practice, ignoring the extent to which such practice is structured by repeatable technique. A canonical articulation of the trope is found in Peggy Phelan's description of performance as ephemeral:

> Performance's only life is in the present. Performance cannot be saved, documented, or otherwise participate in the circulation of representations *of* representations: once it does so, it becomes something other than performance. To the degree that performance attempts to enter the economy of reproduction it betrays and lessens the promise of its own ontology. Performance's being, like the ontology of subjectivity proposed here, becomes itself through disappearance.
>
> (Phelan 1993: 146)

As early as 1968, Peter Brook wrote: "The one thing that distinguishes the theatre from all the other arts is that it has no permanence" (1968: 129). In the same year as Phelan, Alan Read described theatre as "the transient art *par excellence* ... a unique, unrepeatable moment" (1993: 11). More recently, Jill Dolan has identified theatre as "ineffable," its "ontological status" hovering "between appearance and disappearance" (2005: 8). Erika Fischer-Lichte writes: "Performance does not consist of fixed, transferable, and material artifacts; it is fleeting, transient, and exists only in the present" (2008: 75). Each of these statements romanticizes the ephemerality of performance. Phelan raises this commonplace idea to the level of ontology.

The problem is not that practices like dance and theatre are reducible to technique—they are not—but that the performing arts are not exceptional in this regard. To repeat: All practices, including the most mundane, exceed the technique that structures them. Performance in the sense evoked by Phelan—that of theatrical spectacle—is no more ephemeral than any other practice. As Susan Melrose has astutely observed, the apparent ephemerality of performance is an artifact of spectatorship. "The notions of 'ephemerality,' of time and loss, are essentially spectatorial, in the case of live performance. For the performance-maker, the work of making 'the work,' over time, has never been ephemeral" (Melrose and Sachsenmaier 2013: 61). I would add that the privileging of the spectatorial perspective colludes with the fetishization of technology to make the relative stability of material objects and writing appear as the rule rather than the exception. All practice is ephemeral in that it is bound to a specific time and place and can never be exactly repeated. Indeed, the qualities that Phelan and others attribute to performance almost always have their roots in some kind of preparation, often including years or even decades of training in specialized technique. An epistemology of practice like the one developed here allows us to reclaim the importance of repetition and knowledge transfer in all kinds of embodied practice, including the performing arts, without ignoring the centrality of innovation as well.

It is worth recalling here Diana Taylor's warning about the dangers of romanticizing the ephemeral. "Debates about the 'ephemerality' of performance are," Taylor writes, "profoundly political. Whose memories, traditions, and claims to history disappear if performance practices lack the staying power to transmit vital knowledge?" (2003: 5; and see 142). Like Taylor, I reject the idea that the value of a practice lies in its ephemerality. One goal of this book is to draw attention back to that which is relatively stable and transmissible in embodied practice, and to show how much value, as well as danger, is to be found in repeatability. I maintain that locating the value of nonverbal practices in their disappearance, ephemerality, or unrepeatability risks vastly understating their knowledge content. An actor may perform the same role hundreds of times. A dancer may practice the same gesture or movement thousands of times over the course of a lifetime. It is precisely to draw attention to the role of *knowledge* in structuring practice that I have chosen to theorize technique rather than the terms Taylor proposes: repertoire, scenario, tradition, memory, style. Each of these terms, in a different way, replaces or complicates "performance" by working against the liminal norm and shifting emphasis instead to the flows of embodied knowledge that undergird all kinds of embodied practice. Yet none carries the epistemological weight of technique, the causal link between knowledge and repetition.

The inadequacy of a reductive opposition between technique and its excess is revealed with great clarity in a particular example offered by Randy Martin to illustrate his notion of "composite" technique in the bodies of dancers. In this example, Martin demonstrates that what may appear at first to be pure corporeal impulse—or what Philipa Rothfield calls "corporeal flux" (2009: 222)—can also be interpreted as another layer of technique. Recall that, for Martin, composite technique refers to more than the unintentional appearance of elements from jazz or ballet in a modern dance class; it can also include any kind of trained patterning of the body. At one point, Martin observes the manifestation of an involuntary "quiver" in a dancer's thigh. This quiver, he notes, "could be taken as what is archaic" or "primitive" in the body—or as a kind of general "resistance to technical subordination." However, Martin goes on to observe that it might equally result from the surfacing of a different kind of "technical influence," namely one that specifically aims at the release of muscular tension (1998: 175).[17] In other words, the quiver that at first seems to be pure corporeal excess may actually be the result of a different kind of training. Instead of romanticizing the excess or residue of an allegedly pre- or nontechnical body, Martin proposes to grapple with the complexities of practice by recognizing the sheer diversity of technique.

To sum up: Even if it were possible to isolate something like the remainder or residuum of practice—a practice minus its technical content—that remainder would not necessarily have any special value. To single out the unrepeatable, nontechnical remainder of embodied practice as the essence of its value or authenticity is merely to reiterate the binary division between conscious will and unconscious habit that we saw in Bourdieu's definition of habitus and Butler's of performativity. Ultimately, such romanticism amounts to an antitechnical prejudice that is nothing more than the lingering duality of the mind/body paradigm, even if the transcendent power of mind has been replaced by another kind of transcendence. The trope of excess conflates repetition with power and power with oppression—as if freedom were equivalent to change and repetition were always a cage. But there is nothing particularly free about the absence of technique, even if such an absence could be located. The tendency in performance studies to romanticize the ephemeral should be tempered by a greater appreciation of repetition and transmissible knowledge as the basis for all kinds of practice. Just as we avoid reducing technique to language, we should avoid romanticizing embodiment or performance as transcendent excess. The reductive idea of technique implied by the trope of excess damages our ability to appreciate the diversity of embodied practices and the variety of technique that structures them. I have marked this trope here so that I can refer to it in subsequent chapters.

Research in embodied technique

Training—the passage of technique from one person or community to another—is a crucial part of how technique functions. It may include both explicit and implicit pedagogies, active and passive learning, mandatory and optional engagements. Furthermore, training in embodied technique may involve visual and aural mimesis as well as verbal comments, instructions, and physical adjustments. Much of what is trained in any given moment remains unnamed, and we never know all the uses to which the technique we learn may be put. However, training alone is not sufficient to understand the epistemic workings of technique. As a field of knowledge, technique is constituted by the dynamic interplay of *training* and *research*, where the latter refers to the development of new technique through processes of investigation and exploration. The criterion of *newness* here is a relative one, depending on the context of a specific individual or community: What is new to me may not be new to you. Hence, there are different senses of research and different levels of rigor with which the term may be applied. In a weak sense, knowledge can be new relative to an individual. I can be said to engage in this kind of personal research whenever I train in an area of technique that is new to me. A stronger sense of research is invoked when the criterion of newness pertains to an extended community of knowledge. The strongest sense of research would pertain only to the discovery of a pathway that had never previously been known to anyone.

Where does new technique come from? Mauss tells us that a new technique of swimming had been found, but he does not explain who found it or how. In this section, I argue: *If technique is knowledge, then practice can be research.*[18] We know that we are looking at technique, I have argued, when we recognize people in different eras and locations as engaging with materiality and embodiment in similar ways—that is, making use of analogous material and embodied affordances. In some cases, there may be a historical link or lineage between such practices. In others, we may be observing the phenomenon of independent or "multiple" discovery: Because technique is made up of discoveries about the relative reliabilities of the material world, the same channels or pathways may be uncovered by people working in parallel, without contact or communication (Simonton 1979). I have already referred to such discoveries as products of research. I want now to further examine the concept of *embodied research* or *research in embodied technique*, before applying it in subsequent chapters to specific case studies. I begin once again with the sociology of knowledge, and with socially and culturally aware studies of scientific research, such as those undertaken by Karin Knorr Cetina, Andrew Pickering, and various contributors to *The Practice Turn* (Schatzki *et al.* 2001).

New knowledge emerges from the confluence of social and material factors, the "contours" of which are never known in advance. As a result, the knowledge produced by research is simultaneously "objective, relative, and historical" (Pickering 1995: 14, 33). Although Pickering is talking about the technological discoveries of advanced science, his observation applies equally well to the kinds of knowledge studied here. Embodied technique is *objective* in that it can only be developed out of the field of what is materially possible for bodies to do; it is *relative* in that this field is infinitely complex (fractal), and so admits of an infinite number of possible discoveries; and it is *historical* in that particular lines of inquiry give rise to particular discoveries at particular times and places. While theatre, dance, and performance studies have no trouble acknowledging the subjective and historical aspects of embodied practice, they have only recently begun to look for what is objective in such practices. The cognitive turn cited in the introduction locates objectivity in the physiology and neurology of the body as understood by medical science. Here, I want to leave open the question of what material structures make embodied technique possible, while recognizing that every kind of embodied technique is objectively grounded in material reality. From any existing body of knowledge, an unlimited number of research questions might be posed, indicating an infinite number of possible epistemic pathway extensions. However, it is emphatically not the case that "anything goes" (196). Most initial attempts to realize an extension of knowledge will fail. To extend a field of knowledge therefore requires sustained inquiry. The back and forth movement of such inquiry gives rise to what Pickering calls a "dance" of material and human agency, or a "dialectic of resistance and accommodation" (22). Richard Sennett refers to this phenomenon as "the intimate, fluid join between problem solving and problem finding" (2009: 33).

A great deal of work in the sociology of knowledge and practice is dedicated to describing this epistemic relationality, so aptly characterized by Pickering and Sennett as a "dance" or "fluid join." Laurent Thévenot calls this the "realism" of practice, criticizing the antirealism of those who would analyze "the relation between the agent and his environment in terms of symbolic work, meaning, understanding, interpretation, etc.," rather than as a "dynamics of adjustment" (in Schatzki et al. 2001: 64–65). We have already seen these dynamics at work in Mauss's idea of a "compromise between nature and humanity," as well as Foucault's conjoined "power-knowledge." Cetina's "tinkering" (Cetina 1979), Pickering's "tuning" (1995: 14), and De Landa's "tracking" (1991: 26) all name the artisan care with which the practitioner/researcher engages with the material world. Carrie Noland's "experiential groping" (her translation of André Leroi-Gourhan's *l'expérience par tâtonnement*) connotes less care, instead foregrounding the experience of not-knowing and searching-in-the-dark that is essential to research (Noland 2009: 102). And although most of these authors are referring to engagements with materiality outside the human body, there is no reason why the same concepts cannot be applied to research in embodied technique. Like other research, embodied research is not just hermeneutic. It does more than attempt to interpret or explain the body. It is empirical research of the same type that allows for the development of new technologies—only in this case the investigation aims towards the discovery of new pathways in embodied technique.[19]

If these accounts emphasize the objectivity of research through its thick engagement with materiality, Cetina's essay in *The Practice Turn* offers the most compelling account of the subjective or "libidinal" dimension of research, by highlighting the extent to which scientists pursue their work not merely out of intellectual curiosity or to achieve instrumental goals, but also with joy, passion, and pleasure (Schatzki *et al.* 2001: 186). Particularly relevant to my argument are Cetina's descriptions of the "epistemic objects" with which scientific researchers engage. Unlike everyday objects, with which we interact through "absorbed coping," epistemic objects are fundamentally incomplete; their incompleteness is what challenges researchers and provokes them to research. Here too, although Cetina has in mind the objects of science, such as proteins and subatomic particles, her analysis applies equally well to embodied technique. Cetina describes the researcher's epistemic objects as "characteristically open, question-generating and complex. They are processes and projections rather than definitive things. Observation and inquiry reveals them by increasing rather than reducing their complexity" (Cetina in Schatzki *et al.* 2001: 181). Like the scientist, the researcher who works through embodied practice finds that technique seems to expand and open up in proportion to the amount of attention it is paid. What at first seems to be "a" technique, in the singular, is soon revealed as an *area* of technique harboring potentially limitless detail. In contrast to everyday objects, which are like "closed boxes," the objects of knowledge and inquiry "have the capacity to unfold indefinitely." They are like "open drawers filled with folders extending indefinitely into the depth of a dark closet." In my terms, the "closed box" is technique after it has been mastered. It is the habitus, accessed and enacted unquestioningly. The "open drawer" or epistemic object, by contrast, is technique in the process of development and discovery. In research, one discovers or "unfolds" the "internal articulation" of the epistemic territory with which one grapples and wrestles, tinkers and tunes, compromises and accommodates.

At this point, we may return to the spectrum of differentiation proposed above, between weaker and stronger senses of "research." Charles Spinosa offers an example of research in the weak sense when he describes the process of "elaboration" through which practices in general tend to increase in detail and complexity through repetition. He observes, "whenever we learn a new practice, even a very simple one such as jogging, we find ourselves constantly sensitive to new things to which we had paid scant attention before" (in Schatzki *et al.* 2001: 200). These new sensitivities, Spinosa suggests, allow us to discover new possibilities within previously existing technique. For example, while jogging, we might "experiment to find out if we notice the pain in our legs so much if we jog while trying to solve an intellectual problem." Or, equally, we might notice that we have begun regularly "making the second half of our run with the sea breeze in our faces so that the perspiration would not get in our eyes." Such developments are not possible if we do not first enter into and embody the basic technique of jogging. It is only while jogging, at the edge of existing technique, that we can discover new technique. Yet these kinds of discoveries amount to research only in a weak sense. They are new to the individual jogger Spinosa describes, but not to any community of knowledge, and certainly not to humanity as a whole. Like a high school student writing a research paper, the jogger gains something of value from these discoveries, but the resulting knowledge is hardly new in any greater sense. On the other hand, if we look to the practices of world-class runners and their coaches, then we can legitimately ask whether research may be taking place in the strongest and most rigorous sense of that word. Professional athletes are engaged in a socially sanctioned research project to see how far the body can be pushed in a particular direction. By the same token, the development of a jogging practice among older people, or people with disabilities, could constitute research in a stronger sense, insofar as the adaptation of conventional technique to unconventional bodies and contexts might require the elaboration of new technique.

The problem of the substrate

One advantage of the epistemology of practice developed here is that it allows us to compare technical pathways in terms of how obvious they are—how easily discovered—without assuming that this distinction has any inherent ethical or political significance. A pathway that is difficult to discover, and hence relatively rare, is not necessarily more useful or valuable than one that is presents itself so easily as to appear self-evident—and vice versa. The importance of this point will be evident later on, when I consider examples of embodied technique that are more widespread than can be accounted for through historical influence alone. Here, I only want to underscore that the appearance of a given technique in a variety of cultural contexts, across large distances of geography and history, need not mean it is the only way of doing things. Nor does it necessarily suggest historical influence. Rather, certain ways of doing things may simply be more evident, more obvious, and hence more common. This is an epistemological claim, equivalent to identifying the "low-hanging fruit" of a given epistemic field. On the other hand, one might claim that a given line of technique is genuinely new in all of history, and therefore probably quite difficult to discover. Neither claim implies a value judgment, as neither the oldest nor the newest technique is necessarily the best. However, it is often extremely difficult to ascertain whether a given limitation or apparent impossibility should be attributed to materiality itself or to the inadequacy of existing technique. This inescapable dilemma, which I call the "problem of the substrate," can have thorny political implications.

We generally assume that technique operates upon or with an area of materiality that is distinct from it: particle physics works with particles; chemistry with molecules; woodworking with wood; dance with the (physical) body; etc. However, as social epistemologists have shown, this is not quite correct. We cannot separate the substrate from the technique, because we only come to know the substrate through the technique. We know that there is "something" beyond our knowledge because of how difficult it is to produce rigorous, generalizable knowledge at all; but, by definition, we know nothing about what is beyond present knowledge except its contours, its outline as revealed through epistemic encounters. For example, we do not know anything about subatomic particles—including that they exist at all—except via the technique of science and mathematics through which we encounter them. If we adjust that technique, the nature and existence of those particles may appear to change. We then have the task of ascertaining how the old data fits with the new. Likewise, when new dance technique is developed, our understanding of the body as the substrate of that technique also changes. When technique works, we know that we are dealing with some relatively reliable aspects of reality. But we have no way to access these relative reliabilities except through technique. Sometimes a change in context radically alters the effects of technique, making old technique untenable and requiring the development of a new branch of technique: Newtonian physics does not work at speeds approaching that of light; the woodworking technique developed in one country may not work in other climates or with other species of tree; dance technique may or may not work across different kinds of bodies.

Science does not solve this problem; it only extends our encounters with materiality to include reliabilities that are radically more stable than those of artisan craft and embodied technique. Arguably, the purpose and definition of science is the quantification of the reliability of the world. Yet the world is only as reliable as the technique through which we encounter it. In the chapters that follow, the implicit politics of this point will become evident. How might a paraplegic person practice postural yoga (Chapter 2)? How can someone with an uncommon skeletal structure establish a "neutral" body posture (Chapter 3)? The study of (dis)ability raises the problem of the substrate in ways that trouble existing discourses and articulations of technique in physical culture and performing arts. But the best-known example of this problem is that of sexual difference—a central concern and point of ongoing tension for feminist, queer, and transgender theory and activism (Chapter 4). Does a substrate of sexual difference exist independently from the technique of gender? There is no escaping this problem. Technique necessarily makes assumptions about its substrate in order to function. Perhaps the best we can do is to distinguish between the working assumptions of technique and propositional declarations about the structure of materiality. In the terms of social epistemology: We can recognize the ethical and political importance of the incommensurability of diverse fields of knowledge.

We should be wary of declaring things impossible, since technique is never more than an incomplete and unfinished engagement with the affordances of reality. "The body" for technique is not a stable entity but a relative reliability, no more or less constant than the capacity of technique to work across difference. If walking, swimming, and dancing are well-known areas of technique, this is because the aspects of human embodiment they rely upon are widespread and common. We must not on that account leap to the idea of a universal or normal body. These are simply areas of technique, developed in relation to material constancies and always subject to change, transformation, and further research. Crucially, then, the object of research in embodied technique is not "the body" or even "embodiment" as an abstraction, but technique itself. Such research assumes no ideal body, although it must always work through particular bodies in order to discover possibilities that may then travel beyond them. Knowing how to speak with one's voice is very different from asserting that speech is impossible without a voice. Knowing how to walk with one's legs is not the same as asserting that one needs legs to walk.

New technique, in this sense, cannot be identified with new experiences, new aesthetics, or new ideas. It is neither more nor less than concrete knowledge about the possibilities afforded by the relative reliability of the material world, including our own human embodiment. It is therefore quite wrong to think of embodied technique as a small territory or highly specialized interest. We have only to open the box of such technique to see that it is a vast field of knowledge, relatively stable but continually undergoing change, upon which all our technologies are built. How does embodied technique, in this sense, impact society and culture at the largest scale? How does it cross between public and private, the specialized and the everyday, the ethical and the political? In the following chapters, I offer a range of examples from the domains of physical culture, performing arts, and everyday life. Each has been chosen to illustrate how embodied technique is developed through research; how it travels across geographical, historical, and cultural borders; how it is changed by the world; and how, in turn, it changes the world.

Notes

1 This is not the place for an extended analysis of the merits and limitations of cognitive studies for theorizing embodied knowledge. I will however name three important ways in which cognitive studies differs from social epistemology: (1) Like traditional epistemology, cognitive studies focuses on the individual knower, asking for example how emotion shapes thought or how an organism comes to know its environment. In contrast, social epistemology focuses on the circulation and production of knowledge at a social level. (2) Being grounded in the relatively "hard" sciences, cognitive studies attempts to offer closure on the "problematic of realism" (Pickering 1995: 31) by assuming that the objects of science (neurons, hormones, electrical fields, etc.) delineate the fundamental ontology of consciousness. In contrast, social epistemology leaves the problematic of realism more open, allowing one to adopt a less positivist stance. (3) Perhaps as a result, cognitive studies tends to emphasize similarity—between individuals and between cultures—over difference, at the risk of ignoring the important work of several preceding decades of critical theory. Social epistemology, on the other hand, arises out of a deep engagement with the politics of culture and can be seen as an attempt to integrate poststructuralist insights with the reality claims of science. Attempts to ground embodied practice in biology long predate McConachie's "cognitive turn" (e.g., Lex 1979; Pradier 1990). Yet it remains quite premature to conclude that the biological "condition of having a human body guarantees that people's minds will produce a certain number of unchanging, cross-cultural, perhaps even universal structures" (McConachie and Hart 2006: 8). Such overstatements may explain why "sociologists are rightly concerned about the reductionist tendencies in much neuroscience" (Shilling 2003: 16). Additional comments on the cognitive turn in theatre studies can be found elsewhere in these footnotes.

2 From the perspective of traditional epistemology, it may seem necessary to clarify just how and why social epistemology should be counted as "real" epistemology at all (Goldman 2010). On the other hand, when viewed from a social perspective, traditional epistemology can appear as nothing more than an "apologetics" for positivism, with a "vested interest in denying whatever might place conditions on knowledge" and a marked lack of concern for social and historical contexts (Shumway and Messer-Davidow 1991: 216–17).

3 It may be worth clarifying here that my argument rests ultimately not on the word "technique" but on the relevance of an epistemological perspective to society, culture, politics, and everyday life. I have chosen to retheorize

technique because its conceptual genealogy offers a powerful hinge on which to rotate epistemological concerns back into political ones, without losing track of the role of embodiment and materiality in the production of knowledge. There may be another, more appropriate term with which to track the knowledge content and epistemic structure of embodied practice. But in the present context, I use the word technique to name that idea.

4 According to Haney: "Works of art result from techne—the production of tangible objects through the technique of the artist's craft—but ethics falls under the very different domain of phronesis" (Haney 1999: 32). Here, *techne* produces an external object, whereas *phronesis* applies to action. This distinction makes a concept like Foucault's "techniques of the self" (discussed below) inherently paradoxical: Is not the self precisely that thing of which there can be no technique? I retain this tension in the concept of embodied technique: Is the body objectified by such knowledge, as a product of making or building? Or does technique open up into judgment and ethics? In place of a distinction between *techne* and *phronesis*, I posit two aspects of technical practice: *training*—the repetition or transmission of known, established technique—and *research*—the search for new relatively reliable pathways.

5 After reading Foucault, one can begin to see everything in terms of domination and resistance. But a closer reading reveals that Foucault's understanding of the situation is more complicated. He names more than two kinds of technique, listing in one late interview four different types of "technologies" (1988: 18); and even these four basic categories—which could be expanded upon—do not admit of easy analysis in terms of power and justice. Foucault's thinking did not tend towards binary oppositions; his preferred rhetorical strategy was that of a proliferation of terms. Hence, the idea that specific practices may be classified either as "technologies of domination" or as "technologies of the self" is not very Foucauldian.

6 In a later piece, Crossley further explores the potential of Mauss's work on "body techniques" to "remedy" the alleged disembodiment of sociology (Crossley 2007: 93). This essay is part of a special issue monograph from the *Sociological Review* (Shilling 2007), much of which is relevant to the argument developed here.

7 In *The Dynamics of Social Practice: Everyday Life and How It Changes,* Elizabeth Shove, Mika Pantzar, and Matt Watson offer an overview of practice theory that traces it back to the writings of Ludwig Wittgenstein and Martin Heidegger (Shove et al. 2012: 4–8). Other relevant sources include the pragmatic philosophy of Charles Sanders Peirce, John Dewey, and William James, as well as Pierre Bourdieu's *Logic of Practice* (1990) and Michel de Certeau's *The Practice of Everyday Life* (Certeau 2002). Although practice theory is "commonly thought to deal better with routine reproduction than with innovation" (Shove et al. 2012: 122), my focus here is on how practices change through the innovation of technique.

8 For examples of this usage beyond Schatzki's work, see works coedited and coauthored by Elizabeth Shove. In performance studies, a similar distinction—this time between "practice" and "performance"—has been put forward by Edward Schieffelin: "The relation between performance and practice turns on this moment of improvisation: performance embodies the *expressive dimension of the strategic articulation of practice*" (1998: 199, italics original). Although this solves the immediate problem of the ambiguity of "practice,"

the dyad *practice/performance* carries none of the epistemological significance of *technique/practice.*

9   Technique in this sense can be located in the context of contemporary debates over what Gilbert Ryle articulated as the difference between "knowing-how" and "knowing-that" (2000), which Depraz *et al.* trace back to the pragmatic philosophy of John Dewey (2003: 157–58). These are sometimes seen as distinct and irreducible categories. On the other hand, Jason Stanley argues that "knowing how to do something is the same as knowing a fact" (2011: vii). From my perspective, this is less because know-how is made up of facts than because facts are a kind of know-how. The subsumption of propositional knowledge within the larger category of technique makes my argument a variety of what David Löwenstein calls "practicalism," the view that "propositional knowledge is a species of know-how" (2012). The inverse argument is "intellectualism," which subsumes know-how within know-that. For more contemporary post-Rylean arguments, see Bengson and Moffett (2011).

10   To extend the territorial metaphor: Every *epistemic field* is also a *social field* in which a "game" is played over diverse kinds of "capital" (Bourdieu and Wacquant 1992: 94–115). However, an epistemic field engages with the relative reliabilities of a world that exceeds the social.

11   If the branching pathways of technique are truly fractal in nature, then they are so densely packed that they approach—without ever reaching—the dimensionality of practice itself. Technique is thus more than a linear architecture of practice, for there is no limit to how richly it saturates a given practice. At the same time, even the smallest chunk of practice infinitely exceeds the technique that structures it. The classical popular introduction to fractal geometry is Gleick (1987).

12   Ingold has done substantial conceptual work on what I am calling nonspatial linearity. In *Being Alive,* he champions "the idea of life as lived along lines, or wayfaring; the primacy of movement" (2011: xii). To "dwell" in the sense Ingold develops from Heidegger is not to be stationed somewhere but "to be embarked upon a movement along a way of life. The perceiver-producer is thus a wayfarer, and the mode of production is itself a trail blazed or a path followed" (12). Ingold's previous book, *Lines* (2007), is entirely devoted to this topic.

13   It is sometimes suggested that a shift from "knowledge" to "knowledges" pluralizes knowledge. In fact, this shift renders knowledge discrete rather than continuous and so in a sense accomplishes the opposite of what is intended. But there is a use for "knowledges," if the plural is understood— by analogy to water—as suggesting rivers (disciplines) rather than molecules (facts) of knowledge.

14   In this sense, gesture is closer to language than to movement, as has also been suggested by recent work in cognitive studies (see Lutterbie 2011: 123–24). Because of this, I cannot accept Carrie Noland's broad definition of "gesture" as equivalent to what I am calling embodied technique (2009: 15–16 and *passim*).

15   A possible fourth term in this series would be Basil Bernstein's "code" (see Harker and May 1993). Although I do not specifically address the concept of discipline here, its double-edged connotations make it especially well aligned with technique: Discipline suggests both a punishing regime, as in Foucault, and a branch of knowledge.

16 The question of what does and does not count as "performance" is a founding problem of performance studies (Harding and Rosenthal 2011). While some would claim that just about everything can be analyzed *as* performance, the specifically intentional and communicative connotations of the latter are impossible to finally dissolve. Performance is necessarily "set apart from practice" through "self-consciousness" and what Erving Goffman called "framing" (Kapchan 2003: 131). Or, as Herbert Blau wrote much earlier, performance is "a crucial particle of difference" that distinguishes "between just breathing eating sleeping loving and *performing* those functions" (1983: 140). As a result, the "performance" of everyday life can never be more than a metaphor. On the other hand, some scholars now use "performativity" as a flashier alternative to "performance," without any of the Austinian meaning developed by Butler (e.g., Schieffelin 1998: 199; Hargreaves and Vertinsky 2007: 5; Turner 2005: 7). Such ambiguities are symptomatic of the confusion surrounding performance, performativity, and the performative. Andrew Parker and Eve Kosofsky Sedgwick discuss the problem in *Performativity and Performance* (1995: 2).

17 The technique in question here is that developed by Trisha Brown: "Rather than accumulating muscular resistance in the service of a coherent shaping of the body, release technique yields an emphasis on motional qualities as such" (Martin 1998: 172). For the indirect stimulation of "tremors" in the body, see the vocal technique of Catherine Fitzmaurice (Fitzmaurice Voicework 2014). For embodied technique that prioritizes the indirect, receptive, and sensory in physical culture and dance, see my discussion of somatics in Chapter 2.

18 This is the first articulation of the book's subtitle. Mark Fleishman defines "performance as research" as "a series of embodied repetitions in time, on both micro (bodies, movements, sounds, improvisations, moments) and macro (events, productions, projects, installations) levels, in search of a series of differences" (2012: 29). For my take on performance or practice as research in academia, see Chapter 5.

19 Even Deleuze and Guattari acknowledge that the search for what is unknown must begin from what is known. "This is how it should be done: Lodge yourself on a stratum, experiment with the opportunities it offers ... It is through a meticulous relation with the strata that one succeeds in freeing lines of flight" (1987: 161). The "meticulous relation" with strata or structure is precisely technical.

... when for example Ignatius [of Loyola] recommends praying in rhythm by joining a word of the Pater Noster to each breath, his method is reminiscent of certain techniques of the Eastern Church (the hesychasm of John Climaque, or continuous prayer linked to respiration), to say nothing of course about the disciplines of Buddhist meditation; however, these methods (to stay with those Ignatius could have known) were aimed solely at achieving within oneself an intimate theosophany, a union with God. Ignatius gives the method of prayer a wholly different aim ...

(Barthes 1989: 44)

2

THE INVENTION OF POSTURAL YOGA

Yoga and physical culture

No recent example better illustrates what Mauss called "the phenomenon of borrowing and the spread of techniques" (2006: 47) than the invention and meteoric ascent of postural yoga in the twentieth century. Mauss himself was inspired by yoga in theorizing *les techniques du corps* (see Noland 2009: 35–36), although his understanding of it was far narrower than that of the more recent scholarship considered here. Like other contemporary healing (and martial) arts, postural yoga draws on ancient sources but is an invention of modern times. Yet few contemporary areas of embodied technique can lay claim to the extraordinary commercial success that attends postural yoga today, when countless styles of postural yoga are practiced in an ever-increasing number of studios, gyms, classrooms, and other locations throughout the world. The phenomenon that Elizabeth De Michelis calls "Modern Postural Yoga" (2005) is inextricably woven into globalization through discourses of health, fitness, and spirituality. More recently, in the work of De Michelis and others, the practice of yoga has become a topic of academic study. Examining the development of postural yoga in the twentieth century will help put flesh on the conceptual bones elaborated in the previous chapter, and test what I have called an "epistemology of practice" against a concrete historical case study. The emergence and growth of postural yoga offers a fine example of how new technique is produced through research; how its "borrowing" and transmission are interwoven with social change through negotiations of gender, class, and nation; and how embodied technique remains a focal point of cultural exchange, politics, and innovation today.

This chapter does not attempt to offer a comprehensive history of the emergence of postural yoga, its current status in India, or its development and adaptation in Europe and the United States. Excellent historical and sociological work on this topic has been done by scholars like De Michelis, Mark Singleton, and Joseph Alter. In recent years, their scholarship has been supplemented by numerous works directed to a mainstream audience, from journalistic accounts of yoga's rise to popularity (Syman 2010) and current practice (Broad 2012) to medical-anatomical studies (Coulter 2001), as well as countless personal narratives, self-help books, and manuals. My intention here is to intervene in the burgeoning discourse around modern postural yoga by offering a specifically epistemological perspective that treats it as a field of knowledge. Contemporary postural yoga, I will argue, is an outcome of sustained and focused research in embodied technique. Moreover, yoga practice is structured by a complex field of technique in which both training and research are ongoing. Its place in the larger territory of physical culture, spirituality, and cultural politics remains open and mobile. A similar point could be made about any number of dance forms and martial arts, not just in the twentieth century but across history. The spread of postural yoga over roughly the past hundred years is only a particularly clear and commercially successful example of this phenomenon.

I understand "modern postural yoga" (part of the much broader category of yoga in general) as part of the landscape of physical culture. Although the term "physical culture" is most often associated with sport, it can be used to indicate a much wider area of embodied technique, as a few recent definitions will illustrate. Heather Addison defines physical culture as "an umbrella term for those activities that attempt to modify the size or shape of the body to improve health or appearance," noting that such activities may include "dieting, muscle-building, and aerobic exercise" (2003: 1). Susan Grant observes that physical culture in Soviet Russia "was much broader than simply sport and exercise. It in fact covered a wide spectrum ranging from hygiene and health issues to sports, defence interests, labour concerns, leisure, education, and general cultural enlightenment" (2013: 1). Finally, for Jennifer Hargreaves and Patricia Vertinsky, physical culture refers to all "those activities where the body itself—its anatomy, its physicality, and importantly its forms of movement—is the very purpose, the *raison d'être*, of the activity" (2007: 1). In the present context, physical culture will be understood as an area of embodied technique in which the physicality of the body is of primary importance. It is impossible to draw a clear boundary between the physical body and its emotional, psychological, vocal, or imaginative capacities, but clear boundaries are not required to define a territory of knowledge. At the very least, physical culture includes sports, exercise, fitness, gymnastics, martial arts, and the movement technique (rather than the theatrical presentation) of circus and dance. It is within this landscape that contemporary postural yoga—which emphasizes the position, movement, and alignment of the body over other aspects of traditional yoga—has achieved its astonishing global popularity.

A royal success

Much of what is currently practiced under the name "yoga" dates to the early twentieth century. It is not a direct continuation of ancient yogic tradition, but rather a conscious invention of modern times. In *Yoga Body: The Origins of Modern Posture Practice*, Mark Singleton describes the relationship of modern postural yoga to traditional Indian practice as one of "radical innovation and experimentation" (2010: 33). He further observes that premodern or "classical" yoga was never a monolithic entity but was always characterized by "fragmentation, accretion, and innovation" (13). There is no single ancient tradition of yoga, and those very old texts and documents that do exist have strikingly little in common with most current practice. Singleton likens the construction of the "classical" in postural yoga to that which took place in Indian music and dance around the same time (in Singleton and Byrne 2008: 87; and see O'Shea 2006). In each of these cases, the authority of an allegedly ancient and classical tradition was grafted onto a set of distinctly modern practices. They are fine examples of what Eric Hobsbawm and Terence Ranger have called "invented traditions" (1983).

According to Singleton, the growing influence of Indian nationalism in the late nineteenth century provoked a radical period of change in which yoga moved out of the domain of esoteric religious practice and into that of physical culture—a phrase that was just coming into general usage at the time to refer to the growing practice of gymnastic exercises in Europe and elsewhere. In many cases, an explicitly competitive rhetoric surrounded Indian and European physical culture, with innovators like Swami Kuvalayananda (1883–1966) developing his own approach to postural yoga at least partly through direct rivalry with European organizations like the YMCA (Singleton 2010: 91–94). During this period, yoga rapidly expanded through the inclusion of physical technique borrowed from therapeutic gymnastics, calisthenics, and bodybuilding. At the same time, other kinds of technique that had once been included in yoga were left aside as remnants of an earlier age, until gradually the image of the yogi as an isolated Hindu ascetic was replaced by that of the Indian strongman. Numerous individuals played important roles in this dramatic shift, as Singleton and other scholars of modern yoga have noted. However, no one deserves more credit for conducting influential and substantive *research* in yoga technique than Tirumalai Krishnamacharya (1888–1989), a renowned teacher and practitioner whose innovations in yoga technique have been enormously influential.

Krishnamacharya's influence on contemporary yoga practice is both wide and deep. As one article in *Yoga Journal* puts it: "Whether you practice the dynamic series of Pattabhi Jois, the refined alignments of B. K. S. Iyengar, the classical postures of Indra Devi, or the customized vinyasa of Viniyoga, your practice stems from one source: a five-foot, two-inch Brahmin born more than one hundred years ago in a small South Indian village" (Ruiz 2001). My contention is that Krishnamacharya deserves to be called a researcher in the strictest sense of that term. His research in yoga technique was part of a dynamic milieu of experimentation and investigation, which was supported socially and politically by the modernization of India and its nascent political independence. As such, it provides an excellent example of the confluence of social and material factors discussed in the previous chapter. While Krishnamacharya's research would probably never have been conducted without the particular social context that made it possible, its content goes beyond the social and is rigorously epistemic to the extent that it involves the discovery of real and specific possibilities afforded by the relative reliability of human embodiment. It exemplifies what Andrew Pickering calls a "dance" of material and human agency (1995: 22). A brief biographical sketch of Krishnamacharya will illustrate this point. (For more substantial accounts, see Desikachar 2005 and Mohan 2010.)

In the early 1930s—or as early as 1926, according to some sources—the Maharaja Krishnaraja Wodiyar IV of the south Indian kingdom of Mysore invited Krishnamacharya to begin teaching yoga in his palace (Singleton 2010: 177). A highly educated Brahmin with multiple degrees in philosophy and religion from several Indian universities, Krishnamacharya had previously spent seven years in Tibet under the tutelage of a guru named Rama Mohana Brahmacari. The training he received in Tibet went by the name of yoga, but even then many Indians would have considered its technique outdated and extreme. The term *hatha yoga* was then in the process of being reframed and rehabilitated, secularized and nationalized. What Krishnamacharya called "hatha yoga" was primarily aimed at curing and preventing illness. It involved much more than today's practices of *asana*, or postures, along with breathing exercises (*pranayama*), chanting, and meditation. In his 1934 book, Krishnamacharya's illustrated discussion of *asana* is preceded by a discussion of bodily exercises that might well be shocking to many contemporary practitioners. For example, he explains how to gradually cut and pull one's tongue so that, after three years, it will be able to reach out far enough to touch the forehead (1934: 47). Another exercise involves standing in water and pushing the large intestine out of the anus, so as to wash it before putting it back inside the body (39). The contrast between this kind of technique—which Krishnamacharya says should be practiced in an *ashram* far away from crowded cities—and that of today's urban yoga studios suggests the extent of yoga's transformation over the past hundred years.

Krishnamacharya was invited multiple times to take up a highly respected religious position in the Vaisnava Hinduism into which he was born. However, he chose instead to follow the path indicated to him by his guru, to teach and popularize yoga (Desikachar 2005: 79). By 1931, the Maharaja of Mysore had realized how much Krishnamacharya's mission was in line with his own desire to support and promote a distinctly Indian physical culture that could rival those of Europe. Throughout the 1920s and 1930s, the Maharaja had "actively fostered a climate of eclectic, creative physical culture in Mysore State," promoting the development of physical culture "based on a spirit of radical fusion and innovation" (Singleton 2010: 179). Hence, by the time he invited Krishnamacharya to begin teaching, Mysore was already "a pan-Indian hub of physical culture revivalism" (177). Krishnamacharya was among several practitioners working under the Maharaja to rejuvenate the practice of yoga, but through his students he would exert the most profound influence on its transformation and globalization. According to N. E. Sjoman, much of what we now call modern postural yoga was developed during the Mysore period of Krishnamacharya's work (1996: 52). To a certain degree the spread of this technique may be attributed to the entrepreneurial strategies of his students—but there is no doubt that Krishnamacharya himself made concrete technical innovations that would prove to be massively exportable and expandable as the twentieth century progressed.

To popularize yoga for the modern age, Krishnamacharya began to focus more on the practice of *asana*, expanding the number of poses and transforming the way in which they were linked to breath and to each other. While it is impossible to comprehensively enumerate the different strands of embodied technique that Krishnamacharya drew into the practice of yoga during those decades, Sjoman considers Indian wrestling, bodybuilding, and English gymnastics to be important parts of the landscape of physical culture within which Krishnamacharya was working and out of which the modern forms of postural yoga emerged. Through a point-by-point comparison between an 1896 gymnastics manual and the 1966 classic *Light on Yoga* by Krishnamacharya's most famous student, B. K. S. Iyengar, Sjoman shows that what emerged from Mysore during this period was a "syncretism," drawing heavily on gymnastics "but presenting it under the name of yoga" (Sjoman 1996: 55). Singleton likewise affirms that Krishnamacharya drew on Indian wrestling and games as well as European sport and gymnastics in developing his yoga technique. Working at first primarily with flexible young boys, Krishnamacharya's approach to yoga was increasingly physical and postural, leading eventually to "a system whose central component was a rigorous (and oftentimes aerobic) series of *āsanas*, joined by a repetitive linking sequence" (Singleton 2010: 176). This new and much more physical approach to yoga became the basis of contemporary global practice through Krishnamacharya's most successful students.

Singleton's study of the emergence of postural yoga is particularly relevant here because he explicitly invokes notions of research, experimentation, and innovation. While Sjoman's "syncretism" suggests a combination or patchwork of previously existing forms, Singleton hints at a more thoroughly epistemic process that involves active searching and discovery. He describes a laboratory-like environment in which the elements of yoga technique—postures, sequences, transitional movements, breathing rhythms and durations, as well as pedagogical and demonstrative models—underwent continual study and transformation. This was a period of "tests," a "pilot" program, intentionally "experimental" in nature (2010: 186–88). Synthesis is surely part of such experimentation, but we should also recall the notion of "elaboration" borrowed from Charles Spinosa in the previous chapter. Through sustained practice, new details emerge within existing areas of technique—details that were previously unknown and indeed imperceptible. Yoga in this vision is not a single entity or codified system but an unfolding "epistemic object" (Cetina in Schatzki *et al.* 2001). The same exercise might be called gymnastics one day and yoga the next, while much of what Krishnamacharya had learned in Tibet went untaught. Yoga was in flux, but it was not a random flux: It was a research project, led by Krishnamacharya and aimed towards fulfilling specific social and cultural goals.

As A. G. Mohan's biography makes clear, Krishnamacharya was aware of what he was doing. He referred to the necessity of *punaranveshana*—which Mohan translates as "re-search" or "to search once more"—in order to breathe new life into "ancient practices that had declined over time" (Mohan 2010: 115). Yet as Mohan also notes, Krishnamacharya "always credited his teachers with everything he himself taught, even if it was his own discovery or improvisation" (90). Mohan suggests that Krishnamacharya himself composed the *Yoga Rahasya*, a text that is traditionally attributed to the tenth-century sage Nathamuni (120, 136–37).

Krishnamacharya's son, the yoga teacher T. K. V. Desikachar, similarly recalls: "[M]y father never acknowledged that he discovered anything even when I have seen that it was he who discovered it. He has discovered postures but he would say that it was his teacher who taught him. Rarely had he said that it was his 'original' work" (cited in Mohan 2010: 137). In this context, such attributions are not simply an effect of personal modesty, but rather should "be understood as a standard convention in a living (Sanskritic) tradition where conservation and innovation are tandem imperatives" (Singleton 2010: 207). Hence, Krishnamacharya's reluctance to claim his own technical innovations should not be seen as disingenuous. Rather, they refer to a very real sense in which change and continuity commingle in any living practice. Krishnamacharya believed that, in radically changing the embodied technique of yoga, he was nevertheless continuing yogic tradition on another level. Like many other great teachers and practitioners, he believed that yoga itself is constituted not by training alone but by a dialectical relation of continuity and innovation—in epistemic terms, training and research.

Krishnamacharya drew into yoga much that would not previously have been considered relevant or permissible. The *surya namaskara* or "sun salutation"—one of the first things we may think of when we picture the practice of yoga today—was in Krishnamacharya's time considered inappropriate for yoga because of its association with gymnastics and sun worship (Singleton 2010: 180). Indeed, Krishnamacharya seems to have borrowed from the sun salutation the technique of linking one posture to another, and then generalized this to entire sequences of poses or *asana*. What is now called "vinyasa" is a continuous flow between poses, matching movement to breath, which had not previously been associated with the practice of *asana*. Mohan considers vinyasa "essential, and probably unique, to Krishnamacharya's teachings" (2010: 29). While contemporary yoga practices differ greatly in their approach to flow, with some retaining a more static approach to each pose, the discovery of vinyasa marks an important turning point in contemporary yoga. If yoga poses had previously been thought of as discrete entities, it now became possible to assemble them in unbroken sequences, as in the "Primary Series" of Ashtanga Yoga (see Maehle 2006 for a detailed description). Additionally, the use of movement and breath to connect one pose to another fundamentally transforms *asana* practice, bringing it closer to martial arts and dance (see my discussion of yoga and actor training in Chapter 3).

Krishnamacharya's yoga pedagogy continued to evolve and change after he left Mysore in the 1950s. Once he was no longer under the employ of the Maharaja, he reverted to a broader and more religiously grounded approach to yoga that no longer placed so much emphasis on physical exercise and *asana*. Meanwhile, the highly physical approach that had been developed in Mysore was brought to global prominence by Krishnamacharya's students, especially B. K. S. Iyengar and K. Pattabhi Jois, each of whom continued to develop modern yoga technique in particular ways. In one article that exemplifies rigorous analysis of embodied technique, Elizabeth De Michelis juxtaposes photographs from two yoga manuals published by the same organization—one in 1960 and the other in 1983—to show how the technique of physical alignment was developed towards ever-greater precision over the course of those two decades (De Michelis 1995). In addition to physical alignment within a pose, contemporary yoga teachers experiment with visualization and imagery, regulated breathing and meditation, sequences of poses and the poses themselves, chanting and the study of Sanskrit texts, ethical and emotional guidance, and sensation and proprioception, as well as with approaches to pedagogy and the economics of yoga. In doing so, they bring knowledge from other areas into interdisciplinary contact with yoga technique, just as Krishnamacharya did, and they continue the yogic tradition of active research and innovation. Today, as in Krishnamacharya's time, social forces and factors shape the field of yoga by creating the context in which research takes place. At the same time, this research remains an epistemological endeavor, an engagement with and discovery of concrete possibilities of embodiment.

The yoga wars

The question of which areas of technique will be most actively explored is always a matter of social dynamics as well as personal preferences. Yoga teachers and practitioners tailor their technique to meet the needs of those who support their practices socially and financially. In modern economic terms, the "stakeholders" in a yoga practice include not only students, who have particular needs and desires, but also funders and patrons, from the Maharaja to today's corporate sponsors. We have already seen how the Maharaja's interest in developing Indian physical culture influenced Krishnamacharya's approach to yoga during his time in Mysore. It stands to reason that contemporary practitioners would also guide their teaching and research according to financial and other material circumstances as well as their own interests and those of their students and sponsors. This has given rise to the contemporary landscape of yoga practice, with its kaleidoscopic array of schools and styles, traditions and brands. How should these numerous "yogas" be understood in relation to each other? The compact, formal yoga codified by Bikram

Choudhury is not comparable in depth or breadth to the traditions of Iyengar or Jois. What about hot yoga, power yoga, "naked yoga," "kosher yoga," or "yoga for carpal tunnel syndrome" (Wax 2010)? There is even yoga for dogs: "Doga"! Yet as one practitioner objects, "Doga runs the risk of trivializing yoga by turning a 2,500-year-old practice into a fad" (Lyttle 2009). In the context of what Emily Wax calls the "yoga wars," how is the curious practitioner to distinguish between clever synthesis, genuine innovation, and mere rebranding? (For an examination of these distinctions, see Gronow 2009.)

According to Wax, "[m]ore than 30 million Americans practice some sort of yoga in an ever-expanding industry generating an estimated $6 billion in the United States alone" (2010). These figures have only increased since her writing. What Wax calls the "yoga wars" include serious legal battles over yoga as intellectual property, and hence over its commercialization. To prevent such economic exploitation, Wax reports, "an Indian government agency is fighting what it calls 'yoga theft' after several US companies said they wanted to copyright or patent their versions" (2010). A more recent battle concerns the patenting of a specific format of video documentation for yoga classes distributed online (Heagberg 2013). Issues of branding and commercialism, exoticism and appropriation, swirl in the contemporary landscape of yoga. As the editors of a recent anthology on modern yoga observe, yoga classes and workshops can now be found "in virtually every city in the Western world and (increasingly) throughout the Middle East, Asia, South and Central America and Australasia" (Singleton and Byrne 2008: 1). In this context, teachers and practitioners of yoga are under enormous pressure to define what they do in marketable terms, as stable products that can be consumed by any willing practitioner and which reliably lead to predictable results. While legal battles are fought over the authorship and authenticity of its technique, the image of yoga is increasingly used to sell other products, from yoga mats and clothing to cars and yogurt.

If, as I suggest, yoga technique is an "epistemic object" in the sense described in the preceding chapter, then the naming of its various versions and elements can only ever be provisional. With epistemic objects, "a stable name is not an expression and indicator of stable thinghood. Rather, naming, in the present conception, is a way to punctuate the flux, to bracket and ignore differences, to declare them as pointing to an identity-for-a-particular-purpose" (Cetina in Schatzki *et al.* 2001: 184). When we give the same name to different practices, calling them all "yoga," we actively bracket and ignore their differences in order to "punctuate the flux" of the field. In this way, the act of naming may actually work against the "unfolding" and dispersal of knowledge. This certainly seems to apply to the proliferation of yoga schools and styles today. What could be gained if teachers and practitioners of yoga were to resist the commodification and branding of yoga, instead taking a more epistemological perspective on their practices? Could the "yoga wars" be reinterpreted as a lively community of knowledge, using the frameworks of social epistemology to analyze its epistemic contents? Teachers and practitioners might then see themselves not as competitors in a market but as an "epistemic culture" (Cetina 1999)—essentially a culture of training and research—comprising individuals and communities who are bound together by a shared interest in certain aspects of embodiment and potentialities of embodied practice. Could this be the basis for a more accurate and sustainable mapping of contemporary yoga practice?

Bikram Yoga is an extreme example of the standardization and commodification of postural yoga (Bikram Yoga 2012)—one that, for all its founder's claims to universality, seems to have been precisely engineered for an urban, moneyed, Euro-American clientele. Among the technical innovations introduced by Bikram Choudhury are a heated room, which increases sweat and flexibility, and a fixed 26-pose sequence that is repeated in every 90-minute class. By narrowing and standardizing his teaching, Bikram Choudhury has become one of the most commercially successful yoga pioneers, as well as one of the first to successfully copyright a brand of yoga. He has attracted numerous celebrity students and amassed a fortune through the Bikram Yoga franchise. In epistemological terms, Choudhury's research is highly "applied," aiming not towards a general expansion of knowledge but towards the instrumentalization of technique in a particular context. Yet the success of Bikram Yoga must be attributed not only to clever marketing but also to the cleverly applied research that gave rise to his highly saleable and easily standardized version of the embodied technique of yoga. Bikram's product is a particular synthesis of pedagogical and physical technique that, for reasons worth investigating, has had enormous appeal for a relatively privileged class of urban practitioners. We should neither dismiss this achievement nor elevate it above other types and practices of yoga. What we need is an epistemological cartography of the field of yoga: one that comparatively examines the substantive differences between practices in terms of their differing breadth and depth, focus and emphasis, pedagogy and physicality. An epistemological map of this kind could provide a much-needed counterweight to the dominance of commercial models—in particular, the "health and fitness" paradigm, to which I now turn.

Healthism and "performance"

At the start of the twenty-first century, the embodied technique of yoga is inextricably bound up with the biopolitics of health and healthism.[1] In contrast to the complex philosophical concept of health, "healthism" as discourse or ideology puts forth relatively stable and often highly gendered images of health that combine body type and athletic fitness with other kinds of visible success, such as happiness and wealth. In some contexts more influential than religion, politics, or economics, the drive to achieve or maintain physical health has today become a major factor in globalized culture and society, from national health policies and the World Health Organization to the popular diet and exercise regimes that inform so much of today's global popular and commercial culture. Whereas previous generations understood health variously in relation to ethics, morality, or hygiene, the healthist ideal has more to do with athleticism and with the visible shape of bodies. There are many problems with this reductive notion of health, but there is no denying its increasingly hegemonic and global influence today. Indeed, healthism provides the primary context for contemporary yoga practice, even as health itself "has become a major, multi-million pound industry, a topic of routine everyday conversation, a matter of political concern" (Evans *et al.* 2004: ix).

Mark Singleton's work on the origins of postural yoga shows how the interaction of Indian religion and nationalism with European physical culture led to a historical shift in which the "somatic and philosophical framework" of yoga in India was gradually "replaced by a modern discourse of health and fitness" (2010: 7). The recent global expansion of postural yoga must be understood in this context, as part of the rise of healthism and the change in mainstream assumptions about what it means to be healthy and "fit." From the late nineteenth-century physical culture movement to the fitness boom of the 1980s and the "health" magazines of the twenty-first century, healthism has emerged as one of the key discourses that define Euro-American and hence globalized culture. At this point, healthism is more than just one framework among others through which to discuss embodied technique. It has become a totalizing and universalizing discourse that displaces other ways of articulating and evaluating such technique. Increasingly, the diverse goals that motivate embodied practice are eclipsed by an idealized vision of health as universal goal. Correspondingly, embodied practitioners working in many different areas of technique face increasing pressure to describe what they do in terms of its health benefits. Yoga, in this context, is one of many areas of embodied technique that has been influenced and transformed by the discourse of healthism.

The influence of healthism upon the practices it frames goes beyond language to shape the ways in which technique from all over the world is altered and assimilated in order to fit within the relatively uniform environment of the gym, studio, or health club. In this regard, the transformation of yoga is exactly parallel to the "crossover into mainstream fitness" of the work of Joseph Pilates (Hamera 2007: 25–32), the transformation of hip-hop dance into aerobic exercise in fitness clubs (Martin 1998: 139–46), and many other recent healthist reframings of embodied technique. As embodied disciplines like yoga, kungfu (*gongfu*), *taijiquan*, capoeira, hip-hop, and tango are all repackaged to become "health and fitness" modalities, they undergo sometimes radical changes at the level of technique. Certain aspects of the technique that previously structured them are extracted for use, while others are forgotten or ignored. At its most extreme, healthism reduces all forms of embodied technique to different flavors of exercise, all of which are directed towards a single, reductive image of health. It then becomes possible to ask, in all sincerity: "Will yoga make me thin and happy?" (Munyer in Swan 2011: 3). While such a question says little about yoga and virtually nothing about health, it tells us a great deal about today's biopolitical landscape, and about the pressures faced by anyone who hopes to learn or teach yoga within it.

Modern postural yoga has been gradually athleticized. It has achieved its extraordinary popularity through its specific alignment with athleticism and through the dominant assumption that athletic prowess is equivalent to health. This is a significant matter for yoga practitioners, because the equation of athletic ability and health is erroneous. As Nancy Theberge points out in an essay on sports medicine, the idea that top athletes are paradigms of health is incorrect. Theberge cites an interview with an Olympic-level sports medicine administrator, who recalls being asked what it's like to work with "the healthiest people on the planet." The interviewee recounts his response:

"Well, I want to make a distinction here. This is all about performance. This is not about health." These are not healthy people that we are sending to [the Olympics]. These are incredibly high performers and there's a major distinction. If you looked at the medical file of each and every one of these people you would be horrified at the kinds of things they get exposed to. They get sick more often, they get injured more often, they get depressed more often … So, it's not about health. It's about performance.

(Theberge in Hargreaves and Vertinsky 2007: 180)

The aim of high-level sports medicine is not longevity or general well-being, but the achievement of maximum athletic virtuosity. Another of Theberge's interviewees clarifies that "the definitions of health for an elite athlete and the general public" are "quite different" (181). Once "you start training four, five times a week, you're not training for health. You're training for something else. You're training for performance." In other words, elite athletes are not particularly healthy. In fact, they regularly compromise health for the sake of "performance."[2] The sports medicine professionals Theberge interviewed conceptualize health as a midpoint between, on the one hand, injury and sickness, and on the other, elite competitive performance. The purpose of sport medicine in these contexts is the "optimization of performance" rather than the achievement of health, to the point where "being a high performance athlete inevitably means compromising health" (Theberge in Hargreaves and Vertinsky 2007: 185, 190). Yet advertising and other popular media routinely use images of athletes as icons of health. Nor is the confusion of health and athletic ability limited to the realm of professional sports. The ease with which "health and fitness" are combined today indicates the loss of an important distinction between sustainable well-being, or the absence of illness, and athleticism. This elision was notable during the 1980s "fitness" boom, when health and fitness became "synonymous in everyday usage" (Glassner 1989: 181), and it continues to have a profound influence upon the way we conceptualize health today.

It should come as no surprise, in this context, that the athleticization of yoga has probably made it less healthy, in that practitioners are more likely to push themselves into potentially injurious physical contortions. William Broad writes: "It is no surprise that a field that prides itself on the routine performance of twists, contortions, and dramatic bends of the human body can do a lot of damage" (2012: 103). Yet what makes yoga-related injury especially problematic, according to Broad, is "the discipline's image as a path to exceptional health." In other words, the classification of yoga as part of a "healthy" lifestyle hides its intense athleticism and associated risks. (The same could probably be said about many contemporary sports, martial arts, and other intensively athletic areas of technique.) In an environment of hegemonic healthism, the physical dangers associated with athleticism are routinely ignored in favor of the need to get or stay "fit" through vigorous exercise. Such exercise is routinely evaluated in terms of weight loss, which is frequently equated with health itself, despite the fact that the relationship between health and weight loss is far from simple or uncontested. Indeed, the increasingly prevalent idea that fatness or "obesity" is the opposite of health is a result rather than a cause of healthism, deriving more from the idealization of athleticism than from any coherent idea of health as overall well-being (see Rothblum *et al.* 2009). Meanwhile, the athleticization of yoga has made some yoga practices highly competitive—a quality that historically has more in common with sport than with the traditional values of yoga (see Smith 2007).

The diversity of yoga, and of physical culture and embodied technique more generally, calls for a more sophisticated model of practice than can be provided by either an economistic approach to the market or a healthist approach to the body. Yoga is neither a set of consumable products nor a pathway to the achievement of any single goal, be it health or spiritual attainment. Adopting epistemological strategies of naming rather than consumerist or healthist ones could make for a better and more accurate understanding of yoga practice. For example, treating postural yoga as knowledge might give us more nuanced ways to talk about lineage, tradition, and pedagogy. We could then treat brands, schools, or styles of yoga not as closed and coherent entities but as unfolding epistemic objects—in other words, as research projects. Furthermore, because knowledge is fractal, the same epistemological perspective can be applied to every detail of yoga technique. What, after all, is a pose or *asana*? What is it made of? What kind of thing is it? The athletic model suggests that an *asana* is a kind of achievement that may be performed better or worse by a given individual, while the commercial model treats *asana* and their sequences as consumable products. What if we were instead to see each *asana* as a tiny research project? For the individual practitioner, a given pose or posture is a research assignment in relation to their own specific embodiment. This is research at the individual level. At the same time, *asana* and sequences are open to advanced research at the level of extended and even global communities of knowledge. The materiality and epistemic rigor of yoga, in that case, consists not in the achievement of a known posture or shape, but rather in the ongoing discovery of the relatively reliable possibilities of embodiment.

Two studios in the East Village

To examine these issues in greater detail, and to provide a sense of how the embodied technique of yoga can vary from one studio to another even within a small geographic radius, I want to offer a brief account of two different yoga studios in Manhattan's East Village with which I am personally familiar. From early 2010 until early summer 2011, I attended between thirty and forty yoga sessions at East Yoga, a studio located on East 13th Street in Manhattan. Following this, in late summer 2011, I attended between thirty and forty sessions at Ashtanga Yoga Shala

NYC (AYS), just a few blocks away from East Yoga on East 8th Street. Prior to these experiences, I had encountered yoga several times in the context of dance and actor training, but had never practiced it regularly. The two studios are roughly the same size, each having a single large room for yoga practice. In different ways, both studios owe their existence to the research of Krishnamacharya and his students. Both were founded around the beginning of the twenty-first century, but they reflect two very different lines of research and practice in modern postural yoga. In comparing them, my goal is not to evaluate their respective merits but rather to illustrate some of the ways in which diverse approaches to embodied technique produce different kinds of spaces and experiences and give different meaning to the term "yoga." The two studios work differently with poses, sequences, alignment, visualization, breath, and other aspects of embodied technique. They also offer different economic models. Neither goes as far towards commodification as Bikram Yoga, but both grapple with the tensions entailed in selling yoga to the contemporary urban population of New York City.

East Yoga's one-room yoga studio looks out directly onto 13th Street and feels very much part of the fabric of the bustling East Village. Inside, the studio takes an informal approach to yoga and claims only a weak and open-ended relationship to tradition. It offers yoga as an activity that may be useful, meaningful, healthy, and enjoyable, but not necessarily spiritual and certainly not religious. The studio defines its yoga loosely as "vinyasa," meaning simply that movement and breath are linked. (Descriptions of the two studios come from their websites unless otherwise indicated: East Yoga 2013; Ashtanga Yoga Shala 2013.) Greater specification in terms of technique is not possible because the studio offers about thirty-five different classes per week, with a large roster of teachers. At the time of this writing, the website of East Yoga lists seventeen teachers—fifteen women and two men—mostly photographed in yoga poses. Their stated backgrounds include training in theatre, music, dance, and therapy as well as yoga, and they range significantly in level of experience. Classes are defined by type, with the following categories: Beginners, Intermediate, Open, Express, Restorative Vinyasa, Slow Flow Vinyasa, Meditation, Prenatal, Toddler, and Kids. Each of these classes costs $18 (or $10 for students), with multiclass and unlimited passes available. Most classes run for 75 or 90 minutes, with the "express" class lasting just 1 hour. While it is possible, with some effort, to regularly attend the same class taught by the same teacher, this can happen once or twice a week at most, since the teaching schedules are not regular. During my time at East Yoga, I soon discovered which teachers I preferred, but it was not always possible for me to attend their classes on a regular basis. When I did, I found that the sequence of poses taught could be different every time. This provides maximum flexibility for both teachers and students, and fits with founder Kari Harendorf's description of the studio: "The practice is vigorous and creative with a strong emphasis on alignment to keep you safe and injury free ... It is my sincere belief that yoga should be safe and FUN."

At East Yoga, teachers adapt each session to suit their intuitions and desires as well as the perceived needs of the students. The atmosphere is relaxed, and there is no pressure to attend more often or to "advance" in one's practice. Harendorf says that the studio is designed "to cater to the community and my fellow residents," which it does by fitting smoothly into the rhythms of urban life. This approach has both advantages and disadvantages. After several months of semi-regular attendance, I found that I had not developed anything like a repeatable yoga routine that I could practice at home on my own time. The flexibility of East Yoga and its casualness with regard to student–teacher relationships allow one to receive the benefits of a yoga practice without necessarily acquiring the technique needed to practice alone. This does not mean that I did not learn technique at East Yoga—I absolutely did—but it was not structured as a repeatable sequence. Instead, I became acquainted with a large number of poses and began to learn some of the details of alignment that define their rigor. I also learned to search for transitions between unfamiliar poses and to relate my breathing in a flexible but conscious way to any given sequence of poses. The fact that I was not taught a repeatable sequence of poses to practice on my own seems to fit with a business model in which yoga sessions are consumed, like movies or concerts, rather than being conceived of as sites of knowledge transfer. After several months of attendance, I remained dependent on the studio to enact the yoga technique that was slowly sedimenting in my body. Economics also influenced my practice: Since each class was purchased separately, I could always save money by not going, and this discouraged regularity.

In search of a more focused approach, I visited Ashtanga Yoga Shala, located at basement level on East 8th Street. Although much of the core technique of posture, movement, and breath was the same or similar to that of East Yoga, I found radical differences in pedagogy, discursive framing, economics, and many other aspects. As founder Guy Donahaye writes:

> Ashtanga Yoga Shala NYC is a traditional school unlike most modern yoga studios. Based on the teachings of Sri K Pattabhi Jois (Guruji), our aim is to develop a yoga practice for each

student according to his or her individual needs and capacities. Asana practice follows a system of three sequences of postures devised by Jois – primary (yoga chikitsa), intermediate (nadi shodhona) and advanced (sthira bhaga).

Classes in the traditional Mysore style are based on the way Pattabhi Jois taught in his home town of Mysore (India). Students come to class daily and gradually build up a practice over time. The relationship of teacher to student is more like that of a personal trainer, with each student receiving individual assistance and guidance in a group setting.

Elsewhere on the AYS website, Donahaye articulates a strong attachment to the lineage of modern yoga described in the first section of this chapter: "Ashtanga Yoga is a systematic method devised by Sri K Pattabhi Jois with reference to the teachings of his teacher Sri Krishnamacharya, Krishnamacharya's teacher, Ramana Mohan Brahmachari and the teachings of an ancient sage known as Rishi Vamana which were given in an ancient text known as the Yoga Korunta." A large painting of Jois is displayed in the practice room. (For a photograph, see Benjamin Richard Smith in Singleton and Byrne 2008: 155.) Such an exact statement of lineage, unlike anything found on East Yoga's website, is possible only because all classes at AYS are taught by Donahaye himself, except when he is away. According to the website, Donahaye studied with Jois from 1991 until the latter's death in 2009 and is "one of only 40 students worldwide" to receive a teaching certification directly from Jois. The AYS website includes sections on yoga philosophy, interviews, practice guidelines, diet, and lifestyle, none of which are found on the East Yoga site. The business model and class schedule are also different: Students pay $150 or $200 per month to become members of AYS and are expected to attend class as often as possible. Individual classes can be purchased, but this option is only intended for out-of-town visitors. There are just two sessions per day Monday through Thursday (at 7:00 a.m. and 8:30 a.m.), and one each on Friday and Sunday, for a total of ten classes per week. In several ways, then, Donahaye encourages a regular and constant practice: All classes are in the morning, all classes are taught by the same person, and the flat monthly fee makes it cost-effective to practice more often.

In addition to these differences in pedagogical and economic infrastructure, the embodied technique of the classes was more regular at Ashtanga Yoga Shala than at East Yoga. "Mysore style" refers to a pedagogical approach in which students practice simultaneously but separately in a shared space, receiving individual feedback rather than being guided through a group sequence by the teacher. As a result, students work at their own pace rather than in unison. This has a number of advantages, including that students are immediately able to practice at home whatever they have learned in class. On the other hand, the Ashtanga sequence is only adapted in relatively minor ways to suit the needs of individual practitioners and teachers. One can progress more quickly or slowly through the process of learning the sequence, or use props to aid alignment, but the poses and their order remain constant. Hence, one kind of flexibility is exchanged for another. Donahaye, following Jois, places substantial attention on how the breath is matched to the movement—for example, counting exactly the number of breaths in each pose—and on the direction of the gaze at each point in the sequence. I had the impression at AYS of entering into a structure that was both sturdy and precise: The Ashtanga Yoga sequence, with all its technical details, is clearly the product of sustained research over many years. At the same time, I remained curious about the extent to which Donahaye had contributed to the technique as I encountered it, either through the "residue" of other training in his body or through his own intentional research and discovery. Not surprisingly, given his traditional orientation, Donahaye does not claim to be adapting or discovering yoga, but merely passing it along.

Benjamin Richard Smith's critique of Ashtanga Yoga focuses on its athleticism and competitiveness (in Singleton and Byrne 2008). Smith describes the practice at the Ashtanga Yoga Research Institute (AYRI) in Mysore as characterized by intense discipline and a "fiercely imposed authority" that sometimes borders on cruelty (153–54). According to Smith, students at AYRI often internalize these qualities as an aggressive drive to perfect their technique, or that of others, in potentially harmful or dangerous ways. Furthermore, "the sequences of the various *āsana* series are widely regarded amongst Ashtangis as unalterable, despite the fact—obvious to the few students who have visited AYRI across a longer period of time, but not widely recognized amongst the majority of practitioners—that Pattabhi Jois has himself changed the sequence and content of the various series since the 1970s" (154–55). While Donahaye's teaching persona is warm and unassuming, some aspects of Smith's critique are applicable to AYS. I did experience a kind of pressure to "advance" my practice there, and this notion of advancement did not refer only to the cultivation of a regular, long-term practice but also to the accomplishment of increasingly difficult physical postures. Furthermore, while most practitioners at East Yoga were slender, body type at AYS was even more uniform—although it is important to note that there were some older people and some who were not able to do "advanced" poses despite regular attendance. Neither studio took a strong or explicit stance on the availability of yoga to people of diverse body types, but the formal atmosphere of AYS made it feel less accessible in this regard.

I experienced East Yoga, with its informality and lack of religious trappings, as a less competitive environment. Its casual, consumer-oriented atmosphere and flexible scheduling meant that, in accordance with its business model, classes could be taken for personal benefit without reference to any larger or externally imposed scheme. Regular attendance was entirely an individual matter, since no teacher was keeping track. By the same token, however, I left East Yoga without having mastered any definable chunk of sequential technique. At Ashtanga Yoga Shala, on the other hand, the focus on progressing through a predefined sequence, and the presence of familiar faces in the room every morning, provoked in me a sense of competition rather than community. Moreover, since the teacher was always the same, I ulti-mately felt that I had to choose between a more serious level of com-mitment and not attending at all, since anything in between would be perceived as lacking. This finally led me to stop attending class at AYS. By the time I did so, however, I had established a simple yoga practice of about 30 minutes, which I continued to practice—irregularly—for more than a year afterwards.

The comparison of these two studios reveals a number of dimensions or areas of embodied technique with which current yoga practitioners and teachers are experimenting. These include the sequence of postures, the constancy of those sequences, and the transitions from one posture to another; the prioritization of anatomical alignment, sometimes through the use of props, in relation to the overall flow and dynamics of prac-tice; pedagogies based on unison group practice or on individualized practice and feedback (Mysore style); the schedule and assumed reg-ularity of practice; the extent to which progressive achievement of phy-sically difficult poses is valorized; the tracing of lineage and locating of a given practice within a context of past traditions or present practices; the relationship of posture practice to chanting, breathing, diet, and other areas of nonathletic technique; and the relationship of student to teacher or of consumer to service provider. It would be premature to call either studio a site for high-level research in yoga, since I am not arguing that any of their technique is innovative in a strong sense or that it has spread and been taken up in other contexts. However, it is no exaggeration to suggest that studios like East Yoga, Ashtanga Yoga Shala, and hundreds of others in New York City alone, are collectively engaged in a research project in the embodied technique of yoga, continually discovering new possibilities and making them available through diverse models of membership and pedagogy. In the next section, I begin to map the parameters of that research project by situating it within the larger context of physical culture. I argue that yoga has achieved its success in part through its discovery of a particular "sweet spot" in that landscape.

The gendering of yoga

Much excellent work has been done on the gender politics of physical culture (see Hargreaves and Vertinsky 2007). In this section, I consider the well-documented fact that the spread of postural yoga to Europe and North America—and the athleticization of its technique, as described above—was accompanied by a major shift in its demographics. In simple terms, yoga went from being an exclusively male practice to being predominantly female. I consider the gendering of yoga in relation to the notion of distinct male and female spheres of physical culture, which was strongly in place at the beginning of the twentieth century and remains influential today despite the substantial blurring of gender roles. In the following section, I show how the gendering of physical culture maps onto the polarities of athletics and somatics, and link the contemporary success of postural yoga to its particular location between these two poles.[3]

As Barbara Purcell and Andrew Shaffer observe, yoga's current gender configuration "is an oddity limited to the Western world; in India, yoga has actually been dominated by men since its inception" (in Swan 2011: 36). Krishnamacharya was one of the first Indian men to teach yoga to women, and he faced some controversy for doing so (Desikachar 2005: 149–50). Today, in contrast, the majority of practitioners in the transnational phenomenon of postural yoga are well-educated women of European descent. Suzanne Newcombe has examined the growth of yoga's popularity in Britain during the twentieth century, finding that women made up from 70 to 90 percent of yoga students, as well as most of the teachers, in Britain between 1960 and 1980 (2007: 45). Middle-class British women, Newcombe writes, "found yoga an important support in many different practical ways including as an aid to health and beauty, a positive approach to ageing, a complementary support to medical treatment for chronic conditions, social contact with other women and a meaningful hobby" (59). Strikingly, despite major changes in physical culture and gender roles, the demographics of postural yoga in Europe and North America have remained fairly stable since the period studied by Newcombe. Today, the majority of yoga practitioners in the United States are still educated white women, although statistics indicate that the relatively small proportion of male yoga practitioners is growing.[4] Studies published in *Yoga Journal* in 2005 and 2008 suggested that 70 to 80 percent of yoga practitioners were female and most were college educated. Says one former professional wrestler: "Ask a regular guy if he does yoga, and he'll probably say, 'I wouldn't be caught *dead* doing that crap—it's for girls'" (Swan 2011: 36, 109).

European physical culture was heavily gendered long before yoga made its appearance on the scene. As Newcombe observes: "Before the Second World War, middle-class women were taught gymnastics, Swedish drill, and dance at school; middle-class men played team sports like rugby and cricket. After leaving school, men who were interested in physical culture often followed the tradition of George Sandow's exercises, while women joined Mary Bagot Stack's Women's League of Health and Beauty" (2007: 50). There were, in other words, two distinct physical cultures, one for men and another for women. After the Second World War, the lines between these territories of embodied technique began to blur, so that today it is no longer possible to speak of two distinctly gendered physical cultures. Nevertheless, the gendering of different areas of physical culture remains an important factor in who practices what. Men continue to dominate the world of professional sports, both in numbers and economically, while women remain the majority in studio-based physical culture such as dance and aerobics. When placed in this historical context, it is clear that postural yoga has achieved its success by being absorbed into what is still a predominantly feminine area of embodied technique. The relatively small number of male yoga practitioners points to a continuing cultural division between masculine and feminine physical culture.

If the gap between strictly gendered physical cultures has narrowed, this is arguably not because they have both moved towards a middle ground, but rather because the characteristics of what was previously considered a distinctly masculine idea of health are increasingly seen as appropriate fitness goals for all people. Indeed, this is a basic feature of healthist ideology, as described above: Athletics are understood as synonymous with health. As Barry Glassner observes, the new vision of fitness that developed in the 1970s diverged significantly from the "body improvement movements" of the late nineteenth and early twentieth centuries, especially when it came to the gendering of technique. In the earlier body-improvement movements, "prescriptions for men and women differed, whereas typically the prescriptions for fitness in the 1970s and 80s are nearly the same for both men and women." In other words, the previous distinction between masculine and feminine ideals of health has grown less sharp because of the increasingly universal "valuation of traditionally masculine attributes such as strength, endurance, and rational self-control" (1989: 186). A positive result of this shift has been the increased participation of girls and women in mainstream sports and athletics. Less often noted is the absence of a parallel increase in men's participation in areas of physical culture traditionally marked as feminine. While the loosening of gender roles is worthy of celebration, the increasingly universal appeal of traditionally masculine physical culture might lead us to ask what then happens to the forms of traditionally feminine physical culture that were previously taught to and valued by girls and women. I return to this question below.

When viewed in this context, contemporary postural yoga can be seen to occupy a unique position in the shifting landscape of contemporary physical culture. The athleticization of yoga in India during the first part of the twentieth century was based in part on the hope that it could represent a strong indigenous counterpart to the sports and gymnastics of the British Empire. However, as Joseph Alter explains, yoga remained ambiguously positioned within Indian physical culture of that period precisely because, according to the cultural standards of the time, it could not be made sufficiently "masculine." The demand that yoga refute imperialist and racist assumptions about the weakness of Indian men—and by extension the Indian nation—put yoga in an untenable position: Despite its absorption of technique from bodybuilding and wrestling, yoga retained a substantially "holistic" approach to embodiment that could not be fully squared with the demands of the nationalist movement (2007: 35). Even in its radically athleticized form, yoga could not measure up to the European ideal of masculinity. "If not necessarily regarded as effete, *āsana* and *prāṇāyāma* were simply not linked to muscles, masculinity and fitness at a time when that link was of critical national importance" (34). The politics of gender and nation worked together to exclude yoga from Indian physical education. Although it had been athleticized, it was still not athletic enough to compete with bodybuilding and sport for the participation of men. A similar logic may then apply to yoga's development in Europe and North America, where it once again has not been received as sufficiently masculine to achieve commercial success amongst men. Instead, the global success of yoga arrived from a different quarter, as what had been practiced in India almost exclusively by men became hugely successful among women in Europe and North America.

Given that the expansion of healthism and its athletic ideals has gone hand in hand with the continuing dominance of highly restrictive standards of feminine beauty, it is not surprising that many women today are interested in a kind of embodied technique that allows them to engage athletically without stepping too far out of what is still considered proper femininity. In the period studied by Newcombe, yoga classes for women tended to emphasize "body awareness, the deep respect of personal somatic experience and an insistence on non-violence" (2007: 57). Several decades later, during the 1980s fitness boom, Glassner observed that "for women, one result of the fitness movement has been a new ideal of the feminine physique which involves a pulling together of several cultural antitheses: strength with beauty, muscularity with thinness, and hardness with curvaceousness" (1989: 186). At the same time, female athletes may still face rebuke if they appear too "mannish" or masculine (Ross in Hargreaves and Vertinsky 2007: 129). The incredible success of postural yoga among a particular demographic suggests that it may have found a "sweet spot" of physical culture that successfully fuses these polarities. In other words, while postural yoga was never quite athletic enough for Indian men to rely on it as proof of their masculinity (in colonial terms), the same technique seems to be exactly athletic enough for the numerous middle-class white women who are seeking a particular balance between traditionally masculine and traditionally feminine technique. In the context of healthist ideology that pushes women to be athletic, but not *too* athletic, it is no wonder that postural yoga has achieved such popularity among this particular demographic. (The men to whom postural yoga does appeal may be looking for a similar balance, but coming at it from the opposite angle.) A more substantial review of contemporary practice would be required to test this theory, but these changes in the gendering of yoga across the twentieth century clearly indicate the mutual shaping of cultural politics and embodied research.

Between athletics and somatics

Thus far, I have referred to "traditionally masculine" and "traditionally feminine" physical culture as areas of embodied technique historically linked to particular gender roles. This is accurate for historical purposes, but it may not be the best way of thinking about future developments and possibilities. If we imagine a future in which areas of physical culture are no longer mapped onto gender—or in which gender itself works in fundamentally different ways (see Chapter 4)—then it no longer makes sense to think in terms of the historical categories of masculine and feminine. It would be better, in that case, to map the polarities of physical culture in more technical terms, by describing the kinds of technique we are dealing with, rather than by linking it to gender norms that seem increasingly obsolete. I have already suggested that traditionally masculine physical culture is essentially that which is highly athletic. The main features of athleticism include competition, muscularity, measurable achievement, physical strength and speed, resistance to fatigue, and spectacular visual display. What, then, is the technical name for the "other" physical culture—that which is traditionally associated with femininity and which tends to be undervalued by the ideology of healthism?

Newcombe, cited above, associates the traditionally feminine pole of yoga with "body awareness," "somatic experience," and "non-violence." I shall refer to this area of technique as "somatics." In locating somatics within physical culture, I aim to expand the breadth of the latter by affirming that the physical is not equivalent to the athletic. I do not claim that athletics and somatics are the only major branches of physical culture, but they certainly define an important spectrum of technique, with immediate relevance to sport, martial arts, and yoga, as well as to notions of health and fitness. Putting the argument made above into epistemic terms, I am suggesting that postural yoga has risen to such astounding prominence at least in part because its particular balance of *athletics* and *somatics* serves the particular needs of a significant demographic at this point in history. We can expand upon this point by examining some aspects of contemporary postural yoga technique and seeing how they integrate or balance the somatic and the athletic. First, however, it is necessary to further define the somatic. As noted in the previous chapter, it will not be possible to pin down the material essence of the somatic (or, for that matter, the athletic) through anatomical or physiological measurement, even if such analysis may be fruitful. Rather, the material basis for the somatic is simply the relative reliability of embodiment as it is encountered by and through somatic technique. But what is this technique?

As Thomas Hanna wrote in 1976, somatics is "the field which studies the *soma*: namely the body as perceived from within by first-person perception" (in Don Hanlon Johnson 1995: 341). Hanna distinguishes the "soma" from the "body" as perceived by others: "When a human soma looks at itself in a mirror, it sees a body—a third-person, objective structure. But what is this same body when looked at from an internal, somatic perspective? It is the unified experience of self-sensing and self-moving" (346). Hanna's emphasis on first-person experience recalls the phenomenological distinction between *Leib* and *Körper*, while his narrative of an encounter with the mirror image resonates with Lacan's mirror stage and provokes the question of whether self-sensing is necessarily a unified experience.[5] It also prefigures contemporary work on enactive cognition, cited in Chapter 1. Here I understand somatics as a major alternative to athletics, one that is radically *unspectacular* and which emphasizes physical sensation over visual display and "performance" in the sense developed above. My claim is that somatics is a vital part of physical culture, no less important than athletics, but that it is consistently undervalued and marginalized by the contemporary healthist idealization of the latter.

As a field of knowledge, somatics has no clear boundary. Johnson counts among its most important proponents the following individuals: Elsa Gindler, Charlotte Selver, Carola Speads, Marion Rosen, Ilse Middendorf, F. M. Alexander, Moshe Feldenkrais, Ida Rolf, Bonnie Bainbridge Cohen, Judith Aston, Irmgard Bartenieff, Mary Whitehouse, Gerda Alexander, and Emilie Conrad Da'Oud (1995: xi). Philipa Rothfield helpfully glosses a few branches of somatics—also called "bodywork"—indicating the kinds of differences and similarities that define this broad territory of embodied technique:

> Bodywork practices by and large draw attention to the corporeal feelings of movement, although each does so in its own way. For example, Skinner Releasing Technique promotes the maximal release of muscles in the performance of movement ... Other bodily approaches privilege other factors—lines of energy, postural direction (Alexander) or corporeal organisation (Feldenkrais). These fields each constitute distinctive ways of valuing, interpreting and approaching movement.
>
> (Rothfield 2009: 215)

Such differences notwithstanding, Johnson sees diverse somatic practitioners as linked by a shared "desire to regain an intimate connection with bodily processes: breath, movement impulses, balance, and sensibility" (1995: xvi). According to Michael Huxley, two of the earliest pioneers in this field—Frederick Matthias Alexander (1869–1955) and Mabel Elsworth Todd (1874–1956)—defined their work explicitly in opposition to the athletic physical culture of their time, distancing themselves from the idea of "exercise" as a physical endeavor and looking for ways to engage mind and body together (2011: 34–35). In this sense, somatics and athletics can be seen as two poles in European and North American physical culture of the past century. However, the physical culture of somatics is hard-pressed to articulate its value within healthist society. While somatics has increasingly been accepted as part of alternative medicine, especially for pain relief, and has played a major role in the development of postmodern dance and dance/movement therapy (see Eddy 2009), somatic approaches do not fit well into the "health and fitness" paradigm that continues to dominate contemporary physical culture. Thus, while many now accept the value of somatics in healing from injury, few would place it alongside sport and exercise as a fundamental aspect of the routine maintenance of health.

Postural yoga strikes a particular and possibly unique balance between athletics and somatics. Different practices of yoga locate themselves differently with regard to this balance, some tending towards athletics and others towards somatics. But many of the characteristics of yoga technique described thus far can be understood as compromises— or, to put it more strongly, as *research outcomes*—at the border or intersection between athletics and somatics. I am thinking here of the *asana* themselves; the role of competition in yoga pedagogy; the spatial arrangement of the yoga class; and the relationship of movement to breath. Unlike a sport or martial art, there is no direct confrontation between opposing individuals or teams in yoga. Indeed, competition may be explicitly discouraged, especially when the spiritual dimension of yoga is emphasized (Sarbacker in Singleton and Byrne 2008). Yet, as my own experience attests, the display of physical ability is inescapable in the practice of *asana*. In moving through a sequence of postures, one's individual levels of strength, balance, and flexibility are put on view. The visible display of postures cannot help but enable competition, even as the individual focus of the practice and the absence of official winners and losers discourage an adversarial framework. As we saw above, two studios that share a historical and geographic moment may be importantly distinguished by how they place themselves on a continuum from most to least competitive.

Compared to bodybuilding, gymnastics, and sport, postural yoga places more attention on sensation and tends to avoid fostering competition and athletic display, at least explicitly. On the other hand, in comparison with the somatic technique developed by people like Alexander, Todd, Feldenkrais, and Bainbridge-Cohen, postural yoga is extravagant in its celebration of physical virtuosity. Modern yoga studios rarely have mirrors, like aerobics or ballet studios, but the plethora of photographic and video material surrounding contemporary yoga practice highlights the externally visible shape of each *asana* in its apparently ideal form, emphasizing this over less visible effects of the technique upon its practitioner. This makes yoga relatively easy to assimilate within the health and fitness paradigm, as illustrated by one story in which a yoga studio invited a team of advertising consultants to design its new brochure, only to have them pick out the youngest, thinnest, and most conventionally attractive students to photograph (Dunas in Swan 2011). Perhaps the most extreme move in this direction is the attempt to make postural yoga an Olympic sport (Beck 2012). Yet there is also significant resistance towards such developments: While proponents of yoga as sport emphasize its visible, measurable, and competitive aspects, others argue that the most important aspects of yoga are lost when it is athleticized. (For a corresponding view on ballet as sport, see Robb 2013.)

The technique of "vinyasa" is another concrete example of yoga's epistemic location at the intersection or border zone between athletics and somatics. In current yoga discourse, vinyasa generally refers to the counting of breaths in a pose and the matching of half-breaths to the transitions between poses. In the "sun salutation" as I learned it from Guy Donahaye at Ashtanga Yoga Shala, each transitional movement is accompanied by a single in-breath or out-breath. The poses themselves are located at the suspension points between these half-breaths, except for "downward facing dog," during which one takes five full breaths. (This pattern is sometimes explicitly marked in diagrams of the Ashtanga series.) Given the many possible relationships between breath and movement, the technique of vinyasa—which Krishnamacharya seems to have discovered/invented—can be seen as a unique and innovative synthesis of athletic and somatic technique. While breath capacity is essential in sports, it rarely receives direct attention or exercise on its own in athletic contexts. On the other hand somatic technique often consciously places attention on the breath itself—in particular, on the sensation of breathing and the placement of the breath—rather than merely counting breaths or ensuring their regularity. The vinyasa technique of matching the duration of a movement with the length of a breath invites an engagement that is simultaneously athletic and somatic: The dynamic movement between poses and the regulated timing of the breaths keep the practice athletic and limit the extent to which the practitioner can relax into the sensation of breathing. On the other hand, students who tend towards the athletic may find themselves admonished: "Remember to breathe!" or "Focus on the breath!"—directives that return attention to the somatic even during athletically difficult poses.

As research in yoga continues, ideas about gender, health, and spirituality continue to change alongside it. Athletic forms of dance are currently receiving widespread attention through popular films and reality competition shows like So You Think You Can Dance. These shows put a welcome spotlight on embodied technique, but they do so by framing it within a context of fierce competition and rigorous athleticism. The notion of dance put forward by these spectacles is limited in the same way that physical culture is limited when we associate it only with competitive sports. There is no room in such a world for more somatic approaches to dance—such as Contact Improvisation (Thomas 2003: 109) or Authentic Movement (Wyman-McGinty 1998), which cannot be rendered competitive—let alone for bodywork that emphasizes sensation over movement. It is therefore not surprising to find trends within yoga that push it towards the extremes of athleticization, such as turning it into an Olympic sport. In the following section, however, I would like to touch upon some examples of contemporary practice that suggest a growing interest in somaticizing yoga through a turn (or return) to more patient and gentle technique. Whether such adaptations constitute a reversion to the premodern Indian roots of yoga, or a new branch of research entirely, is less important than recognizing *how* a more somatic yoga serves contemporary practitioners and *whom* it could be designed to serve.

A therapeutic turn

Perhaps in response to injuries of the kind William Broad describes, some yoga practitioners are actively engaged in the promotion of yoga as a therapeutic rather than an athletic practice. In 2012, when I moved from the East Village of Manhattan to the Greenpoint neighborhood of Brooklyn, I encountered a third yoga studio, which can be usefully contrasted with the two discussed above. Founded and run by J. Brown, Abhyasa Yoga Center's mission is "to provide instruction, practice, and products that encourage individual and communal health" (Abhyasa Yoga Center 2013). Yet Brown's idea of health is not defined by athletic fitness or virtuosic performance. Instead, Brown's explicit goal is to work against the dominance of athleticism in contemporary postural yoga and against "workout-based schools and classes that are more concerned with physical prowess than any behavioral or spiritual component." Classes at Abhyasa Yoga Center are slow, careful, and meditative, with an emphasis on bodily sensation that can rightly be called somatic. Brown emphasizes: "No struggling. No straining. No striving. Just strong and calm, even and measured work." As a teacher, he overtly prioritizes the embodied technique of *ujjayi* or "ocean-sounding breath" over the achievement of difficult poses, fitting movement within breath rather than the reverse. On the map of contemporary physical culture, J. Brown's establishment of Abhyasa Yoga Center carries a flag for the somatic side of yoga. In epistemic terms, it may indicate a therapeutic turn in embodied research within the field of yoga.

An even more extreme example of yoga as somatic rather than athletic technique may be found in the autobiography of Matthew Sanford, a paraplegic yoga teacher. Like many pioneers of somatic bodywork, Sanford arrived at the need to explore sensation and internal alignment because of an injury—in this case, a catastrophic one. As Johnson reminds us, much of the most important work in somatics has been done in response to injury, illness, and disability. "Gindler had tuberculosis; F. M. Alexander had chronic laryngitis; Gerda Alexander had rheumatic fever; Moshe Feldenkrais, Bonnie Bainbridge Cohen, and Judith Aston had severe accidents leaving crippling bone fractures" (1995: xi). Despite a common origin in sickness and injury, the research projects these practitioners launched in response to their own physical illnesses and injuries generated knowledge with applications that extend far beyond their own bodies or even the healing of similar problems. Sanford's memoir, *Waking* (2006), is written in autobiographical style and does not lay claim to research outputs in the sense I have defined. Nevertheless, towards the end of his memoir, Sanford articulates what I understand as a clearly framed research question in embodied technique. He asks: "How do you interact with a body that you cannot feel directly but is conscious nonetheless?" (185). Although Sanford would not describe his practice in epistemological terms, his encounter with yoga has undoubtedly done more than simply help him as an individual to manage the pain of his physical condition.

The premise of what I have identified as Sanford's research project is a relatively uncommon physical state in which the spinal nerves have been severed so that the brain cannot send commands or receive sensations from the lower part of the body. This situation constitutes the relative reliability of Sanford's embodiment. Conceived as a research project, the interaction between two parts of Sanford's body—one connected by nerves to the brain and one not—is the substrate of his research, the zone of embodiment in which it takes place. The methodology is Iyengar yoga. As Sanford recalls his introduction to yoga through a teacher named Jo, it is evident that his paraplegic body constitutes an unknown territory for postural yoga:

> After meeting me the first time, Jo called two senior teachers in the Iyengar method for advice. Their recommendations of one or two seated poses and some shoulder and arm stretches were of little help. She had already exhausted their ideas in our first session. She was left to her own devices, to her own creativity, to an uncommon openness that would guide our work together. She didn't have to be the expert. She knew Iyengar yoga—that

was clear. I was her student—that was also clear. But we explored the possibilities of yoga and paralysis together. She made me a partner in a great experiment.

(Sanford 2006: 187–88)

The reference to "senior teachers" indicates that Sanford's practice may constitute research on more than an individual level. It may in fact take place at the edge of a substantial field of existing knowledge, in this case that of Iyengar yoga. The senior teachers of Iyengar yoga are experts in their field, but they have no idea what to do with a partially paralyzed body. Hence, the problem posed by Sanford—how to practice yoga given his specific bodily capacities—is beyond the limits of knowledge held by that epistemic community. Sanford's question indicates a "research edge" of this field. Indeed, some practitioners of Iyengar yoga might have assumed that no engagement could be found between their technique and the substrate of Sanford's body. However, this turned out not to be the case, as Sanford is now a teacher of yoga who works with a wide range of students, "from the very advanced traditional student to the beginner with disabilities" (Matthew Sanford 2013). The field of yoga that could be practiced by Sanford had to be discovered through embodied research—that is, through an exploration of "the possibilities of yoga and paralysis."

Although modern medicine had saved Sanford's life after a severe accident, and given him a certain limited mobility, it was not able to restore to him an organic relationship with his body. Surgeons had inserted metal into Sanford's body in order to keep him upright, but they could not tell him what to do with the bottom half of his body. At one point, Sanford asked his doctors to amputate his legs, but they responded that he needed them as counterweight to keep his upper body upright. As a result, Sanford came to experience his lower extremities as dead weight. It was only through his encounter with yoga, described in the latter part of his book, that Sanford began to look for other ways to relate to those parts of his body. By the end of the memoir, it would no longer be correct to say that Sanford's lower body is disconnected or that he cannot move it. He can move it and is connected to it through touch, balance, and sensation, despite the absence of a link through the central nervous system. Describing this phenomenon, Sanford writes, "the mind is not strictly confined to a neurophysiological connection with the body. If I listen inwardly to my whole experience (both my mind's and my body's), my mind can feel into my legs" (2006: 193). Sanford's technique for accomplishing this includes new approaches to touch and balance—both valuable ways to interact with his lower body—as well as physical sensations that do not pass through the spinal cord but through some other channel. The fact that medical science could not offer him these pathways in practice suggests the importance of what I previously called the incommensurability of diverse branches of knowledge. Medical science saved Sanford's life, but it was helpless to map the field of embodied technique to which he still had access. For this, embodied research was needed.

It is impossible for me to say whether the extended proprioceptive sensation discovered by Sanford is the same or different from that taught by other somatic pioneers. Perhaps Sanford only rediscovered pathways of technique that Feldenkrais or Bainbridge-Cohen already knew and taught. This would still be research, but in the weaker sense of individual discovery. On the other hand, it is possible that Sanford has discovered some technique that is genuinely new, constituting research in the stronger sense. Either way, as a teacher of Iyengar yoga, Sanford offers knowledge that extends beyond what Iyengar himself would have imagined: knowledge derived from his own sustained investigations of embodiment. Sanford's research moves yoga decisively away from its current tendency to athleticize and instead extends its somatic dimension. It is possible to describe this research in terms of the gendered division of physical culture, as Sanford himself does when he writes that the integration of his mind and body brought with it a "deeper connection with the more vulnerable, feminine aspect" of himself (2006: 202). However, given all the work that has gone into dismantling restrictive gender roles in physical culture, it seems preferable to understand vulnerability as part of somatic technique rather than as archetypally feminine.

The argument of this chapter has been that, from Krishnamacharya and Iyengar to J. Brown and Matthew Sanford, the development and extension of modern postural yoga as a field of technique is quite distinct from scholarly or scientific research *on* yoga as a cultural and historical phenomenon. These are examples of research *in* yoga technique, understood as an important field of knowledge in its own right. The global but also diverse impact of such research suggests, among other things, that the success of postural yoga cannot be attributed to its "exotic" origins alone, or to a desire among Europeans and North Americans to appropriate Indian culture. Certainly, the initial appearances of yoga in Europe and North America were framed by discourses of Orientalism that were in many ways similar to those attending the rise of Chinese and Japanese martial arts.[6] Yet as Benjamin Richard Smith observes: "Western practitioners of Ashtanga Vinyasa Yoga do not appear to be simply mimicking practices drawn from 'another culture.' Rather, they seem to be successfully engaging in a set of supposedly exogenous bodily techniques and modes of somatic attention" (2007: 40). In other words, although Orientalist fantasy and misperceptions about yoga's ancient pedigree may play a role in its popularity, these cannot explain the intense commitment of the many non-Indian practitioners for whom yoga has become a regular activity or even a central part of life. Such practitioners are committed less to the idea or the name "yoga" than to the exploration of a specific area of embodied technique. Their engagement with yoga therefore cannot be understood through cultural analysis alone, but requires a close examination of technique.

What is physical education?

The remainder of this chapter takes a speculative approach to the project of reconceiving or remapping physical education in light of the foregoing discussion of physical culture. The term "physical education" is used by Mauss to refer to education and training in embodied technique, not just in childhood but throughout life (2006: 85). Today, physical education has a much more limited meaning. In my own high school, the division was stark between "health" and "physical education" classes, on the one hand, and dance and theatre, on the other. Health and PE were taught by the same teachers, the former in classrooms and the latter in a large gym or field house, where we engaged in competitive sports like tennis or swimming and in athletic training such as running and calisthenics. Dance and acting took place in a different building: the former in a studio with mirrors, ballet barre, and a wooden floor; the latter in a "black box" theatre studio.[7] At the time, it seemed to me that these two universes had nothing in common. They involved completely different kinds of physical and social effort. They also seemed to be intended for different types of people, different economic classes, different genders and sexualities. I felt intimidated by the men involved in sports and never dreamed of playing on a team. In contrast, men were a minority in the dance and theatre world, where I devoted countless hours to after-school rehearsals and productions. It did not occur to me then that, in contrast to all the other classes I took, both PE and acting/dance involved the use of my entire body. Both PE and performance classes relied less on reading, writing, and discussion than on embodied engagement. Looking back, it seems obvious that this set them apart from every other subject: math, science, literature, languages, etc. At the time, however, their differences were so great that I scarcely noticed their similarities.

The amount of embodied technique transmitted both explicitly and implicitly throughout the educational system is enormous. Chris Shilling writes: "The study of physical education has traditionally been a low-status subject within sociology, yet there is little justification for this as *all* education involves a physical education of the body" (in Evans *et al.* 2004: xx–xxi). One 1969 report on nursery school children revealed that "children experienced as many as thirty physical constraints on their behaviour in each hour, a figure which translates into thousands of corrections over a single year" (xvi). Shilling reminds us of Antonio Gramsci's pertinent observation that people must be "trained to acquire the stamina necessary to endure long hours of relative physical passivity," if they are to engage with activities like reading and writing at the levels modern societies demand (xxi). Yet in much contemporary education, embodied technique goes unmarked. Children train in physical practices of stillness and sitting, but these are not considered part of the content of lessons. In PE, on the other hand, embodied technique is the explicit content. But does physical education live up to its name by providing a substantive education in physical culture? Sociologists of education John Evans and Brian Davies call on us to deconstruct "common sense categories, such as the 'good' and 'able' child, 'intelligence,' 'physical ability,' 'skill,' 'health,' 'fitness' and 'educability,'" which are generated and endorsed by sometimes questionable scientific and scholarly research (Evans *et al.* 2004: 7). What happens if we examine physical education from an epistemological perspective?

Today, physical education—like yoga, martial arts, and increasingly even dance—is understood primarily through the ideology of healthism. As a result, it fails to offer students anything like an open-minded introduction to the range of physical culture that exists, let alone to physical culture as a field of ongoing research. Like the instrumental logics that impel teachers and schools to "teach to the test" in mathematics and history, the healthist ideology that equates athletic performance with health has led to a narrowing of physical culture to the point where it rarely involves more than sport and aerobic exercise. This is not to suggest that there could be anything like a "neutral" physical education curriculum. All education imposes limits by teaching certain pathways and implicitly foreclosing or ignoring others. But in light of the existing diversity of physical culture, it seems worthwhile to push back against the narrow concept of physical education as sports and athletics. Furthermore, an epistemological perspective suggests that physical education need not justify itself in terms of the dominant framework of health and fitness. It need not follow the commercial marketplace or popular culture in dismissing somatic technique as relevant only in the case of injury. On the contrary, physical *education* is precisely the context in which epistemological concerns should take precedence over economic ones. Rather than understanding physical education as a means to the acquisition of skills or the maintenance of health, we could see it as a critical and embodied introduction to physical culture in a broad sense. This suggests a mandate for physical education that is vastly greater, more challenging, and more urgent than is commonly ascribed to it.

Richard Tinning has critiqued the dominance of healthism and "mesomorphism" (the idealization of a certain body type) in physical education. In *Pedagogy and Human Movement*, Tinning attempts to rethink the field of "Human Movement Studies" by "moving outside the comfort zone afforded by the sub-culture of the active mesomorph" and engaging with perspectives on movement that go beyond sports and athletics (2010: 114).[8] In his examination of physical education trends in Australia, Tinning shows how what we can now identify as relatively somatic approaches to physical education were overtaken by more athletic technique. One approach, called "movement education" and based on the work of Rudolf Laban, emphasized "individualization" and "problem solving," asking students to explore and experiment with movement rather than to drill particular forms (54–56). Instructors in this line of practice did not give physical demonstrations, but instead asked students to respond to verbal cues in their own ways. In epistemological terms, "movement education" taught students how to conduct their own individual research in and through movement. As Tinning recounts, this approach was marginalized during the 1970s, giving way to "more scientifically focused forms of PE (including fitness training and circuit training) on one side, and to sports and sports skills on the other" (55). Once again, this "marginalization had a strong gendered dimension," since "movement education was very much (but not solely) the preserve of women PE teachers and the science and sports focus were largely championed by men." Here, the gendering of physical culture is inscribed not in adult society but through the physical education of young people.

Tinning sees the physical education teacher—a much maligned figure in today's popular culture—as a serious educator. In his view, physical educators and scholars of human movement studies have a joint responsibility to continually re-envision physical education and to determine what kinds of knowledge will be passed along to the next generation. What could happen if we took physical culture seriously, as one of the major areas of knowledge in which schools prepare children for adulthood, alongside literacy and math, humanities and sciences? What if we called upon physical education to introduce students to a wide range of embodied technique—not just sport and exercise, but also somatics, dance, martial arts, and yoga? With this remit, physical education would be obliged to offer a curriculum that is both broad and deep, introducing students to many kinds of movement-based technique while also helping them understand what it means to explore a narrowly framed area in greater depth. The relevant question would then no longer be how to keep kids healthy or compel them to exercise, but rather how to provide the best and most comprehensive introduction to the embodied technique of physical culture, where the latter is understood as a field of knowledge rather than a means to a known end. As a result, students would be better able to navigate the kaleidoscopic—but not necessarily epistemically diverse—array of fashionable new "Techniques" offered by today's health and fitness marketplace.

Consider the following three examples of new physical culture forms, drawn from the official websites of Zumba, Bokwa, and Nia:

> Zumba Fitness® is the only Latin-inspired dance-fitness program that blends red-hot international music, created by Grammy Award-winning producers, and contagious steps to form a "fitness-party" that is downright addictive. Since its inception in 2001, the Zumba program has grown to become the world's largest—and most successful—dance-fitness program with more than 12 million people of all shapes, sizes and ages taking weekly Zumba classes in over 110,000 locations across more than 125 countries.
>
> (Zumba Fitness 2012)

> BOKWA … is an intense cardiovascular workout combined with South African war dance, Capoeira, Kickboxing and Steps. It has been proven to burn a great amount of calories making it easier for weight loss goals. Through the use of fast paced extreme movement, a fun, challenging, and energizing total body workout was created.
>
> (Bokwa Fitness 2012)

> Nia is a sensory-based movement practice that draws from martial arts, dance arts and healing arts. It empowers people of all shapes and sizes by connecting the body, mind, emotions and spirit. Classes are taken barefoot to soul-stirring music in more than 45 countries … Step into your own joyful journey with Nia, and positively shape the way you feel, look, think and live. Nia draws from Tai Chi, Tae Kwon Do, Aikido, jazz dance, modern dance, Duncan dance, yoga, Alexander Technique and Teachings of Moshe Feldenkrais.
>
> (Nia Now 2012)

How rigorous are the research projects that underpin these allegedly new inventions? How different are they from each other and from the practices on which they draw? To what extent are they new areas of technique, rather than simply efforts to rebrand and repackage, say, the aerobics of the 1980s? Which areas of embodied technique does each explore, and what do they leave out? While Nia is apparently influenced by somatics—citing healing rather than health, welcoming "people of all shapes and sizes," and listing Alexander and Feldenkrais among its sources—all three of these accept the basic premises of healthism, offering individuals a packaged and consumable way to alter themselves through movement.

A meaningful physical education would prepare students to encounter such newly trademarked movement brands alongside practices that name themselves after more established traditions—from ballet to *taijiquan*, and of course postural yoga—with an understanding of the epistemic landscape within which they function. Physical education, in other words, could see itself as providing the resources to navigate a movement world that is far richer and more varied than the one envisioned by healthist athletics. This may sound far-fetched, but it is no more radical than the kinds of pedagogical changes that have swept other areas of general education over the past decades. The difference is that physical education is not usually understood as a field of knowledge. Like dance and theatre, it tends to receive little serious attention in discussions of academic curriculum. The critique of education has neglected the body and underestimated the importance of embodiment in schooling (Evans *et al.* 2004: xv), too often seeing bodily practices as "unworthy of critical reflection" and "unlikely agents of change" (Markula 2008: 389). As a result, ideas that have been hotly debated in the context of English composition or math pedagogy are only now beginning to receive consideration in the field of physical education. This may be why, as Tinning writes, "many young people still graduate from our schools oppressed by the tyranny of the cult of the body" (in Evans *et al.* 2004: 219). If we already know "what a body can do," then the job of physical educators is merely to discipline and athleticize young bodies, rather than to introduce them to a lifelong process of individual embodied research. Collectively, we must recognize that embodied technique is not a by-product of theory, but a site and methodology of research in its own right. To renew and reinvent physical education, we must place critical theory and pedagogy alongside embodied technique, laying them side by side as *contiguous* rather than hierarchical fields.

Consider, for example, the technique of breathing, which is rarely introduced as part of childhood physical education. What could be more physical than breath? Yet at the same time, what could more intimately, viscerally, and undeniably connect the physical to other kinds of embodied technique? Breath, as noted above, is essential to athletics because it underpins competitive abilities—most obviously in the case of swimming, but actually in every sport. Yet a more explicit focus on breath, as we saw with J. Brown's Abhyasa Yoga, tends to immediately shift the emphasis of a practice towards the somatic pole. The linking of breath to movement in "vinyasa" was one of the principal innovations of Krishnamacharya, a synthesis of somatic and athletic technique that undoubtedly contributed to yoga's meteoric rise to global popularity. This is just one small example of breathing technique as a keystone of physical culture. In the epigraph preceding this chapter, Roland Barthes compares the use of breath in Catholic and Orthodox prayer to that found in Buddhist meditation (1989: 44). Elsewhere, Don Hanlon Johnson imagines an unwritten "volume on embodied breath that would include Ilsa Middendorf, Elsa Gindler, hatha yoga, Taoism, and Russian hesychasm" (1995: xiii). Jane Boston and Rena Cook have attempted to compile a volume along these lines, bringing somatic bodywork together with martial arts, acting, and dance (2009). Brian Lande has studied what it means to breathe "like a soldier" by analyzing "two situations (running, and shooting) where a specific technique of breathing anchors the soldier's body in the military world" (2007: 99). Studying and practicing different forms of breathing technique could serve as a gateway to a world of diverse practices. It could ground the study of history and culture in the relative reliability of embodiment and reveal the contiguity of physical culture with other areas of knowledge. Such possibilities suggest a very different kind of physical education.

Notes

1 On biopower and biopolitics, see Rabinow and Rose 2006. On healthism, see Rich *et al.* 2004: 178–81; Tinning 2010: 177–80. On the historical and philosophical concept of health, see Canguilhem 2008; Csordas 2004.

2 This usage of "performance" to indicate measurable competitive output is another reason why I prefer the term "practice" to designate the specific doings that are structured by technique. For more on corporate, military, and other uses of performance, in relation to those of theatre and performance studies, see McKenzie 2001.

3 I argue in Chapter 4 that gender itself can be conceived as an area of technique. This would make gender and physical culture distinct but contiguous fields of knowledge, which would then be subject to interdisciplinary interaction— rather than, as is usually assumed, two different dimensions or axes of social practice. My argument in this chapter is simpler and more conventional in structure.

4 The disproportionate number of famous yoga teachers who are male (Krishnamacharya, Iyengar, Jois, Bikram Choudhury, etc.) surely reflects a patriarchal bias in culture at large rather than the specific gendering of yoga.

5 The *Körper/Leib* distinction is commonly attributed to Maurice Merleau-Ponty. Hans-Peter Krüger (2010) clarifies that it was originally put forward by philosophical anthropologist Helmuth Plessner. See also Drew Leder's essay, "A Tale of Two Bodies: The Cartesian Corpse and the Lived Body" (in Welton 1998: 117–29).

6 If anything, the impact of Orientalist fantasy in the transmission of embodied technique has been even more pronounced in martial arts than in yoga, due to the phenomenon of spectacular and entertaining martial arts films. See essays in Farrer and Whalen-Bridge 2011 and Green and Svinth 2003.

7 In the 1990s, the Cambridge Rindge and Latin School had a very strong performing arts department, led by Judith Contrucci, Gerry Speca, Steve Hall, and Barbara Ehrlich. Its material resources were due in part to its being the only public high school in the city of Cambridge, Massachusetts.

8 The privileging of the mesomorph and of athletic technique are not identical phenomena. There are plenty of world-class athletes whose body types do not match that of the current aesthetic ideal, as compellingly illustrated by the photography of Schatz and Ornstein (2002). Placing 300-pound Olympic weightlifter Cheryl Haworth next to 85-pound Olympic gymnast Olga Karmansky reveals the absurdity of equating ability with body type. One can acknowledge this while still romanticizing disciplined physical training, strength, and competitive mastery as representative of the greatest human achievements. Nevertheless, Tinning is surely correct that the privileging of the mesomorphic body is linked to the dominance of certain kinds of technique in physical education.

In the beginning of our activity we too believed in the "myth of technique," something which it was possible to acquire, to possess ... This faith in technique as a sort of magic power which could render the actor invulnerable, guided us also in the domain of the voice ... For a long time the "myth of technique" nourished our work. Then gradually it brought me to a situation of doubt. I had to admit that the argument for technique was a rationalization, a pragmatic blackmail—if you do this, you obtain that—which I used to make others accept my way of working ...

(Barba 1972: 49–53)

What form was communicated over the decades and three continents, in the medium of muscle and bone? What hospitality made that possible? What precisely traveled over that time and space?

(Roach 2011: 36:45–37:02)

3

ACTORS WITHOUT A THEATRE

Craft and presence

This chapter analyzes acting technique as a field of knowledge, situating the craft of acting within a broader epistemic context and applying the theoretical framework developed thus far to the study of theatre and performance. I begin by arguing that much of what goes by the name "actor training" is more accurately a kind of research in acting technique. Focusing on *training* without also naming *research* does a disservice to the epistemic field of acting and limits our understanding of the diversity of acting practices. From this premise, I turn to a close examination of particular elements of the work of Konstantin Stanislavski (1863–1938) and Jerzy Grotowski (1933–99), examining aspects of each through an epistemological lens. In both cases, I am looking to identify specific *research outcomes* and to analyze these in technical terms. I first examine Stanislavski's "method of physical actions," as described in the memoir of Vasily Toporkov, and then look at songs and other epistemic objects investigated by Grotowski and his colleagues at the Workcenter in Pontedera, Italy. Following this, I critique certain recurring ideas in contemporary discussions of acting—the commonplace notions of "neutral," "extra-daily," and "empty" technique—and I ask what it would mean to cultivate a more explicit and robust *research culture* in this field. I conclude with a discussion of two major interdisciplinary lines of inquiry that characterize current research in acting—its intersections with physical culture and with cultural identity—and with a call for a revised concept of the contemporary theatre laboratory.

A few boundaries should be clarified regarding the scope of this analysis. First, I am concerned here with contemporary Anglophone pedagogical and critical discourse on the craft and technique of acting, including both academic texts and the language of actor training. Although I closely examine some aspects of the work of Stanislavski and Grotowski, I do not offer an overview of their careers or legacies, nor do I intend to add substantive new information to the historical record of these figures. Instead, I draw key examples from their practices to enrich the discussion of embodied knowledge and research developed thus far. I do not dwell on the relevant Russian or Polish cultural contexts or make use of sources in those languages. In the case of Stanislavski's "method of physical actions," I rely heavily upon the account of a single individual. While I hope this discussion will shed new light on the work of both figures—in particular, how we think about their relevance to contemporary practice—my primary goal is to further develop the epistemology of practice by extending the notion of research into the field of acting technique. Likewise, my discussion of interdisciplinary links between acting, physical culture, and cultural identity is not intended to comprehensively survey these vast areas, but only to indicate how an epistemological perspective could help reframe the practice of acting. More than a historical study, this chapter proposes an alternative conceptual framework for acting, which I hope may be of use to both theorists and practitioners.[1]

Anglophone discourse around acting in the past hundred years has displayed a profound ambiguity with regard to the question of what might constitute *transmissible knowledge* of the craft. As John Lutterbie observes: "No one seriously doubts the importance of technique in acting. However, it is also viewed with ambivalence" (2011: 131). Whether or not they explicitly refer to technique, many of the best-known Euro-American teachers and practitioners have taken great pains to reject the notion that acting is transmissible or that it could be subject to systematic articulation. Surveying the essays collected in Alison Hodge's *Actor Training* (2010), one finds that Stanislavski asserted, "There is no System" (23); Joan Littlewood "denied the existence of any method or way of working to a system" (130); Joseph Chaikin expressed "a resistance towards describing exercises, and a resistance to 'recipe-books' that document exercises" (168); Grotowski "became increasingly wary about providing descriptions of specific physical and vocal exercises" (201); and Jacques Lecoq, Monika Pagneux, and Philippe Gaulier "would strenuously deny that their teaching practice represents a 'method,' and most certainly would be dismayed to have their work yoked together in a common 'system' or 'technique'" (215). This otherwise diverse sampling of artists and teachers is striking in its united rejection of the idea that acting can be standardized or rendered methodical. Their energetic repudiation of notions like *philosophy, system, exercise, recipe, method*, and *technique* reveals an acute sense of caution about how the verbal or written analysis of embodied practice can lead to reductive misunderstandings.

Rather than risk such confusions, many artists prefer to underestimate the transmissibility of what they know.

At its most extreme, the denial of system and method in the work of actors can lead to a dichotomy in which the repeatable and transmissible aspects of acting are radically divorced from a reified quality of "presence" in the actor. It then becomes possible to describe specific exercises or techniques, while at the same time implying that these ultimately have little to do with what makes an actor or ensemble effective or captivating. In this vein, Jane Goodall identifies "two models of human presence" that "remain at the core of the western theatrical tradition":

> To the first belong all the regimes of training and technical prowess: elocution and vocal technique, deportment, the aesthetics of gesture and facial expression. The second is suggested in the more mysterious qualities of magnetism and mesmerism, a sense of inner power being radiated outwards ... The scientific and the uncanny, mystique and technique, may be frequently in tension but they are also hand in glove.
>
> (Goodall 2008: 8–9)

Such dualism plays into what I have called the trope of excess. In this romantic view, skill and technique deserve respect and can even be impressive, but they are ontologically—and perhaps also ethically— inferior to real presence, which is understood as a quasi-mystical power: Hodge calls it "intrinsic, mysterious, essential," and "innate" (2010: xxii). As noted, the trope of excess is most often used to rank practices according to a spectrum that ranges from the "merely" technical to the "more than" technical. In the teaching of acting, this trope may appear through the idea of talent, conceived as "an elusive quality that cannot be taught or learned" and which "seems to exist separately from skill, technique, and knowledge" (Nigel Rideout cited in Prior 2012: 21). The real effect of the trope of excess is to allow those who evaluate performances to avoid articulating their own values and priorities. Instead of clarifying what exactly they perceive in a given performance, this trope allows critics and theorists to appeal to a reified and exaggerated notion of sheer presence, talent, or quality, as distinct from embodied technique.

We saw in Chapter 1 how the denigration of technique as mechanical repetition can be traced back to its first English usage by Samuel Coleridge in 1817. In the twentieth century, such wariness has more to do with an increasing sense of alarm concerning technology and the rapid technologization of society. This can be seen in the work of late twentieth-century philosophers who criticize the "illusion of technique" (Barrett 1978) or the "lure of technique" (Dunne 1992). In theatre, a similar rhetorical move underpins what Eugenio Barba has called the "myth of technique." In the first epigraph preceding this chapter, Barba evokes a narrative that is familiar by now, even cliché: One begins with technique and follows it to a certain point, after which it must be abandoned lest it become stultifying and restrictive. Significantly, Barba derides the "argument for technique" as based not just on error, but on a kind of "blackmail": a lie about the reliability of the world and our ability to control the outcomes of organic processes. In this way, he repeats the romantic underestimation of technique. Using what I have identified as the trope of excess, Barba dismisses yoga, ballet, mime, and gymnastics as stepping stones on the way to a practice that will transcend mere technique (1972: 48). Tellingly, Barba associates technique with Asian performance traditions that are based on a "purely technical apprenticeship" in "codified" and "mechanically" learned "virtuosity." He posits an "essential difference" between this and a European approach based on "personal attitude" or "inner necessity" and the actor as "creator" (49, 52, 48).[2] Reading this through an epistemological lens allows us to strip away Barba's cultural essentialism and progressive narrative. Rather than distinguishing the merely-technical from the more-than-technical, we can then identify two branches or areas of technique: one that works on the composition of the performer's body and voice and another that works with imagination and personal associations. To identify either of these with "presence" would be a mistake.

Yet it would be misleading to characterize Barba as simply opposed to technique. While the cited essay rejects the "myth" of technique—the idea that it has a deterministic relationship to practice, so that "if you do this, you obtain that"—the notion of technique I propose is in some ways close to the comparative embodied knowledge that Barba has long sought to investigate through his International School of Theatre Anthropology (see Watson 2002). The *Dictionary of Theatre Anthropology* (Barba and Savarese 1991) is one of the boldest attempts thus far to develop a comparative epistemic mapping of embodied performance technique. Elsewhere, Barba divides technique into three more nuanced categories: daily, virtuosic, and extra-daily (1995: 16). It seems likely that Barba's understanding of technique grew more comparative and less hierarchical between the early 1970s and the later publications related to ISTA. (This development mirrors that of Grotowski—discussed below—as well as larger cultural and intellectual trends.) In a sense, Barba's concept of theatre anthropology can be seen as a precursor to the epistemology of practice developed here, although it does not attempt to integrate "the study of man in a theatrical situation" into the broader discipline of cultural anthropology and the analysis of everyday culture (Barba 1988: 14). Later in this chapter, I return to the notion of "extra-daily" technique. First, however, I want to examine a term that has become even more central in contemporary discussions of acting: "training." In his earlier essay, Barba uses this word to name that apparently deeper and more individualized process—"a process of self-definition, a process of self-discipline" (1972: 47)—of which technique is one aspect. In part due to his influence, this has since become a standard way of thinking about the relation between technique and training—one that, I argue, may need revisiting.

Beyond "actor training"

The past two decades have witnessed a slew of scholarly publications focused on the training of actors and performers (Watson 2001; Bartow 2006; Evans 2008; Margolis and Renaud 2010; Matthews 2011; Prior 2012). In addition to these volumes, the journal *Theatre, Dance and Performance Training* takes training as its central unifying concept. Training also figures centrally in a variety of works that focus on acting and the actor's work (Zarrilli 1995; Krasner 2000; Nascimento 2009). In general, "training" in these texts functions to extend the study of acting beyond the bounds of public performance and into various kinds of preparation and rehearsal processes. It is in this sense that actor training can be seen as "arguably the most important development in modern Western theatre making" (Hodge 2010: xviii). But how did training come to occupy such a central place in our understanding of theatre and performance? What function does the word "training" have, and is it really the best name for the processes and practices discussed and analyzed by these authors?

Despite the important work that has been done in its name, the concept of training is limiting insofar as it emphasizes the transmission of knowledge over its creation, discovery, or production. From an epistemological point of view, to speak of *training* without in the same breath mentioning *research* suggests that a field of knowledge is being sustained without being extended: that is, existing knowledge is being passed along, but new knowledge is not being developed. Clearly, the practices discussed in the works just cited go beyond training in this sense. However, the discourse of actor training suggests no distinction between the transmission of knowledge and its production. Even more troublingly, this discourse tends to subsume research practices under the rubric of "training," thereby flattening out the epistemic depth of the field by failing to acknowledge the gulf of expertise that separates the novice from the advanced practitioner. What is the difference between training in a form and conducting research in a field? And where, after all, do the forms of training come from? It is customary to juxtapose training with "creation" or "performance." Alternately, we may speak of individuals combining or synthesizing diverse approaches to training. However, neither creation/performance nor the synthesis of previously existing forms can adequately account for the substantive development of new technique. At present, there is no commonly accepted term for this missing link, which is really an essential third term alongside training and performance. We can talk about the development of new approaches to actor "training," or about the creation of new performances, but not about the *discovery of substantively new areas of acting technique*. This linguistic gap is particularly strange given that the major innovations in acting—such as those discussed by the contributors to Hodge's *Actor Training* (2010)—are neither varieties of training nor components of specific performances. Rather, they are innovations in technique or craft, in the very fabric of what constitutes acting. To understand such innovations, we cannot do without a concept of *research in acting*.

Two clarifications are needed: First, I am not suggesting that there is a lack of actual research in acting technique. Quite the opposite—there is a great deal of research in acting technique, but it usually goes nameless and misrecognized because it appears under the inaccurate label of "training." Virtually every area of technique that structures contemporary acting practice—from Stanislavski's active analysis to Strasberg's Method acting, from Decroux's corporeal mime to Staniewski's musicality, and from Boal's Theatre of the Oppressed to Bogart's Viewpoints—is an innovation resulting from *research in technique*. None of these can be reduced to a matter of "training." Secondly, I am not suggesting that there is a lack of *scholarly research* on the topic of acting. All the publications cited above, and many more, analyze and theorize acting from various perspectives that include the historiographic, semiotic, phenomenological, and pedagogical. There is already a substantial "research culture" in the scholarly field of research *on* acting. What is missing is a conceptual framework that would allow us to name—and thereby analyze, critique, and support—a parallel but distinct research culture *in* acting as an epistemic field. While research *on* acting produces scholarly and intellectual knowledge about acting, research *in* acting produces new acting technique. The latter must be acknowledged if we hope to understand how acting changes, or to compare acting practices, across time and space.

Returning to an issue raised briefly above, we can now ask: What is the transmissible knowledge content of any given practice of (theatrical) acting or performance? Current discourse offers a plethora of terms that could in some cases describe transmissible knowledge, but which are rarely defined with precision. In addition to *work* and *training*, these include *style, school, teaching, method, mode, model, craft, approach, convention, brand, exercise, principle, process, protocol, procedure, discipline, form, strategy*, and *tool*. Some of these, like *protocol* or *regime*, have Foucauldian connotations. Others, like *craft* or *style*, recall earlier periods and eras and their quite different practices of theatrical production. *Method* and *model* are quasi-scientific, while *school* and *pedagogy* suggest coherent lineages and underscore the importance of the personal relationship between student and teacher. *Convention* evokes social constructionism and semiotics. Of these terms, *approach* is perhaps the most useful because it is so vague. Who could deny that there are many different "approaches" to acting? But what exactly constitutes such an approach? How do approaches relate to styles, brands, methods, or pedagogies? Most often, these terms are used interchangeably, as in the following passage:

> I use "Method" to include all the major American approaches to acting based in Stanislavsky's fundamental principles and strategies. Though this lacks subtlety, the term allows us to place these related approaches together and refers explicitly to two of the main forms, Stanislavsky's method of physical actions and Strasberg's Method.
>
> (Rhonda Blair in Krasner 2000: 217n1)

Within these few lines we encounter each of the following terms: *approach, principle, strategy, form, method*. Should these be taken as synonyms? Or are there significant differences between them? I quote this sentence not because it is exceptional, but because it illustrates a common trend in the scholarship of acting: There exists a common pedagogical vocabulary, but little work has been done to more rigorously define the terms in which acting is analyzed.

With this in mind, let us reconsider the relation between training and technique. Some recent discussions of acting and performance continue to use the trope of excess to define this relation, as we saw in Barba (1972) above. More recently, John Matthews has coined the term *askeology* to name a comparative study of training across the domains of performance, physical therapy, and monastic life (2011). As noted in the introduction, there are significant parallels between Matthews's proposal for askeology and my own notion of embodied technique. However, the limitations of training as an overarching concept for theorizing embodied knowledge and practice become evident when one notices that Matthews's book addresses only the effects of established training regimes upon individuals and groups, and not the question of where such regimes come from and how they develop. In contrast, a robust epistemology of practice must be as concerned with the invention of technique as with its transmission and effects. Mark Evans and Simon Murray run into a similar problem when they state, within the span of a single page, first that "training must ultimately aim to transcend mere demonstration of technique" and then that "training is inevitably more than just the acquisition of technique" (2012: 141). The explicit contradiction between these assertions reveals the untenability of the trope of excess when applied to a wide range of practices. If we replace training with "practice," then we can affirm the second statement (practice is always more than the technique that structures it) and recognize the first as an example of the trope of excess (the idea that we have to work in some special way in order to escape the limitations of "mere" technique). It may well be that what Evans and Murray want training to "transcend" is not technique but athleticism. In any case, I suggest that we have a responsibility as theorists to articulate the aims of our practice using more subtle instruments than the trope of excess. We must name the contents of the "more than."

It is ironic that "technique" has today come to refer to the dimension of practice that most approximates formulaic repetition, while "training" has been elevated to the status of "more than" technique. In contemporary actor training, the word "technique" reeks of the merely known, while training is increasingly theorized as encapsulating both technique and something "more": the leap into the unknown, into phenomenal presence, into vitality. Yet if we consider the roots and histories of these words, we find that training has stronger and deeper associations with mechanical repetition and externally imposed forms than does technique. As Simon Shepherd points out, "[t]he word 'training' only started to become associated with the activity of education in the early to middle sixteenth century," while the "application to theatre and music came pretty late in the history of training" (2009: 5–6). Before this shift, training was primarily a military concept, "associated not only with transmitting skill and technique but also with creating coherent group entities" (6). Derived etymologically from a French verb meaning to "pull" or "drag," training suggests the effects of external constraints and forces upon a passive object, as in a train of wagons or railroad cars (OED Online 2012). It thus carries none of the epistemological associations of technique, which as we saw in Chapter 1 derives from one of Aristotle's basic modes of knowledge. Much more than technique, the word "training" suggests the enactment of previously known forms, or travel along well-established pathways. It does not tell us where these forms come from or how these pathways are laid down.

I propose that, like any other field of knowledge, acting technique is sustained by the ongoing and dynamic *interaction of training and research*. Technique therefore exceeds training in a very precise sense: It involves both the known and the unknown in relation to each other. Training may then refer to any practice in which existing knowledge is intentionally passed along, inculcated, or absorbed. This includes mandatory or imposed training, self-directed training, military training, dance training, actor training, spiritual training, strength training, physio-therapeutic training or "re-training," the training of animals, and more. In other words, training can refer to any practice that works through previously established pathways of practice. Training can be an ongoing, even lifelong process: a continual and iterative encounter with technique. What training cannot logically signify is the development or discovery of *new technique*: new pathways in materiality, newly recognized patterns and forms in which one might then proceed to train. One cannot "train" in a discipline that does not exist. When Matthews, Evans, and Murray suggest that training is "more than" technique, they are pointing to exactly this potential of discovery, on both individual and social levels. But rather than attribute this difference to the mystifying and hierarchical trope of excess, an epistemological model allows us to articulate the content of the "more than" as precisely *research*. Without research, there would be no forms or disciplines—no technique—in which to train. If training is the transmission of what is known, then research is the edge of any epistemic field.

Although "training" is the key term organizing Hodge's *Actor Training*, the word "research" also appears in some of the essays, especially when authors strive to articulate the innovative character of what was done, its newness in comparison with what went before. Thus Hodge refers to the "deep research processes of Jerzy Grotowski, Eugenio Barba, and Włodzimierz Staniewski" (Hodge 2010: xix), and Dorinda Hulton describes Joseph Chaikin as working in a "research theatre" (173). Without explicitly invoking research, Augusto Boal clarifies the purpose of a workshop called "New Techniques from the Theatre of the Oppressed" by noting, "techniques don't come out of the blue sky" (312, 322n15). In each of these cases, research is invoked as a necessary process through which new technique is developed. The word "research" is also found in the names of some theatre and dance institutions, where it seems to indicate the extent to which their work extends beyond either training or performance: Peter Brook's International Centre for Theatre Research (2012) in Paris; the Centre for Study of Jerzy Grotowski's

Work and for Cultural and Theatrical Research in Poland, now called the Grotowski Institute (2012); and the organization Movement Research (2012) in New York City, which continues the legacy of Judson Dance Theater's "movement research" (Burt 2006: 57).[3] To my knowledge, none of these institutions has offered a precise definition of the "research" they conduct, as distinct from academic or scientific research. Nevertheless, the nature of their relationships to the artistic fields of dance and theatre suggests something very like the "research and development" wing of a wider community of knowledge.

There is more to be said about the notion of "research in acting" and what it might look like to more explicitly foster research culture in this field (as distinct from research in the history or theory of acting). Before considering these broader issues, it may be useful to explore two relatively narrow but historically significant examples of research in acting. Each of these illustrates not only the potential to discover new technique through research, but also the breadth of impact that such discoveries can have through their subsequent transmission.

Stanislavski's threshold[4]

Towards the end of his life, Konstantin Stanislavski gathered together a small number of actors to work on Molière's *Tartuffe*. According to Vasili Toporkov, a member of the group, Stanislavki chose that play for its small cast and because it would allow him to prove that the acting technique he had spent a lifetime developing was not limited to the genre of realism (2004: 104). This was to be a period of "work on technique, on the re-education of the actor and the acquisition of a new method of working on oneself" (154). Stanislavski had no intention of premiering *Tartuffe,* and indeed the production was not mounted until after his death in 1938. Although Toporkov suggests that "Stanislavski had undertaken his work on *Tartuffe* purely for teaching purposes" (114), it seems more accurate to describe this period of work as a kind of research. More than the transmission of existing knowledge (actor training), *Tartuffe* was to be a site for the continuation of Stanislavski's lifelong investigations in the field of acting technique. In this section, I reread Toporkov's memoir as an epistemic trace of embodied research. I am less interested here in how Stanislavski was inspired by the science of his day, or understood his own work as scientific (see Pitches 2006), than in how his contributions to acting technique may be understood as research outcomes in the sense defined in Chapter 1.

According to the epistemology of practice developed thus far, if Stanislavski indeed conducted research in acting, then we should be able to: identify the precise points at which his research branched off from previous technique; articulate the results of that research in terms of new technique; and compare this new technique with other kinds practiced before and since. As Sharon Marie Carnicke observes, Stanislavski "never envisioned his System as complete. He suggested no final answers, only various experiments. As he cautioned, 'There is no system. There is only nature'" (1998: 61). The word "nature" here suggests—as in Marcel Mauss's "compromise between nature and humanity"—the empirical and realist dimension of embodied research.[5] There is "no system," as Stanislavski declared, because such pathways are never entirely reliable—particularly when the substrate of technique is as diverse and developmental as human embodiment—and also because the goals of embodied technique continually change along with changes in society. But there is also "no system" because, if the goal is to explore what people can do—in this case, what actors can do—that search is never-ending. One may encounter revolutionary findings, but one is never finished, because there is always more to be known, more areas of technique to explore. Carnicke and others have recently highlighted the diversity of Stanislavski's interests and pointed to the fact that he focused on different kinds of acting technique in different periods of his life. According to Carnicke, each time a generation of Stanislavski's students began to transform his most recent discoveries into fixed routines, he would start up a new studio or group with which to continue his research (46).

There is an explicit epistemology underpinning Toporkov's memoir, but it is not the one I have elaborated here. Toporkov treats knowledge as progressive, as if it moves from one hypothesis to another until arriving at final truths. He describes Stanislavski's approach as a "new, improved, more effective acting technique" and dismisses other approaches as mistakes, dead ends, or failures (2004: 101). Toporkov attributes a kind of finality and completeness to Stanislavski's findings that is not compatible with the always-provisional findings of genuine research. In other words, he subscribes to the "illusion," "lure," or "myth" of technique discussed above: the idea that technique develops through progressive improvement towards perfection, rather than through successive or parallel explorations of adjacent areas. As translator Jean Benedetti notes, Toporkov is "toeing the [Communist] party line" when he extols Stanislavski's technique as uniquely valid. However, Toporkov's claim that "Stanislavski achieved results that were unprecedented in the history of world theatre" should be distinguished from his assertion that these results constituted a "most perfect weapon in our struggle for great ideas on the cultural front" (162–63). The first claim is epistemological and should be assessed in those terms. I will argue here that Stanislavski may indeed have discovered historically unprecedented areas of embodied technique. This has nothing to do with the assertion that what he discovered was superior to all previous technique. As Carnicke writes, we should avoid "investing the System with linear and teleological development" (1998: 150). Instead, we should see it as a series of research outcomes, guided by precise questions and at the same time limited, like all research, by the scope of investigation.

By the time Toporkov went to work with him, Stanislavski was already well known for his "bizarre methods" and the "new kind of acting" he promoted (2004: 8–9). As Benedetti explains, acting pedagogy at that time "consisted mainly in students preparing scenes that were then reworked by the tutor. Sometimes a student would prepare only one or two scenes throughout his entire studies and would merely learn to copy his master's tricks" (Stanislavski 2008: xvii). Toporkov's description of his own substantial acting career prior to joining the Moscow Art Theatre adds detail to this picture, as he describes great actors struggling to pass along their abilities to their students. One great actor named Davydov, we are told, would regale his pupils with inspiring stories and provide brilliant analysis of dramatic scripts. When he was done, his "students would rush onstage and start rehearsing, only to realise that they could not do what had seemed so simple, clear and easy a moment before. *Their technique was inadequate.* They couldn't achieve even a hundredth of what their beloved teacher had so clearly explained" (Toporkov 2004: 2). Other teachers faced similar limitations. As Toporkov observes, they "could not explain to their pupils" the secrets of acting technique, "although they tried to do so with all their heart and soul" (2004: 3). These actors knew "secrets" of acting in that they had found relatively reliable pathways through their own personal embodiment. But they had not generalized these pathways as more widely transmissible knowledge in the form of technique.

A radically new area of research is often one that branches off close to the roots of previously existing knowledge. Instead of taking existing knowledge for granted, and seeking to discover new possibilities at the edges of what is known, radically new research may locate a hidden doorway or threshold—a branch of technique that had previously gone unseen or been dismissed as unimportant—and dive through it into hitherto unexplored territory. One way to understand Stanislavski's research in acting is to see it as based on the realization that some of the most important technique employed by the "great" actors of his day was not directly perceptible to the audience. In other words, Stanislavski realized that acting technique can involve not only practicing how to move or speak onstage but also engaging with the content of a play in ways that become perceptible in performance only indirectly. The term "indirect" here is borrowed from Nick Crossley, who uses it to describe embodied technique that achieves its ends via the stimulation of unconscious processes—such as closing one's eyes in order to fall asleep, or marching and chanting in order to arouse anger at a protest (2004; and see Chapter 1). In the case of acting, a distinction based on direct or indirect uses of technique is more precise than one that distinguishes between "inner" and "outer" approaches.[6] In what follows, I refer not to the inside and outside of the actor but to direct and indirect uses of technique, as well as to the gap between the repeatable and the perceptible—that is, between what actors reliably do and what audiences reliably perceive.

Stanislavski's contributions to acting technique can be seen as resting upon the idea that the perceptible dimension of performance is to a great extent an indirect effect or by-product of layers of embodied technique that are largely imperceptible. But the indirect use of technique in acting, by itself, would not have made Stanislavski's work radically new. There is ample historical precedent for indirect acting in this sense, as Mel Gordon illustrates when he argues that "substitution as an acting strategy" has a history as old as acting itself. Gordon offers two evocative examples of actors in other eras focusing on memories from their own lives rather than on those of the fictional characters they played—one from classical Greece and another from nineteenth-century England. During an ancient Athenian performance of *Electra*, Gordon tells us, "the tragic actor Polus placed the actual ashes of his dead son in an urn that was supposed to contain the remains of Orestes." Similarly, Edmund Kean in 1814 "reflected upon his deceased adopted uncle when he held up the skull of 'Poor Yorick' in *Hamlet*" (Gordon 2010: 54).[7] In these examples, actors do things that are hidden from the audience in order to achieve perceptible results. Likewise, James McTeague argues that Steele MacKaye's adaptations of François Delsarte's theories anticipated Stanislavski's work by focusing on spontaneity and on the emotional and imaginative relationship between "inner state" and "outward manifestations" (1993: 10). These are pre-Stanislavskian precedents for indirect acting technique.

We can surmise that countless performers throughout history have enhanced their performances using embodied technique that was only indirectly perceptible to their audiences. Yet how many of them explored the indirect use of technique as a comprehensive approach to acting? How many of them taught what Gordon calls "substitution as an acting strategy" to their apprentices, not merely as a trick of the trade but as a substantial area of technique alongside movement, gesture, and vocal production? From an epistemological perspective, there is a vast difference between using something as "a" technique and treating it as a starting point or gateway into an *area* of technique. In European theatrical traditions, including those of dance and opera, it had long been assumed that what one rehearses should coincide with what one wants the audience to see. It seems only logical that one should practice what one is going to perform! But Stanislavski made a radical break with this assumption: Rather than seeing the indirect use of technique as a single idea or exercise, he treated it as a threshold opening into an entire area of technique. Stanislavski did not simply want to add substitution as another trick or tool of actors. He wanted to comprehensively map the territory of indirectly scoring performances, making it widely available and thereby substantially altering the practice of acting. This desire to thoroughly investigate a previously under-developed area of embodied technique is what made Stanislavski a researcher as well as a teacher, and what allowed his work to depart so radically from prior technique that it could change the very definition of acting.

Stanislavski drove a wedge between the actor's score and those aspects of performance that are perceptible to the audience. This was the first problem Toporkov encountered when he joined the Moscow Art Theatre, where he found himself continually admonished by Stanislavski for thinking too much and too early about what an audience would perceive. The borderline of the perceptible is plainly at issue when Stanislavski scolds Toporkov for trying to "set" (make repeatable) his movements and vocal production too early in the rehearsal process: "At best you were trying to find ways of saying the dialogue, how you would deliver your first line, when you open the window to your office, when *the part of your role the audience can see* begins. You didn't put down roots through which to feed your role" (Toporkov 2004: 18, italics added). In this example, and many others as well, Stanislavski exhorts Toporkov to explore what lies beyond the threshold of audience perception. The metaphor of a tree's roots suggests an analogy for indirectly perceptible acting technique: The roots of a tree cannot be seen directly, but their flourishing or withering will be indirectly evident in what is visible above ground.

This was a radically counterintuitive step for an actor at that time, as Toporkov recalls: "It was absorbing, fascinating, but, it seemed to me, had nothing to do with the practicalities. Of course, I can achieve certain limited results by doing as he says, but *that's not what the audience is going to see*" (2004: 19, italics added). Toporkov had conceptualized the indirect use of technique as an additional trick or add-on that can "achieve certain limited results." He had not yet realized that, for Stanislavski, this was actually the largest and most important area of acting technique. It is no wonder that Stanislavski's methods were considered bizarre, since they seemed to be predicated on ignoring the audience. Toporkov was shocked to observe: "During an intensive, active rehearsal period, nobody appeared to give a thought to the end result—the performance—they *seemed to ignore the audience* who would come to see them, and, very strange indeed, they paid far greater attention to *things the audience wouldn't see*" (20–21, italics added). Instead of practicing movements and line-readings that would be directly perceived by future audiences, Stanislavski's actors worked on various kinds of embodied technique—such as improvising scenes that were not part of the play—which Toporkov only retrospectively understood as having profound indirect effects on what the audience eventually witnessed.

The turn away from the audience marks a significant branching-off point in the embodied technique of theatre. By postponing the question of what the audience would actually see, Stanislavski opened the door to a territory of embodied technique that, in the history of theatre as public spectacle in Europe (and the United States), had perhaps never been thoroughly explored. In the early stages of his research, Stanislavski turned to psychology and yoga, two contemporary areas of embodied technique that he suspected might indirectly bring depth and power to an actor's performance. The best known of these experiments are those relating to "affective memory," a concept Stanislavski borrowed from French psychologist Théodule-Armand Ribot and which became central to the understanding of Stanislavski in the United States. During the same time period, Stanislavski also worked with what he knew of yoga, drawing on the writings of Yogi Ramacharaka (William Walker Atkinson) and the experiences of his colleague Leopold Sulerzhitsky at a Canadian commune (Carnicke 1998: 138–45; Gordon 2010: 9; White 2006; and see Kapsali 2010; Zarrilli 2009: 65–72). Later on, he shifted to what he called the "Method of Physical Actions" and then to "Active Analysis" (Carnicke 1998: 156). What remained constant throughout the phases of Stanislavski's research was his emphasis on the indirect use of technique, for it was in the gap between technique and its effects that what he called "organic" reactions took place.[8] As in Crossley's examples of indirect technique, Stanislavski saw acting less as the composition of a perceptible score than as a sustained investigation of the relationship between embodied technique and its indirect, organic effects.

Such an approach requires the actor to surrender a significant degree of control over the perceptible dimension of performance. The actor must relinquish, to some extent, the responsibility of directly shaping what the audience will see, turning instead to the creation of a score that will give rise to the perceptible performance indirectly. For example, if one's score is defined by a task or short-term goal, the precise way in which this will be achieved remains open-ended. In Stanislavski's words to an actor:

> You must hide Marianne from her cruel father. That's what you have to do. So, how? If you use the usual actors' clichés, you will hide her by putting out your hands behind your back and looking anxious, etc., but if you are creative, *I don't know how you will do it*. But the main thing is "to hide" her.
>
> (Toporkov 2004: 111, italics added)

The repeatable score here is the task of hiding Marianne. This is repeatable in the sense that the actor can try to hide Marianne again and again throughout the scene, as well as each time the scene is repeated. However, the perceptible manifestation of this task—how it is visibly accomplished—may be different every time. Thus, the score becomes perceptible only indirectly, and a degree of genuine spontaneity is introduced in the gap between the repeatable and the perceptible. Significantly, the playing out of such genuine spontaneity was of such value to Stanislavski that he was ready to dismiss all other kinds of acting technique as uninteresting, because they aimed directly rather than indirectly at the perceptible dimension of performance.

The degree to which control is surrendered and unpredictability introduced into the actor's process can vary tremendously. In the example just given, Stanislavski seems to imply that there are countless ways to accomplish the task, all of which are permissible. Yet in the work on *Tartuffe,* and in his own acting and directing, Stanislavski did not leave such enormous room for unpredictability in performance. Although he worked extensively with open-ended improvisation in rehearsal, he would not have permitted it to govern a public performance. Ultimately, then, Stanislavski was not interested in pushing the idea of indirectly perceptible technique to its extreme, as in what we would now call "improvised" theatre. Rather, Stanislavski looked for ways to weave together the perceptible and the imperceptible in an actor's score, so that what the audience saw could be reliably composed and at the same time involve a certain degree of genuine spontaneity.[9] In what he called the "Method of Physical Actions," Stanislavski looked to preserve just enough genuine spontaneity between score and perceived performance to make the actor fully convincing and believable in a dramatic role. A close reading of Toporkov's memoir will help illustrate this process.

The method of physical actions

The heart of Toporkov's account is a fascinating turn in Stanislavski's work back towards perceptible technique that is nonetheless used in an indirect way to stimulate the actor. This is the method of physical actions.[10] I want now to give a brief explication of this "method" as I understand it—not because it is the final result or ultimate achievement of Stanislavski's research, but because it represents a clearly framed and historically unprecedented research outcome in embodied technique. Toporkov's memoir is of course merely a single window onto a complex and much-analyzed practice. Yet this book offers detailed description of a practice that is clearly delineated in both space and time. For an epistemological analysis like that proposed here, it makes more sense to deal with such a focused account than to wrestle with the nebulous territory of "Stanislavski's work." The question is whether a written account like Toporkov's can be understood as a document through which new knowledge—new technique—is disseminated. Just as studies in social epistemology may focus on a single moment of invention in order to develop a more general epistemological theory (e.g., Pickering 1995: 37n1), my analysis of the method of physical actions is intended to be illustrative. I have chosen this example because, like postural yoga, it appears to constitute a genuine research outcome that has proven to be influential well beyond its original context of discovery.

As Toporkov describes it, the method of physical actions is a way of developing a performance score based on the relationship between the imperceptible thoughts, intentions, and feelings of the actor and their perceptible movements and vocal utterances. Unlike the embodied technique of affective memory or yogic "rays of energy," which Stanislavski had previously explored, the method of physical actions does not proceed in one direction only, from the imperceptible to the perceptible. Rather, it works in both directions at once, or alternates quickly between them. In the example of the task "to hide her," cited above, this could work in the following way: During the course of successive improvisations, that task would give rise to different movements, different possible ways of executing the task, each of which will be visible to an observer. At a certain point, one of those ways—one particular "choice"—will be chosen and "set" as part of the actor's score. The next time the scene is done, it will not be the imperceptible task "to hide her" that is repeated, but this perceptible movement. However—this is the crucial point—according to the method of physical actions, the question of which movement choice to set will not be determined by reference to a future audience but to the organic reactions of the actor. In other words, when a perceptible movement is set, this will not be because it "worked" in the sense of fitting into an overall, audience-oriented composition—for example, by conveying the meaning of the story, or creating a strong stage image. Instead, whether a given movement is set will depend on whether it is expected to provoke a fuller engagement on the part of the actor. Only when the physical movement is deemed likely to be more deeply engaging for the actor than the imperceptible task will it be made part of the repeatable score. On this basis, Toporkov draws a technical distinction between "expressive movement representing action," which is set because of its perceptible qualities, and "genuine" psychophysical "action," which is set because of how it affects the actor (2004: 110).

The method of physical actions is defined neither by painstaking work on highly detailed, perceptible movements, nor by the genuine commitment of the actor to accomplish certain tasks, but by a relation between these two domains and the "organic" unfolding reactions that take place in the gap between them. This means that the actor continually weaves and layers multiple kinds of technique in creating the repeatable score: movement technique, "tasks" that can be accomplished in various ways, imaginative associations, and more. Some of this layering is directly perceptible to the audience, but much appears only indirectly—through the unfolding, unconscious reactions that Stanislavski called organic and which he prized as the bounty of genuine art. The purest version of the method of physical actions would then include only two kinds of perceptible movement: that which is intended to provoke organic reaction and that which results from organic reaction. This does not mean that Stanislavski never asked his actors to incorporate movements simply because they looked right or "worked" from an external, spectatorial perspective. But it does seem that, during the work on *Tartuffe,* he strove to go as far as possible in the opposite direction, to the point where even the rooms in the rehearsal space "were not to be allocated with the performance of a dramatic episode in mind, but in response to a genuine, real-life question of how to divide up a house with twenty rooms" (Toporkov 2004: 116). In this case, even the marked location of a potential future audience was erased, so as to avoid influencing the movement of the actors and to ensure that they developed their scores entirely on the basis of the method of physical actions.

This technically dense example illustrates the need to conceptualize technique as a network of branching pathways rather than a flat array of choices. In choosing to study how imperceptible technique can give rise to perceptible performance, Stanislavski opened up what had previously seemed like a single trick (or "a" technique), and found within or beyond it a vast territory worthy of ongoing exploration. In Cetina's terms, discussed in Chapter 1, Stanislavski took a closed or stable object and turned it into an epistemic one by treating it as worthy of intensive study. In addition, Stanislavski's approach to physical action shows how an epistemological perspective on embodied technique can explicate the value of certain discoveries without implying that they are universally superior. For Stanislavski—and for many who followed, from Strasberg to Grotowski—the search for movements arising organically from an imperceptible score came to exceed what I consider its epistemological value and took on elevated aesthetic, spiritual, and moral meaning. Rather than seeing "physical actions" as a new and fascinating area of technique, Stanislavski heralded it as the only honest and legitimate way of acting. He rejected what Toporkov calls "expressive movement representing action" as if it had nothing to offer—as if it were a dead end in the branching networks of technique. Such "zealotry" (Pitches 2006: 49) amounts to a policing of disciplinary lines, in this case between "acting" and dance, mime, or any other area of embodied practice that works extensively with the direct perceptibility of the body. In effect, Stanislavski redrew the border around acting even as he expanded the field, by defining true acting in opposition to the structuring of movement and voice with spectator perception in mind.

To conclude, it is worth noting that Stanislavski's turn away from what had previously been understood as acting technique—the direct composition of what the audience will eventually see—may offer a key to understanding the importance of acting (and "actor training") in the twentieth century. For in the gap between repeatable score and perceptible performance, it has become increasingly common to recognize not only yoga, ritual, and therapy, but every imaginable kind of embodied technique. Arguably, everything that one has experienced in life—from childhood to adulthood to just five seconds ago—may be *indirectly* perceptible in one's actions. The repeatable, if it is not required to be directly perceptible, is synonymous with technique itself. As a result, every kind of embodied technique can now be seen as preparation for acting. Psychology, physical culture (both athletics and somatics), religious ritual, and even the technique of everyday life are now understood as part of what an actor brings to performance. They can, therefore, be considered as part of the training and preparatory work of actors. There is nothing, after Stanislavski, that cannot be understood as part of "actor training."

While the perceptible is the specific issue of the performing arts—their domain, their definition, their (research) problem—Stanislavski discovered that it need not constitute the boundary of performance technique. Even as he policed the borders between acting and other, more "artificial" genres of performance, Stanislavski reconnected acting to the much larger field of embodied technique that exists outside theatre. "This is no longer theatre," he declared. "Don't think about the audience, there isn't one, it does not exist as far as you are concerned" (Toporkov 2004: 122). Far from being tied to an aesthetics of realism, Stanislavski's work should be seen in the context of the radical expansion of acting technique surveyed in works like Hodge's *Actor Training*. For this reason, his work remains extremely valuable for any attempt to reframe acting technique as an area of ongoing training and research. Understanding Stanislavski's work in this way also allows us to examine, more precisely and in technical terms, similarities and differences between his work and that of other practitioners.

Grotowski's legacy

Of all the teachers and practitioners studied here, Jerzy Grotowski is the one most closely associated with the idea of research. Today, there is considerable consensus that research is an appropriate framework for understanding Grotowski's work, even if it does not capture the more esoteric dimensions of his life's calling. Grotowski himself used the language of research as early as 1967, when he compared the Laboratory Theatre to the Niels Bohr Institute, saying: "An institute for methodical research is not to be confused with a school that trains actors ... Nor should this activity be confused with theatre (in the normal sense of the word)" (1968: 97). By that time, the Laboratory Theatre had already moved to Wrocław and added a subtitle to its name: the "Institute for Research into the Actor's Methods" (Kolankiewicz in Allain 2009: 55). Later, as Grotowski broke away from the institution of theatre, the notion of research remained central to his work. In 1969, Grotowski referred to his paratheatrical work as a "type of research" that had "most often existed outside theatre" (Grotowski 2008: 39). Of his "Theatre of Sources" period, he wrote: "In this research, the approach was rather solitary ... [W]e were looking mainly for *what the human being can do* with his own solitude" (Grotowski 1995: 120, italics added). Grotowski's version of the Deleuzo-Spinozan question was made concrete precisely as a question of technique. Or as Thomas Richards— Grotowski's artistic heir—puts it, summarizing the relationship between Grotowski and Stanislavski: "[B]oth dedicated their lives to research on *craft*" (Richards 1995: 5, italics original).

In taking up the question of Grotowski's research, my project continues that of Lisa Wolford Wylam to "demystify" his work (Wolford 1996: xx). Like Wolford, I want to oppose the image of "Gurutowski" that, as Wolford said, came "to dominate critical discourse, particularly in America, obscuring any more pragmatic understanding of Grotowski and his work" (107). I also want to respond to Rustom Bharucha's critique of Grotowski as insufficiently cognizant of the vast differences in cultural and economic power that enabled much of his later work (1993). In her book, *Grotowski's Objective Drama Research,* Wolford does much to frame these later phases as a kind of research. As the title suggests, research was the primary framework through which the Objective Drama project at the University of California (1983–86) was articulated. Indeed, the "objectivity" of drama is precisely what I have sought to link with philosophical realism through the notion of relatively reliable pathways in practice. Wolford makes frequent reference not only to research and knowledge but also to "investigations" and "experiments" with and through performance technique (1996: 15). She also asserts that Grotowski's research in technique can and should be distinguished from the mystical orientation that informed his work from the beginning and became increasingly explicit in his later years: "Not only is it *possible* to separate Grotowski's metaphysics from the body of artistic knowledge that informs his artistic practice, but, I would suggest, it is *advisable* for anyone who wishes to apply these techniques outside the specialized context of Grotowski's own research" (139–40).[11] A grant proposal for the Objective Drama program echoes this distinction and prefigures the epigraph cited at the beginning of this book: "Grotowski's work codes may be religious by origin, but they are in the process of being isolated into technical codes by means of the work of the laboratory" (in Schechner 1985: 256).

Wolford does not explicitly problematize the notion of research or provide analytical tools that would allow us to tease apart Grotowski's technique from the personal and spiritual uses to which he put it. Her methodology is largely descriptive, using theory to provide context, but not to present substantive alternative views on Grotowski's achievements. The essays in a recent volume edited by Paul Allain, *Grotowski's Empty Room,* go further in seeking to articulate the nature of Grotowski's "research methodology" (Allain 2009: xv). For instance, Leszek Kolankiewicz asks: "What made [Grotowski] borrow these scientific terms—'laboratory,' 'institute'—and use them as names? Why did he constantly place his artistic work in the context of scientific research?" (58). Kolankiewicz argues that Grotowski's research bears the same relationship to science as does alchemy to chemistry (60). Noting that alchemy always developed "in close relationship to one or another mystical tradition," he attempts to articulate the rigor of Grotowski's work in alchemical terms (64). In my reading, this sidesteps the important issue of technique and the question of what is transmissible. Such parallels could be useful if our goal were to contextualize Grotowski's work alongside the history of mysticism and the emergence of new and New Age religious movements in the twentieth century. But they do not shed much light on the relationship between Grotowski's practice and concurrent developments in ensemble theatre, postmodern dance, drama therapy, postural yoga, and physical culture, with which it has less in common ideologically and more at the level of technique.

Although Grotowski came to emphasize the personally transformative and revelatory dimensions of his work, he never abandoned embodied practice based on repeatable technique as the field in which such mystical experiences could occur. During his "paratheatrical" phase (roughly 1969–78—see Schechner and Wolford 1997), Grotowski did temporarily set aside a certain kind of highly specialized technique. This period of work bordered closely on therapy or applied theatre insofar as it was the facilitators rather than the participants who had specialized training. At the time, Zygmunt Molik even led workshops in "Acting Therapy" (Campo and Molik 2010). Yet as Wolford suggests, Grotowski's mid-career "attempt to de-emphasize structure and technique provided sufficient empirical evidence" that such work was not for him (Wolford 1996: 14). Following this period, Grotowski concluded that a certain degree of specialized technique was necessary on the part of the doers in order to realize the embodied possibilities that interested him. "Once Grotowski arrived at this awareness, his research was guided by a renewed emphasis on structure and mastery." The return to expertise in Grotowski's trajectory indicates that he was not primarily interested in personal or individual research, of the kind that so powerfully impacted many participants of paratheatre, but rather in research that pushes forward the boundary of what is known to be possible on a larger, socially epistemic level. But if Grotowski was a researcher in this sense, what are we to make of the distinctly mystical and esoteric qualities that attended his later work, from the paratheatrical "Holiday" (Schechner and Wolford 1997: 215–25) onwards?

In principle, there is no reason why spirituality or mysticism cannot be combined or intertwined with empirical research within a given practice or life. As Cetina notes, scientists pursue their work not merely for reasons of instrumentality or intellectual curiosity but also with joy, passion, and pleasure. This is the "libidinal dimension or basis of knowledge activities" (in Schatzki *et al.* 2001: 186). Many scientists have strong spiritual or even religious beliefs and do not find them incompatible with their research. Yet, as Richard Schechner has noted, Grotowski was "of a double mind" regarding the dissemination of research outcomes proceeding from his practices (2008: 11). He was not simply a researcher whose spirituality informed his investigations. Rather, his dual orientations towards research and mysticism were often in tension. Grotowski was exceedingly cautious about sharing the results of his research through any medium other than direct, interpersonal communication. Despite their taking place at a public university, the research outcomes of the Objective Drama project were never disseminated as such:

> Neither during the course of the work, nor after its completion, were the hypothesis and results subjected to any open discussion; they were made known only to a small coterie or to select individuals from within the circle of Grotowski's supporters. They were never verified in the way scientists do, by publishing their findings in journals.
>
> (Kolankiewicz in Allain 2009: 60)

Although Grotowski spoke of knowledge and research, his notion of transmissibility was very different from the one I have employed here. Transmission for Grotowski referred above all to a long-term relationship of great intimacy, as in his thirteen years of intensive work with Thomas Richards. Grotowski was highly skeptical of the capacity of modern forms of mediated communication to disseminate the kind of knowledge he valued.

Grotowski ultimately saw his ideal working conditions as "almost invisible," giving rise only to "anonymous influences" in the wider world (Grotowski 1995: 135). In one sense, such anonymity sets his research apart from scholarly and scientific research, which, as Kolankiewicz notes above, must verify their findings through channels of publication that ensure transparency within a community of knowledge. On the other hand, there is a sense in which Grotowski's notion of "almost invisible" and anonymous influence perfectly describes the potential impact of advanced research. Such research, unlike the public spectacles of performing arts, only reaches the public sphere indirectly—for example, when apparently obscure discoveries in physics lead eventually to the mass production of new technologies. In this way, researchers can make substantial contributions to mainstream culture without ever appearing in the limelight as public figures. We might then attribute the tensions that arise in any consideration of Grotowski's work and legacy to the disjunction between visible and invisible influences and their histories. Grotowski became famous as a director, but he almost immediately left that role behind to focus on a much narrower research project. It is difficult to compare the impact of these two aspects of his work, because they operate on very different levels socially— perhaps, by analogy, like that of a research scientist and a popular science writer.

As Wolford observes, numerous "21st-century theatre artists continue to promote their work by emphasizing a linkage to Grotowski," while scholars like herself have worked to maintain distinctions between those who were inspired by Grotowski's productions, ideas, or short workshops; those who have genuine claims to an indirect lineage via one or more generations of practice; and those who worked closely with Grotowski for an extended period (Wylam 2008: 127–28). Too often, such discussions proceed from the assumption that there is a single Grotowskian ideal to which practitioners more or less closely hew, rather than a complex area of embodied technique in which Grotowski worked and with which others might also engage. But as Nando Taviani points out, the implied "his" in "Grotowski's work" refers as much to a sense of belonging—as in "his country" or "his time"—as to any kind of possessive ownership (in Schino 2009: 168). Virginie Magnat's recent study of women in the Grotowski diaspora is perhaps the first sustained attempt to examine contemporary post-Grotowskian practices using a comparative rather than hierarchical approach. Invoking once again the metaphor of branches, Magnat recalls Rena Mirecka's suggestion that "Grotowski's work and legacy are like a tree with many branches and leaves" (2013: 74). Indeed, an epistemological perspective postpones the evaluative ranking of practices in favor of a more detailed analysis of similarity and difference at the level of technique. In the next section, I examine a particular phase of the Workcenter of Jerzy Grotowski and Thomas Richards from such a perspective, suggesting that it offers a rigorous example of embodied research.

Songs and other epistemic objects

As with Stanislavski above, I focus here on a specific period of Grotowski's practice, in order to show how an epistemology of practice can shed light upon its meaning and value. In this case, I want to address the multiple sources of technique that became central to the practice of the Workcenter of Jerzy Grotowski and Thomas Richards before and immediately following Grotowski's death. This period of practice is known as "Art as vehicle" or "ritual arts."[12] In particular, I want to consider two strands of embodied technique that intersect in the Workcenter's practice: the method of physical actions, as described above; and traditional songs, or what Grotowski called "songs of quality" (Wolford 1996: 40), which in the case of the Workcenter are largely derived from Afro-Caribbean diasporic traditions. I maintain that, in recent writing both from and about the Workcenter, the relationship between these areas of technique has been obscured. As a result, discourse surrounding the Workcenter has been problematic in two ways, each of which can be articulated in epistemological terms: First, there has been a failure to acknowledge the importance of the songs as knowledge and to adequately credit and cite the individuals and communities that developed them. Second, there has been an oversimplification of the Workcenter's practice, which has rendered its research outcomes less comprehensible and potentially less useful in a broader context. I analyze each of these problems below and suggest how an epistemology of practice might contribute to a more accurate and productive analysis of the Workcenter's valuable research.

Grotowski understood his own work to a large extent as a continuation of Stanislavski's—especially in the area of "physical actions," which Richards describes as the "axis" of his own first book, *At Work with Grotowski on Physical Actions* (Richards 1995; and see Grotowski 2008; Biagini 2008). As I have argued, Stanislavski's notion of physical actions, as distinct from expressive movement, arose from a fundamental premise: namely, that the actor should work to some extent, or for some time, without thinking about what an audience will eventually perceive in the moment of performance. This step, I suggested, marks a significant branching-off point in performance technique. In Toporkov's book, we see that Stanislavski's rehearsal techniques were considered "bizarre" because they involved dedicating an extraordinary amount of time and energy to "things the audience wouldn't see" (2004: 21). The same can be said of Grotowski's work following his departure from theatre around 1970. During the last three decades of his life, Grotowski took Stanislavski's turn away from the audience even further, deeply investigating areas of embodied technique that would directly affect the practitioners or "doers" and only indirectly affect someone who might be watching. Echoing Stanislavski, Grotowski wrote: "The actor should rather seek to *liberate* himself from the dependence on the spectator, if he doesn't want to lose the very seed of creativity" (Richards 1995: 124). From this angle, Ryszard Cieslak's score in *The Constant Prince,* the experiments of paratheatre and "Theatre of Sources," and the Workcenter's "Art as vehicle" can each be seen as distinct research projects within an area of technique that was first opened by Stanislavski, when he took acting beyond the threshold of audience perception.

Stanislavski's work on *Tartuffe* is particularly significant in this regard, because it was not aimed towards public performances. Describing the founding of the Workcenter, Richards recalls a statement made by Grotowski in 1988, when he paraphrased Stanislavski's invitation to the actors as they began to work on *Tartuffe*: "I want to transmit to you the technique of work, and only the technique of work. We are not going to do a premiere, we are just going to work to understand what the technique of work is" (Richards 1995: 71). During rehearsals for *Tartuffe*, as mentioned above, no physical location for the audience was established. Rather, the rooms in the rehearsal space were organized "as if" in real life (Toporkov 2004: 116). To an even greater extent, Grotowski's work in Pontedera took place without the kind of audience-focused spatial awareness that defines most theatrical rehearsals. Richards recalls: "*Downstairs Action* was constructed without any consideration for someone who might be in the room watching ... We never even thought about the angle a visitor might see that opus from" (2008: 27). However, even when there were no external observers, repeatability and perceptibility remained fundamental to the Workcenter's practice. In contrast to Grotowski's earlier "paratheatrical" work, these links to theatricality remained in place at the Workcenter. Richards affirms: "Our basic elements are the same as the basic elements of acting. And on a level related to an aspect of craft, the work is the same for an actor in public theatre and a person who is doing this work" (13). This similarity is found above all in the use of physical actions and songs as embodied technique for structuring repeatable scores.

Richards's book, *At Work with Grotowski on Physical Actions*, resembles Toporkov's *Stanislavski in Rehearsal* and Stanislavski's *An Actor's Work*, each of which uses the voice of a student recalling a learning process to render accessible a considerable amount of technical detail.[13] In this volume, Richards offers a clear and precise account of Grotowski's approach to physical actions, including many technical details that could be useful for actors in general. On the other hand, no such clear technical discussion is offered regarding the work on "songs of quality." It is true that *At Work with Grotowski* treats only the first few years of Richards's apprenticeship with Grotowski, ending just when Richards is beginning to "rediscover the process hidden in the work on the ancient Afro-Caribbean and African songs" (1995: 92). Yet songs and singing already constituted a major portion of the work. Published in 1995, the book comes six years after the filming of the Workcenter's *Downstairs Action*. It describes the period after that of Wolford's book, in which traditional songs (such as those of the American Shaker movement) already figure prominently. Furthermore, Richards devotes three short final chapters to analyzing the difference between Stanislavski and Grotowski in their approach to physical actions, impulses, and organicity. There he asserts that Stanislavski "worked on physical actions within the context of the common life of relations: people in 'realistic' daily-life circumstances, in some social convention" (99). According to Richards, Grotowski wished "to remove the actor's art from the realistic foundation, dear to Stanislavski, and to reach a higher level" (101). Richards's book places Grotowski in relation to Stanislavski, and perhaps for that reason underplays the importance of dynamic physical and vocal technique in his own work. But it is not possible to grasp the relation between Stanislavski and Grotowski—or Grotowski's interest in a "higher level" of acting—without reference to songs and expressive movement.

Even if Stanislavski's work had been defined by realism, Richards's reference to a "higher" level lacks specificity and is troubling in its implied ranking of performance genres. Yet it is not at all the case that Stanislavski worked with "daily" or "common" situations. Like Grotowski—and probably most theatre artists throughout history—Stanislavski was interested in emotional climaxes, extraordinary moments, and matters of life and death. Even in Chekhov's plays we do not witness "everyday" interactions, but moments of extreme tension, emotion, and crisis. This is truer still for Stanislavski's adaptations of Kataev's *The Embezzlers* or Gogol's *Dead Souls,* where—as Toporkov makes clear—the characters are constantly on the verge of total destruction. There is nothing "daily" about the situations depicted in these plays. Finally there is *Tartuffe,* which as I have noted represented a special challenge precisely because it is a classical play, originally written in verse. Instead of reducing Stanislavski to "realism" and "daily-life circumstances" (which are quite different things), it would be more accurate to say that Stanislavski worked primarily from dramatic scripts, whereas the Workcenter's opuses are primarily structured by songs. This is a major difference in embodied technique. It is misleading to attribute the differences between Stanislavski and Grotowski to the latter's search for a higher level of acting without connecting this to Grotowski's specific interest in the song (and, to a lesser extent, dance) technique of a variety of global folk and ritual traditions.

Grotowski hated to be associated with "physical theatre," as in mime or clown, preferring ultimately to contextualize his work in relation to Stanislavski. Yet there is no escaping the role of non-Stanislavskian physical and vocal technique in every phase of Grotowski's work, from the Laboratory Theatre to the Workcenter.[14] Such technique is already evident in *Towards a Poor Theatre,* in a passage cited by Richards:

The human being in a moment of shock, of terror, of mortal danger or tremendous joy, doesn't behave "naturally." The human being in this type of *inner maximum* makes signs, rhythmically articulates, starts to "dance," to "sing." Not common gesture or daily "naturality" but a sign is proper to our primal expression.

(Richards 1995: 104, italics original; and see Slowiak and Cuesta 2007: 50)

The problem, for Grotowski—and it is precisely a *research* problem—was to find a way for an actor to enact song and dance as "believably" (to use the classic Stanislavskian criterion, which Grotowski also employed) as actions arising from dramatic scenarios like those of Chekhov or Molière. Grotowski resisted the "multiplication of signs," which he associated with traditional Asian theatre, and called instead for the "*distillation* of signs by eliminating those elements of 'common' behavior which *obscure pure impulses*" (cited in Richards 1995: 104, italics original). A survey of his practice, however, reveals that what Grotowski sought, or at least what he found, was not only "pure" (organic) "impulse," but also new technique. If Grotowski looked for the "inner maximum" that appears in moments of "mortal danger or tremendous joy," he also returned, again and again, to the criteria of repetition and perception. Questions of technique are therefore essential in understanding his practice. No matter how pure the connection may be between an impulse and the dance or song to which it gives rise, it cannot be repeated unless one is willing to ask: Which song? What kind of dance? The fact that these choices were often made with the energetic engagement of the performer in mind, rather than the perception of the spectator, does not make questions of repeatability—and hence technique—any less relevant.

Grotowski's oeuvre can be seen as a series of successive research projects that engage in different ways with this question: How can technique that is composed according to its direct perceptibility, as in dance or song, be made to arise organically out of human embodiment? Or, to put this another way: How can human embodiment be brought to enact precisely composed, directly perceptible technique, without losing its organicity? In my discussion of Stanislavski, I defined the organic as taking place in a gap between the repeatable and the perceptible. "Organicity," then, is the unconscious, embodied unfolding of one thing into another, as when an action manifests organically through movement, or a movement organically evokes an association. In this sense, organicity is profoundly related to training and to technique. In an iterative process, the imperceptible score both proceeds from and is shaped by the perceptible performance. Grotowski put it this way: "The fundamental thing … is always to precede the form by what should precede it, by a process which leads to the form" (Richards 1995: 90). We should not see form and process here as two discrete entities. It is rather a question of iteration and layers, of the sedimentation of technique through practice, and the shaping of future impulses and possibilities through technique. Grotowski wrote: "Organicity is something which one has more of when one is young, less of as one gets older. Obviously, it is possible to prolong the life of organicity by fighting against acquired habits, against the training of common life, breaking, eliminating the clichés of behavior" (66–67). Yet, if this is a fight to retain a wide range of technique—a wide range of embodied possibilities—as organically accessible to the individual, then it is a fight that takes place through daily repetition, through practice.

Grotowski thoroughly explored *movement*—distinct from physical action—as structuring technique for the performer. Towards the beginning of his career, he listed the following sources: "Dullin's rhythm exercises, Delsarte's investigations of extroversive and introversive reactions, Stanislavski's work on 'physical actions,' Meyerhold's biomechanical training, Vakhtangov's synthesis," as well as the "training techniques" of Chinese opera, Kathakali, and Noh (1968: 16). Later on, through extended research, Grotowski and his actors developed new areas of technique, two of which were called the "plastiques" and the "corporeals." The former were based on technical details taken from Delsarte, Dalcroze, and European pantomime, among other sources, while the latter were adapted from the *asana* of modern postural yoga (Slowiak and Cuesta 2007: 137–40). In a letter from 1963, Grotowski recalls the moment in which "the imaginative factor" was introduced into all the physical exercises, leading to their visible transformation (Ruffini in Allain 2009: 98). A precise research question is apparent here: How can physical and imaginative technique be combined? Like Krishnamacharya and his students, Grotowski wanted yoga to be more athletic and less meditative, with more fluid and choreographed movement between poses. Unlike them, he sought continual movement without stillness, and he wanted the actors to be able to interact with each other and with imaginary partners while moving through the poses. Still later in his life, Grotowski oversaw the development of "Motions," which Richards compares to postural yoga (1995: 54; and see Lendra in Schechner and Wolford 1997). Despite this, explicit analysis of movement technique is frequently avoided in discourse surrounding the Workcenter.[15]

Much of the current language surrounding the Workcenter's practice derives from yoga and is similar to that which attends some practices of modern postural yoga. Indeed, the embodied and pedagogical technique of yoga is an explicit source of the Workcenter's practice. As Maria Kapsali notes, "yoga played a considerable role both in Grotowski's life and work" (2010: 186), from the threads of posture visible in the work demonstrations of Ryszard Cieslak to the later phase of "Art as vehicle." Grotowski's idea of a passage from "coarse" to "subtle" body (Richards 1995: 125) echoes the interpenetration of the "gross" physiological body with the "subtle" or "energetic" body that Benjamin Richard Smith identifies as a central goal in the Ashtanga Yoga lineage of K. Pattabhi Jois (in Singleton and Byrne 2008: 145). Moreover, Smith's analysis of the "styles of interaction" that define the "performance of spirituality" at Jois's Ashtanga Yoga Research Institute in Mysore (151) resonate with some of my own experiences of Workcenter pedagogy. These parallels beg the question of why similar esoteric or spiritual goals should be carried out through the particular kinds of embodied technique that Grotowski developed at the Workcenter. Why develop a "yoga" based in song and physical action rather than posture, movement, and breath? Why unfold this particular epistemic object? The answers to such questions are deeply felt by the researchers, but they are also resolutely technical. An exploration of physical movement is not the same as an exploration of song. A sequence of individual postures is not the same as a coordinated group structure. Without a detailed discussion of technique, there is no way to articulate and value the richness and diversity of these distinct epistemic pathways, or to understand the profoundly technical reasons why people choose to pursue one kind of long-term practice rather than another.

Songs are central in the Workcenter's embodied technique. Associate Director Mario Biagini articulates what I understand as a well-formulated research question, posed to himself and Richards by Grotowski: "That Polish gentleman threw us a challenge: 'Sing—can something happen?'" (2008: 170). In Biagini's essay, the "something" that can happen is described as an experience of unity with the world and expansion or dispersal of the ego. But more concrete research questions are also implied: Sing—now, what can happen while you are singing? What can be done without breaking the song? What movements, interactions, experiences, and physical actions might the song provoke, and how might these transform your way of singing? How far can you go physically and emotionally before the structure of the song breaks? What are the differences between various songs and song traditions in this regard? How can physical and imaginative technique become indirectly audible in singing? How can song become indirectly visible in movement? How does the imperceptible give rise to the perceptible, and vice versa? A whole area of research is here, focused on the intersection of Stanislavski's method of physical actions with a particular body of songs, and with a secondary emphasis on movement technique (as in Motions and the Haitian *yanvalou*). There may of course be other lines of technique informing this practice of which I am unaware. The point remains: Even if the aims of the project are primarily personal or metaphysical, its epistemic content can be described in technical terms. In fact, I worry that significant dangers attend the avoidance of such description.

Wolford writes that the aim of *Action* is "to facilitate a special process that can occur within practitioners performing with and around certain songs taken from African and Afro-Caribbean ritual traditions" (Schechner and Wolford 1997: 409; and see 499n1). She describes the songs in some detail, but neither traces their origins nor analyzes them technically. Richards is complicit in this tendency insofar as, despite his frequent reference to the details of practice, he avoids offering thorough technical descriptions throughout his more recent book of interviews. We are told only that the songs are mostly Haitian, African or West African, and Afro-Caribbean (2008: 6). Richards does make an effort to distinguish between technical descriptions of the work and the "intimate language" or "personal mythology" that merely "witnesses" his own "personal experience" (2008: 7, 20, 10, 25, 93). As one might expect, following his trajectory at the Workcenter from assistant and disciple to leader, Richards's "personal" language is more prominent in his earlier interviews, while in later conversations he moves towards fuller technical descriptions and towards a notion of "research" that resonates with the one presented here. "My attitude is that of a researcher," he says (134). "What does it mean for me to be the leader of this research? It means to carry forward an in-depth practical study of a know-how, one step at a time. In that way we can gradually discover its potential development" (115–16). However, critical writings by and about the Workcenter have not maintained this important distinction. Instead, such writing tends to fall into some of the same anti-intellectual traps that plague the discursive framing of other practices, such as postural yoga (see Singleton and Byrne 2008: 3).

By failing to adequately distinguish between personal mythology and critical analysis, discourse surrounding the Workcenter mystifies what might otherwise be recognized as a rigorous and valuable project of embodied research. In a recent essay by Kris Salata, Richards describes his work in terms of "tempo-rhythm" and "tuning," noting that a "moment may arrive in which it's as if the limits of what you perceive as 'I' expand, become more transparent ... " (Salata 2008: 119). In the citation, Richards shifts from the technical language of tempo, tuning, and rhythm to the mystical or psychotherapeutic language of an expansion of self. Yet Salata follows up only on the latter—linking it to Martin Buber's formulation of the "I–thou" relationship—and not on the former. In doing so, he repeats a pattern also found in the writings of Richards, Biagini, and Wolford. Salata continues this approach in his more recent book, *The Unwritten Grotowski,* which relies throughout on a dualism that separates the Workcenter's focus on "true," "deep," or "essential encounter"—the focus of Salata's book—from its embodied technique (2012: 24 and *passim*). As an analytical strategy, this is risky—even problematic—because it is not finally the search for meaningful encounter or dissolution of the self that makes the Workcenter's practice unique. The expansion of the "I" and the possibility of authentic meeting are goals found in many spiritual and artistic traditions. To suggest that this is the defining characteristic of the Workcenter's practice is to ignore or dismiss countless parallel endeavors that work through radically different technique to achieve similar goals. Furthermore, Salata seems to consider the Workcenter's practice not simply as unique in its detailed content, but rather as uniquely "alive" in contrast to much performing arts—and perhaps much of life itself—which he characterizes as "dead" (46). Rather than seeing human encounters as layered through the complexity of technique, Salata starkly divides form from content, using the trope of excess to elevate the Workcenter's achievements above other theatrical and everyday practices.

Framing the Workcenter in this way obscures the sources of their practice and makes it difficult to place them in a wider context—whether that of "physical theatre," Haitian ritual, song, martial arts, or expressive arts therapies. In this regard, Salata's approach is part of what Jacques Rancière has identified as the "familiar landscape of contemporary thought" according to which art is understood—in more or less exactly the language employed by Salata and Wolford—as bearing "witness to an encounter with the unpresentable" (Rancière 2004: 10). To understand the Workcenter's practice as both unique and contextually situated—like all practices—we would do better to take Grotowski's advice: "If possible, let's always speak technically" (Salata 2012: 134). Following this suggestion, we might begin by asking about the origins and structure of the songs that form the core of the Workcenter's practices. We might then investigate the Workcenter's approach to physical actions and think about how these two areas of embodied technique intersect and augment one another in practice. The technique of song, movement—or even physical culture—and physical action is not an empty shell into which personal desires or mystical yearnings are inserted. Rather, this technique is the very structure of the practice. The search for contact and interpersonal connection between the performers is a kind of embodied technique, as is the work on memories and personal associations. If we avoid technical analysis, stressing instead the extent to which the work is "more than" mere technique, we risk entering into two serious epistemological problems, which I mentioned above and will now elaborate.

First, we risk failing to acknowledge the importance of the songs— and other directly perceptible technique—as a body of knowledge that derives from a particular people and place and has come to the Workcenter through particular channels. It is hardly necessary to invoke Linda Tuhiwai Smith's critique of the stealing of indigenous knowledge (1999) in order to suggest that it may have been incumbent upon Grotowski—and may now be upon the Workcenter—to name the sources of their songs. The fact that doing so would significantly demystify their practice is an additional reason for doing so. As Wolford notes, "Grotowski traveled to Haiti, Nigeria, Mexico and Bengal to study traditional bodily techniques" (1996: 8). Yet he rarely spoke publicly of these encounters, instead declaring:

> I always looked to frequent people that were in an unbroken relation with this or that technique or tradition. And there, in different fields, I received a direct transmission. I have been helped a lot in my life from this point of view. There are also certain figures or "elders" for whom I feel an enormous gratitude. In Central Asia, in India, in Latin America, in China, in the Caribbean ...
>
> (Grotowski cited in Wylam 2008: 133)

Why not mention the names of these elders? If Grotowski sought to protect their identities, why not at least describe what he did with them in technical terms? If he believed they would prefer not to be credited individually (as with Krishnamacharya), why not name the lineages or traditions to which they belonged? Which songs came through Haitian practitioner Maud Robert, for example, and which from audio recordings? What specific traditions do these songs come from, and across what historical or geographical transitions are they "unbroken"?[16] An honest account of the sources of knowledge is an essential premise for any claim to research. To conceal such information is to deny the broader context, the field of knowledge in which the research intervenes.

This is particularly ironic in the case of Grotowski, given his own recurrent frustration upon learning of people who claimed to work in his name or spirit after having had only brief contact with him.

The second epistemological problem, less overtly political but in my view no less important, is that failing to acknowledge the technical content of the work on song and movement risks oversimplifying what the Workcenter does in such a way as to render it less useful and less meaningful to those who encounter it. If the Workcenter's practice consists in taking Stanislavski's approach to acting and transforming it into a spiritual, metaphysical, or personal practice, then this will be of interest mostly to those who have direct, interpersonal contact with that practice. If, on the other hand, the Workcenter's practice constitutes rigorous and sustained research in an area of embodied technique—defined by the intersection of physical actions, movement technique (what kind?), and particular groups of traditional songs (which groups?)—then, I would argue, it may have value beyond personal and interpersonal connections, value in the public sphere and for society at large.

Understanding the Workcenter as a site of embodied research would allow us to ask in detail about its methodology. Grotowski said: "This whole family of ritual practices which we can sum up as African and Afro-Caribbean, constitutes a field of study where the tools of dramatic techniques, in the sense of organicity, can be applied" (Fumaroli in Allain 2009: 212). This is a significant research outcome in and of itself: *It is possible to work on physical actions and organicity, in Stanislavski's sense, within the structure of African and Afro-Caribbean ritual songs.* It is not the mere idea of combining "Stanislavski" with "Afro-Caribbean folk songs" that makes for compelling research, as Grotowski would have been the first to point out. What is interesting is the area of technique—the epistemic object—that may be discovered at their intersection. Only with competence in both fields can this intersection be explored, leading to an area of technique that may indeed be historically unprecedented.[17] Certainly, the Workcenter's technique is radically different from that found in opera or musical theatre. It is also very different from other song-based research projects in experimental performance, such as those of Meredith Monk, or of Włodzimierz Staniewski and the Gardzienice Theatre Association (see Spatz 2008). While there are points of commonality, neither Monk nor Staniewski works with anything like a Stanislavskian conception of physical actions. On the other hand, this area of technique is also radically different from any religious ritual with which I am familiar, not least because of the level of detail at which repeatable scores are elaborated. Only the

Workcenter, and perhaps some younger companies directly influenced by it, uses the method of physical actions to create precisely elaborated and repeatable scores within sequences of folk and ritual songs.

When I have witnessed *Downstairs Action* or *Action,* live or on film, I have seen performers who are rigorously trained in choral harmonic singing and who, while singing mostly Afro-Caribbean songs together, pass through a score of actions and interactions that are extremely believable as well as physically dynamic. The resonance of the singing, and the way in which it seems to derive from the performers' interactions, is indeed so powerful that the "vibratory qualities … become the meaning of the song" (Grotowski 1995: 126). I understand the actors to be working both with real-time interpersonal contact and with memories and associations, much like Stanislavski's actors. If I squint, I can see an entire drama unfolding before me, through the structure of *song-action*, with such committed and believable acting that I am not bothered by the lack of an explicit narrative. From an epistemological perspective, the discovery of this technique is a substantial legacy in its own right. There is no need to claim *sui generis* legitimacy through reference to mystical attainment, or to seek historical or anthropological knowledge from this practice—as if singing these songs could tell us what life was like at another time or in another culture (Wolford 1996: 158–59). To describe Grotowski's legacy and the Workcenter's practice as a return to a mythical or idealized past merely reverses the progressive fallacy of Stanislavski's teleological justifications, this time locating higher truth in the past rather than the future. These are both oversimplified and reductive epistemologies. Instead, we might better assess the Workcenter's practice in terms of its extraordinary depth of knowledge and the value of its ongoing research in embodied technique.

A research culture in acting

I have argued that the exploration of embodied technique is research in precisely the same sense as scientific or scholarly research. It is even *empirical* in that, as one unfolds an epistemic object, it reveals specific details or contours that could not have been predicted beforehand. Whether the objects of inquiry are songs and movement patterns, proteins and particles, or archival documents and vanished histories, the researcher finds pleasure in establishing contact with something that has its own structure. The notion of "encounter" explored by Salata is thus not unique to the Workcenter. It is rather a fundamental aspect of artisanal practice, and of research, in any field. Although the epistemic objects described by Richards are located within the researcher rather than externally, his language plainly echoes that used by Cetina, Pickering, and other sociologists of (scientific) knowledge:

> A doorway opens in you, and you touch something and something touches you. And ah, it exists! You might then think that's the end. That's it, I've discovered it. And then a year later, you see that it wasn't the end. There's a whole other territory that's now open. And then, year after year, it's like you see that what can be growing and extending through some inner channel is almost endless. It seems there's no point of arrival.
>
> (Richards 2008: 36)

The "something" that touches and is touched by the researcher is not imaginary or metaphorical. It is the concrete manifestation of relative reliabilities in the materiality of the world. What if we conceived of acting and performance technique in this way—as an epistemic field, full of epistemic objects yet to be unfolded, and constituted by the mutually sustaining relationship of training and research? What doors could be opened by such a theory?

At the present time, the notion of research *in* acting—as distinct from historical, theoretical, or even neurological research *on* acting—is hardly thinkable. The countless teachers and practitioners who conduct what amounts to research in acting technique generally conceive of it in other terms: as experiments in pedagogy, syntheses of lineages, or innovations in actor training—but rarely as *research* in the full epistemological sense of that term. Yet, as I have argued, the concept of actor training is insufficient insofar as it suggests only the practice and transmission of existing technique and not the development of new technique. Despite the fact that the "training" practices lauded by Hodge and others are all outcomes of sustained research, there is as yet no broad-based institutional framework to support research in acting. Lacking such support, and without a coherent theoretical framework around which to articulate research in this field, contemporary teachers and practitioners often have no choice but to promote their work according to the instrumental logic of the marketplace.[18] Like the teachers and practitioners of postural yoga, actors and acting teachers constitute a research community—or what Cetina calls an *epistemic culture* (1999)— but they rarely see themselves as such. In the rest of this chapter, I ask what it might look like to develop a more robust and explicitly epistemic research culture in the field of acting. What kinds of research questions or problems might this culture address, and how would it go about doing so? What would it look like to organize, fund, and carry out research in acting under its own name, without hiding behind the more accepted frameworks of training and production?

In the current situation, teachers of acting—like teachers of yoga and other areas of embodied practice—are under considerable pressure to brand and market themselves either as torch-bearers of authentic tradition or as the inventors of a hot new method. This leads to a double bind: Either one appropriates the name of a previously established figure, or else one sets out to achieve brand recognition under one's own name. Both lead to misunderstandings and petty territorial disputes. On the one hand, we have countless teachers framing their work by oversimplified references to the theories or principles of Stanislavski, Grotowski, Brecht, or even Artaud, and erroneously implying continuity and tradition even when there is little evidence of actual technical commonality. On the other, we have the emergence of "new" techniques like the Margolis Method™ (Potter 2002) and Rasaboxes™ (Schechner 2001), whose legally trademarked status hides their debt to previous generations of work. In both cases, the complex web of influence and inspiration that nourishes a field of knowledge is replaced by a reductive notion of discrete "training" approaches or "Techniques" with a capital "T." Unlike fields of knowledge in the sciences and humanities, the technique that structures embodied practices like acting and yoga is still thought of in terms of discrete or even conflicting approaches, schools, and styles—each leading to an outcome that may be instrumentally useful in particular artistic or commercial contexts—rather than as a dense network of branching investigations that map divergent possibilities. At the same time, theorists and teachers of acting are increasingly looking for alternative models that would allow them to escape or resist the dominant economic framework (see Margolis and Renaud 2010; Prior 2012). The epistemology of practice developed here is one such alternative.

An active research culture is one that acknowledges the value of a diverse array of ongoing research projects. There may be a spectrum between pure and applied research, but an active research culture depends on both. In research, there is no such thing as perfect knowledge, as every area of discovery contains further detail to unfold. The notion of a single coherent line of progressive improvement is the opposite of research culture. While recognizing the achievements of specific individuals and institutions, a vibrant research culture downplays individual glorification in favor of an epistemic ecology that sustains and is sustained by many small independent projects. Research, in this sense, is diametrically opposed to the celebrity/genius culture fostered by commercialism. To envision a research culture in acting technique is therefore to propose a significant paradigm shift. Institutions that provide actor training, both within and outside academia, might have to let go of some of the shorthand notions of quality and success that currently define acting, in order to start thinking instead about ongoing, parallel projects that explore different areas of technique.

One of the most harmful shorthand notions in circulation among actors today is the idea that diverse approaches to acting, despite their obvious differences, all finally aim to achieve the same kind of success. Phrases like "the craft" or "the actor's work" suggest a single actor who scales a single ladder of capability or quality. On the contrary, in an epistemic field, precisely those branching points that are deemed uninteresting at one moment may be revisited later as thresholds to new areas of exploration. One person's dead end is another's unexpected pathway into the unknown. In his memoir, Toporkov refers to an actor's attempt to provoke his own feelings directly as the "forbidden path," as opposed to the "correct path" of physical actions (2004: 4). From this perspective, movements exaggerated for comic effect "lead nowhere" and amount to "a big lie" (22). But comic exaggeration is not a big lie; if explored thoroughly, that embodied pathway can lead to clowning, melodrama, and other areas worthy of exploration. Even Joseph Roach's otherwise excellent historical study of acting technique and science is marred by this reductive impulse, ending as it does with a "gotcha" moment in which one theory of acting apparently triumphs over another. Rather than seeing the divergent theories of Diderot and Grotowski as describing two different branches or types of acting, Roach characterizes Grotowski's as an error to be eventually corrected (1993: 226). But why must the same explanation illuminate the greatness of both David Garrick and Ryszard Cieslak? Could not these two renowned actors have worked in substantially different ways? There is nothing contradictory about the idea that different actors use different kinds of technique, or even that the same actor may work differently from one day to the next. Perhaps some actors experience intense emotions onstage, while others do not, each appearing fascinating or dull to particular spectators who likewise have their own preferences and investments. The desire to explain the greatness of actors through a single mechanism is like the discredited attempts of early philosophers of science to establish "the unity and universality of science" on the basis of "one scientific method and one knowledge" (Cetina 2007: 362). It is time for a fuller recognition of the "epistemic diversity" of acting technique (364).

An epistemological comparison of pathways in acting technique must analyze both similarities and differences. While there is no such thing as "the craft" in a universal sense, there is such a thing as *craft*: discoverable and transmissible knowledge that may link actors together even when they do not share a common history or aesthetics. The notion of a singular goal approached by different means is just one of the commonplace ideas that hinders the development of explicitly research-oriented frameworks for the development of acting technique. In the present context, three others are worth mentioning, each of which is still used with some frequency by teachers and theorists of acting, at least in Anglophone contexts: These are the concepts of "neutral," "extra-daily," and "empty" technique. The first need only be glossed here, since it has been thoroughly critiqued elsewhere. Mark Evans has traced the concept of the "neutral" body back to that of the "natural" body, showing how both fail to work across differences in ability, gender, and ethnicity (2008). Here, we can reformulate this as a reductive approach to what I have called the problem of the substrate, namely that we only come to know material reality through technique. When conceived as a stable object or goal, the substrate of embodied technique becomes an image of the ideal body against which actual bodies can then be measured and assessed. Carrie Sandahl reveals the danger of implementing such an ideal in her discussion of how actor training fails to account for disabled bodies that do not share the assumed reliability of common anatomy (Sandahl and Auslander 2005: 259). In an interview with Victoria Anne Lewis, Sandahl recalls an acting class in which students were instructed to imagine that the sacrum bone was the "seat of their soul"—an upsetting command for Sandahl, given that she has never had a sacrum (Margolis and Renaud 2010: 187). Rather than suggesting a special category of differently structured or differently abled bodies, this example should serve to remind us that all embodied technique is only ever *relatively* reliable.

The concept of "extra-daily" technique, championed by Eugenio Barba, is similarly problematic in that it seems to suggest a universally applicable division between mundane and extra-ordinary technique. However, in the *Dictionary of Theatre Anthropology*, Barba acknowledges that the "social use of the body is necessarily the product of a culture" and refers to "training" as the development of a "second colonisation" of the body (Barba and Savarese 1991: 245). It is striking that Barba, who is so deeply associated with the idea of training as individual empowerment, should here characterize it in terms more readily associated with the cultural criticism of Bourdieu, Foucault, and Butler. Indeed, the *Dictionary* reveals considerably more technical specificity and nuance than is commonly associated with the idea of "extra-daily" technique. There is no question that specialized training works to transform its practitioners so that they no longer embody the technique of everyday life. The question is, first, whether daily and extra-daily are conceived of as two poles or as a multitude of positions; and second, how malleable the borders of these territories are thought to be. From the perspective of epistemic diversity, it is important to remember that the dividing line between daily and extra-daily technique is at least partly culturally specific. Technique is "daily" when it is part of the common explicit and implicit curriculum of a given society or culture. This means that different cultures have different everyday technique. It also means that the extra-daily can be made daily, and vice versa. The daily and the extra-daily are not fundamentally different kinds of technique, but are constituted by an epistemic borderline that every society continually redraws through the implementation of training. Whatever is trained on a daily basis becomes "daily" technique.

Finally, there is in practice no such thing as "empty" or purely mechanical technique. Technique may serve many ends, both predictable and unknown. It can produce multiple outcomes, including those that are unintended. Technique can be trained to the point where it is no longer conscious, but this does not make it empty or mechanical in the sense of lacking intention and meaning. In fact, as we saw in Chapter 1, training technique to the point of automaticity can be a way of sedimenting and thereby increasing or expanding agency. Every practice is structured by different kinds of agency and intention, overlapping and intersecting with each other through the residues and sediments of embodied technique. The notion of "empty" technique, which reformulates the trope of excess critiqued above, has no place in a discussion of actor training. It is a red herring that most often works to conceal the variety of goals and desires motivating practice. When Toporkov describes his sense of failure in delivering a monologue before Stanislavski—"There was not one living line, not a spark of real-life feeling, it was all dead, empty, artificial" (2004: 25)—we should not take this notion of emptiness at face value. Instead, we should ask: What emotions was the actor feeling at that moment, however inappropriate to the character? There is nothing "empty" about delivering a monologue while feeling nervous and embarrassed, even if the sensation of emptiness is sometimes used metaphorically to describe such states. Similarly, there is nothing "empty" about performing a dance while thinking about an unrelated topic. It is the responsibility of the teacher or critic to unpack, in technical terms, what is taking place in a given moment of practice, rather than relying upon the reductive concept of "empty" technique.

The epistemology of practice developed here suggests a way to analyze acting and performance technique without reference to reductive notions like that of a single goal to which all practices aim, or of "neutral," "extra-daily," or "empty" technique. (As we will see in the next section, these harmful tropes are still alive and well today.) Drawing on social epistemology allows us to replace linear and hierarchical models of knowledge with multivalent, fractal fields that reveal rather than conceal epistemic diversity. It then becomes possible to revisit the notion of *research in acting technique*, without presuming that such research will move progressively towards superior technique or objectively greater "presence" for the actor. Instead, every research project must map its own epistemic territory, defining its desired outcomes and situating itself in relation to multiple fields of both commonplace and specialized technique.

Interdisciplinarities

The two primary modes of research are disciplinarity (specialization) and interdisciplinarity. Although these are not exclusive categories, the founding gesture of a research project is usually either to delineate a small, underexplored area within a field of established knowledge, or else to point towards the possible intersection of two previously existing areas. The latter should not be confused with the commonplace idea of acting as a "toolbox," which lacks any concept of epistemic depth. Rather, epistemic synthesis or interdisciplinarity involves substantive and complex interactions between fields of knowledge, each of which has its own (incommensurable) depth dimension. Many of the best-known twentieth-century research projects in acting technique were both intercultural and interdisciplinary, drawing extensively on specialized technique that was not considered to be part of "acting" at the time. In some cases the sources of what seemed to be new and exciting technique were appropriately credited, but very often they were not. In any case, due to unequal power relations, the nature of the relationships between practitioners was frequently obscured. Even when the sources of such "exotic" technique were acknowledged, they were rarely understood in epistemological terms. Accordingly, the development of a more explicitly framed research culture in acting technique could shed light on the meaning and continuing relevance of the practices conducted under the banner of experimental theatre during the twentieth century, by analyzing them in terms of the exchange, transmission, and appropriation of knowledge.

In the final sections of this chapter, I want to briefly consider two major areas of current research in embodied technique, both of which are defined by the interdisciplinary intersections of acting with another area of technique: first, the interdisciplinarities of acting technique with physical culture; and second, its interdisciplinarities with sociocultural identities. In both cases, I argue that the second "discipline" constitutes an epistemic field in the same sense that acting does. (I made this argument regarding physical culture in the previous chapter, while the argument for analyzing *identity* as technique will not be made fully until the next chapter.) I aim to show how acting technique intersects with both physical culture and cultural identity not through a hierarchical relationship but as a contiguous field of knowledge. In other words, in the first case, yoga and martial arts are not "tools" that may be added onto an actor's set of skills; they are fields of knowledge in their own right, which interact with the technique of acting in interdisciplinary, epistemic ways. By the same token, identities of gender, race, and class are not stable facts or factors with which acting and actor training must deal; they too are epistemic fields, which intersect with acting most directly at the level of technique.

Daniel Mroz has usefully traced the integration of *taijiquan* into actor training programs, historicizing the process and debunking the common assumption that it is "an archaic and quasi-religious system of movement training concerned with health maintenance and personal enlightenment" (2008: 127; and see Frank 2006). According to Mroz, "different schools of *taijiquan* served a spectrum of needs that ran from militia training, to bodyguard skills, to personal self-defence, to health enhancement, to national identity construction, with plenty of overlap between categories" (130). In a more recent book, Mroz traces the impact of Chinese "body technologies" on European and North American theatre, before describing his own research at that particular juncture (2011: 17–31). Similar historical tracings are needed to show how research in physical culture, from the athletic to the somatic, has interacted with research in acting in Europe and the Americas. In addition to recognizing the importance of technique from China, India, and Japan, such a perspective should acknowledge the impact of the somatic pioneers discussed in the previous chapter upon Euro-American dance and actor training. For example, Alexander Technique and other somatic approaches are now "considered a standard component in [actor training] programs throughout the United States" (Barker 2002: 35). Whereas Stanislavski's actors might have cross-trained in ballet or fencing, contemporary actors in the United States are more likely to experience the embodied technique of yoga, *taijiquan*, Feldenkrais, or Alexander, as a supplement to monologues and scenes from dramatic scripts. The interdisciplinary project unfolding at the borders of acting technique and physical culture is far from complete. An epistemological perspective may therefore help to clarify both the strengths and weaknesses of current discourse on "psychophysical" acting.

Phillip Zarrilli has played an important role in the advancement of acting technique as a field of research. His book, *Psychophysical Acting: An Intercultural Approach after Stanislavski,* begins by critiquing American "method" training as hyper-intellectual, unable to fully integrate the mind and body of the actor (2009: 17). Zarrilli then proposes a "psychophysical" approach to acting based in his own practice, highlighting the extent to which Asian martial arts may help the actor to engage the full "bodymind" rather than working in an overly intellectual way. Zarrilli's project is exemplary in its sustained effort and in the impact it has had upon theories of acting. His work, including his much older anthology, *Acting (Re)Considered*, is cited not only in theatre and performance studies but also in the emerging field of martial arts studies (Farrer and Whalen-Bridge 2011: 9). However, Zarrilli's theorization of acting does not go far enough to escape the reductive notions described above, or to offer an alternative view of the field. Throughout *Psychophysical Acting,* Zarrilli relies on precisely the concepts of "neutral," "extra-daily," and "empty" technique I have just critiqued. The same problems recur in Zarrilli's more recent book, co-written with Jerri Daboo and Rebecca Loukes (Zarrilli *et al.* 2013), and in the special issue of *Contemporary Theatre Review* that he co-edited with Bella Merlin (Zarrilli and Merlin 2007). In general, Zarrilli fails to precisely articulate the sources and technical framing of his own practice. As a result, he seems to put his own work forward as a universal solution for the problems of "the actor," rather than as a research project in a particular area of technique. In critiquing Zarrilli's work, I do not mean to underestimate the value of his contributions to acting theory. On the contrary, it is because his contributions have been so influential, and have shaped current discourse on acting to such a degree, that his writings can serve as the basis of a critical analysis of the limitations of this discourse as it stands today.

In *Psychophysical Acting*, Zarrilli draws on some of the same theoretical sources in the science of embodiment to which I have referred. His notion of the performative score as a "horizon of possibilities" resonates with my image of technique as a network of branching pathways, and he beautifully describes the way in which embodied repetition can lead a practitioner to the discovery of unknown possibilities within that horizon: "As one continues to repeat a particular form or structure over time, a larger field of experience accumulates as an expanding field of possibilities. Ideally one is able to improvise within this larger field" (2009: 49). Yet when it comes to the question of how different kinds of training relate to one another, Zarrilli does not take us much further than where Barba had arrived in the 1970s. For one thing, Zarrilli continues to rely on an ahistorical notion of the extra-daily. "What, precisely, is acquired or brought to accomplishment through long-term bodymind training?" he asks. The answer: "To become accomplished is to achieve an optimal level and quality of relationship between the doer and the done where 'the body(mind) becomes all eyes'" (213). Phrases like "to become accomplished" and "optimal level" bypass the variety of technique in favor of a unitary notion of quality and success. Indeed, throughout this book, Zarrilli develops a model in which "long-term bodymind training" apparently leads to a singular and universally desirable goal: the development of "a non-ordinary, extra-daily bodymind that is totally open in the moment" (89). This is troubling insofar as it does not distinguish between different kinds of training, different kinds of bodymind, or different kinds of openness "in the moment." Surely there are many different approaches to "long-term bodymind training," and these do not all produce the same "non-ordinary" body! How should we understand Zarrilli's approach in relation to that of Stanislavski—or, for that matter, to the "psychophysical" technique of Mabel Todd or F. M. Alexander (Huxley 2011)?

Zarrilli elevates his own psychophysical approach to acting above other practices that he considers too intellectual, too physical, or too technical. As in Barba's early writing—and that of many contemporary yoga practitioners—sport and athletics receive strong criticism, with Zarrilli dismissing his youthful (pre-Asian) "sports body" as masculine, aggressive, and dominated/dominating (2009: 23). At one point, Zarrilli seems to suggest that playing a sport, unlike psychophysical acting, does not usually involve emotional work (87). It is certainly valid to critique normative masculinity for its aggressive and objectifying approach to the body, as many others have done. (This was part of my critique of athleticism and healthism in the previous chapter.) But Zarrilli does not unpack the specific ways in which sport worked upon his body, or the technical and embodied differences between *kalarippayattu* as a martial art and the games of (American) football and soccer. He does not explain the differences between how sport and acting engage with emotion and affect. Instead, the reader is given to understand that some technique trains the "bodymind," while other technique trains only the body or only the mind. In addition, the reader is repeatedly warned of "the tendency for form training to become empty and habitual" (97). To avoid this, according to Zarrilli, we have to engage "consciously" with our practice. This is an old account of agency in which the empty shell of the body is animated by conscious intent. It is a common rhetoric among practitioners in many areas of embodied technique, but surprising given Zarrilli's theoretical sophistication in other respects.[19] We clearly have a long way to go before acting and physical culture can be understood as distinct but parallel epistemic fields, coming into contact via interdisciplinary research.

The second area of current research I wish to mention here is the intersection between acting technique and cultural identity. While just one or two essays in the earlier volumes edited by Zarrilli (1995) and Krasner (2000) address identity politics, many of the essays in Margolis and Renaud's more recent collection (2010) do so. I hope this indicates an increasing interest in this important area. Yet as these essays show, there is a significant gap between the theories used to analyze acting technique, on the one hand, and identity, on the other. Discussions of acting technique, for the most part, continue to assume a neutral or unmarked body that transcends or ignores divisions of race, gender, and ability. Meanwhile, those who theorize identity are often working from a strategic essentialism that prioritizes identitarian categories over a recognition of how embodied technique moves between bodies and practices. I propose that an epistemology of practice can be the basis for a conceptual framework within which "acting" and "identity" might come into more thorough and rigorous dialogue. In order to see acting and identity as contiguous, however, we have to recognize the extent to which socialization and vocational training intersect in what Randy Martin calls the "composite body" of technique (1998: 139). This means, on the one hand, that the sedimentation of acting technique in the body contributes to and can even transform a person's identity; and, on the other hand, that identity itself is trained and practiced to a large degree as embodied technique. The latter argument will be more fully developed in the next chapter, but I hope to set the stage for it here by showing how acting intersects with identity in ways that go beyond the politics of representation.

Actors and acting teachers today sometimes get themselves into hot water by asserting that social identities like class, gender, or race cease to exist within the space of the acting classroom or rehearsal studio. The problem with such assertions is that, unless they are backed by a strong awareness of historical and contemporary oppression, the well-intentioned desire to be rid of identity-based hierarchies can easily shade into the privileged assumptions of hegemony. Yet treating identities as immutable realities that can only be represented and not transformed by the technique of acting and performance leads to a disappointingly superficial understanding of the latter. What do people mean when they say that sociocultural identity categories change or disappear in spaces of focused embodied practice? Although this observation can stand in for domination and privilege, it does not always do so. It was James Baldwin who wrote that "nakedness has no color" (1972: 23). At issue here are questions of scale and intimacy: how to deploy identity categories that describe populations on a social level in contexts of long-term, intimate, interpersonal interaction. Epistemologically, there is also the matter of the incommensurability of disciplines. Bringing together diverse areas of specialized technique cannot be a matter of collage, or of subsuming one within another, but rather of making space for complex interdisciplinary interactions. What might it look like to conceive of a given identity category not as a stable reality, which acting then depicts, nor as a field of discourse in which acting intervenes, but as an epistemic field parallel to but distinct from the field of acting?

Over two decades ago, Sue-Ellen Case wrote:

> Social conventions about the female gender will be encoded in all signs for women. Inscribed in body language, signs of gender can determine the blocking of a scene, by assigning bolder movements to the men and more restricted movements to the women, or by creating poses and positions that exploit the role of women as sexual object. Stage movement replicates the proxemics of the social order, capitalizing upon the spatial relationships in the culture at large between women and the sites of power.
>
> (Case 2008 [1988]: 117–18)

Case is concerned here with the extent to which acting technique unwittingly replicates the sexist power dynamics of everyday life. In Rhonda Blair's formulation of the same period, this process works in the other direction as well, since "performing a role is a kind of 'training for life,' a rehearsal and patterning of a way of being in the world" (1992: 16). There is thus a flow in both directions, between the technique of gender and that of acting. From a feminist perspective, the danger is not just that acting will re-present hegemonic sexism onstage, but equally that it will support the ongoing reproduction of inequality by offering training in normative gender under the guise of actor training. This is confirmed by Elizabeth C. Stroppel's suggestion that "acting classes claiming to free students physically, in order to develop characters from a more neutral basis of gestures, in fact allow students to remain locked into gendered behavior" as long as gender is not explicitly problematized as part of the process (in Krasner 2000: 123n19). Rosemary Malague (2012) has further investigated how acting teachers like Lee

Strasberg and Sanford Meisner—and even Stella Adler, to a lesser extent—reproduced and reinforced conventional gender by demanding it of their students.

Judith Butler's work in the 1990s seemed to many to confirm the interpenetration of gender and performance (even though, as previously noted, Butler herself did not believe the gap between everyday gender performativity and theatrical performance could be so easily bridged). Yet if hegemonic cultural identity can be perpetuated through an approach to actor training that replicates assumptions about how men and women use their bodies, then it should also be possible to open up alternatives to this hegemony through innovative approaches to actor training. Given the complexity of present-day thinking on gender and sexuality, this would probably not be as simple as "cross-casting" male actors as female characters and vice versa. Instead, it would require a more thorough unpacking of gender technique in technical terms—such as the "proxemics" mentioned by Case—combined with an experimental attitude towards the training and transmission of this technique. To articulate gender in technical terms is already a step forward, one that I will pursue more thoroughly in the following chapter. To offer gender technique as an area of training and research available equally to everyone is a potentially radical move. The idea of *alternative training* in gender is distinct from Butler's notion of parodic citation and suggests quite a different approach to political transformation.

Gender is the category of identity explored most fully here and in the following chapter. However, it may also be possible to consider other kinds of identity as involving differences in embodied technique that can both feed into and be influenced by explicit training in fields like acting. The past fifty years have seen substantial discussion of race, ethnicity, sexual orientation, and most recently (dis)ability in the context of theatrical representation. Yet just a few scholars have addressed these types of socially and politically urgent difference in the context of acting technique and actor training. David Wiles has argued that Method acting fails to provide actors with "tools for forging a relationship" with the audience (in Krasner 2000: 172). This is not surprising, given my previous discussion of Stanislavski's turn away from audience-focused composition. In the work of Stanislavski and Grotowski, the actor's implicit trust in the director's vision is assumed, because the actor does not establish a direct relationship with the audience. What happens if this trust is not present?

Wiles recalls performing a role in which he was subjected to a racial slur, noting that his relationship to the performance "changed depending on who was in the house from show to show" (in Krasner 2000: 174).

Several essays in *The Politics of American Actor Training* focus on similar conflicts between "becoming" a fictional character and avoiding the reproduction of oppressive stereotypes: Derek Mudd recalls being directed to speak a line in *The Exonerated* in a homophobic way; Micha Espinosa and Antonio Ocampo-Guzman describe the impact of mainstream stereotypes upon Latino actors; and Victoria Anne Lewis remembers being rejected by an acting conservatory because her visible disability meant, in their eyes, that she could never become a "professional" actor. Each of these examples evokes the powerlessness actors may experience when the alignment of hegemonic acting technique and hegemonic cultural values allows directors, teachers, and producers to enforce stereotypes through the language of training and craft. Yet these essays only scratch the surface of the collusion between acting technique and repressive social norms. It is easy enough to argue for more "diversity" in actor training programs and in mainstream theatre institutions, but such arguments risk implying that acting technique itself is a stable edifice into which "others" might enter. We would do better to conceive of both acting technique (extending well beyond the European tradition) and cultural identity (including white and other dominant identities) as operating substantially in and through embodied technique. We can then begin to conceive of embodied research projects that explore their mutual transformation.

Cláudia Tatinge Nascimento has written a rare monograph-length work that explicitly tackles the intersection of race and ethnicity with the field of actor training. Nascimento draws on her own experience, as well as her connections with performers Ang Gey Pin and Roberta Carreri (whose work has been deeply formed by their relationships with Grotowski and Barba respectively), to theorize intercultural theatre and acting at the level of embodied technique. While Nascimento duly acknowledges the importance of representation and the public dimension of theatre, she wants to draw our attention to deeper layers of embodied technique that are, as I have also argued, not directly but only indirectly perceptible in the moment of performance:

> It is unavoidable that the actor's body is an obvious visual marker for the viewer, an instrument that unequivocally displays her race ... That which remains invisible—the length of her apprenticeship, the way in which she acquired a given performance technique, her personal experience in crossing cultural borders, her artistic justifications to do so—is seldom taken into consideration.
>
> (Nascimento 2009: 75)

160

Throughout *Crossing Cultural Borders*, Nascimento emphasizes the difference "between the trivial utilization of foreign elements in performance and the long-term embodiment of foreign performance techniques" (18). While the first takes place at the level of representation and can be critiqued in relation to an assumed public sphere, the second involves the transmission of embodied knowledge on a level that exceeds the domain of the public.

Nascimento's critique of a merely representational analysis of intercultural theatre resonates with Saba Mahmood's discussion of the ways in which Islamic practices are reduced to signs and symbols in the discourse of Europe and the United States (2005). As discussed in Chapter 1, Mahmood argues that it is not enough to "read" practices of prayer or dress, like the wearing of the veil, as cultural signs. Rather, such practices must also be understood as embodied technique that ethically and politically shapes individuals and communities in complex ways. For my purposes, the crucial point illustrated by both Nascimento and Mahmood is the continuity between the domain of public spectacle and the domain of everyday life at the level of embodied technique. When critics assess publicly visible performances only in terms of their symbolic meaning in the landscape of discourse and representation, they miss the ways in which such performances also operate as embodied technique. Furthermore, as is clear in the writing of both Nascimento and Mahmood, this problem attends not only the technique of acting and religion but also supposedly stable identity categories like those of race and gender. Nascimento observes that the "transmission of knowledge" through long-term training is often downplayed by critics of intercultural theatre, who instead "privilege the individual performer's race or nationality over how rigorously that actor acquired a certain technique" (2009: 26). But if we understand acting as a field of knowledge, then we must also recognize that some of what we refer to with categories of race, ethnicity, and nationality is acquired in the same way that a profession or a religion is acquired: through training. Culture itself "is not natural but, rather, a learned and embodied practice" (58).

Nascimento borrows the concept of intersectionality from Cherríe Moraga and Gloria Anzaldúa's *This Bridge Called My Back*, applying it here to the question of how culture itself can be learned through processes of actor training and ensemble creation (2009: 29–30). These two points are equally important: first, that identity categories are acquired through embodied training; and second, that professional training constitutes identity no less fundamentally than does cultural training or socialization. As Nascimento reminds us, training in performance has a permanent effect upon the actor. Through training, actors acquire technique so deeply that it becomes second nature: the actor's "process of embodying such techniques is irreversible" (74; and see 106).[20] In applying the concept of intersectionality to actor training, Nascimento suggests that it is not just gender, race, and sexuality that intersect in the body of each individual person. Rather, as I have tried to show, specialized and explicit training like that of athletes and performers interfaces with these kinds of identities through intersectionality. What Randy Martin calls the composite body, with its residue of technique learned in diverse contexts, is not only the body of the trained performer. The notion of technical residue applies to the learning of everyday identity as well. We can therefore legitimately speak of "intersectionality" between what are usually dichotomized as professional versus cultural identities: acting and race, for example, or dance and gender, or sport and sexuality. An analysis of intersectionality in these terms is not the same as one that treats race, gender, and sexuality as stable categories that may be represented or explored through embodied practices like those of acting, dance, or sport. Instead, such an analysis requires that we examine all kinds of identity formation and training processes at the level of embodied technique.

Turning somewhat aside from a politics of the public sphere, such an analysis might ask how the various kinds of training we receive in life work to enable certain embodied possibilities while obscuring or foreclosing others (see Ahmed 2006). Nascimento's book defends the validity of deep research processes, which may become caught in the net of public discourse when they emerge into the public sphere. I do not wish to deny the responsibility of artists to consider how their work will be perceived at the level of cultural representation. However, I agree with Nascimento that critics and scholars should take a more sophisticated view of embodiment, one that acknowledges the depth of technique as well as its symbolic meaning. (This is what I tried to do in my critique of the Workcenter of Grotowski and Richards.) It may be that what has been called "intercultural theatre" is more accurately a kind of "research theatre" in which interculturalism is the methodology. Such theatres ideally work against the alignment of actor training with racism and sexism, not by inserting "other" identities into existing theatrical infrastructures, but by conducting sustained explorations in the border zones between performance technique and cultural identity. I suspect that this is what David Wiles has in mind when he asks us to go "beyond race and gender" in considering what "diversity" means in the context of actor training programs (in Margolis and Renaud 2010: 123–36). Surely Wiles does not mean that we should ignore race and gender, returning to earlier racist and sexist models of "neutral" bodies and training.

Rather, I understand Wiles as calling for a richer understanding of cultural identity that has the potential to more thoroughly transform acting and theatre than the conventional notion of diversity.

Laboratories

At a recent academic conference, Courtney Elkin Mohler discussed the complexities of "color awareness" in casting (2013; and see Banks 2013). She asked: How do audiences interpret various approaches to the relationships that may be set up between the racial and ethnic identities of actors, their visible physical characteristics, and the fictional characters they portray? Mohler wished aloud for a "laboratory" in which to explore different configurations of these relationships and receive audience feedback on the reception of different casting choices. Elsewhere at the same conference, in a panel I organized on the possibilities of "Training Queer," Dana McConnell made virtually the same point about gender (2013). Describing a recent project that explored cross-gender casting across multiple plays within a laboratory-type setting, McConnell wondered aloud why such work is not considered a vital part of theatre research in the United States. At least part of the answer is that we do not yet have a robust theoretical framework with which to describe and assess such projects *as research*. One can easily imagine a center of scholarly research that would focus *on* the topic of acting (or dance) and race (or ethnicity)—but what about a center of embodied research that explores this intersection through epistemically organized embodied practice? Can we envision projects that use embodied methodologies to develop substantive new technique for dealing with race or gender and acting/performance as overlapping areas of practice?

Mohler's stated wish for a "laboratory" in which to explore the intersection of racial phenotype, racial identity, and character-based acting technique calls to mind the mixed legacy of theatre laboratories in the twentieth century. "A laboratorial situation," Mirella Schino writes,

> implies not only paths of artistic production but also varying existential processes: paths of knowledge, transmission of knowledge, research and study of the deepest structures of the theatre. To progress along these paths, this type of theatre is concerned not only with the impact a performance can have but *also* with the theatrical sphere that starts from the actor's everyday life ...
>
> (Schino 2009: 220, italics original)[21]

Stanislavski and Grotowski both invoked the notion of the laboratory at certain points in their careers, while simultaneously distancing their artistic and creative practices from the objectivity and reproducibility of science. However, as sociologists of science have demonstrated, science is also a creative practice, and the sharp distinctions that once separated the sciences from other fields no longer seem watertight. Developing an epistemological perspective on acting technique means reclaiming the notion of "experimental" theatre as distinct from the physical or ensemble-based theatre with which that term is commonly associated. Experimentation is not a matter of aesthetics but of epistemology. We must then distinguish between experimentation, in an epistemological sense, and the particular results of prior experiments— for example, those of Grotowski's Theatre Laboratory. It may be time to reinstate the notion of the theatre laboratory, this time with a much wider remit that would include all kinds of interdisciplinary embodied research.

Bryan Brown offers a powerful triadic model—drawn from twentieth-century Russian theatre—in which *laboratory* operates as a valued third term alongside *theatre* and *school* (2013: 44–48). This trio of spaces reflects the epistemic structure of acting as a field of knowledge: the school, for training; the laboratory, for research; and the theatre, for the public display and dissemination of knowledge made accessible to a general audience. (The trio also maps directly onto the three basic functions of the university: teaching, research, and public engagement— see Chapter 5.) In this context, the laboratory does not occupy a higher position than the theatre or the school. Each space has its own values and requirements. Yet the laboratory has a unique power, as Bruno Latour boldly affirms: "Give me a laboratory and I will raise the world"! (1983). Laboratories, for Latour, are places where a researcher "actively modifies" society by directly and literally altering the landscape of possibilities for action (156). They are sites for the emergence of "fresh politics" and even "future reservoirs of political power" (157, 168). The power of laboratories, Latour suggests, inheres in their ability to "displace society and recompose it by the very content of what is done inside them, *which seemed at first irrelevant or too technical*" (168, italics added; and see Cetina 1992). As Brown suggests, laboratory studies—part of the sociology of scientific knowledge—could be a powerful resource for reenvisioning embodied practice today. At the very least, the sociological concept of the laboratory suggests a significantly different way to think about the politics of acting: Rather than intervening through spectacle and representation in the public sphere, the epistemic politics of the laboratory are more like the "anonymous influences" that Grotowski wished his later work to have: a politics of gradually spreading knowledge and slowly shifting priorities.

The history of performing arts is full of examples of epistemic continuity between schools, laboratories, and theatres of embodied practice. To name just one, Sharon Marie Carnicke has drawn a distinction along exactly these lines between the Actors Studio and the Group Theatre. "The Studio did not attempt to create an alternative theatre, as had the Group," she writes. "Instead, it set its sights on a vast arena. Studio actors would infiltrate and transform from within the entire commercial system that had spelled the doom of the American Laboratory and Group Theatre" (Carnicke 1998: 48). The current theoretical framework of performing arts in the public sphere cannot account for such a subtle but influential politics, which unfolds in a laboratory or studio rather than upon a public stage. Yet there can be no doubt as to which institution, the Theatre or the Studio, has had a more substantial long-term impact upon American and global theatre. For it is not ultimately performance but embodied research that opens new pathways in how we live our lives.

Notes

1 As noted in the introduction, there is some overlap between my approach and the "cognitive turn" in theatre studies. Like the cognitivists, I am interested in how diverse approaches to acting work with and through the relative reliabilities of human embodiment. Unlike them, I do not believe that science holds the keys to finally understanding these reliabilities. Rather, branches of acting technique must be understood on their own terms as epistemic projects. While interdisciplinary connections between acting and cognitive science are worth investigating, neither area of knowledge can explain the other. They are epistemically incommensurable.

2 The distinction is particularly clear in Barba's discussion of vocal practice, where the choice to explore one kind of technique rather than another is characterized as a transcendence of "calculated work" and "pure 'technicity'" in favor of "courage" and "transparent" encounter (1972: 52–53). Here, Barba extends the specific progression or epistemic linearity of Odin Teatret's development—from imitating sounds and movements to the development of individual forms—to an allegedly universal (at least in a "Western" context) rule. This leads to two problematic conclusions: first, that the practice of mere "gymnastics" lacks "personal justification," a reductive view of athleticism; and second, that the "exterior forms" of the work "are of no importance," when in fact the turn to "courage" and "transparency" can only produce *theatre* if the actors are already well-trained to exteriorize (54).

3 Marijke Hoogenboom also names the Surrealists' "Bureau de Recherche" and Brecht's concept of "Versuchen" as part of the "long tradition of lively artistic research" (in Gehm *et al.* 2007: 84).

4 A slightly revised version of this and the following section is currently in press with the *Journal of Dramatic Theory and Criticism*. That version uses

the spelling "Stanislavsky" and cites the 2009 second edition of Carnicke's *Stanislavsky in Focus*, among other minor differences.

5 This is "realism" in the sense given by Laurent Thévenot (see Chapter 1), rather than the literary sense that has long been associated with Stanislavski. It refers not to a mimetic resemblance between theatrical production and everyday life (aesthetically "realistic") but to a systematic grappling with the contours and resistances of the material world (philosophically "realist").

6 The latter is still in use even by those who acknowledge its limitations (see Zarrilli *et al.* 2013: 179, 190).

7 Gordon does not provide sources for these stories. The earlier anecdote can be found in Eric Csapo and William J. Slater, *The Context of Ancient Drama* (1995: 264). According to Aulus Gellius (*c.*180 AD), the ancient actor "took his son's urn from the grave and, embracing it as the urn of Orestes, filled everything about him not with representations and imitations, but with real living grief and lamentation. The audience was deeply moved to see the play acted this way." My thanks to Judith Milhous for locating this source.

8 I discuss the concept of the organic further below. On Stanislavski's idea of the organic, see Benedetti's introduction to Toporkov 2004: xi. Kris Salata notes that a fully organic reaction can be understood as a "natural signifier" of the underlying cause, which Grotowski also called a "symptom" (2012: 83).

9 Joseph Roach is therefore wrong to describe Stanislavski's technique as "a means of manipulating levels of consciousness to achieve certain specific effects on the body, especially the illusion of spontaneity" (1993: 206). If this spontaneity is illusory, it is so only in the sense that one can always analyze ever-deeper layers of hidden technique at work, including those that have nothing to do with professional training. The actor's spontaneity, then, is no more or less illusory than that of everyday life.

10 I do not capitalize "method of physical actions" for the same reason that I do not capitalize "modern postural yoga." Capital letters imply a stable, proper object, while lower-case letters suggest the porous borders and processual development of an epistemic object or field.

11 In the context of higher education (see Chapter 5)—as in the Soviet context that shaped the careers of both Grotowski and Stanislavski—"research" would be an officially legitimate framework, while mysticism would not. This should not be taken as invalidating the epistemic content of their practices (see Osiński in Schino 2009: 141–48). For more on Grotowski's strategic compromises with Communism, see Baumrin (2009).

12 I will not here address the more recent practice of the Workcenter, such as its division into two distinct teams led by Thomas Richards and Mario Biagini respectively. The practice examined here—in particular, that of *Downstairs Action* and *Action*—is described in Schechner and Wolford (1997) and in Richards (2008). It is also regularly shown on video, although not publicly available as of this writing. For more on recent developments, see Salata (2012).

13 This approach can be contrasted with the format of the technical manual, as in Iyengar (1966). The student narrative and the technical manual are two of the most common genres for writing embodied technique.

14 Even in the productions of the Polish Laboratory Theatre, which were mostly based on classical scripts, the musicality of the voice signaled an important difference between Grotowski and Stanislavski. According to James Slowiak

and Jairo Cuesta: "One could even say that all of Grotowski's performances were sung" (2007: 107).

15 In particular, one may critique Richards and his colleagues for failing to acknowledge the centrality of a certain kind of athleticism in their practice. As defined in the previous chapter, athleticism is an area of embodied technique that emphasizes virtuosic physical performance, especially that which is visible and measurable. In contemporary globalized Euro-American culture, athleticism is further associated with what Richard Tinning identifies as the "mesomorphic" body type (see Chapter 2). We can assume that contemporary dance and theatre companies favor highly athletic, toned, mesomorphic bodies because they are considered attractive and appealing to spectators. The need to privilege such bodies is then far from obvious in a practice that is not primarily directed towards spectators at all. I do not deny that there could be legitimate reasons for favoring certain body types even in a practice not designed with audience perception in mind. However, in the absence of a clear articulation of research methods, the culturally dominant aesthetic of the slim and "beautiful" young body remains unacknowledged as a factor in determining the composition of the Workcenter's team(s). On this level, the Workcenter more closely resembles mainstream dance and theatre companies—as well as health and fitness studios—than the discourse surrounding it admits.

16 Dominika Laster has begun to explore the importance of "Afro-Haitian song and movement" in Grotowski's later work (2010: 240–48). See also Kolankiewicz (2012). However, a clear articulation of the sources of the Workcenter's songs has not yet been made.

17 From this perspective, Grotowski's repeated assertion that he was not producing something "new" but rather something very old (Salata 2012: 113; Magnat 2013: 204) should be understood in the context of a performing arts industry that values newness in the sense of fashions and trends rather than epistemic innovation. The new of research should not be confused with the new of capitalist production. In today's mediatized world, to conduct research in embodied technique is indeed to undertake a very old practice. By continually searching for the new in the oldest medium of all—embodiment—Grotowski resolutely stood for a very old set of values.

18 Theatre practice has an ambiguous position in academia for exactly this reason: The logic of the marketplace does not apply, but no truly epistemological framework has yet been proposed. I discuss the role of embodied research in academia in Chapter 5.

19 In *Acting: Psychophysical Phenomenon and Process* (Zarrilli *et al.* 2013), a similarly problematic assumption is evident in Zarrilli's continual reliance upon an uncritical notion of virtuosity as the goal of diverse training practices. Moreover, the idea of "psychophysical" acting (and likewise the "bodymind") is problematic insofar as it defines itself in the very dichotomous terms it seeks to discredit—as Jerri Daboo acknowledges in the same volume (190). There is also a troubling misapplication of cognitive science at work here, as when Rebecca Loukes implies that the work of Mark Johnson and others supports the legitimacy of certain types of acting and actor training (227–54). The argument made by Johnson and his peers is that cognition is *inherently* embodied. This is quite different from the idea, stated or implied by Zarrilli, Loukes, and others, that specific kinds of training can make people *more or*

less embodied. As tempting as it may be to use cognitive science to bolster the validity of a particular training pathway, such arguments usually do not hold.

20 John Lutterbie makes a similar point without specific reference to cultural identity: "Actors do not simply learn new skill sets, however; in the process of gaining control over their technique, a new image of the body emerges that has strong ties to the emotional centers and redefines the values and beliefs that structure their identity as performers and human beings" (2011: 148).

21 Schino's discussion of the concept of the theatre laboratory is drawn from conversations between herself, Eugenio Barba, Franco Ruffini, Leszek Kolankiewicz, and others who have participated in the International School of Theatre Anthropology. It resonates in many ways with my analysis here.

There's an essay by the philosopher Gilles Deleuze called **"What Can a Body Do?"** And the question is supposed to challenge the traditional ways in which we think about bodies. We usually ask: What is a body? Or: What's the ideal form of a body? Or: What's the difference between the body and the soul? That kind of thing. But "What can a body do?" is a different question. It isolates **a set of capacities and a set of instrumentalities or actions,** and we are kind of assemblages of those things. And I like this idea. It's not like there's an essence and it's not like there's an ideal morphology—you know, what a body should look like. It's exactly not that question. Or what a body should move like. And one of the things I've found in thinking about gender, and even violence against sexual minorities or gender minorities—people whose gender presentation doesn't conform with standard ideals of femininity or masculinity—is that **very often it comes down to how people walk, how they use their hips, what they do with their body parts.** What they use their mouth for. What they use their anus for. Or what they allow their anus to be used for. There's a guy in Maine who—I guess he was around 18 years old, and he walked with a very distinct swish. You know, hips going one way or another, a very feminine walk. But one day he was walking to school and he was attacked by three of his classmates and he was thrown over a bridge and he was killed. And the question that community had to deal with—and indeed the entire media that covered this event—was, you know: How could it be that somebody's gait, that somebody's style of walking, could engender the desire to kill that person? And that makes me think about the walk in a different way. **A walk can be a dangerous thing.**

(Judith Butler in Astra Taylor 2008)

4

GENDER AS TECHNIQUE

How to slice a cheese

Once, when I was a child, I was told that cutting off the tip of a wedge of soft cheese, so as to leave a short new edge, is the "Jewish" way. It is not Jewish, I was told, to slice the wedge along an acute angle, leaving a pointed end in place for the next person. Such a distinction makes sense only within a limited cultural context: "Jewish" here refers to secular and assimilated (white) Jews in the northeastern United States. Yet I remember being struck, in that moment, by how the most mundane technique—how to slice a cheese—could stand in for a whole social and cultural identity. It was, somehow, part of the technique of being Jewish. Such technique hardly deserves to be called epistemic, since both ways of slicing are obvious, no research being needed to discover how to proceed along either pathway. But cooking itself—long a topic of interest in studies of everyday life—certainly deserves to be analyzed in epistemological terms.[1] If every culture has its own cuisine, this does not simply result from preferences and choices; empirical research is involved. The Persian style of crispy rice called *tadig*, for example, is evidently a product of research. Some experimentation was needed, however long ago, to discover this particularly delicious pathway in the relative reliability of rice, yogurt, water, and heat. While it is not quite "embodied" in the sense I have defined—as a field of knowledge, cooking works as much with the properties of ingredients and heating processes as with human embodiment—it is certainly an area of everyday technique in which practical knowledge becomes indistinguishable from the *being* of identity: cultural, ethnic, gendered, religious, and more.

The preceding epigraph from Judith Butler marks a joint in this book, between specialized areas of technique and that of everyday life. While Chapter 1 laid out an epistemology of practice, Chapters 2 and 3 used this framework to analyze practices that are fairly well bounded, even if their borders are continually in dispute. As a result, it may seem confusing to follow a chapter on yoga and a chapter on acting with a chapter on gender. Are these not wholly different kinds of thing? I analyzed the gender dynamics of twentieth-century yoga in Chapter 2, but that is quite different from analyzing gender itself as an area of technique. At the end of Chapter 3, I suggested that professional identities like that of an actor, dancer, or yoga teacher are not fundamentally different from cultural identities of gender, race, and class, insofar as each of these is constituted to a large extent by training in embodied technique. This suggestion may appear counterintuitive: The more common view is that physical culture and performing arts are fundamentally different types of things than are gender, race, class, ethnicity, religion, (dis)ability, or age. However, my readings of Mauss, Noë, Schatzki, Pickering, Crossley, Martin, Bourdieu, Butler, Mahmood, and Nascimento, among others, suggest that apparently very different modes of cultural practice may be contiguous at the level of embodied technique. In this chapter, I propose that what Certeau called the "practice of everyday life" (2002) can be analyzed using the same epistemology of practice that I have previously applied to physical culture and performing arts. I examine the materiality of sexual difference as an example of what I call the problem of the substrate and consider the implications of this for feminism and feminist studies of masculinity. I also consider the "inertia" of gender technique—its resistance to change—and survey some contemporary research projects in gender.

Charlotte Canning recently asked: "Where do the limits of performance and everyday life intersect?" (2013: 179). In my view, theorists of performance and everyday life are skipping a step if they fail to develop a substantive theory of practice. Without a notion of practice, performance remains stuck within the old problem of representation: How do we get from the extraordinary (or at least consciously framed) moments of "performance" to the mundane repetitions of daily life? Here, as in previous chapters, my primary goal is to further develop and extend the epistemology of practice. To the social and cultural analyses of everyday life found in the writings of Bourdieu, Butler, and Certeau, I bring a new emphasis on the epistemic dimension of practice: the extent to which practice is structured not only by habit (or habitus) and performance (or performativity), but also by knowledge. I do not deny that gender is at times both a habit and a performance. However, I argue that habits and performances are determined as much by knowledge, in the form of technique, as by the social dynamics of power. In addition, I claim that technique is a result of ongoing research that continually tests the limits of similarity and difference between bodies. My focus in this chapter is therefore not on theatrical performances of gender, but on the doing of gender in everyday life. Following Butler, this "doing" has sometimes been referred to as the performance or performativity of gender. I nonetheless deem it wise to distinguish between performance and practice in this context.

Gender is not something that one simply chooses to have or to do, nor is it a specialized area of technique practiced by a particular group of people. Postural yoga may be increasingly found in gyms, classrooms, and studios across the globalized world, and acting technique may be an important part of many school curricula as well as the film and television industries, but to be a serious practitioner of yoga or acting is still to be in the minority. On the other hand, while most people do not identify as athletes, yogis, or stage performers, everyone has a gender identity of some kind—or so it is usually assumed. Judith Butler has described having a gender as a basic "condition of cultural intelligibility" (2004: 52). Gender in this sense is not specialized ("extra-daily") but emphatically *everyday* technique. There are spectacular displays of gender—many of which overlap with physical culture and performing arts—but examining these will not necessarily tell us how gender works in everyday life. Much gender practice in everyday life goes unnoticed and unlabeled as such. Of what then does the practice of gender consist? What does it mean to "have" a gender, and why must everyone have one? Can male and female, or masculine and feminine, be seen as technical specializations? Are binary divisions the best way to think about and understand gender? How might an epistemological perspective on gender reconcile current tensions in queer, transgender, and feminist theory? To begin addressing these questions, I want to offer an alternative to the call for a "revolution in everyday life" put forward by Situationists like Raoul Vaneigem. In its place, I will outline an approach to radical social and cultural transformation that I call *research in everyday life*.

My focus on gender derives from my own attachments to and personal entanglement with issues of gender, sexual difference, and sexuality. However, as in the preceding chapters, I understand gender as a specific example within the broader context of what I am calling the *technique of everyday life*. This is technique which, like that of physical culture and performing arts, structures embodied practice at every level: from the smallest details of gesture and physicality to the literal shaping of bone and flesh; from the briefest moments of intimacy to the grandest historical trends; and from the "thin band" of consciousness to the layers of deeply sedimented agency that define who we are as individuals and communities. What distinguishes the technique of everyday life is that it is not optional. When a certain kind of physical culture is taught to young children as a basic necessity of health, it passes into the common curriculum of society and becomes part of the technique of everyday life. By the same token, when particular ways of doing gender are taught in specific classes or hidden away behind closed doors, they deserve to be called specialized in the same sense as the specialized technique of professional athletes and performers. In this chapter, I argue that what it means to "have a gender" is substantially—though not entirely—a matter of everyday embodied technique. The difference between gender and athletics is then one of degree rather than kind, having to do with how the technique is framed and with who is compelled or allowed to practice it. However, before turning to a thorough consideration of gender as embodied technique, I want to briefly mention some of the ways in which ideas related to embodied practice and technique have previously been used to theorize class, religious, ethnic, and racial identities.

Social class is a founding site for the theorization of embodied knowledge and practice, thanks to the work of Pierre Bourdieu. It was Bourdieu who first attempted to study everyday practice from an epistemological perspective, as structured by a special kind of "practical" logic or knowledge. Bourdieu himself analyzed gender as habitus (Bourdieu 2001; Jagger 2012) and scholars studying many other aspects of everyday life—including religious and racial formations—have since taken up his concept of habitus. Saba Mahmood's previously cited analysis of Islamic religious practice in Egypt (2005) is an important intervention in the strained public discourse surrounding contemporary relations between Islam, Christianity, and secularism. Drawing on Aristotle, Bourdieu, and Foucault, Mahmood argues that the politics of the Egyptian Piety movement can only be grasped if we understand Islam—and, by extension, other religions—as constituted by embodied practice as much as belief. Philip Mellor and Chris Shilling propose the concept of "religious habitus" with which to understand "religious life as a form of embodied pedagogics" (2010: 28). While these theories deal with religion itself, scholars like Mahmood, Charles Hirschkind, and Talal Asad have also begun to theorize secularism along similar lines, asking whether there could be such a thing as a "secular body" (Asad 2011; Hirschkind 2011). If there is such a body, it is no doubt trained in and structured by particular kinds of embodied technique.

There is likewise ample precedent for theorizing specialized technique as a form of cultural and ethnic identity—as in my anecdote about the "Jewish" way of slicing a wedge of cheese. When scholars like Thomas DeFrantz analyze Alvin Ailey's dance as an "embodiment of African

American culture" (2004), they emphasize spectacular performance technique as a site of identity. However, this idea of embodying culture can also be extended to everyday life via critical concepts like Bourdieu's habitus, as Harvey Young does in *Embodying Black Experience* (2010). Young's notion of a "black habitus" calls to mind playwright August Wilson's evocative description of culture as layered and sedimented from childhood:

> Growing up in my mother's house at 1727 Bedford Avenue in Pittsburgh, Pennsylvania, I learned the language, the eating habits, the religious beliefs, the gestures, the notions of common sense, attitudes towards sex, concepts of beauty and justice, and the responses to pleasure and pain that my mother had learned from her mother and which you could trace back to the first African who set foot on the continent.
>
> (Wilson 1998: 494–95)

To this Young adds a specific recognition of how common experiences of racism and prejudice may contribute to the habitus of an oppressed group. The concept of habitus allows Young to explain how blackness can be both "socially constructed and continually constructing its own self." It also highlights *automaticity*, the forgetfulness through which race is enacted: "Like driving a car or riding a bicycle, each action becomes an 'intentionless invention of regulated improvisation'" (Young 2010: 20; and see Ahmed 2006: 129–42). However, there are limitations to the concept of habitus as applied to racial, cultural, and gender identity. The apparent unity of the habitus forces Young to define identity as a "sum total of a series of overlapping *habiti*" (21, italics added)—an image that suggests the discrete experience of code-switching rather than the continuity of a hybrid or newly synthesized identity. Habitus also fails to indicate the epistemic depth of identity and the role of embodied knowledge in racial formations and racializing projects. I therefore wonder if an epistemology of practice could enhance current discussions of race, ethnicity, religion, and social class, by highlighting the ways in which cultural identity is sustained not merely by habit but also by the active transmission and production of knowledge.[2]

Research in everyday life

Michel de Certeau's work on everyday life is the best known today, but it should not be our only reference point for understanding how *research in embodied technique* transforms the everyday. In a small but incisive work, John Roberts (2006) traces the history of the concept of the everyday from revolutionary Marxism through the Situationist movement and into the cultural studies of the 1970s. According to Roberts, the "everyday" of Certeau and his successors is a heavily diluted version of a concept put forward by Marx and further developed by Trotsky and other revolutionaries. In the 1960s, Situationists like Raoul Vaneigem called for a "revolution of everyday life" (2001) that would entail a complete overhaul of social practice at every level. This would be a revolution in both the technique and the technology of everyday life, completely restructuring human relations and, in a great utopian vision, doing away with hierarchical power entirely. The tradition Roberts traces called for the application of artistic creativity across all aspects of life and for the dissolution of "the barrier between artistic technique and general social technique" (2006: 52). Rather than being a specialized domain, these revolutionaries saw artistic creation as a model for reality in general. In the early years of the Russian Revolution, hopes were high for "new forms of cultural production and the revolutionary transformation of the everyday" (54).[3] According to Roberts, Certeau's notion of everyday tactical resistance actually marks an "unprecedented reversal" in the history of the everyday: Even as globalization and capitalism rendered daily experience more uniform, the new field of cultural studies began to study the everyday as an "irreducible symbolic remainder" and "a hugely expanded site of interpretative freedom, cultural activity and popular pleasures" (121).

Like Roberts, I find Certeau's notions of tactics and *perruque* (the latter is similar to Butler's *catachresis*) limited in comparison with the more radical calls for transformation of the everyday that came before it. Yet in place of—or alongside—the Situationist demand for a *revolution of everyday life*, I would like to propose a way forward that is more patient and subtle, but no less radical or far-reaching: the task of conducting *research in everyday life*. Such research aims to produce neither a total revolution, as in the Situationist slogan, nor mere tactical resistance, as in Certeau. Instead, it combines the aim of radical transformation with a slower, more enduring, but equally determined approach to discovering exactly *which* aspects of the everyday can be altered and *how* this can be done. Inasmuch as embodied research has the potential to effect deep-seated change in the fabric of everyday life, it has more in common with the revolutionary tradition traced by Roberts than with the cultural studies represented by Certeau. Yet in calling for research as opposed to revolution, I also want to recall the images of sensitive "tinkering" and "tracking," of "fine-tuning" and "experiential groping" discussed in Chapter 1. We should bear in mind that a revolution cannot effect positive change unless it proposes genuine workable alternatives to what has gone before. This is a difficult challenge, because workable alternatives to everyday life are rarely just lying around awaiting implementation. Substantive alternative ways of life must be discovered through research.

Like some approaches to performance, the "situation" of the Situationists privileges instances of radical disruption or what Roberts calls "that non-heteronomous gesture or action that stands out from the instrumental continuum of the everyday as a critique of the totality" (Roberts 2006: 80). Here, I am less interested in extraordinary moments than in small discoveries of the kind that might go unremarked in the moment of discovery—perhaps because they seemed "irrelevant or too technical" to make a difference in the world at large (Latour 1983: 168)—only to spread and proliferate later in radically unexpected ways. I therefore champion the humble researcher, who knows that no amount of effort or planning can guarantee large-scale impact, because in searching for what is possible, one never purely creates or invents reality. Reality always pushes back, through the relative reliabilities of materiality and of embodiment itself. In research, as previously noted, it is just not the case that "anything goes" (Pickering 1995: 196). Most experiments result in failure—not epistemic failure, but the discovery that a given pathway does not "work" as hoped, which is its own research outcome. Taking this into account in formulating social and political goals suggests a need for patience and honesty in proposing alternative social structures. This does not mean that social struggles become less urgent. It simply acknowledges the debt that meaningful social and political activism owes to ongoing, daily, usually anonymous research in everyday life. It may also suggest that the gradual renovation of the ordinary may ultimately be more transformative than any attempt to produce a special moment, no matter how extraordinary. In any case, there can be no revolution in power without research into possibility.

Technique, once discovered, becomes available for dissemination. As knowledge, it has the potential to travel beyond its community of origin and to effect widespread transformations far beyond the imagination of its original discoverers. Previous chapters illustrated how the technique invented by Tirumalai Krishnamacharya, Konstantin Stanislavski, Jerzy Grotowski, and others has impacted the broader fields of physical culture and theatrical performance. Today, it may be as difficult to imagine somatic bodywork or Grotowskian "song-action" being universally taught as it must have once been to imagine a society in which almost everyone could read and write. But the spread of literacy—to return to this striking example—shows how malleable the common curriculum of everyday life can be. If literacy has now become everyday technique in many countries, this is not because it is natural or easy but because years of mandatory schooling make it so. We should therefore not underestimate the potential of research in everyday technique to radically remake the world. Indeed, we might say, whatever now constitutes the everyday was at some point discovered through research. There is then no reason to dismiss current innovations in embodied technique as the practices of fringe minorities. The same technique that is highly specialized today may become the technique of everyday life in days or years to come. Nor is there any reason to think that changes in embodied technique are less constitutive of reality than changes in technology. Once discovered, embodied technique may be picked up, appropriated, and transmitted across time and space. Gradually, *what we do* becomes *who we are*. Actions sediment into identities and what was once specialized becomes the new landscape within which daily life unfolds. Research in technique can therefore be the basis for a slow reworking of reality. There are undoubtedly limits to how extensively everyday life can be transformed, but those limits are permanently unknown. The rest of this chapter examines one particular area in which embodied research is currently leading to widespread and radical change in everyday practice: the technique of gender.

We live now in a time of intense research both *in* and *on* gender, in which new ways of doing gender are continually being put forward—and often violently censured, as well. There exist numerous divergent approaches to gender, to which people and communities are deeply attached. Any attempt to define male or female, masculine or feminine, as areas of technique is riddled with danger for this reason. Yet I want to initiate a conversation along these lines by asking a basic epistemological question: *What kind of technique is gender?* We can learn something about how to answer this question from the examples studied in the previous chapters. There, we saw how arguments over the precise boundaries of a label, while they may be politically expedient or necessary in particular circumstances, tell us little about the technique those labels name. For example, two practices, both called "yoga," may be far more different than two other practices, one of which is called "yoga" and the other "fitness." The debate over what does or does not count as "yoga" or "acting" remains meaningful only insofar as it continually refers back to the detailed technical structure of practices. Here I propose that the same logic applies to gender. Some voices in late twentieth-century feminism argued for the complete dissolution of masculinity and femininity, or even male and female, as categories (e.g., Harding in Alcoff and Potter 1993: 74; and see Stoltenberg 1989, discussed below). On the other hand, what Judith Butler has more recently called the "new gender politics" (2004: 4), including queer and transgender theories and activism, acknowledges the value or even the necessity of gender for many people and rejects or indefinitely postpones the project of eliminating gender. In theorizing gender as technique, I try to avoid a reductive policing of boundaries and to focus instead on the complexity of its spread, borrowing, and innovation.

The remainder of this chapter is located at an underexamined point of convergence between thinkers who write about "the body" in specialized and virtuosic practices and those who write about it in the context of everyday life. Theorists of postural yoga, sport, health and fitness, physical culture, physical education, actor training, and the history of acting generally have much to say about embodiment—but they tend to assume a neat binary division between male and female. (My own discussion of the gendering of yoga technique followed this model: I offered reasons why yoga in the United States is primarily taught and practiced by women, but I did not problematize the category of women as such.) On the other hand, theorists of complex gender rarely draw substantively upon discussions of specialized embodied knowledge, such as those found in dance, theatre, and performance studies. In splitting the difference between these two lineages of contemporary thought, I acknowledge certain risks. Theorists of yoga and acting may find my approach to gender too radical, while theorists of gender may find it not radical enough. Nevertheless, I agree with Eve Kosofsky Sedgwick that we cannot hope to analyze any social phenomenon today without an awareness of gender and sexuality (1990: 1). By the same token, I cannot now imagine a satisfying account of gender—or any other identity—that fails to take a critical perspective on embodiment. A useful epistemology of practice must therefore engage seriously with both perspectives.

The problem of sexual difference

In previous chapters, physiological difference was considered in regard to anomalous cases requiring the extension of technique—as in Matthew Sanford's yoga practice (Chapter 2) or Carrie Sandahl's experience in acting class (Chapter 3). In this chapter, the dissimilarity of bodies moves to the center of the discussion via the heavily debated but still unresolved notion of sexual difference and its relationship to gender. In Chapter 1, I borrowed Laurent Thévenot's definition of philosophical realism as "the relation between human agency and material environment." According to Thévenot, practice goes beyond "symbolic work, meaning, understanding, [and] interpretation" insofar as it engages with a material world that continually "responds" with the force of its own reality (in Schatzki *et al.* 2001: 58, 64–65). In my terms, this is what makes embodied practice *epistemic*: We come to know ourselves, others, and the material world through the myriad pathways of technique. As a result, the reality that one encounters "depends on the different ways one has to 'take hold' of the environment" (Thévenot in Schatzki *et al.* 2001: 59), which Pickering refers to as "grips on the world" (Pickering 1995: 190). My own analysis suggests that this engagement with the material world is not limited to an external "environment" or to the "machinic" grips of technology. Rather, the primary site of *taking hold* and *gripping* the world is embodiment itself—its capacities and limitations—which we come to know through embodied technique. Realism in Thévenot's sense suggests a continual engagement between technique and materiality. What I call the "problem of the substrate" is the inescapable fact that we cannot know the material reality with which technique grapples except through that same technique. This is a fundamental characteristic of knowledge, independent of field or discipline: We come to know "history" (the reality of past events) through history (an area or branch of knowledge); we know "mathematics" (abstract patterns) through mathematics (another branch of knowledge); and we know "wood" (the relatively reliable material) through working with it— whether in the craft of woodworking or the science of molecular biology. The premise of realism is that materiality pushes back against technique, making some channels or pathways more accessible than others. However, technique itself is our only way of knowing which pathways are possible and how they can be reached.[4]

Feminist, queer, and transgender accounts of gender are all centrally engaged with the problematic of realism in this sense. The question of what is material in human embodiment—as opposed, usually, to what is cultural—has been at the heart of many productive but also divisive debates about sex and gender.[5] On the one hand, a realist account of gender must acknowledge the material and physiological differences that exist between bodies and the extent to which such differences may affect subjectivity and experience. This means, in my terms, recognizing that not all technique is equally available to all people; different bodies afford different technical pathways and possibilities. On the other hand, we cannot know in advance exactly which bodies are capable of which kinds of technique. Technique tells us what is possible; it does not tell us what is impossible. Because the material reliabilities with which technique deals are only ever relative, there is always a chance that technique will not work when it is expected to, or that it will work when it is not expected to. How then should we think about the relationship between the materiality of bodies and the range of possible technique? This is a central question for theories of gender, where the "materiality of bodies" has most often been understood as referring to a binary division between female and male.

Applied to gender, the "problem of the substrate" gives us a useful way to rethink the vexed issue of sexual difference. In 1975, Gayle Rubin defined the "sex/gender system" as "the set of arrangements by which a society transforms biological sexuality into products of human activity, and in which these transformed sexual needs are satisfied" (1975: 159). Rubin's anthropological model of gender reiterates Simone de Beauvoir's observation: "One is not born, but rather becomes, a woman" (Beauvoir 1953: 273). However, Rubin's formulation adds to Beauvoir's comment the notion of a material substrate upon which gender works—a ground upon which gender is constructed—which Rubin calls "biological sexuality" and later simply "sex." In the context of 1970s feminism, Rubin's essay opened new possibilities for gender by distinguishing it from mere biological sex. This idea has now become commonplace and has sometimes even been framed in epistemological terms, as when Linda Nicholson defines gender as not just "the social organization of sexual difference" but also "the *knowledge* that establishes meanings for bodily differences" (1994: 79, italics added). Yet it is important to remember that we do not have access to "sexual difference" except through different kinds of technique—above all, that of gender itself. It is therefore legitimate to ask whether we can say anything at all about the materiality of sexual difference without already beginning to enact (a particular kind of) gender as technique. This problem is evident in Nicholson's slippage from "sexual difference" to "bodily difference," for it is precisely the technique of gender that determines which bodily differences are understood as sexual.

In *Bodies That Matter,* Judith Butler critiques the idea that sexual difference is materially distinct from gender, arguing that the former "is never simply a function of material differences which are not in some way both marked and formed by discursive practices" (1993a: 1). For Butler, sex is not a biological reality separate from gender, but rather a socially constructed "regulatory ideal." The risk in this kind of discursive analysis is that the materiality of the body drops away, leaving one to imagine that there is no substrate for gender, no relative reliabilities upon which it depends and with which attempts to transform or innovate gender must grapple. In the epistemological model proposed here, gender is understood as an area of embodied technique that tinkers and tunes, tracks and grapples with some of the relative reliabilities of human embodiment and materiality. It is therefore not wrong to think of the substrate of gender as sex, sexuality, sexual reproduction, or sexual difference. The substrate of gender can include all of these. However, the precise boundaries of the substrate of gender cannot be defined except through gender itself. We can think of Rubin's sex/gender paradigm as shorthand for the relationship between gender technique and its substrate, as long as we remember that the substrate can never be finally defined apart from its technique. The technique of gender determines what counts as sexual difference. For example, it may seem clear that the embodied technique of gender is initially founded on the politics of reproduction, and that gender is a way of organizing and handling kinship. But could there be gender technique that has no relation to kinship and reproduction? How many genders could there be? Which parts of the body are gendered? Can gender operate without a notion of sexual difference? The goal of my argument is not to answer these questions, but to show that they are substantive *research questions*, which must be answered through embodied research. Such questions do not have final theoretical or scientific answers. They are challenges to discover new pathways in embodied technique.

Butler was not the first to critique the sex/gender distinction or to observe that a binary approach to sexual difference is itself a cultural phenomenon. Suzanne Kessler and Wendy McKenna's "ethnomethodological" approach to gender (1978) is an important precursor to my argument and perhaps the first attempt to analyze gender as something like embodied technique.[6] Predating Butler's work by over a decade, Kessler and McKenna reject the existence of a material foundation for binary sexual difference upon which gender would then be constructed. Instead, they see gender as a set of culturally organized "methods" for dealing with a complex array of physiological and psychological variations across a population. This prescient rejection of the sex/gender dichotomy (they use the term gender exclusively) has been borne out by subsequent decades of scientific and critical thinking. Recent trends in queer and transgender theory likewise draw on current science to support a more complex theory of bodily variation.[7] In nature as measured by science, including biology and the life sciences, there are no ideal paradigms of maleness or femaleness; there are only populations of individuals, each of which possesses a particular set of attributes. Measuring these traits provides quantitative data, which may reveal correlations between these attributes, but such data is statistical in nature. It can tell us how particular attributes are distributed across a population, but not how to get from individuals and populations to ideal categories. Hence, the reproductive and evolutionary mechanisms of sexual dimorphism do not in any way imply a sexual binary.[8]

To demonstrate this point, Kessler and McKenna provide a list of physiological traits, none of which is perfectly correlated with gender: chromosomes (XX or XY), gonads (ovaries or testes), internal reproductive organs (e.g., uterus, sperm ducts), external reproductive organs, prenatal hormones, and pubertal hormones (1978: 47–55, 59–68, 73–75). (A similar breakdown of the complex and imperfectly correlated dimensions of gender was proposed by Magnus Hirschfeld as early as 1910—see Germon 2009: 193–95.) As it turns out, the only time when a physiological trait is perfectly correlated with a binary sex category is when the appearance of external genitals is used to classify a newborn child as either male or female—an example that emphasizes the socially produced character of the binary. In all other cases, the relationship between a person's gender and these physiological traits can vary to greater or lesser degrees. Neither chromosomes nor any other quantifiable measurement of the body can tell us with certainty what gender a person is.

As Kessler and McKenna observe, this means that scientists do not possess special tools with which to assess a person's gender. On the contrary, scientists generally use the same everyday technique as everyone else to determine whether someone is male or female, and then organize their research around that assumption. Many individuals do not fit neatly within the binary classification scheme at all. Yet scientists, doctors, and others actively maintain binary gender technique, working tirelessly to "construct dimorphism where there is continuity" and complexity (1978: 163). In some cases, this construction is literal, as when doctors surgically operate upon newborn babies to make their genitals more closely match either the male or the female cultural ideal. This amounts to more than a cultural policing of "what a body can do." As Jennifer Germon points out, the violence of the genital surgery routinely performed on intersex babies includes the foreclosure of unknown possibilities of embodiment. Particular avenues of embodied technique are then not merely forbidden but rendered physically impossible, as the bodily formations that would afford such alternative technique are surgically altered, returning the body to within the "normal" range of technique. As one intersex individual recounts, "all the things my body might have grown to do, all the possibilities, went down the hall with my amputated clitoris" (Germon 2009: 178–79). Doctors and surgeons recognize that the body after such surgery may have a smaller range of technique than "normal" bodies—such as less erotic sensation or infertility—but find this more acceptable than the existence of bodies that suggest unknown, perhaps "monstrous" (Stryker and Sullivan 2009) sexual possibilities.[9]

The literal construction of binary gender is not limited to intersex surgery. As Esther Rothblum points out, the embodied technique assigned to women often "focuses on physical characteristics (e.g., size of feet, body weight) that are already smaller in women and attempts to curtail its size even more" (2011: 175). These examples illustrate not only the material, disciplinary force with which dimorphism is constructed out of continuity, but also the range of bodily variation that may be considered part of sexual difference. In some contexts, the size of a person's feet would not be thought of as gendered, whereas in other cases this is an important substrate of gender technique. In any case, the reification of two normative body types or "sexes" leads to the identification of bodies as abnormal or disordered if they do not fit neatly within either category. Once the dimorphism has been constructed, the continuity and complexity of physiological variation is no longer perceptible as such. Instead of seeing continuous natural variation, we begin to perceive bodies as either normal or abnormal, prioritizing imaginary ideals of male and female over the reality of diverse embodiment and sexual variation. A woman who turns out to have a Y chromosome may then be seen as a defective or abnormal female, rather than as a case that reveals the insufficiency of the binary paradigm. This is a standard attribute of a paradigm in Thomas Kuhn's sense: Data that do not fit into it are routinely ignored (Wray 2011: 69). In Kuhnian terms, then, we may now be approaching a paradigm shift in gender technique, as what were once considered anomalous cases move to the center of attention.

If we were to avoid constructing this dimorphism, instead acknowledging continuity and variation where it exists, then we might arrive at a very different notion of sexual difference. Certainly, bodies differ in terms of their chromosomes, reproductive gonads, internal and external organs, and hormonal patterns. Not only do these measurable physiological traits vary between people, but they also change radically throughout the lifetime of an individual, leading Judith Kegan Gardiner to suggest that age categories "should form a more integral part in feminist theories of gender so that all gender would be conceptualized developmentally" (2002: 94). Such a complex field of similarity and difference cannot be adequately described by a binary model, or even by a linear spectrum with male and female poles. The important question is not why some bodies are difficult to classify as one or the other sex, or whether a classification scheme with a different number of sexes (three in Herdt 1993; five in Fausto-Sterling 1993) would be more accurate. As long as there are categories, there will be bodies that fall in between or outside those categories. Instead, what we have arrived at are essentially questions for embodied research: What can be done with or made of the complex materiality of sexual variation? Given the distribution of phy-siological attributes in a population, how might sexuality, reproduction, kinship, and other areas of life be structured and organized? These are research questions in embodied technique, which takes as its substrate bodily difference and physiological variation as well as similarity.

From an epistemological perspective, gender is an ongoing exploration of the possibilities afforded by the variation of bodies in a population. Such a perspective does not forget or ignore the materiality of sexual difference, but reconceives it as the substrate of a field of knowledge continually in development. Furthermore, once the complexity of sexual variation is acknowledged, the border between it and other kinds of physiological and anatomical variation—such as height and weight, body shape, skin color, and (dis)ability—becomes porous. Part of the technique of gender is the determination of which kinds of variation are relevant to it and which not. Different approaches to gender may therefore take different aspects of anatomy and physiology as their substrate. This does not mean that gender has an arbitrary or merely symbolic relation to the distribution of physiological traits. Rather, gender engages, wrestles with, and comes to know its material substrate through embodied research. Gender is open-ended, because we can never say that we have discovered all the possible ways of organizing and working with sexual and bodily variation. Just as we may yet find new ways of working with steel or electricity, the material substrate of gender may still afford new pathways that have yet to be discovered (or are long forgotten). As Elizabeth Grosz writes, the body

> is constrained by its biological limits ... whose framework or "stretchability" we cannot yet know, we cannot presume ... Processes and activities that seem impossible for a body to undertake at some times and in some cultures are readily possible in others ... The scope and limit of the body's pliability is not yet adequately understood.
>
> (Grosz 1994: 187, 190).

Today, it is possible to reshape bodies—through surgery and hormonal injections—in ways that were previously unimaginable. That which was presumed to be a stable and necessary substrate for gender has been rendered plastic. At the same time, we continue to search for new embodied technique with which to make use of and come to know the materiality of sexual difference and sexual variation. The Deleuzo-Spinozan injunction applies as well to gender as it does to postural yoga or acting technique: *We do not yet know what a body can do.*

An epistemological approach to embodied technique places us in stubborn middle ground between theories that reify and essentialize sexual difference and those that try to open it up to unlimited play. Conceiving gender as technique can help explain the fact that societies and cultures of virtually every period and region have developed concepts roughly analogous to those of female and male (or feminine and masculine), without attaching value judgments to this fact. The ubiquity of binary gender is sometimes taken as proof that it is natural or unavoidable. However, there is another explanation for this phenomenon, based on the idea that pathways in the relative reliability of embodiment may be more or less obvious (Chapter 1). If a binary approach to gender is found in many cultures, this could be because it is an easily discovered pathway in that area of technique. After all, the physiological differences between bodies are real, and some of them correlate with one another, including several that cluster around reproductive sexuality. It is therefore not surprising that many societies have defined two types of person based on these correlations. The fact that binary gender is very common across cultures need not be taken as an endorsement of its value, because the most obvious technical pathway is not necessarily the only one or the best. In the previous chapter, I suggested that Stanislavski was able to discover a genuinely new approach to acting because he broke away from the "obvious" technical pathway according to which performers should rehearse what they are planning to do onstage. In taking seriously the idea that actors might prepare for performance by extensively exploring scenarios that would never be performed, Stanislavski found a hidden pathway in the embodied technique of acting. The fact that this pathway is less obvious than the other does not make it better or worse. It simply illustrates the fact that technique is structured epistemically—as knowledge—and that it is therefore possible to discover new, unknown pathways even in areas that are thought to be well-explored.

Fracturing the feminine

Feminism is the founding critique of gender. Jennifer Germon shows that it was sexologists like John Money who invented gender as a social category in the mid-twentieth century, borrowing the term "from linguistics (philology), where historically it had been used to signify relations between words rather than between people" (2009: 32). However, the idea of gender in sexology was not yet a *critique* of gender, because it did not engage with issues of power. Feminism, on the other hand, has been foundationally concerned with disentangling the feminine from

186

the female, and with separating embodied technique from its biological substrate, in order to transform unequal power relations among individuals and gendered classes. This has led to an ongoing tension within feminism, between the desire to undo binary gender and the simultaneous need for gender categories as the basis for a critique of power relations. Could an epistemology of practice suggest a new synthesis between these dual feminist projects? Might a reconception of gender as technique offer new ways of thinking about the interplay of bodily variation and social power relations?

While distinguishing sex from gender—as Beauvoir and Rubin did—has been a crucial aspect of the feminist project, the separation of sex from gender has never been finally achievable, since, as Butler observes, many feminists still assume "that in order for feminism to proceed as a critical practice, it must ground itself in the sexed specificity of the female body" (1993a: 28). Even Grosz's call for a "corporeal feminism" ends with a call for "new productivity between and of the two sexes," leaving the assumption of underlying binary sex intact (1994: 210). In contrast, other theorists of gender—like Kessler and McKenna and Germon—have argued that there is no singular "sexed specificity" in which binary categories of male and female might be grounded. At issue in tensions between cultural and materialist feminist theories—or what Eve Kosofsky Sedgwick calls "more and less historicizing" approaches to feminism (1985: 11)—is once again the question of *realism* in the relationship between gender and sexual difference. While "more historicizing" feminists emphasize differences between the gender technique of different periods and regions, "less historicizing" feminists emphasize the relative reliability of human embodiment that affords those differences transculturally. There is no inherent contradiction between these perspectives, as long as the question of what kinds of technique are afforded by material reality remains open. After all, the relatively reliable materiality of bodies is precisely what makes ongoing research in gender technique possible. Both the variability of gender technique and the reliability of its substrate can be affirmed if we understand gender as a field of knowledge. From an epistemological perspective, there need not be any unified basis of sexual difference with which gender technique works. Rather, every kind of gender technique defines its own substrate, picking and choosing from the different kinds of physiological and anatomical variation that human populations afford. For every example of gender technique, there may be a different referent for "sexual difference."

Iris Young's work on differential bodily training and experience carefully navigates the intersections of physiology, ability, and training.

In her 1980 essay, "Throwing Like a Girl," Young describes the everyday discipline through which girls may be conditioned to exclude athleticism from their embodied technique. While this essay may now seem dated, it offers a pointed example of how technique can sediment in the body to the point where it is mistaken for physiological inevitability. Young observed girls being taught, through both formal and informal education, to "sit, stand, and walk with their limbs close to or closed around them" (in Welton 1998: 267). She analyzes this training as not a "lack of practice," but rather a "specific positive style of feminine bodily comportment," albeit one that emphasizes restraint and containment over action and accomplishment. Through such training, a girl may learn "actively to hamper her movements ... Thus she develops a bodily timidity that increases with age. In assuming herself to be a girl, she takes herself to be fragile" (270). Young's emphasis is on disentangling the technique of gender from assumptions about male and female physiology, so as to show that throwing "like a girl" is a product of sexist training rather than any kind of "feminine essence" (269; and see Noland 2009: 23–31). Her discussion also recalls the way in which disciplined training, particularly at a young age, can permanently shape the physical body at the level of anatomical structure. If differential training in gender can literally shape bodily difference, this would presumably help to conceal the extent to which agency and oppression are involved in such training. This is then a classical example of the feminist critique of embodied technique.

Young's later writings complicate her original project by turning towards a more positive valuation of some kinds of "feminine" embodied technique. In "'Throwing Like a Girl': Twenty Years Later," Young reexamines her classical essay, observing that its focus on exposing "how male-dominated society excludes women from highly valued male activities" had prevented her from pursuing the equally important project of contesting the devaluation of traditionally feminine activities (in Welton 1998: 289). Taking up this latter charge, Young begins to expand the notion of feminine technique beyond the simply oppressive, calling for an exploration of "specifically feminine forms of movement" that would celebrate their value. Although Young does not mention somatics, it is not hard to draw a connection between her call for a revaluation of feminine technique and my discussion of less athletic approaches to physical culture in Chapter 2. However, Young also proposes a different kind of "specifically feminine" technique to celebrate. In her essay on pregnancy, she describes the experience of carrying a child in admiring terms: The "pregnant subject ... often experiences her ordinary walking, turning, sitting as a kind of dance ... she glides through space in an immediate openness" (in Welton 1998: 278). The celebration of pregnancy would seem to most readers to be grounded not only in a difference of technique, but also in a more fundamental kind of bodily capacity. This apparently marks a limit in the relative reliability of embodiment that has yet to be crossed. Are we then dealing with two kinds of ability—one that results from training in technique and another that precedes or undergirds such training? Is the definition of pregnancy necessarily narrower, and therefore more limited by its material substrate, than the definition of athletics? Or can pregnancy also be seen as a kind of technique, which may or may not be identified with the category of the female? And is the focus of Young's celebration actually the "female" capacity to be pregnant? Or might it rather be the "feminine" (somatic) technique of "dance," "gliding," and "openness," which may or may not attend that state?

Luce Giard's work on the everyday technique of cooking—to return to that mundane example—offers yet another example of how knowledge in the form of technique may be interwoven with categories of gender identity. Cooking is a common example of everyday technique that evidently combines sophisticated knowledge of materials and recipes with the literally "everyday" need for nutritious provisions. Giard, a colleague of Certeau, offers an evocative account of cooking as a field of knowledge in which "tradition and innovation"—that is, training and research—matter equally (in Certeau et al. 1998: 151). She is highly aware of the oppressive patriarchal conditions under which women in France have been associated with the everyday activity of cooking in the domestic sphere; her project is a critique of this history. Nevertheless, Giard also recognizes the value of cooking as an epistemic field that is constituted through the transmission of knowledge (157). Drawing on Certeau's valorization of everyday technique, she highlights ongoing innovation in cooking and the development of new knowledge in response to advances in technology (e.g., 172–73). For Giard, reclaiming cooking means reclaiming its epistemology, its depth and breadth as knowledge. This, for her, is no less urgent a project than that of freeing women from the burden of that knowledge. Following Giard, we might then suggest that the project of reclaiming traditionally feminine technique (above, somatics; here, domestic cooking) be placed alongside that of redistributing traditionally masculine technique, as part of feminist politics and epistemics. Feminism would then have two distinct but interwoven referents: the category of women as defined by prevailing gender technique and the epistemic category of traditionally feminine technique, even (or perhaps especially) when this is practiced by individuals classified as male.

The debate over sex and gender within feminism continues—as seen, for example, in a series of linked essays in the recent anthology *Embodied Selves* (Gonzalez-Arnal *et al.* 2012). Here, in her critique of Linda Alcoff's too-easy acceptance of binary sex categories as the material basis upon which gender is culturally constructed, Kathleen Lennon echoes many of Kessler and McKenna's points about the complexity of human physiological, anatomical, and reproductive variation. Lennon's notion of "the natural as that which constrains discourse" functions much like my idea of the substrate of technique (in Gonzalez-Arnal *et al.* 2012: 30). It attempts to give the relative reliabilities of embodiment—and the "natural history" of humans as a species—a central role in the development of sex and gender categories, while at the same time avoiding a deterministic approach to sex or a reductive, binary account of biology. The examples of pregnancy and sport are precisely those that provoke Lennon's question: "If we do not view our everyday sexed categories as biological categories, what kind of an account can we offer of them, which recognises their bodily nature, and is such that a division of labour in biological reproduction might make them unsurprising, even while we might claim it does not necessarily justify them?" (38). Her answers align with mine: "Practices"—what I am calling technique—

> require a community for whom the use of the term makes sense. With innovation there can be divisions, and sub-practices may emerge where the application of the term becomes contested, but the debates here are not stipulative. They are about the *possibilities for communal ways of life.*
>
> (41, italics added)[10]

I do not think I am wrong to read in this passage the suggestion that theoretical discussions about the meaning of gender and sex categories will be most likely to produce genuine innovation if they are linked to concrete *projects of embodied research* in the technique of gender.

The technique and discourse of mainstream gender still wrestle with the apparently inextricable link between women and pregnancy. Meanwhile, transgender communities—see below—are already developing the technique of transmasculine pregnancies: the pregnancies of those who identify as transmen or simply as men (see j wallace in Bornstein and Bergman 2010; Leonard 2008; Spottiswoode 2013). In this context, it is important to recognize that conflicts between different communities of practice result not only from hierarchical power dynamics but also from the fact that research is unevenly distributed, with different communities pursuing different lines of inquiry and different varieties of technique simultaneously. I have argued that every area of gender technique selects and organizes its own material substrate from among the differential distributions of bodily potentials and capacities. It is therefore impossible to disentangle technique from its substrate. This does not mean that gender is merely discursive or symbolic. Rather, we should recall Andrew Pickering's description of knowledge as simultaneously "objective, relative, and historical" (1995: 33). If it is deeply misleading to assert the existence of two sex categories with different inherent abilities, it is equally so to imagine that gender can function without some recognition of bodily differences that exist beyond the power of technique—embodied or otherwise—to alter. To assert a link between sport, cooking, or pregnancy and the category of "women" is then not to make true or false statements about the material reality of sexual difference. It rather amounts to the declaration or founding of a field of gender technique, in which a particular kind of knowledge—and its material substrate—will be used to define and produce "a" sex. One can then conduct research in that field and indeed found whole disciplines of practice upon it—to the point where it can easily be forgotten that the original act of grouping individuals into mutually exclusive categories was never either more nor less than the first step along a pathway of technique.

Masculinities

Like feminism proper, the feminist study of masculinity offers an attempt to disentangle embodied technique from what may at first appear to be a stable biological substrate. The problem of the substrate comes up as soon as the feminist project of separating the feminine from the female is extended to the relationship between masculinity and males. In *The Masculinity Studies Reader*, Rachel Adams and David Savran ask: "Does the study of masculinity need to consider men at all? What is the role of the sexed body in the analysis of masculinity?" (2002: 2). More pointedly, Eve Kosofsky Sedgwick calls for the study of masculinity "to drive a wedge in, early and often and if possible conclusively, between the two topics, masculinity and men" (1995: 12). Following earlier feminist scholarship, these passages take as their starting point the sex/gender paradigm, according to which "men" is a stable category, defined by "the sexed body," from which the embodied technique of masculinity can be distinguished. Yet as I have suggested, the classification of some bodies into the category of "men" is already technique, insofar as it draws on the distribution of a variety of anatomical, physiological, and genetic variations in human populations and uses these to construct or invent a binary classification scheme. From an epistemological perspective, every kind of "masculine" technique works with the materiality of sexual difference in a different way, picking and choosing which kinds of bodily variations to engage. Thus, if masculinity can be shown to vary across history and culture (Arnold and Brady 2011), so too does maleness itself.

One thinker who acknowledges the role of embodied technique in constructing maleness as well as masculinity is John Stoltenberg, who argues against the very category of "man." To be a man, for Stoltenberg, is not merely to fit within a particular range of physiological variation. Rather, the word already implies an area of embodied technique linked to domination and oppression. Stoltenberg's rejection of the category of man is analogous to the feminist concern that the very "concept of woman" may be "radically problematic" and "crowded with the over-determinations of male supremacy" to the point where "every source of knowledge about women has been contaminated with misogyny and sexism" (Alcoff 1988: 405–6). For Stoltenberg, rejecting the hierarchy of gendered domination requires the denial of manhood as a category— what he calls "refusing to be a man" (1989). This argument is notable in its rejection of the sex/gender paradigm, according to which we might try to salvage a safe or harmless reality of "man" from beneath layers of oppressive "masculine" technique. Like Kessler and McKenna, Stoltenberg understands binary sexual difference as a particular kind of gender technique, which for him intrinsically suggests a hierarchical relation- ship. In his writing, Stoltenberg replaces identity categories like "boys" and "men" with anatomical descriptors, like "the child-with-a-penis" or "some of us with penises" (42, 27). While the penis is only one aspect of anatomical variation—one that itself eclipses the real variety of sexual anatomies—such descriptors remind us of the material substrate out of which gender produces its categories. For Stoltenberg, any gender tech- nique that begins by sorting people into (two) categories is already dangerously ripe for the installation of gender-based inequity and vio- lence. Without necessarily accepting Stoltenberg's conclusions, his call to refuse even the apparently basic categories of maleness and men is an important counterpoint to the more familiar studies of masculinity just cited, which work according to the sex/gender paradigm.

Moreover, Stoltenberg is surely correct in suggesting that the need to disentangle the technique of sexual violence from the distribution of body parts and types is one of the most pressing sociopolitical issues today. As feminists like Andrea Dworkin and Catharine MacKinnon have argued, rape is not an isolated crime, but part of the fabric of gender in many contemporary and historical societies (Dworkin 1987;

MacKinnon 2006; and see Butler 2004: 53). Although many people nei-ther experience nor commit rape, feminism has revealed the ubiquity of *rape culture* as a field of everyday gender technique in which the possi-bility of rape figures centrally to define the differentiated experience of men and women. As a paradigmatic "intersection of domination and sexuality" (Sedgwick 1985: 9), the continuing and highly gendered pre-valence of rape must be an important consideration for any critical analysis of contemporary masculinity as embodied technique. Insofar as rape culture is a field of everyday technique that constitutes all men as potential rapists and all women as potentially raped, these roles could be said to reflect or incarnate different kinds of embodied training that determine how people understand and relate to their own bodies and those of other people. If girls are taught from a young age to see them-selves as "fragile," as Iris Young suggests, then the teaching of boys to see themselves as physically dangerous and sexually needy is part of that same embodied education in gender. Yet altering the everyday train-ing of "girls" and "boys" is not necessarily the same as dismantling the binary categories according to which children are sorted in the first place.

What then is the relationship between training in masculine gender and the complex materiality of physiological and anatomical variation? To what extent do the characteristics of bodies simply *afford* the possi-bility of rape? Susan Brownmiller's classic work on the subject offers a biologically deterministic analysis of this relationship, according to which rape is a direct result of the physiology of sexual difference. In her view, "we cannot work around the fact that in terms of human anatomy the possibility of forcible intercourse incontrovertibly exists. This single factor may have been sufficient to have caused the creation of a male ideology of rape" (1975: 14). But this is too simple: Women can and do sexually violate men, and men sexually violate other men, but that is not what feminists mean by rape culture—except insofar as the violation of men may be conceived as a kind of feminizing. The culture or technique of rape clearly goes beyond the affordances of bodies. In contrast to Brownmiller, Sharon Marcus defines rape as "a scripted interaction which takes place in language and can be understood in terms of conventional masculinity and femininity as well as other gender inequalities" (1992: 390). By analyzing rape as language, Marcus follows the discursive turn in cultural theory and emphasizes the social construc-tion of sex and gender. But taking language as a metaphor for practice risks dematerializing the bodies involved—as I noted in Chapter 1—and overlooking the way in which rape makes use of bodily differences that exceed those produced by training and technique. Sexual violation does not require any particular kind of body, but rape culture does work through and with the distribution of anatomies in human populations. Hence, rape is neither biology nor discourse, but embodied technique.

Rape culture works, using Kessler and McKenna's phrasing, to "construct dimorphism where there is continuity." In place of complex variations in sexual anatomy, desire, and sensation, rape culture constructs a sheer dichotomy between those who need sexual release and those from whom it can be obtained. As embodied technique, this construction is dependent upon, though not determined by, certain relative reliabilities of sexual difference, which are its material substrate. It is, then, one way of handling the possibilities afforded by sexual difference—in this case, through the starkest hierarchical dichotomy. Masculinity as practiced by (heterosexual) rape culture locates sexual pleasure in the female body. In doing so, it does not merely structure the relationship "between" men and women; it also helps to define these two categories. The identification of women as objects of pleasure simultaneously exaggerates and intensifies binary sexual difference *and* works to elide differences between men, who through this identification create a male "homosocial" domain in which homosexual contact is forbidden (Sedgwick 1985; Rubin 1975). Other kinds of masculine technique, such as that which makes the body feel hard and impenetrable—indeed, precisely those kinds of technique that prevent bodies from being "fragile" and which are central to athletic and military training—can also be seen as part of the everyday technique that makes rape so common and so profoundly gendered. This everyday technique is part of the "common curriculum" of some societies. Whether we look for solutions within or beyond the binary, the continued prevalence of sexual violence suggests the need for embodied research to find new ways of doing gender.

Some ways forward may be found in queer theory, where masculinity is less often understood as equivalent to domination than as a legitimate and potentially valuable area of embodied technique—including for people identified as female. Some of the clearest discussions of masculinity as technique can be found in studies of butch lesbians and other women, where something like a technical analysis of masculinity is enabled by the absence of any possibility to ground gender in biological sex. Judith (Jack) Halberstam offers several examples of "fully realized nonmale masculinities," including "lesbian fatherhood, butch identities, drag king performances, [and] female sports icons" (in Gardiner 2002: 352; and see Halberstam 1998a). For each of these, an epistemological perspective might lead us to ask how this particular technique of masculinity relates to the materiality of bodies. For example, why lesbian fatherhood? What does the word "father" do in this phrase? To what does it refer? The notion of lesbian fatherhood seems to reclaim something positive about fatherhood from a version of feminism that would equate it with patriarchy. Fatherhood here suggests more than just the situation of raising a child that one did not give birth to, for that applies equally to many adoptive and lesbian mothers. To be a lesbian father is then to engage with the child-rearing technique that other fathers—including male ones—have developed in the past. Whether one hopes to learn from this technique, transform it, or reject it outright, the notion of lesbian fatherhood puts the lesbian parent in dialogue with a field of knowledge developed and passed along by prior fathers. Fatherhood in this sense is not primarily a material or physiological fact, but an area of embodied technique. From a psychoanalytic perspective, the father provides a bridge from domesticity to the larger social world, enabling the child to move out of the family unit and into the public sphere. The notion of lesbian fatherhood may suggest the continuing value and validity of such technique, independent of any presumed maleness or heterosexuality.

The other kinds of "nonmale masculinity" enumerated by Halberstam suggest other aspects of masculine technique, each of which may take as its substrate a different aspect of the materiality of sexual difference and variation. What Halberstam calls "butch identities" may refer to the technique of flirtation, seduction, sexual encounter, romance, and intimacy. Such identities could involve everything from the ways bodies are dressed to the ways they dance or make love. In her essay on butch lesbian identities, Gayle Rubin surveys a wide range of butch identities, from the "tough yet sensitive" motorcycle-riding icons of the 1950s to butches who are "tough street dudes," jocks, scholars, artists, and much more. She observes:

> Butches vary in how they relate to their female bodies. Some butches are comfortable being pregnant and having kids, while for others the thought of undergoing the female component of mammalian reproduction is utterly repugnant. Some enjoy their breasts while others despise them. Some butches hide their genitals and some refuse penetration. There are butches who abhor tampons, because of their resonance with intercourse; other butches love getting fucked.
>
> (In Stryker and Whittle 2006: 473–75)

This passage indicates how different types of masculinity may relate in radically different ways to the materiality of bodies and their variations. The fact that each area of technique works with a different substrate of embodiment means that neither biological nor discursive explanations alone can account for their variety. Some kinds of masculinity may be easily transferred across all kinds of bodies, while in other cases sustained research may be necessary to make a particular kind of technique available to those whose bodies do not afford the relative reliabilities for which it was developed. Such research could be as simple as getting masculine technique to "work" for bodies with certain traditionally female attributes. But it could also lead to the development of new technique designed specifically for such bodies, which might then require another round of research in order to be practiced by bodies with correspondingly "male" attributes. From this perspective, the "border" zone between butch lesbians and transexual men (Halberstam 1998b) could be reconceived not as an embattled boundary, but as an area in which research in embodied technique is especially active. By analogy with the earlier example of the "yoga wars," it might be possible to conceive of different identity categories as parallel lines of research, rather than alternatives from which one must choose.

From this discussion, it should be clear that masculinity is neither limited to "men" nor entirely unrelated to the physiology of sexual difference. Because every technique of masculinity works with a material substrate, gender is not simply whatever we choose to make of it. Our freedom to develop new approaches to gender is dependent upon our understanding of the potentials afforded by differences and similarities that exist in actual bodies. Recognizing this could perhaps help us achieve better theoretical "grip" on the practice of gender, by acknowledging the very real sense in which gender is a grappling-with and coming-to-know the possibilities of human embodiment. However, it need not imply closure on the technique of gender. Embodied research may yet generate substantially new areas of technique that go by the names "femininity" and "masculinity." While mainstream discussions of gender assume that it arises from and is caused by sexual difference, some theorists attribute too much power to the play of language, implying that embodied technique has no material substrate.

I have suggested here that the complex interaction between gender and sexual difference may best be understood not as a linear correspondence, nor as purely discursive production, but as the engagement of technique with its material substrate. It is not the case, in other words, that everyone can have or be whatever gender they choose. This would only be possible if gender were epistemically flat, consisting entirely of the play of signs (energetically inexpensive technique, as defined in Chapter 1), rather than materially engaged with the relative reliabilities of embodiment. On the other hand, neither is it true that the substrate of bodily variation causes or mandates the implementation of any particular (e.g., binary) gender technique. As embodied technique, gender is both constrained and enabled by the relative reliabilities of the materialities with which it works. Gender is both open-ended and finite. It is neither a prison nor a zone of free play, but an area of knowledge.

Identity and inertia

The previous sections suggest that, alongside the potentially exhilarating project of radically transforming gender, we must acknowledge what Eve Sedgwick has called the "inertia" of gender, its "slowness." This is

> the process that mediates between, on the one hand, the biological absolutes of what we always are (more or less) and, on the other hand, the notional free play that we constructivists are always imagined to be attributing to our own and other people's sex-and-gender self-presentation.
>
> (Sedgwick 1995: 18)

Thus far in this chapter, I have attempted to rethink both the "biological absolutes" of sexual variation and the "free play" of gender technique. Now I would like to consider the "inertia" that makes gender so resistant to change, even when new technique has been developed.

The testimonies and theories of transexual and transgender individuals have been a key point of resistance to the assertion that gender is a matter of "doing" rather than "being." As Henry Rubin acknowledges (2003), a basic point of tension between feminist, queer, transexual, and transgender narratives has been the recurring idea that one's material body is not merely different from what one wants but also "wrong" in a fundamental or essential way. Body dysphoria is an integral part of the medical analysis of transexualism, which sees it as a disorder that can be at least partially alleviated through surgical intervention and/or hormonal treatments. Butler suggests that the "wrong body" trope may partly be an artifact of a medical system that requires it in exchange for certain services (2004: 91; and see Stryker and Whittle 2006: 231, 350–57). However, this hardly explains the fact that many transgender and transexual individuals, including those who do not pursue surgery, experience a sense of wrongness that is located firmly in the physiology and anatomy of the body. Such accounts contrast strongly with the transgender movement as articulated by Kate Bornstein, who writes that both her gender and her sense of fashion "are based on collage. You know—a little bit from here, a little bit from there? Sort of a cut-and-paste thing"

(1994: 3). Bornstein's account seemingly has little in common with that of people for whom the goal is to become—socially and/or physically—a particular sex that one already feels oneself intrinsically to be. In queer theory following Butler, claims to being intrinsically male or female may be rejected as naïve essentialism when they are made by cisgender individuals—those whose gender identity matches their gender assignment. But the same assertion cannot be so easily dismissed when it contradicts social expectations and is both personally and politically risky.

For Butler, the free play of gender "performance" is preceded and constrained by the performativity of social discourse, which takes the form of norms and ideals. Thus, the "sedimentation" of gender takes place through the continual "citing of power" and the "history of imaginary relations" out of which subjectivity emerges (1993a: 15, 74). I have argued that, in addition to the social reproduction of power relations, embodied technique is also sedimented more literally *in* and *as* the body of its practitioner. If the layers of gender that constrain daily choice are made out of "power" and "history," these are concretely realized in the body as technique: knowledge of what to do, ways of doing things, pathways through the world. And if the topmost layer of gender technique is that which may be chosen on a daily basis—such as clothing, or some aspects of posture and gesture—there are countless layers of gender technique below this that are less easily altered. To take just one example, Joy Ladin describes the lengthy process of developing a vocal range that would allow her to be read as female in everyday life (in Bornstein and Bergman 2010: 249). Ladin's training in gender technique explicitly resembles the training of actors, who practice for lengthy periods in order to be able to change their voices, postures, and gestural patterns. There may also be layers of sedimented gender technique that are even more difficult to change, such as internal structures from early childhood that are difficult to modify through even the most rigorous of training regimes in adulthood.

In this sense, the *experiential* depth of gender identity derives from the *epistemic* depth of gender technique. The sedimentation of technique at the deepest levels of our being explains how and why gender may be felt to "arrive from elsewhere" (Salamon 2010: 83), despite its being produced through processes that are undeniably cultural and historical. We can then comprehend both the felt strength of gender identity and its potential for sociocultural formation, without dismissing either of these. Gender is real not in spite of being learned and trained, but precisely because it is learned and trained in and as embodiment. By way of comparison, it is clear that years of training in ballet or martial arts can lead to an embodied state in which one "is" a practitioner of those forms in a way that goes far beyond conscious choice (or explicit identification). A ballet dancer can wake up one day and decide to stop performing, to stop practicing, and to stop identifying as a dancer—but the deep sedimentation of technique within that dancer's body is not thereby removed. As we recall from Mauss, it is difficult to unlearn one's technique, especially that which is learned in childhood. Having seen how dance and other specialized training can shape us at every level, from the structure of breathing to the structure of our bones, we should not expect gender to operate upon us any less deeply or shape us less permanently. In fact, we might expect gender identity to be even more deeply sedimented in the body, and less accessible to change, than other kinds of embodied training. For even the strictest regimes of training in dance or martial arts usually begin no earlier than age six, whereas training in gender begins at birth.

This does not mean that gender is learned without agency. On the contrary, as the analogy with physical culture and performing arts suggests, the learning of gender over the course of one's life is profoundly agentic, not only in the moment of learning but also after it has been fully absorbed, mastered, and rendered automatic. Children do not absorb gender passively any more than they do other kinds of technique. Rather, children reject and struggle with gender, they embrace and revel in it, they test its limits and play with its content. They do all of this through interactions with parents, teachers, peers, and the rest of society, including but not limited to representations of gender in books, movies, and other media. The child who has been classified a "girl" is more often praised for enjoying what her cultural context understands as appropriately feminine, while being scolded or teased for taking on what is seen as masculine, and vice versa. Yet these interactions are complex enough to ensure that each child's gender will be somewhat unpredictable and may or may not develop as others intend. The fact that some technique is forbidden does not mean the child will not learn it. Nor does the fact that one is assigned to learn certain kinds of technique mean that one will actually do so. Some children fit well into their assigned gender; others, to differing degrees, do not. Children learn gender in the same way they learn language, through practice: "They hear and retain, imitate and repeat, make mistakes and correct themselves, succeed by chance and begin again methodically, and, at too young an age for explicators to begin instructing them, they are almost all ... able to understand" (Rancière 1991: 5). Because this process of learning is complex and active, we cannot predict what kinds of gender an individual will learn any more than we can predict which infants will become athletes, writers, or scientists. In every case, the individual takes an active role in learning and engaging with available pathways of embodied technique. The acquisition of gender, like the acquisition of language or any other technique, is an accomplishment as much as a prison. By the same token, when we grapple with gender or look for new ways of doing it, we are to a certain extent fighting with our own sedimented agency.

To paraphrase Butler, there is no subject that precedes technique; the subject is formed through the sedimentation of technique. Only an account of gender that remains cognizant of its epistemic depth can explain "how essential becoming a gender is to one's very sense of personhood, one's sense of well-being, one's possibility to flourish as a bodily being" (2004: 100). If becoming a gender simply meant agreeing to fit neatly within one of two categories, then we could hardly call this essential to personhood or flourishing. But gender is more than its categories: It refers to a vast and complex area of embodied technique, in which numerous and variable physiological traits are woven into the fabric of everyday life. If gender is technique that deals with the materiality of bodily variation—and with reproduction and sensual desire in particular—then it will be crucial in structuring sexual attraction and sexuality, friendship and intimacy, reproduction, familial relations, and many other areas of human life. This is the sense in which we need gender. As bodily beings, we cannot do without technique in these areas, however that technique is labeled. We may not need the categories of male and female, masculine and feminine, gay and straight, transgender and cisgender—but we do need the areas of embodied technique that currently go by those names.

Recognizing the depth of gender as sedimented identity may also help to explain why some people react with rage and horror to experiments and innovations in gender technique. As Butler writes, those who threaten violence against queer and transgender people proceed "from the anxious and rigid belief that a sense of world and a sense of self will be radically undermined if such a being, uncategorizable, is permitted to live within the social world" (2004: 34). Such anxiety underscores the elemental importance of embodied technique, insofar as it can be understood as stemming from the fear of a world in which one's own ability to reliably find and offer intimacy will be compromised. Many people no doubt fear that the gender crossings and transformations of others will prevent them from practicing gender competently in their own lives. If, as I have suggested, gender technique is a basic human necessity, then a person who is deprived of such technique—not because they fail to acquire gender, but because the gender they learn as a child turns out to be incompatible with the world they encounter as an adult—may experience a terrifying sense of disorientation and isolation. The political irony, of course, is that such punishing incompatibility with the dominant technique of everyday life—the fear of which all too often motivates violence against those who practice alternative gender—is precisely that which is already suffered by gender nonconformists.

Consider straight male anxiety around gay men. One need not even accept these two categories to recognize that what becomes unstable for the heterosexual man is the boundary between sexual and nonsexual technique of intimacy, as well as the technique of bodily relation he expects to encounter in others. "Heterosexual masculinity" is nothing more than the (hegemonic and highly valued) technique that some men use to guide themselves in knowing when to pay attention to the pleasures of touch and when not. Straight men have learned—and it has sedimented in their bodies at a much deeper level than conscious thought—to base the distinction between sexual and nonsexual contact upon the categories of female and male. When those categories are disrupted or complicated, the result is not only that the technique of straightness no longer guides the man in knowing how to move towards or away from others. More fundamentally, he no longer knows how to handle his own sensations. In this sense, gender is part of the way in which we navigate fundamental issues of bodily integrity, contact, and sensation. The privilege of the straight man is being able to assume that his gender technique will function reliably wherever he goes. His fear is that his daily technique of touching, from rough to gentle, will no longer function if homosexuality (or transexuality) becomes commonplace. The fact that this fear can be located historically—as Sedgwick notes, there have been many societies in which masculinity was not threatened by homosexuality (1985: 26–27)—does not make it any less powerful for someone whose identity has been sedimented in these ways.

A related fear may also fuel the rejection of transgender women by other women, including certain "radical" feminists.[11] A central concern for some feminists is that the politics developed around reproductive rights will be lost if the category of woman is substantially deconstructed. Although this branch of feminism no longer has much legitimacy within academia, it continues to fuel debate online and elsewhere. Indeed, it may be true that some queer and transgender activism, like the rest of society, has failed to acknowledge the centrality of reproductive politics in the politics of gender. If sexual reproduction is an important part of gender technique, then there can be no truly radical politics of gender without a politics of reproduction aimed at empowering those whose bodies do the work of pregnancy and childbirth. For feminists who prioritize this point, some transgender rhetoric may seem premature or utopian, especially in a global context where "women" appears to be the only available name for the class of people who bear children. But equating the reproductive category with the category of women may not be the only or the best way to politicize it. Doing so puts women who don't or can't have children into a difficult position not unlike that of transwomen. It also leaves out transmen, for whom many aspects of "female" reproductive healthcare are essential (Sherbourne Health Centre 2013).

As useful as the sex/gender paradigm has been, it is a kind of shorthand. It opens up "gender" to innovation, but does so by leaving binary "sex" intact as a reliable material substrate with which gender works. In the context of current debates, this tactic now appears outdated, because it leaves out the extent to which the categories of binary sex are themselves constructed through technique—as well as the extent to which gender, once deeply sedimented in the body, can become the substrate for other kinds of technique.[12] We might then do better to accept that it will never be possible to determine conclusively what is and is not potentially mutable through technique. Technique actually becomes material as it sediments in the body, while even the most apparently material facts can be rendered malleable through the discovery of new technique. Each theory, each social movement, each area of embodied technique defines its substrate in a way that opens up certain possibilities and forecloses others. For some, the new instability of the material body made possible by advances in technology suggests the end of binary sexual difference. For others, the same unfixity only underscores the reality of sex and gender as identities located elsewhere in the body or psyche. The relationship between technique and its substrate is not fixed. Technique, sedimented, becomes substrate; substrate, investigated, is revealed as technique. In a research context, the goal cannot be to conclusively determine what bodies are, but rather to support the continued investigation of what they can do.

Butler asks: "What if new forms of gender are possible?" (2004: 30). We can now expand upon this by returning to our growing list of questions for embodied research: What kinds of gender technique are possible? How can society be organized, given the relative reliability of the substrate of gender technique? Is it necessary or advantageous to locate individuals within two main categories? Could we think of these as positions rather than identities, with possible transit between them? Is it possible to be rid of the binary altogether? Could there be gender technique that is entirely independent of the statistical dimorphism that underpins sexual reproduction? That is, could the technique of sexual reproduction be fully delinked from that of sexual desire and gender identity? And given that different geographic and cultural regions practice gender differently, how might individuals navigate between these? What kinds of interdisciplinary translation would enable diverse branches of gender technique to converse? What links these questions to the development of new yoga or acting technique is the fact that they cannot be answered by theory alone, but must be investigated in practice.

Current research in gender

The past few decades have witnessed a blossoming of research not only in gender studies but also in gender technique. The latter has produced a diverse and innovative field of alternative gender(s), concretely answering research questions like those just enumerated. Among feminist, gay, lesbian, bisexual, queer, transexual, transgender, and other communities, new forms of gender are currently being discovered through processes of embodied research that are formally analogous to that which has led to new forms of physical culture and performing arts. The difference is that this research investigates the terrain of everyday life. As a result, innovations in gender tend to come not from controlled laboratories, but from deeply engaged and intensely personal research projects, undertaken by individuals and communities whose very lives may be at stake in the discovery of new practical possibilities. In what remains of this chapter, I cannot hope to do justice to these everyday research projects either ethnographically or historically. Instead, I want to emphasize that what Butler calls "the new gender politics" (2004: 4) is underpinned and enabled by an epistemic field of new embodied technique. While the invention of technique cannot ensure or determine a shift in politics, it is hard to imagine a meaningful politics that does not incorporate, as part of its primary agenda, an alternative field of technique. Knowledge is, after all, "the magnetic field of power" (Sedgwick 1994: 23): the epistemic engagement with reality through which social relations become material.

Sedgwick's "queer tutelage" (1994: 21) finds its complementary epistemic pole in William Haver's notion of "queer research" (1997). The embodied research projects I survey in this section can be understood as queer in the broad sense of exploring concrete possibilities of gender and sexuality that branch away from standard or mainstream technique. Some of them experiment with gender directly, while others work with neighboring areas of technique. Some are undertaken by mainstream institutions, such as schools or governmental bodies, while others are the work of fairly enclosed subcultures. Identity categories like "queer," "poly(amorous)," "kinky," and "asexual" (citations below) work explicitly with sexuality, but they also extend into the domain of gender. As Michael Warner points out, "sexual desires themselves can imply other wants, ideals, and conditions," so that "what queers want" is much more than just a certain kind of sex (1993: vii). While it is certainly possible to be queer, poly, kinky, or asexual on the basis of binary gender, it is arguable whether this is precisely the same gender binary as that which underpins monogamous, "vanilla" (non-kinky) heterosexuality. In any case, it is neither desirable nor possible to establish a firm definition or boundary between sexuality and gender, or between "mainstream" gender and its most radical alternatives. Instead, as before, we might think of these as forming an ecosystem or "research culture" that involves and supports multiple ongoing investigations in parallel.

Significantly, the research projects explored here are not those of individuals or small groups, but of communities. My discussion of yoga and acting in previous chapters could perhaps have led to the idea that embodied research only takes place in small, isolated contexts, where a few people explore new possibilities under the protection of the state. Current research in gender looks nothing like this. In the first place, it frequently takes place without official support—if not actively outlawed and repressed by the state, then certainly not funded by it as were Krishnamacharya, Stanislavski, and Grotowski. (However, see below for some recent state-supported exceptions.) In the second place, because gender deals with sexuality and sexual difference, including the physiology of reproduction, significant innovations in gender rarely result from the experimental practice of individuals. Rather, gender as technique functions above all at the level of community. Focusing on research at this level has the additional bonus of pointing us away from the question of whether any single person's gender is progressive, transgressive, or regressive, and towards an emphasis on communities of practice as sites for the development of new gender technique. As Leslie Feinberg has declared, "No one's gender expression is any more 'liberated' than anyone else's" (1998: 53). Because gender is interpersonal, attempts to locate the queerest or most transliberated gender in a single individual will inevitably fail. Queering gender cannot mean the same thing for each person. Instead, at a cultural or social level, it can refer to a general tolerance for sexual and gender variation—or, more radically, to the active and explicit cultivation of research culture in gender. As Butler reminds us, no individual can transform gender "outside the context of a radically altered social world" (2004: 101). Ultimately, gender is technique for dealing with relationships, families, and populations—not just individuals—and it is at this level that the most significant innovations are likely to occur. Luckily, the "radically altered social world" to which Butler refers need not be the whole world or even a whole country. It only has to be large enough to create the context for concrete, practical experiments in alternative technique.

This point is borne out by recent attempts to raise genderless children. Halberstam envisions a system of "gender preferences" whereby a person would be considered to have "gender neutrality until such a time when the child or young adult announces his or her or its gender" (1998a: 27). A single family cannot do this. Although one family can attempt to raise an ungendered child, if they live in a society based on standard gender technique, their child-raising practices will be interpreted not as avoiding gender but as keeping the gender of the child "secret" (Daily Mail Reporter 2011). As one headline reads: "Parents of 2-Year-Old Refuse to Reveal Child's Gender" (Mieszkowski 2009). Moreover, raising a child without a gender in a culture that demands one sets that child up for many difficulties, including that the individual will be viewed as "fundamentally unintelligible" or even "an impossibility" by the larger community (Butler 2004: 30). This need not be so, however, if an entire community makes the shift, as in the case of the Nicolaigarden school in Sweden, where "teachers avoid the pronouns 'him' and 'her,' instead calling their 115 toddlers simply 'friends'" (Tagliabue 2012). This project—which is backed by state legislature as well as the school itself—aims to produce not a single ungendered child but a community in which gender technique functions differently at scale. It represents a slow but undeniable sea change in official governmental policies, attested to globally by landmarks like the official recognition of third genders in Germany (RT 2013) and India (BBC 2014) and by Canada's new Family Law Act, which allows birth certificates to list more than two parents (CBC 2014).

The Nicolaigarden experiment posits important questions about how the developmental process of aging complicates the standard binary model of gender. How early does a person need gender? Why force gender on children before they need it? If children grow up without (binary) gender, what kinds of embodied technique might they develop later in life? The Nicolaigarden experiment tests a kind of gender minimalism. At the other end of the spectrum are communities in which gender is expanded and proliferated rather than reduced or neutralized. David Valentine offers a rich account of some of these in his ethnography of the category of "transgender," which both constitutes and is constituted by a variety of communities that in some cases have little in common beyond that label. One undated postcard from the NYC

Commission on Human Rights lists the following members of the transgender community:

> bi-gendered, crossdresser, drag king, drag queen, femme queen, female-to-male, gender bender, gender blender, gender gifted, gender queer, male-to-female, new man, non-operative transexual, passing man, passing woman, post-operative transexual, pre-operative transexual, shemale, third sex, trannie/tranny, trans, transbutch, transexual/transsexual, transgender, transgenderist, transie, transperson, transexed man, transexed woman, transvestite, transwoman, two-spirit.
>
> (Valentine 2007: 198)

Even if some of these are simply new names for old practices, such a proliferation of terms often indicates the ferment of new technique. It recalls, for example, the proliferation of new subatomic particles in the 1960s (Pickering 1995: 71), when new technology made possible the discovery of a new bestiary of subatomic particles, dubbed the "particle zoo." Although new genders are not likely to be as stable as new particles, the explosion of terminology in both cases indicates an encounter with complex contours of resistance in an area that had previously been unexplored. Upon entering into this area through sustained research, a new territory of "flora" and "fauna" appears, requiring a new lexicon of terms. In this sense, each new identity category may also constitute a distinct research project or embodied experiment in gender.[13]

Earlier in this chapter, I touched upon what Halberstam calls "lesbian fatherhood" as an area of contemporary research in gender. It should be clear by now that the intersection of "lesbian" and "fatherhood" is not a matter of labels but of deeply sedimented identities—that is, of embodied technique, from the most superficial to the most profound—and that such an intersection constitutes a research project in its own right. A related but distinct project of this nature could be the "mothering" practices of gay and transgender men within the Black and Latino house/ball scene described by Marlon M. Bailey (2011; see also 2013).[14] An earlier epoch of this subculture was the focus of Jenny Livingstone's 1990 film *Paris Is Burning* and of much subsequent discussion by Judith Butler and others. Both Bailey and Valentine treat the balls as sites in which new genders are continually under development. According to Bailey, house/ball culture is based on a "six-part gender system" comprising butch queens, femme queens, butch queens up in drags, butches, women, and men—although these categories are not permanent and new ones are continually emerging (2011: 375; and see 385n9). But "gender" here is not just a matter of individual performance. Among the most significant aspects of this research must be counted the development of *alternative kinship*. Drawing connections between the house/ball scene and the national debate over marriage equality for gay and lesbian couples, Butler points out the pressing need to "rework and revise the social organization of friendship, sexual contacts, and community to produce non-state-centered forms of support and alliance" (2004: 109). She also affirms that practices of alternative kinship are not imitative but experimental. They are high-stakes research projects aimed at finding new ways to structure intimacy, care-taking, and generational continuity, outside the gender-normative family structures of mainstream society. Butler's analysis of the house/ball scene is supported by that of Bailey, who describes the houses as "familial structures that are socially rather than biologically configured" and which "provide guidance and life skills for their 'children' of various ages, races/ethnicities (usually Black and Latina/o), genders and sexualities, and from cities and regions throughout North America" (Bailey 2011: 367). Bailey's work shows how layers of technique depend upon each other, linking the spectacular gender display of the balls to the mundane but life-sustaining kinship practices of the houses. This example illustrates the contiguity of research in performing arts and everyday life and underscores the extent to which research in gender impacts other aspects of everyday life. Because gender is the basis for so much of our daily technique, changes in gender may have profound ripple effects elsewhere.

An epistemology of practice allows us to claim and comprehend the epistemic or knowledge-producing dimension of investigations like these—kinship as technique. From this perspective, reconfiguring the family is not merely a question of political will, important as that may be. There are also substantive questions here that can only be answered through practical experimentation: What kinds of communal kinship technique could replace that which is grounded in heterosexual institutions like marriage? When the state sanctions family-building relationships between pairs of individuals, without requiring them to consist of one man and one woman (as in gay marriage), what possibilities for gender does this open up, and what does it foreclose? If, on the other hand, the state were to renounce its power to legitimate particular relationships through the bond of marriage, what kinds of alternative family and kinship practices might be enabled? In short, how might society structure the relations between people, and what does or doesn't this have to do with sexual reproduction, long-term committed relationships, the raising and education of children, healthcare, and the law? My point here, again, is merely that such questions are not answerable through any amount of scientific or sociological research, which can only measure and document current practices and make educated guesses about the future. The actual new technique that will structure future kinship practice can only be developed through embodied research.

The examples presented so far in this section have dealt explicitly with gender. However, research in gender may also take place implicitly, through research in sexuality and other kinds of embodied technique. Contemporary practices of polyamory (Barker and Langdridge 2010) and asexuality (Cerankowski and Milks 2014) reconfigure relationships and kinships through changes in the basic categories of sexuality. The extent to which such changes indirectly transform gender seems to vary depending on their specific implementation. In some cases, changes in sexuality seem to produce concurrent changes in gender, while in others, sexuality is put into play in a way that isolates it from a substrate of (binary) gender that remains fairly stable. Thus, according to Margot Weiss (2011), the San Francisco community that practices "BDSM"—a portmanteau acronym combining bondage and discipline, dominance and submission, and sadism and masochism—is fairly conventional in its kinship structures, as well as in its structuring of racial and class identities. Nevertheless, BDSM's explicit focus on consensual power exchange can still be seen as interacting with the technique of gender in experimental ways. In BDSM, power is explicitly separated from gender insofar as either men or women can equally be "tops" (dominants) or "bottoms" (submissives) in a sexual encounter or partnership. If hierarchical power relations are a significant part of what defines male and female identities, then making those dynamics explicit, and detaching them from gender identity, could be a significant modification of gender as well as sexuality. We should therefore take Weiss seriously when she writes that the "bodily experiments" of BDSM give rise to "new forms of power and knowledge—of technique" (Weiss 2011: 139–40).[15]

In other contexts, the embodied technique of BDSM may be more explicitly bound up with that of gender. According to Robin Bauer, BDSM in the "dyke+" community has resulted in the development of "new subcultural skills" that are "much more sophisticated than those of sexual 'majorities'" (2008: 236, 240). Although Bauer frames these new skills as part of BDSM, they seem to have as much to do with gender as with power and pleasure, and they overlap extensively with the innovative technique of queer and transgender communities that do not practice BDSM. For example, Bauer describes the "recoding" of "body parts and sexual practices" that takes place when a "dildo" is treated as—and therefore becomes—a "dick" (2007: 184). In the context of BDSM, this suggests an exploration of how power and desire become sedimented in a particular body part or object. In *Bodies That Matter*, Butler uses the language of psychoanalysis to ask why it is "assumed that the phallus requires that particular body part [the penis] to symbolize, and why it could not operate through symbolizing other body parts" (1993a: 84). Bauer's notion of "new subcultural skills" suggests that "symbolization," with its connotations of an arbitrary relation between signifier and signified, does not adequately account for practices such as these. Instead, what we are dealing with is substantive research into an area of skill or technique, in this case located at the intersection of gender and sexuality.

These brief glosses and references barely scratch the surface of contemporary research in gender technique. Although my focus has been on the epistemological dimension of these practices, nothing here should be taken to diminish the political concerns and movements that labels like feminist, queer, dyke, trans, poly, or kinky enable. Instead, my aim has been to suggest a way of integrating the strategic and social concerns of Butler's "new gender politics" with an epistemology of practice that grounds them in an empirical engagement with the real possibilities and resistances afforded by the relative reliabilities of human embodiment. The idea that social identities constitute new knowledges and new ways of knowing has precedents, but the grounding of this assertion in a critically realist epistemology of practice could add rigor and nuance to the articulation and analysis of these practices and their politics.

New paradigms

The division of people into binary sex categories remains widespread and basic in many if not most cultures today. At the same time, the critique of normative gender coming from some queer theorists can make it seem as if binary sex categories are simply wrong. But the question is not whether there are "really" two sexes, but whether and how it is possible to develop robust and workable nonbinary alternatives at the level of society. The embodied research practices explored above suggest that such alternative gender technique exists and that several of its variants have already been tested and are on their way to expanded implementation outside the communities that developed them. Could the wider acceptance of such technique lead to a truly radical and widespread global transformation in the landscape of gender? Is the experimental technique of lesbian fathers, gay and transgender mothers, BDSM "kinksters," and Nikolaigarden's "friends" destined to thrive only within these isolated pockets of alternative gender? Or could this technique find itself "borrowed" and "spread" (Mauss's terms) to other communities, even to the point of becoming widely accepted by a social majority?

In fact, terms like *femme* and *butch*, or *topping* and *bottoming*, are already in use outside the communities that invented them. Might this represent a significant change in the technique of everyday life? Could this be the future of gender? We have seen how Krishnamarchya's yoga and Stanislavski's acting technique grew from being highly specialized practices, known only to a select few, towards global dissemination. It is worth noting, however, that the large-scale spread of technique usually involves a kind of dilution as well. If "yoga" is now a household word, and "Stanislavski" now a common reference point in theatre schools across the globe, this does not mean that the average actor or yoga practitioner has a deep understanding of the practices of Krishna-macharya or Stanislavski. Indeed, it is eminently debatable which aspects of this technique have spread globally and which have been forgotten or remain known only to specialists. It is surely important to ask how much of the knowledge produced by an embodied research project has become widely known and to what extent the technique may have spread in name only. However, perhaps the more important question is: How substantially has everyday life been transformed by the spread of this technique? For even if only a small part of the knowledge discovered in these laboratories of practice has been widely transmitted, it has had a considerable impact on the everyday. Might we not expect the same from gender?

I recently attended an academic meeting in which, at the beginning, each person was asked to share their name, departmental affiliation, and "preferred gender pronouns." The meeting was about labor relations and had nothing to do with queer or transgender theory or activism. However, the technique of explicitly providing one's preferred gender pronouns was added in a simple way to the standard protocol for introductions. Not everyone identified their preferred pronouns when invited to introduce themselves, and those who did revealed few surprises. (One person preferred "they" over "she." I said that I go by male pronouns "mostly," taking the opportunity to queer my otherwise fairly standard gender presentation.) Yet, simple but significant, this technique changed in a subtle way how gender was practiced at that meeting. It did not just create a safe space for queer and transgender individuals, but slightly queered the entire meeting, inviting cisgender folks to recognize the privilege they experience in having their preferred pronouns attributed to them on a daily basis. Being asked to state one's preferred gender pronouns changes how we perceive our own gender and the genders of other people. Instead of seeing men and women, we may now see people who prefer particular pronouns, and these pronouns can no longer be taken as transparent or mandatory indications of having particular genitals or any other physiological traits. This is an example of technique that was developed in queer and transgender contexts spreading into the common technique of everyday life.[16]

As we saw above, state governments have slowly begun to implement alternative gender, sexuality, and kinship technique through policy reforms that officially sanction such possibilities as three or more genders, three or more parents, and nonheterosexual marriage. The passage in Taiwan of a legislative act intended "to validate diverse gender and sexual subjects and ensure equality between them" could be particularly relevant here, insofar as its focus on "transforming gender and sexual ideology in Taiwanese society by focusing on educational environments" recalls my discussion of physical education in Chapter 2 (Hsieh 2012: 75). In the same way that physical education could be reconceived as a broad introduction to a wide range of physical culture and technique— rather than a narrow healthist training in athletics—the curriculum of sexuality education could perhaps be redesigned to reflect the diversity of gender technique across history, geography, and culture (see Allen 2011). Both "phys ed" and "sex ed" are significant areas of pedagogy and training in the transmission of embodied technique from one generation to the next. The opposition with which even minor changes in these curricula are routinely met underscores the profound importance of officially sanctioned pedagogy in determining the future of everyday practice.

In any case, there can be little doubt that such small but important shifts in legislature are evidence of the transmissible research outcomes of feminist, queer, transgender, and other areas of embodied research. To restate my basic argument: These are research projects in and through gender, whose outcome is not new knowledge about gender but rather *new gender*. The examples provided demonstrate that the invention of new gender is not just a matter of power and desire. Rather, to discover new ways of doing gender requires a searching engagement with the relative reliabilities of embodiment. In this sense, research in gender is similar to research in yoga, acting, and other fields: One cannot simply do whatever one wants, but must tinker with and attune to the materials at hand. To develop male femininities and female masculinities, or to fracture the very categories of male and female, masculine and feminine, is a project—actually, multiple-related projects—of embodied research. Furthermore, because so much of the substrate of what we call gender has to do with relationships—desiring, reproductive, and otherwise—it will rarely be possible for an individual to single-handedly produce new gender technique. Instead, we should look for and support the development of new gender in communities. I have tried to provide examples of what this could mean, but in the context of my larger argument could hardly offer more than a few brief examples. Others will surely have more and better insight into the current status of research in gender. I hope that the epistemological framework proposed here may serve to validate and garner support for their important work.

Notes

1 Mauss includes a section on cooking in his catalogue of techniques (2006: 115–16) and Certeau lists it among the areas of "tactical" practice in *The Practice of Everyday Life* (1984: xiii). Schatzki cites cooking more than once as an example of a practice (see Chapter 1). For contemporary anthropologies of cooking, see Sutton (2014).

2 A more thorough investigation of class, religious, ethnic, and racial identity as embodied technique is beyond the scope of this book. For the application of a "post-positivist realist theory of identity" to racial identity, see my citation of Paul Taylor in note 8 below. For disanalogies between race and gender as they relate to biological variation, see Linda Alcoff's essay in Gonzalez-Arnal *et al.* (2012).

3 As Roberts puts it: "The arrival to power of subaltern consciousness of the everyday into the experience of a shared, common culture was to enact the promise of the total dehierarchization and dealienation of capitalist production and social relations" (2006: 120). At least one current thinker has returned to this radical sense of the quotidian through an epistemological analysis of *lo cotidiano* in Latino/a experience (Isasi-Díaz in Isasi-Díaz and Mendieta 2012: 48–51).

4 The very distinction between "field" and "discipline" repeats this same problematic: We can only know a field through a discipline, but in defining the discipline we preemptively shape our encounter with the field. Even something as apparently simple as *breathing*—to return to an example from Chapter 2—does not allow for a conclusive distinction to be drawn between technique and substrate. We know there is "something" there, a zone of material embodiment with which we engage. Holding one's breath is difficult; the longer one holds one's breath, the more one feels material reality push back against technique. But it is not possible to say, for example, how long the breath can be held. We can only cite the longest recorded breath held thus far. And we cannot define the substrate of breathing except tautologically, as the zone of relative reliability with which the technique of breathing works.

5 For an overview of recent debates between feminist, queer, and transgender theorists and activists, see Elliot 2010. On the terminology of tran(s)sexual and transgender, see Stryker *et al.* 2008; Valentine 2007; Salah 2007; and Namaste 2005. Here, I use *transgender* in the inclusive, ethnographic sense proposed by Valentine. I also use words like *transwomen*, *transmen*, and *cisgender* (normatively gendered), all of which are part of the emerging vocabulary of alternative gender technique.

6 The fundamentals of Harold Garfinkel's *ethnomethodology* are similar to the theory of practice offered here—with the key difference that "method" implies rules rather than knowledge. See also Erving Goffman's "The Arrangement between the Sexes" (1977; and see Germon 2009: 13).

7 For an overview, see Lane 2009. According to J. Edgar Bauer, the seeds of a more complex view of gender can already be found in the writings of Charles Darwin, whose *Origin of Species* "marks the inception of sexual Modernity" in its foregrounding of variation and change over the categories of sexual as well as species taxonomy (Bauer 2012). However, one does not have to go that far back to recognize that binary gender is less a product of science—as a mode of investigation that seeks to quantify the reliabilities of the material world—than of the social world in which scientists operate. Recent disability studies offer related grounds for a "theory of complex embodiment" (Siebers 2008: 25).

8 More precisely: The reproduction of humans and other sexually dimorphic species depends upon a general distribution of reproductive capacities that can be mapped as overlapping bimodal distributions. To create from this statistical *dimorphism* a *binary* model of sex requires two steps of abstraction: first, the overlapping but nonidentical graphs of the various relevant physiological traits must be combined to produce a single bimodal distribution; second, that distribution must be divided into two sectors, with the middle part discounted as anomalous. The first move reduces a multivariable equation to a line, treating the complexity of sex, sexual difference, gender, and sexuality as a single spectrum ranging from female to male. The second reduces even that limited spectrum to a binary model with an arbitrary cutoff point between the two categories. Paul Taylor makes a similar argument with regard to racial categories, emphasizing the distinction between *groups* and *populations* (2013: 48–51). Following literary theorist Paula Moya, Taylor offers what he calls a "post-positivist realist theory of identity," according to which "identities are ways of approaching the world" (115).

9 For more on intersex bodies and infant genital surgery, see Fausto-Sterling 2000: 78–114, and Butler 2004: 63–67.

10 To illustrate the way in which physiological and reproductive variation underpins but does not determine the categories of sex, Lennon suggests a fascinating analogy with the "bodily expression of emotions": "It is not possible to specify physiologically what unites all the faces which are expressing joy or sadness ... Living with someone whose facial muscles have suffered paralysis, we may at first be unable to detect emotion in this face, or maybe respond to it as though it is expressing some untold terror. Living closely alongside such a face, however, we come to grasp what range of movement there is, as expressive of pain or joy. We come to perceive a continuity with our perception of a smile in physically very diverse faces, due to the way the materiality is woven into our form of life" (in Gonzalez-Arnal *et al.* 2012: 39, 42–43). Here again, physiological variation classified as (dis)ability offers a useful lens for thinking about sexual difference, and vice versa.

11 The classic example is Janice Raymond's *The Transsexual Empire* (1979), critiqued by Sandy Stone in Stryker and Whittle 2006; and see Valentine 2007: 217–20.

12 Mainstream culture appears to have responded to the rise of the sex/gender paradigm, not by deconstructing the latter term, but instead by simply co-opting

the word "gender" to refer to a categorical division that remains binary. This point was brought home to me when an X-ray technician asked if my partner and I would like to know the "gender" of our unborn child at 18 weeks of gestation. If an unborn fetus has a "gender," then the power of the sex/ gender paradigm to disrupt the binary would seem to have been exhausted.

13 An up-to-date lexicon of gender and sexual technique today would be far more extensive. The Identity Project's online alphabetical photo gallery (2014) "seeks to explore the labels we choose to identify with when defining our gender and sexuality." The first 23 of its 141 distinct labels are as follows: "androgynous queer top," "artsy femme," "baba," "bad ass queer femme mama," "barely legal," "bearded gay," "bearded queer," "besties," "bisexual," "big bro little bro," "bitter queens," "black gay queer feminist cisgendered man," "boi," "boos," "born again transgenderqueer," "boyfriends," "brainy gender queer drag king," "brilliant black beautiful," "butch," "butch daddy poet," "butch dandy gentleman," "butch lesbian," "butch mama," and "butch queen." While some of these identities may have less epistemic depth than others, the project as a whole indicates a vibrant and innovative culture of embodied research in gender, racial, vocational ("poet"), and other identities.

14 For an earlier precedent to theorizing male motherhood, see Ruddick (1995). A recent documentary short on transexual, transgender, and gender fluid parenting is Huberdeau (2012).

15 As with the queer and transgender communities described above, the depth and variety of this new technique can be glimpsed in the proliferation of terms that BDSM practitioners use to identify themselves: "perverts, voyeurs, masters, masochists, bottoms, pain sluts, switches, dom(me)s, slaves, submissives, ponies, butch bottoms, poly perverse, pain fetishists, leathermen, mistresses, and daddies" (Weiss 2011: 11). Another lexicon, another area of knowledge. Indeed, with its endless paraphernalia, drop-in classes, and language of "scenes" and "roles," BDSM has much in common with modern yoga and acting technique and with recreational sports like rock climbing (17, 28). There is even a familiar debate within the BDSM community about whether too much emphasis on "technique" has allowed people to engage in the practice "without feeling, just by following the rules" (75).

16 There are multiple ways to open up and innovate the narrow but consequential practice of gendered pronouns in everyday speech. Some of the possibilities for new pronoun technique include: having individuals state their preferred pronouns, as in this anecdote; the invention of new gender-neutral pronouns (see Wikipedia 2014); and the playful or indiscriminate use of pronouns (see Bailey 2014: 504n15). These innovations are neither exhaustive nor mutually exclusive. Research is ongoing: What can a pronoun do?

Ideas of the university in the public domain are hopelessly impoverished. "Impoverished" because they are unduly confined to a small range of possible conceptions of the university; and "hopelessly" because they are too often without hope, taking the form of either a hand-wringing over the current state of the university or merely offering a defence of the emerging nature of "the entrepreneurial university." Against this background, the questions arise as to **what, if any, are the prospects for imagining the university anew?** What role might the imagination play here? What are its limits and what might be its potential for bringing forward new forms of the university?

(Barnett 2013: 1)

5

EMBODIED RESEARCH IN THE UNIVERSITY

Blue skies?

Chapters 1–3 argued that the various branches of physical culture (sports, martial arts, somatics, yoga) and performing arts (acting, dance, song) are products of sustained research in embodied technique. They are not only styles or genres of practice, but also areas of knowledge about the possibilities afforded by the relative reliability of human embodiment. Chapter 4 then argued that everyday identity categories like those of gender can also be understood as areas of embodied knowledge in this sense. My discussion of physical culture, performing arts, and everyday life has emphasized the spread of technique beyond the context of its original practice and showed how technique may be put to use for quite different purposes than those for which it was originally intended. My hope is that, by understanding embodied practice through the epistemological lens of technique, we can begin to find more adequate ways of valuing, articulating, and supporting ongoing research and education in areas like these. In order to theorize embodied knowledge, I have drawn heavily on the concepts of social epistemology. I have occasionally made reference to formal education, as in the school curricula of physical or sexual education. However, I have not yet addressed the relationship between embodied knowledge, embodied research, and academia. My emphasis on epistemology throughout suggests that research in embodied technique could perhaps find an appropriate home within academia. However, there are several challenges that must be addressed before it will be possible to argue for embodied technique as knowledge in a specifically academic or scholarly sense. This final chapter considers the place of embodied research in the university.

Any serious discussion of the future of the university must begin from the recognition that it has reached a significant turning point in its history. In the US and UK, one increasingly hears talk of a "crisis" in academia—nor is the global status of the university by any means certain. Contributors to a recent volume on the future of the university (Barnett 2012) report on radical changes and disjunctive histories of the university as a social institution in Australia, China, Latin America, and Africa, as well as Europe and North America. The university system, we are told, is undergoing a process of transformation from "elite" through "mass" to "universal" higher education (Wheelahan in Barnett 2012); from a "pyramid" structure through one defined by "pillars" to that of a "network" or "web" (Standaert in Barnett 2012); and from its original dependence upon the church through analogous relations to the sovereign state, the nation, the professions, and most recently the corporation (Kavanagh in Barnett 2012). Ronald Barnett sums up the situation this way:

> [G]lobally, the university is being incorporated into "knowledge capitalism," a process that is closing off spaces of the university such that its dominant activities—teaching, research and public engagement—are being steered in that direction. And yet, there remain spaces for more emancipatory and publicly-oriented stances on the part of the university. Wisdom, care, purpose networking, sustainability and openness are just some of the ideas offered here that imply that spaces may even be opening anew for the university in the twenty-first century ... It is not necessarily the case that the spaces of the university are being closed; or at least, even amid closure, new spaces may be opening. The university has not yet been suffocated.
>
> (Barnett 2012: 202)

Resolutely optimistic, Barnett has written prolifically of the need to imagine new possibilities for the university rather than simply lamenting its demise. Nevertheless, it seems certain that official (if not also public) opinion is rapidly moving towards a narrower and more instrumental view of both education and research.

Countless essays and editorials in *The New York Times, The Chronicle of Higher Education*, and elsewhere warn of the continued shrinking of academic focus and the narrowing of the university's mission to accommodate the needs of the market rather than to deliver broad education in the name of public good.[1] Whatever the outcome of these developments may be, it is clear that, in the present era, not only the case for academia, but the case for knowledge itself, must be made anew (Wheelahan 2010). If knowledge is not to be reduced to information, education to vocational training, and research to product development, then new epistemological groundwork must be laid. This groundwork must support rigorously epistemic work without falling into the pitfalls of positivism and imperialism that have been so rightly critiqued within academia over the past decades. Postcolonial and poststructuralist theories must be incorporated into our understanding of the "politics of research" (Kaplan and Levine 1997), so that the case for knowledge can be made both convincing and ethical. While such a broad analysis is beyond the scope of this book, the crisis—or transformation—of the university is the necessary backdrop for a consideration of embodied research in academia.

In this chapter, I argue that embodied technique could be conceived as a major branch or division of human knowledge, alongside the sciences and the humanities, and that universities could legitimately design and support major research projects in this field. In making this argument, I will not seek to justify or explain the outcomes of embodied research in terms of marketable products. Previous chapters—especially Chapter 2—have shown how it is possible for new embodied technique to become commercially viable on a global scale. My interest here lies at the other end of the spectrum, in the realm of so-called "blue skies" research, or "research without a clear goal" (Bell 2006: 33). Such research is worth supporting, as it is often the source of the most innovative discoveries in any field. Moreover, "blue skies" research is less likely to be supported by capitalist market forces, and thus stands to suffer the greatest losses if academia continues to move towards an instrumental conception of knowledge. Of course, in the present context, advocating for support of blue skies research in embodied technique could be seen as wildly unrealistic. When even the sciences are having trouble funding open-ended research (Travis 2009), how can one imagine finding support for it in areas of embodied technique? Yet as Barnett and others suggest, a structural crisis is the right moment in which to consider radical changes. The response to the current situation cannot simply be a call for the university to remain as it was. Instead, proposals must be made that match and oppose the model of the corporate university. Now is the time to put forward bold ideas about what the university can and should be: "A new poetry of the university is now needed; nothing less" (Barnett 2012: 204). In that spirit, I consider the place of embodied research in the university as one possible aspect of a transformed epistemic landscape.

The university has awesome strengths at its disposal, and it is precisely these that I have tried to harness through my construal of social epistemology as underpinning research in a much wider variety of fields than those to which it is usually applied. The validity of such an approach is based on the assumption that academia has more than an adaptive and reactive relationship to society as a whole. Indeed, the university as conceived here has a profound epistemological and ontological role to play in shaping the world. As the authors of one quantitative study of disciplinary shifts argue, academia is "definitionally committed to mapping reality" (Frank and Gabler 2006: 14). This suggests that the organization of knowledge into disciplines—first and foremost, through the explicit epistemological systems of education and research—is a primary human engagement. Disciplinarity maps reality and in this sense could be said to determine what kinds of projects, institutions, and social movements are thinkable. Academia could even be called the premiere social institution designated to map the contours of being. Curricular and programmatic shifts in higher education might then be seen as actively driving the social and cultural formation of reality by producing epistemic diagrams of what is known. On the largest possible scale, academia undertakes epistemic "tinkering" and "tuning" as it continually revises its curricular and research programs. In this sense, academia and epistemics are no less responsible than arts and aesthetics for determining what Jacques Rancière calls the "distribution of the sensible" (2004). Rather than being a site for stagnant and formulaic training, the university is precisely the institution most responsible for determining which areas of technique will be explored and expanded, practiced and taught, at the core and at the edge of current knowledge.

This is a far grander mission and responsibility for academia than current discourse favors, perhaps even harkening back to the earlier history of the university as a site of universal truth (Barnett 2013: 58). In a slightly less dizzying register, we could articulate the power of educational and research institutions as follows: *Knowledge is politics in the long term.* In that case, the university by definition cannot be neutral with respect to politics. It can only take on a particular view—the longest possible view, the *longue durée*—and a politics appropriate to that view. While the university is just one aspect of formal education— to say nothing of informal and implicit education—it is an important one. As the top of the academic hierarchy, university research influences what is taught at all levels of formal education, down through primary school. Despite its historical links to empire (Smith 1999; Isasi-Díaz and Mendieta 2012), academia remains a crucial site for sustaining and extending knowledge beyond the instrumental focus of the present cultural moment. It is crucial, then, to develop what Christopher Newfield calls "a new framework for higher education's nonmarket purposes," in which the university can be reimagined as a "noncapitalist domain" on the basis of substantive "postcapitalist alternatives" (2008: 13), or what Barnett calls "feasible utopias" (2013: 26–28).

With this in mind, I now turn to examine current debates over the relationship between theory and practice in academia at a more concrete and discipline-specific level. Embodiment is a central issue for a wide range of academic fields today, including theatre, dance, and performance studies, anthropology, religious studies, gender studies, cognitive science, philosophy, and more. In the words of Jill Dolan, many of these fields remain fundamentally "shaped by tensions between those who purportedly 'do' (as if one could ever 'do' without thinking) and those assumed only to 'think' (as if thinking could ever be merely so)" (2001: 1). The division between "theory" and "practice" is grounded in the methodologies that have historically characterized many if not all scholarly fields, wherein the scholar is defined as one who studies—and therefore does not participate in—a given practice of theatre, dance, ritual, or everyday life. The epistemic distance that separates scholar from subject has been seen as enabling objectivity and has historically been accepted as a key standard for academic rigor. Before embodied technique can be accepted as an area of scholarly knowledge, these fundamental issues of objectivity and epistemic distance must be faced.

The epistemic impulse

In the past few decades, the division between theory and practice has continually been tested, in part through the development of new research methodologies—such as action research, participant observation, and qualitative research methods—that make possible a different relationship of the researcher to the object of research. However, none of these have gone so far as to suggest that those who are framed as research subjects—such as the makers of theatre and dance, or the practitioners of ritual—possess knowledge in the sense that scholars do. In many cases, theorists and practitioners remain divided and even suspicious of one another. In theatre departments, for example, "practice" refers to the making of theatre productions, if not with the theatre "industry" in mind, then within the larger cultural domain of the "arts." Although scholars of theatre might concede that theatre practitioners possess a different kind of knowledge, the nature of this knowledge, and its relationship to scholarly knowledge, has never been thoroughly analyzed. Theatrical production has always had an uneasy relationship with theatre studies, as the scholarly field that studies it, even when the two approaches are housed within the same academic programs and departments. According to Marvin Carlson, the tension between theatre studies and theatre practice in university departments in the US grew more pointed in the 1960s and 1970s, when it was widely felt that "both theatre research and theatre production should become more *professional*, more specialized, more 'serious'" (2011: 119). This has led to, among other things, a strong division between MFA and PhD tracks in US graduate education. It may also help to explain why universities, despite having all the necessary resources to conduct sustained and even large-scale embodied research projects in performance technique, have for the most part not done so.[2]

Other academic departments and fields have their own definitions and versions of the tension between theory and practice. In religious studies, practice may refer to pedagogical approaches that involve doing or performing rituals in addition to reading about them or observing them in ethnographic fieldwork. Such approaches have been of interest to some scholars and teachers since the 1960s, but they remain on the fringes of acceptable methodology (see Bell 2007). For example, the practice of yoga may raise eyebrows when introduced in a traditional classroom setting, whereas the historical or sociological study of yoga would not. One teacher recalls being asked by the head of Religious Studies at his university to stop teaching *asana* in a course called Yoga in Theory and Practice, because she was afraid it might "give evangelical Christians an argument for permitting prayer in university classes" (Liberman in Singleton and Byrne 2008: 112). This course was later transferred to the Folklore Program, which apparently was more open to embodied pedagogies. In queer and gender studies, as Dolan explains, practice usually refers not to artistic production or to ritual but to an activist engagement with political movements. In business schools, on the other hand, practice may refer to an engagement with "real world" businesses, as opposed to more theoretical economics. Medicine and the sciences have their own differently structured but analogous divisions between theorists and practitioners, where similar sentiments of competition and mutual "suspicion" may be at play (Cetina 1999: 16). In some fields, there are differentiated doctorates, as in the parallel pathways of the PsyD (Doctor of Psychology) and ThD (Doctor of Theology), both practical degrees that are distinct from the PhD in psychology or theology.

Alongside academic skepticism over the value of practice within academia, practitioners report considerable mistrust of academics and academia. Mark Singleton and Jean Byrne observe that "teachers and practitioners of yoga in modern times have often been in the habit of expressing their distaste for academia, which they may view as elitist, disembodied, and irrelevant to the real task at hand," or even "antithetical" to the practice of yoga (2008: 3). D. S. Farrer and John Whalen-Bridge make the same point with regard to mutual dismissal between martial artists and cultural historians and scholars of martial arts (2011: 7). Ross Prior encountered "strongly anti-academic sentiments" among acting teachers in England and Australia (2012: 176). As Dolan writes, "those who teach the practical business of theater and performance—acting, directing, playwriting, speech, voice, design, movement—are often simply hostile to theory" (2001: 2). Carlson attributes such hostility to an "anti-intellectual bias" (2011: 121). However, there are also legitimate reasons why teachers invested in "practice" might be skeptical of academic theories about their work. As Dolan points out, the value of academic support for fields like critical race studies and women's studies must be considered in light of "what the costs have been of institutionalizing knowledge that began on the street, in the vernacular, and came kicking and screaming into the academy" (2001: 30). Linda Tuhiwai Smith's indictment of academic research as complicit with colonialism suggests a larger historical context for such mistrust: In some circles, "research" is "one of the dirtiest words" (1999: 1). In short, there are considerable obstacles—stylistic, institutional, epistemological, and more—to the integration of theory and practice in academia. These obstacles cut in both directions and require substantive address.

Implicit in the tension between theory and practice is the idea that "practice" is not epistemic in nature. It is assumed, in other words, that "knowing" is a matter of "thinking" rather than "doing." This assumption remains in place despite the work of sociologists of knowledge who, ever since Bourdieu's *The Logic of Practice* (1990), have argued that practice has its own logic and that academic knowledge production is itself a kind of practice. Semantically, a basic ambiguity continues to confuse conversations about "practical" knowledge: It is often unclear whether the adjective "practical" refers to *embodiment* or to a *pragmatic* (in the colloquial rather than philosophical sense) engagement with the world. The study of acting, for example, is sometimes referred to as "practical," because it must be accomplished through embodied practice (Evans 2008: 176). Yet, as many well-meaning parents of undergraduate students assert, there is nothing "practical" about getting a degree in acting! Acting as a subject is practice-based, but not pragmatically oriented. Indeed, "blue skies" research in a field like acting is both deeply "practical," in the sense of being embodied, and at the same time highly *impractical*, in the sense of being epistemically distanced from immediate (e.g., economic) concerns. As Richard Sennett observes:

Practice and *practical* share a root in language. It might seem
that the more people train and practice in developing a skill,

the more practical minded they will become, focusing on the possible and the particular. In fact, the long experience of practice can lead in the opposite direction ... [T]he better your technique, the more impossible your standards.

(Sennett 2009: 46, italics original)

In this book, I have tried to show how an epistemic impulse—rather than a commercial or otherwise instrumental one—can be at the heart of the most deeply embodied practices. To "practice" in an embodied sense, then, is not necessarily to follow a "practical" logic as Bourdieu intended.

To illustrate the epistemic impulse in embodied practice, I have worked through a series of examples of research projects undertaken with little or no support from academia. In some cases, "research" and related terms are already in circulation among artists and practitioners outside academia, as in Grotowski's theatre "laboratory" and later "research" on the actor's craft; the New York City organization Movement Research (2012); the Centre for Performance Research in Wales (2012) and a dance studio with the same name in Brooklyn; or the Ashtanga Yoga Research Institute in Mysore, India. In none of these cases does the term "research" imply academic support or the use of academic models of knowledge production.[3] It should therefore be clear at this point that academia does not have a monopoly on either the idea or the practice of research. Research in embodied technique has long taken place outside of academia and does not need academic support to proceed. Nevertheless, it is worth asking whether the epistemological alignment between embodied research projects and those of academia— the fact that both proceed through sustained investigation to discover new knowledge in clearly framed areas—might provide the basis of a new framework for embodied research within academia and a new solidarity between researchers in these areas. If there is indeed a strong alignment between the epistemic impulse at work in projects like those I have described and the mission of academia as a social institution, then might academia offer an appropriate home for such projects?

Placing embodied technique next to the sciences and humanities— acknowledging it as a fundamental sector of humanity's inherited knowledge—could have major implications not only for higher education, but for the entire educational pathway, beginning with early childhood. How might academia go about supporting education and research in embodied technique? What would be the benefits to academia of offering such support—and what would be the benefits to embodied practitioners of placing themselves within an academic context? Since none of the projects discussed in previous chapters were supported by academia, might we not conclude that such research has no need of academic support? Is the argument for embodied research in academia simply a plea for new sources of funding? On the contrary, I believe that academia can offer more than financial support to embodied researchers. The university is the only social institution that explicitly stands for the depth dimension of knowledge, for specialization as a potential in any field, and for particular kinds of epistemological rigor. It is in this capacity that academia can legitimately champion areas of unconventional, subaltern, or subjugated lines of knowledge: not by virtue of their historical disempowerment alone, but by asserting their epistemological depth. Tim Ingold's notion of an "experimental" anthropology suggests a move in this direction (2011: 15), as does Richard Tinning's call for a more experimental, research-oriented, and socially aware approach to physical education (2010). In the field of theatre and performance, these tensions are currently playing out through the debate over "Practice as Research" and its cognates.

"Practice as Research"

Some of the most radical attempts to house embodied practice within academia are currently unfolding in many countries under the banner of "Practice as Research" and related terms. These programs and projects offer a useful starting point from which to consider the questions posed in the previous section in more concrete terms. "Practice as Research" (PaR) is one of a handful of phrases that are currently circulating within academia in the United States, Europe, Australia, and elsewhere, through which ongoing tensions between theory and practice are being tested. Other terms in this family include practice-based research, practice-led research, research through practice, performance as research, and arts-based or artistic research. Each of these has its own genealogy and connotations, which are too numerous and geographically specific to examine here.[4] Nevertheless, a review of the literature shows that they have much in common, with many of the same issues at play.

The British paradigm of PaR offers a useful starting point for a discussion of how and to what extent embodied research of the kind I have described might legitimately find a home within academia. According to Heike Roms:

In contrast to the incorporation of vocational training in American universities and the continuing (if slowly dissolving) separation between the practice of art and its study in the

European tradition, the British model ... with its attempted integration and mutual interrogation of practice and theory within research and pedagogy, may have created a situation of persistent anxiety, but it has arguably also produced an ongoing problematization of the position of performance practice within the academy that has proven highly productive. Over the last 15 years or so, this problematization has been concentrated around the notion of practice-as-research.

(Roms 2012: 58–59)

In England, practice-based masters and doctoral degrees in theatre, dance, and other arts are now common. However, on a theoretical level, the discussion surrounding PaR has not yet convincingly engaged with the established standards of academic rigor, nor has it established a credible epistemological framework of its own. Contemporary discussions of PaR usually describe it as a recent trend developing within academia, in which hybrid artist-scholars or scholar-practitioners synthesize and combine academic research with artistic or creative practice. This assumption sets PaR afloat, without historical reference points, and has led to a vibrant and kaleidoscopic but often incoherent debate over the definition and purpose of PaR. In contrast, I have argued that embodied research is a major historical area of research and knowledge production. The examples I have given, spanning roughly the past century, indicate the depth and breadth of this field, while the theoretical argument developed throughout proposes a coherent framework for research in embodied technique. Although there are many similarities between PaR as an emerging academic field and embodied research as a historical phenomenon, there are also substantial differences. A comparative examination may help make my proposal for embodied research in academia more concrete, while simultaneously offering challenges to the ways in which PaR has been theorized up to this point.

Baz Kershaw is a key figure in the PaR debates, having directed the Practice as Research in Performance (PARIP 2012) project at the University of Bristol (2001–6), from which came the volume *Practice-as-Research in Performance and Screen,* a collection of essays with attached DVD that documents a wide range of PaR projects in the UK and elsewhere (Allegue *et al.* 2009). Kershaw also has two chapters in Shannon Rose Riley and Lynette Hunter's *Mapping Landscapes for Performance as Research* (2009), the only volume that examines the more recent development of PaR in the United States; a chapter on PARIP in Hazel Smith and Roger Dean's *Practice-led Research, Research-led Practice in the Creative Arts* (2009); and a chapter on PaR in his and Helen Nicholson's *Research Methods in Theatre and Performance* (Kershaw and Nicholson 2011). Kershaw's support for the field has been open-ended and has supported the growth of complex dialogue around a cluster of related issues. Rather than putting forth a clear statement about what PaR should be, he has helped to create space for multiple voices and perspectives. While this has led to an expansion of both the discourse and the constituency of PaR, the predominance of essay collections over monographs in this field also illustrates the fragmentation that characterizes PaR today. (See also Biggs and Karlsson 2011; Barrett and Bolt 2007; Gehm *et al.* 2007.) From these multivocal conversations, nothing like a consensus has emerged regarding best practices in PaR, or what the category of PaR should or should not include, on either a practical or theoretical level. Moreover, the emphasis on interdisciplinary in these works means that essays in the same volume may draw their examples and assumptions from fields as diverse as dance, theatre, performance art, visual art, design, media studies, engineering, architecture, poetry, painting, film, and music. Most book-length, single-author treatments of PaR focus on the visual arts and have little to say about the specific role of embodiment in the production of knowledge (Sullivan 2010; McNiff 1998).

Two volumes worth considering in greater depth are John Freeman's *Blood, Sweat & Theory: Research through Practice in Performance* (2010) and Robin Nelson's *Practice as Research in the Arts* (2013). The former interweaves Freeman's own reflections on PaR with first-person narratives from a wide cross-section of artists and practitioner-researchers. While Freeman acknowledges that he is not putting forth a coherent framework or model for PaR, but rather a series of juxtaposed and sometimes contradictory essays, his warnings about the facile "celebration of newness" that attends much PaR discourse resonate with the position taken here (2010: 7, 23, 60). Nelson's book, on the other hand, stands as the clearest articulation to date of PaR as an academic methodology. In laying out a clear formula for the framing and development of academic PaR projects, Nelson does much to clarify the existing situation. However, as I argue below, his view of PaR is far more limited than the concept of embodied research I propose. Curiously, both Freeman and Nelson write almost exclusively about the structure of PaR projects at the doctoral level—the PaR PhD—rather than at higher levels of research. There is little sense, in other words, of a larger epistemic field, distinct from the world of professional theatre and contemporary performance, into which such PhDs could lead. This suggests one of the main problems faced by PaR: the risk that debates over its meaning have more to do with handling changes in the funding and administrative landscape of academia than with shaping a substantive field of inquiry. It is difficult to imagine another context in which the legitimacy of an emerging scholarly discipline would be hashed out primarily around the issue of PhD theses, rather than the formation of new departments, programs, and advanced research projects.

Freeman mentions Stanislavski, Meyerhold, Brecht, Grotowski, Barba, and Brook as examples of practitioners in whose work "the investigative and research qualities were clear to see," although his position on the validity of their practice as research is not clear (2010: 151, 237, 265, 282). The difference between these practitioners and the PaR projects of today, Freeman suggests, is "the sheer scale of practice-based research. That which was once in the sole domain of some of the world's greatest thinkers and makers in their chosen theatrical forms now peppers the pages of countless curriculum vitae" (2010: 151). Freeman offers a welcome critique of "the false certainty that practice is always already research," an assumption within which "both practice and research are reduced to facile terms" (199). Moreover, the varied case studies interwoven throughout the volume include some of the most rigorous as well as the most relevant to the present discussion. To give just one example, Yves Knockaert documents a Belgian research project that explored the vocal, aesthetic, and gendered dimensions of the romantic *Lied*. While the interdisciplinary premise of the project is hardly uncommon in the context of PaR, Knockaert's detailed description of its elaboration of vocal technique suggests a type of research outcome that is more in line with my epistemology of practice than with other models of PaR in circulation. Likewise, Freeman's call for "a different kind of support" for PaR—neither "evangelical" nor "defensive"—suggests that a more coherent epistemology is needed to subtend this blossoming but unstable field (283).

In contrast to the avowedly "schizophrenic" nature of Freeman's book (2010: 7), Nelson's monograph attempts to provide a comprehensive foundation for PaR—although, as I noted, this is understood primarily as a format for PhD theses rather than a field of advanced research. Having supervised numerous PaR projects at Manchester Metropolitan University and London's Central School of Speech and Drama for over a decade, Nelson is well positioned to critique and clarify the development of PaR in the UK. His book also includes brief essays on how PaR operates in New Zealand, Australia, continental and Nordic Europe, South Africa, and the United States—where, according to Shannon Rose Riley, "there are only one or two established PhD programmes in theatre or performance framed up as practice-based programmes or as having a substantial and required practice component" (in Nelson 2013: 175).

Drawing on some of the same sources I cited in Chapter 1—including Judith Butler, Pierre Bourdieu, Francisco Varela, and Theodore Schatzki—Nelson attempts to propose a more rigorous epistemological framework for PaR. He puts forward a model of PaR as a "third species of research" alongside established qualitative and quantitative methodologies (Haseman in Nelson 2013: 56). Like Freeman, Nelson is concerned about a lack of epistemological rigor in practice-based projects and hopes to offer the outlines of a more coherent methodology. One of Nelson's main arguments—with which I agree—is that not all practices constitute research, and that it is therefore incumbent upon the defenders of PaR to explain exactly what kinds of practice are research and why. Nevertheless, Nelson's model retains some of the problematic assumptions found in other, less thorough explications of PaR. These assumptions make Nelson's proposals both more realistic, in the short term, and more epistemologically limited, in comparison with the notion of embodied research proposed here.

First, Nelson sees PaR as recent and interdisciplinary, whereas embodied research as defined here is ancient and very often disciplinary in form. What I have called the epistemic impulse in embodied practice has existed for as long as humanity has searched for relatively reliable pathways through its own embodiment and has often led to the establishment of highly disciplined and regimented traditions of practice. Nelson acknowledges that the drive "to address a problem, find things out, establish new insights ... is apparent in the arts throughout history" (2013: 3). However, he does not explain the relationship between historical research of this kind and contemporary PaR. In fact, Nelson specifically deemphasizes the importance of a historical perspective on PaR: "Though historical knowledge is not effaced, my notion of a practice review focuses on what other practitioners are achieving in synchronous space and time" (54). As I argue below, a diachronic perspective is essential in establishing the rigor of any research, including embodied research, yet surprisingly few champions of PaR emphasize this point.[5]

In addition to favoring the synchronic over the diachronic, Nelson sees PaR as radically interdisciplinary, rather than grounded in existing disciplines. Although he takes care to illuminate several ways in which rigor can be applied to interdisciplinary projects, Nelson gives little attention to the kinds of narrowly focused research projects that might help to establish the validity of an emerging field. The rigor of PaR, Nelson argues, is "in syncretism, not in depth-mining" (2013: 34). Its conceptual framework "is more typically wide and interdisciplinary rather than narrow and specific" (102). As a corollary, Nelson suggests that the establishment of mastery or even competence in existing fields is often not relevant to the successful framing and completion of a PaR project. For Nelson, PaR is "less dependent upon a specific body of knowledge requiring prior mastery" (34). Accordingly, while some projects might require high levels of prior training, many will not. However, for interdisciplinarity to have any meaning, it must be based on competency in at least one discipline. Interdisciplinarity moves from one discipline towards another—"producing new forms of knowledge in its engagement with discrete disciplines" (Moran 2002: 16)—rather than escaping from the requirement of competence in any field. Nelson characterizes PaR as resembling the postmodern "rhizome" of Deleuze and Guattari, as opposed to a modernist "surface/depth" model (2013: 54). I would argue, in contrast, that a sophisticated theory of knowledge must involve both horizontal and vertical movements, surface and depth, disciplinarity and interdisciplinarity. Although knowledge has no center, any given field or research project must establish its starting points and research edges. In the present academic milieu, an emphasis on interdisciplinarity over disciplinarity additionally risks playing into the arguments of those who want to reduce support for sustained pedagogy and research in general. As I argued above, the case for knowledge itself must presently be made, and this case must involve the recognition of epistemological depth as well as breadth.

Another problem is that Nelson situates PaR within the context of interdisciplinary arts, a domain that includes "dancing, music- or theatre-making, writing, painting, sculpting, filming" (2013: 62). As a result, he sees performing arts as presenting a specific problem for academia because of their alleged ephemerality. Drawing on Phelan's "ontology of disappearance" (critiqued in Chapter 1), Nelson considers theatre and performance to be uniquely difficult to document and assess: "Numerous instabilities in the diversity and ephemerality of performing arts practices pose particular challenges to ideas of fixed, measurable, and recordable 'knowledge'" (4). The notion of embodied research proposed here, on the contrary, places live performance alongside an entirely different set of sibling practices: martial arts, yoga, sports, somatic bodywork, and ritual, as well as gender and other categories of identity. In this context, the absence of a material product is hardly anomalous and requires no special explanation. Placing theatre and dance alongside martial arts and gender allows us to recognize the stability of practice insofar as it is structured by technique. In contrast, many contemporary ideas about art and art-making work directly against the epistemological demands of research. By grounding his vision of PaR in the arts rather than in embodiment, Nelson puts himself at the mercy of prevailing assumptions about ephemerality, uniqueness, and radical breaks from history in the making of art. Whether or not these assumptions are useful or true, they work against any recognition of the transmissible knowledge that structures all kinds of artistic and embodied practices. The term "art" itself carries very different connotations across the martial, healing, performing, literary, and visual arts. As I have argued, art can only be research if it is understood in terms of craft (Latin: *artes*; Greek: *techne*). In this sense, the association of PaR with "the arts" is damaging insofar as it ignores the relationship that live performance has to other kinds of embodied practice outside the domain of "art" in the modern sense.

Finally, and perhaps most fundamentally, Nelson's model does not sufficiently explain what kinds of knowledge outcomes might be expected to result from successful PaR projects. His proposed methodology for PaR is essentially a triangular relationship between three modes of knowing: "know-that," "know-how," and "know-what" (2013: 37). The first and second of these come from Gilbert Ryle, who distinguished between propositional knowledge "that" something is true and practical knowledge of "how" to do something.[6] The concept of "know-how" is problematic here, insofar as it conflates knowledge, ability, and experience. Since neither ability nor experience are transmissible, "know-how" in this sense cannot be a rigorous research outcome. "Know-that" is certainly a potential research outcome, but there is nothing new in this idea, since for Nelson this category is equivalent to "traditional 'academic knowledge'" (45). This leaves only "know-what" as a possible new type of research outcome. Nelson defines "know-what" along lines very similar to my concept of technique. It includes, he writes, "what can be gleaned through an informed reflexivity about the process of making and its modes of knowing. The key method used to develop know-what from know-how is that of critical reflection—pausing, standing back and thinking about what you are doing." This process is "rigorous and iterative," leading to a knowledge that consists in "knowing what 'works,' in teasing out the methods by which 'what works' is achieved and the compositional principles involved" (44). Nelson does not offer a more thorough explanation of how "know-what" is produced, nor does he give explicit examples of it in contrast to "know-how" and "know-that." If "know-what" is essentially technique as I have defined it, then there could be significant overlap and compatibility between my proposal and Nelson's. But whereas Nelson shows three "modes" of knowledge interacting equally, the epistemology of practice developed here would locate technique at the top of the triangle—or in its center— to illustrate how experience, ability, and the archive can each inform the development of new technique.

Nelson is very clear about the possible forms the material product of a PaR dissertation can take, including suggested proportions for written and audiovisual materials (2013: 100–102 and *passim*). But no amount of detail regarding the format of the output can replace an epistemological theory of its content. What is an example of a substantive research outcome in PaR? The question is not: What does it look like, how many pages, and what is the format of the DVD? But rather: What kind of transmissible knowledge does it contribute, and to which field(s)? Early on, Nelson mentions Pina Bausch—unquestionably an innovator of embodied technique alongside Krishnamacharya, Stanislavski, and Grotowski—as an example of someone whose work constitutes practical or artistic research findings that are "paradigm-shifting." But, he rightly points out, "to set the bar for *new knowledge* at the level of the paradigm shift is to set it too high," since such instances "are rare—and, indeed, often not recognized in their own time" (27, italics original). How then should we conceive of smaller, more modest contributions to practice along similar lines? What are the "substantial new insights" (47) to which PaR projects ought, at a minimum, to give rise? The underlying problem here is once again the lack of a clear distinction between practice and the knowledge that structures it. Nelson insists that "the practice itself," or "the work itself," or "the artwork" can stand as part of the research outcome (83). In contrast, I have argued that practice itself is not equivalent to knowledge, because it is neither repeatable nor transmissible. A live event cannot constitute a research outcome, because it is bounded in time and space. We must therefore have a way of naming the transmissible knowledge that a live event or practice may discover, explore, demonstrate, clarify, reveal, illustrate, or incarnate. Technique, as knowledge, can be a research outcome of practice.

My concern, when reading the work of Nelson and other theorists of PaR, is that the concept of "research" may lose its meaning as a result of being too easily and broadly applied. Working alongside practitioners of yoga, dance, martial arts, and acting/performance, I have seen how the word research can be used to name a particularly *epistemic* impulse in practice. In this precise usage, "research" in yoga or actor training identifies a type or dimension of those practices—which can be distinguished from their health or psychological benefits, as well as from their use value in creating public works of art or entertainment—on the grounds that it is a *search for transmissible knowledge*. Yet both theorists and practitioners are also guilty of using the word research as a catch-all term: "Research is whatever you need" (Burrows 2010: 43). In most current theories of PaR, including that of Nelson, the defining characteristic of research as an *epistemic endeavor relative to a field of knowledge* tends to be lost. The problem is less that this is definitionally wrong than that it overwrites the particular and hard-won epistemic sense of "research" that has been developed over centuries by scholars, as well as more recently by embodied practitioners like Stanislavski and Grotowski.

Most often today, instead of naming an epistemic impulse already at work in many embodied practices, the "research" in PaR refers merely to an interdisciplinary relationship between embodied practice and theoretical knowledge. I call this the "weak" conception of PaR, or "Practice *and* Research." In it, practice is invited to be in dialogue with more traditional forms of research, but how practice may itself constitute research is not adequately shown. A stronger conception of PaR—more like the notion of embodied research developed here—would argue on epistemological grounds that practice can itself be a research methodology, leading to the discovery of new knowledge in the form of new technique. The potential for interdisciplinary exchange between this and other kinds of knowledge would then be a worthy but secondary concern. Moreover, PaR would be seen less as an interaction of two previously existing communities—artists and academics—than as a special kind of pursuit that is already at work in a variety of contexts, including but not limited to the arts and academia. This would constitute not an additive model of *practice* + *research,* but rather an argument for certain kinds of practice: those in which *practice* = *research*.

Michael Biggs and Daniela Büchler exemplify the weak conception of PaR when they define it as the interaction of "two different communities presenting conflicting claims: the community of academic researchers working in contexts such as university departments, and the community of professional practitioners working in contexts such as the concert hall or the art gallery" (in Biggs and Karlsson 2011: 83). According to Biggs and Büchler, the academic community values "the archiving and dissemination of outcomes," while the creative practice community tends to value "the singularity of the event" and "the direct encounter with the artifact" through exhibition and performance (87). Yet, as I have shown, some practitioners are deeply concerned with the dissemination of research outcomes far beyond the singularity of the event. Moreover, such an interest in dissemination is not limited to fringe elements, but can be identified with the foundational moments of fields like yoga and acting. Far from being secondary to the production of singular events, the development and transmission of knowledge in the form of technique can be seen as the primary activity of many practitioners in physical culture and performing arts—the ground upon which the "singular event" can be realized and without which there can be no event at all.

The weak conception of PaR pays no attention to those practitioners who hold the (epistemic) values that Biggs and Büchler associate with academia and yet do not work in academic contexts or receive academic support.

The archive and epistemic distance

Many of the significant differences between my notion of embodied research and current discussions of PaR converge around the issue of documentation. Very often, the starting point for considering the documentation of PaR is the claim that recording technologies "fail" to capture the complexity of live events. After all, if the written word cannot "capture" live performance, then neither can film, tape recording, or digital video. Even the best documentary video cannot record smells, flavors, or the feeling of being in the room when something happens. As Nelson writes, "there are experiential aspects of many PaR performance projects which can only be thought-felt live in the here and now" (2013: 78). For this reason, he explains, there is "an informal consensus in the UK" that "ephemeral practice in the context of PaR PhD must be experienced live by the examiners" (105). Simon Jones takes this argument even further, asserting that PaR actively "flees textual practices" and "the known," and is therefore "*outside of judgement*" (in Allegue et al. 2009: 30; italics original). Such an avowedly "outrageous" conception of PaR is an example of what I have called the trope of excess. It is no wonder that conversations about PaR documentation run into difficulties, when PaR is sometimes defined as that which, by definition, cannot be documented. I agree, of course, that the fullness of live performance cannot be captured on DVD. However, as I have argued, this fact is not specific to artistic or theatrical performance—it is true of practice in general. No chunk of practice, defined by its boundaries in time and space, can be fully captured, articulated, or enumerated by any system, logic, or documentation strategy. To exalt certain practices as "fleeing" judgment is to take an unacceptably dismissive attitude towards practice in general. Practices of theatre and performance are no less subject to "capture" by discourse, knowledge, and judgment—and no less structured by technique—than are those of everyday life.

PaR theorists like Kershaw, Nelson, Biggs and Büchler, and Jones no doubt feel they are taking the more radical stance by demanding that academia accommodate and support even those aspects of practice that are ephemeral, evanescent, undocumentable, and unknowable. In my view, however, such proposals romanticize artistic practice and make light of academic standards. The bolder stance would be to demand of embodied practitioners that they produce stable, transmissible documents of the technique that structures their practice. This opens the door to a radical transformation of academia, not through the dismantling of its standards but through an extension of the logic of scholarly epistemology itself. Calling on academia to recognize and accept the ephemerality and transience of live performance is not an original move. After all, it is largely scholars who have described performance as uniquely ephemeral in the first place, leading some theorists to accuse performance studies of unconsciously privileging the perspective of the spectator—from which performance appears ephemeral—over the knowledge of the performer (Melrose 2003; Roms 2012: 61; Ness in Noland and Ness 2008: 22). I propose instead that we call upon academics and practitioners alike to acknowledge the relatively stable and transmissible knowledge content of embodied practice and to find ways of documenting and assessing this content. Rather than focusing on those aspects of practice that multimedia recordings fail to capture, we might ask how new multimedia and network technologies are making new territories of knowledge available for the first time to academic scrutiny through the long-established protocols of peer review and citation. In this respect, we might also do well to remember that academia itself only became possible through the development of certain "new" technologies of documentation and distribution, beginning with the printed word. A proposal for embodied research in academia should therefore begin with a closer examination of the epistemological relationship between scholarship and the archive.

The idea that scholarly knowledge is contained in written texts, whereas practical knowledge inheres in ephemeral events, is deeply misleading. On the contrary, scholarship in every field is in large part tacit and embodied. Consider the following description of a research practice:

> In place of the familiar alienation between theory and practice, we find an action/cognition mesh to which the received notion of a theory can no longer be adequately applied. According to the [researchers], theories in research are more akin to policies than creeds. Such policies blend interpretation with strategic and tactical calculations, and are sustained by methodological "how-to-do-it" projections. Like the concern with making things work, policies are necessarily tied to an interest structure. Pure theory, then, can be called an illusion …

This passage could easily be from a contemporary PaR text, like those cited above, that argues for the exceptionality of PaR in comparison with other kinds of allegedly more objective or generalizable research. However, it is actually a description of laboratory science put forward as part of the emerging sociology of knowledge more than three decades ago (Cetina 1981: 4). As this passage shows, the difference between embodied research and other kinds of research practice, including the scientific, has been seriously overstated.

Scholars and scientists do not have direct or conscious access to all the knowledge they possess any more than do actors, dancers, or yoga teachers. They do, however, have recourse to an archive of relatively stable documents, and it is this that distinguishes *academic* knowledge from other kinds. To a large extent, academia is defined by the relationship between a community of knowledge and its archive—from cutting-edge research to the pedagogical processes that make each archive legible to successive generations. Of course, the stability of this archive can and has been questioned (Piccini and Rye in Allegue *et al.* 2009). But there can be no doubt that the circulation of documents—written words and also visual materials—is essential to academic knowledge production. On the other hand, if scholarship were purely archival, and not grounded in embodied encounters, there would be no need for education: Students could simply read the texts of whichever field they wanted to master. Books and articles "fail" to capture the pedagogical work of professors—the vocal nuances and context-dependent remarks of a lecturer as much as the more intimate event of a seminar—in the same way that they fail to capture dance, theatre, and ritual events. What distinguishes scholarly knowledge is not that it is textual—there is no such thing as purely textual knowledge—but rather its particular use of documentary technology to capture and disseminate not even "language" but just those particular aspects of language that can be recorded in written, printed, or digital words.

The scholarly archive is both synchronic and diachronic, and each of these is essential to its working. The synchronic dimension of the archive makes possible "blind" peer review: the evaluation of work by people who are specialists in the field but who do not have a personal investment in the success or failure of a given author. Michèle Lamont has examined peer review through a study of interdisciplinary panels that award high-level grants and fellowships. Drawing on interviews with scholars from disciplines as diverse as history, philosophy, anthropology, literature, economics, and political science, Lamont finds a great deal to appreciate in the "imperfect but satisfactory system" of peer review (2009: 156). Like Cetina's ethnographic work with scientists, which she cites (22–23), Lamont incorporates the social dimensions of knowledge production without reducing the latter to mere strategy and power play. "Strategic voting, horse-trading, self-interest, and idiosyncratic and inconsistent criteria all are unavoidable parts of the equation," she notes (156). Nevertheless, peer review manages to achieve meaningful epistemological goals despite or because it is social in nature (10). Countering Bourdieu and others, Lamont finds that peer review is not "driven only or primarily by a competitive logic". Rather, the experience of shared learning, exchange of knowledge, and even "collective effervescence during deliberations," amounts to an epistemic practice that is more than just a "self-serving illusion" (20, 36). Strikingly, Lamont's findings hold true across the humanities and social sciences. Her study shows how peer review functions not only within disciplines but also between them, at the level of scholarship in general, where it enables scholars to parse the sometimes radical epistemological differences (incommensurability) between diverse fields of knowledge.

Synchronic comparison, as in peer review, is one of two keystones of scholarly epistemology. The fact that my work can be assessed by someone far away, who has never heard of me (and, in the case of "blind" review, who does not even know my name), enables a particular kind of rigor in knowledge production, which we can call *synchronic rigor*. With the advent of computer networks, this dimension is growing exponentially. The diachronic dimension of the scholarly archive, on the other hand, allows for comparative engagements to occur across time. The depth and rigor of diachronic engagement is necessarily limited by the unreliability of the archive, its gaps and errors, and by the limitations of archival materials themselves. Generally speaking, the further back in time we reach, the more fragmentary the evidence, the more difficult to ascertain its reliability, and the more complex the issues of translation and interpretation. Nevertheless, this dimension of the scholarly archive is also growing exponentially, and it makes possible what we can call *diachronic rigor* in the production of scholarly knowledge. Without such rigor, scholarship would be limited to a discussion among those who are currently living, engaging through oral tradition with the memory of what their teachers (and their teachers' teachers) said. The diachronic dimension of the scholarly archive makes it possible to go back to the writing of earlier thinkers and wrestle with them in the present. However imperfect this engagement with historical thinkers may be—and it certainly fails to capture the singular "event" of any life—it adds a temporal dimension to academic knowledge that could not otherwise exist. Taken together, synchronic and diachronic comparison define the particular rigor of scholarly epistemology.

According to Lamont, there is more consensus about what constitutes quality in the discipline of history than in other academic disciplines, in part because of shared "agreement on what constitutes good historical craftsmanship, a sense of 'careful archival work'" (2009: 80). Throughout this book, I have occasionally used history and mathematics as examples of research, precisely because these disciplines have achieved a kind of methodological consensus that allows them to articulate what they are doing beyond the confines of their own fields. Both history and mathematics, as well as many other disciplines, offer a clear sense of how the researcher may engage through skill and attention with something that exists beyond the community of knowledge itself. Their methodologies could hardly be more different, yet the grappling of historians with the past, and of mathematicians with abstract patterns, have this in common: the grappling, the tuning, the tinkering, the tracking, the tracing, the "experiential groping" (citations in Chapter 1) with a zone of materiality, a substrate that exists beyond themselves. To understand how embodied practice can function analogously, we need to shift emphasis away from individual idiosyncrasies—like ability and talent—and towards relative reliabilities with which we can meaningfully engage across time and space—and, more importantly, the transmissible technique these reliabilities afford.

The problem of the substrate: Do scholarly disciplines like history and mathematics really engage with some material reality that lies beyond their respective archives? Or is the archive itself the subject of each discipline? We do not have to answer this question in order to recognize that the synchronic and diachronic dimensions of academic rigor are made possible by the existence of the archive. Without reference to an archive of circulating documents, there could be no peer review; no publication or citation; no historical depth—in short, no community of knowledge beyond interpersonal connections. Oral traditions may pass along valid and valuable knowledge across many generations, but they do not possess the distinctive synchronic and diachronic dimensions that a shared archive makes possible. The relationship between a community of knowledge and a relatively stable synchronic and diachronic archive is the distinctive feature of academic fields. In this sense, the issue of documentation is fundamental to academic epistemology. The "theory vs. practice" debates, and the discussions of PaR cited above, can thus be seen in a new light: Rather than thinking of performance and embodied practice as uniquely ephemeral—an exceptional phenomenon that "flees" textuality or "evades" judgment—we should instead recognize the extraordinary power of writing and printing technologies to render some aspects of practice stable over hundreds or even thousands of years. If the fragile relationship between the written word and embodied knowledge has made possible all the fields of academic knowledge that exist today, what new fields might be founded in the wake of technologies that can capture light and sound waves as never before, making them available across time and space in unprecedented ways?

It is not then performance that is a special case in its ephemerality. Rather, academia—with its foundational relationship to the archive—is the special case. All of life is ephemeral. Not just performance but every moment of practice exceeds our ability to "capture" or articulate it in words, images, or digital information. Scholarly knowledge is a special kind of knowledge—that which to some perhaps small degree avoids the general ephemerality of life—and it does so through the painstaking construction, maintenance, and interpretation of a rich synchronic and diachronic archive. Academic fields are what they are because of their relations to particular kinds of documentary technology. These fields do not exist prior to the question of documentation. The question of documentation is the basis for any academic field, insofar as it determines what will constitute its scholarly archive. Until very recently in the history of human society, scholarly rigor has been limited to those fields that are founded upon printed materials (words, drawings, "ephemera," etc.) and other kinds of physical objects (such as fossils or antiques). Yoga, dance, and other embodied practices have been documented in writing for hundreds if not thousands of years, and in this sense have indeed been exchanged and assessed across synchronic and diachronic distances. However, the new media of the past century enable us to approach these fields of knowledge with a new rigor, making available many dimensions of practice that were previously inaccessible to the mechanisms of scholarship.

It has now become possible to develop a synchronic and diachronic archive that allows moving images and recorded sounds to travel far beyond their original context, where previously only paper documents and static images could go. Certain dimensions of embodied technique—especially sound and the moving image—can now be accessed and assessed across the kind of *epistemic distance* that defines the rigor of scholarship in other fields. It could even be argued that the growth of theatre, performance, and dance studies, as well as the increased discussion of embodied knowledge in other fields, is substantially a result of the development of recording technologies over the past 150 years. Mark Singleton, for example, argues that the advent of photography enabled the physical culture movement (2010: 163–74). We could equally chart the development of phonograph, photograph, film, and video techniques alongside the rise of theatre and performance studies. Does the advent of such technologies make thinkable the question—fundamental to these disciplines—of how one performance of a script or score differs from another? Might the birth of performance studies be closely linked to the appearance of cheaper and more widespread recording technologies, which make more instances of embodied practice accessible to scholarship? In any case, it is quite backwards to conceive of performance as a special kind of phenomenon that escapes or eludes capture. Rather, scholarly notions of performance and embodied practice have emerged from the growth of multimedia technologies precisely because these technologies can so successfully record aspects of practice—like movement and rhythm—that otherwise could not be archived.

Without a citable synchronic and diachronic archive, there can be research, but not scholarly research. Researchers like Krishnamacharya, Stanislavski, and Grotowski all operated within specific communities of knowledge. They were each aware of a range of practices related to their own and extremely interested in the differences and similarities between them. In addition to drawing on personal encounters and apprenticeships, they were extremely well-read, making powerful use of the print and visual archive to move forward with their embodied research. But they did not have recourse to multimedia documentation of historical practices. Today, multimedia documentation makes the comparative study of embodied technique possible in unprecedented ways: Singleton uses photographs to illustrate the technical link between European contortionism and Iyengar yoga (2010: 60–63); video stills documenting the physical training of Ryszard Cieslak show the migration of embodied technique back to Europe via India (Kapsali 2010: 193). Audiovisual recordings bring another giant step forward in this archive. There are grainy black-and-white films of Krishnamacharya performing a yoga sequence, and of Stanislavski directing *Tartuffe*— both in 1938, and both available through a simple search on Google or YouTube—but nothing like the teaching and rehearsal videos that now abound. These kinds of documents are part of the growing archive of specialized embodied practice, although scholarly publications have yet to begin citing them as serious references. The film of Grotowski's *Akropolis,* and that of Ryszard Cieslak leading physical training at Odin Teatret, are widely known in theatre studies, but even these are usually cited only as complete works and not in specific detail. The films of the Grotowski/Richards Workcenter's *Action* and *Downstairs Action*, discussed in Chapter 3, are now shown regularly by Thomas Richards and Mario Biagini, but as of this writing they are not available to purchase or watch except in their presence. We are clearly a long way from establishing a scholarly multimedia archive, but there are many signs that we are moving in that direction.

If scholarly rigor is defined by the relationship of the researcher to a synchronic and diachronic archive, then the place of embodied practice within academia depends upon the establishment of such an archive. Of course, we will never have audio or video footage that predates the development of those technologies. But we can begin to develop the archive from the present moment onward. There are many substantive questions to be asked along the way. What would a multimedia document look like, if its purpose were to make the embodied technique of a given practice available to interested parties across geographic and temporal distance? How would this differ from a documentary film intended for general audiences? How might one cite a multimedia document, not simply by giving the reference and time code but by including an excerpt, as with verbal citations? In addition to written documents that cite multimedia documents, can we imagine archives of multimedia documents that actively cite one another? Such archives would do more than simply make audio and video materials available to scholars for whom the required research outcome is a written essay or book. They would become sites of and for scholarly debate in their own right. The question today is how a scholar could produce a multimedia document of embodied practice that would cite and engage with other such documents, be submitted to rigorous peer review in that context, and then itself become available for citation. Nothing less can meet the established standards of academic knowledge production.

This argument is based on the supposition that yoga, martial arts, dance, acting, sport, therapy, ritual, and other embodied practices have greater affinity with multimedia documentation than with purely textual media. That simply means that multimedia captures more of the embodied knowledge that structures such practices than does the written word. I am not suggesting that multimedia documents capture everything that happens in practice, or that such documents are conclusive or final. As previously stated, it is impossible to capture or articulate all the technique that structures any practice. The question is: To what extent does multimedia documentation make new areas of knowledge available to the mechanisms of scholarly rigor? (The extent to which new media can be used to improve the scholarly archive in more tactile and proprioceptive fields of technique, like somatic bodywork, remains to be seen.) In any case, the founding of a scholarly field is, to a large extent, equivalent to the founding of its archive. A single, unique artistic event can never attain scholarly rigor, because it can never be assessed or cited by anyone who was not present at the time it occurred. Likewise, a teaching tradition that is only passed down through personal contact cannot claim scholarly rigor, because such rigor is based on assessment and citation that extends beyond interpersonal contact. This does not mean that such events and traditions cannot produce valuable, transmissible knowledge. It simply means that they cannot meet the scholarly standards of assessment and citation by a community of knowledge across synchronic and diachronic distances. The question of whether and how embodied research can find a home within the academy is therefore substantially a question of the extent to which it can be documented. Documentation is not a secondary, logistical question, but an essential part of academic epistemology. Documentation, in the broadest sense, is the difference between knowledge, which may or may not be documented, and scholarship, which necessarily engages with an archive across epistemic distances both synchronic and diachronic.

Research design and methodology

The problem with contemporary conversations about documentation is that they focus on, and attempt to capture, the wrong object. It is neither possible nor desirable to "capture" or document a *performance* in the sense of a unique live event or moment of practice. The debate around documentation would substantially shift if we were to stop trying to capture *works of art* and instead try to document "art" itself—that is, technique. This is more plausible, more feasible, and also more useful, because technique is precisely that which is not tied to specific bodies and local contexts. Watching a document of a unique event can only prompt either historical inquiry or nostalgia—unless we are able to derive from it concrete pathways and possibilities that may be put to use at other times and places. As Peter Hulton—a pioneer of multimedia documentation through the Arts Archives at Exeter—has asserted: "We need a portrait of presence, not a discourse of disappearance ... [A]rchives and documentations are not defined by their attempt to rescue things from oblivion, but are provocations rendered a-new into present reality each time someone encounters them" (2009: 341). This suggests a very different set of questions about the formatting of documentation, since the goal is no longer to capture the event itself, but rather the transmissible knowledge that structures it.

Scholars are understandably skeptical when it comes to the outcomes of embodied research. As Joseph Roach recently remarked: "I hesitate to use the word 'laboratory' only because it was so overused at another time in the development of theatre studies: the 'laboratory theatre.' But the problem with that was, there was never any research outcome. The show went up, and the show came down, and that's it" (2011). Yet as we have seen, it is not true that there was never any research outcome from Grotowski's work. The embodied technique developed by Grotowski—at the intersection of song, physical culture, and physical action—has had an enormous impact on practitioners worldwide and continues to be practiced and brought forward through ongoing research today. However, Grotowski's continual emphasis on live interactions, his mistrust of documentation, the Workcenter's continued reluctance to articulate its practice in technical terms, and the lack of any serious epistemological framework for Grotowski's research can easily lead to the idea that there were no substantive research outcomes from the Theatre Laboratory. Painstaking archival and analytical work will be required before the embodied technique Grotowski and his actors invented could be placed in the kind of synchronic and diachronic context that would allow it to warrant the title of "research" in a scholarly sense. Research may be the discovery of new knowledge, but in academia it also refers to the documentation of that knowledge in stable, transmissible form.

I have attempted to offer a framework for understanding how physical culture, performing arts, and everyday life are all structured by knowledge in the form of embodied technique. This should make it possible to design research projects in which (1) methodology is clear and outcomes are transmissible; and (2) research is undertaken through embodied practice. In other words, we should no longer have to choose between meaningful outcomes and practical or practice-based methods. If practice is to be research, the outcome of that practice cannot just be more practice. There must be new technique. How might academia support embodied research as I have defined it? What shape might be taken by projects, programs, and departments in embodied technique? Having worked for the past decade in the United States, I am writing now from a position that straddles the Atlantic, between the US and the UK. I also write after five years of participation in the "Performance as Research" Working Groups of the International Federation for Theatre Research and the American Society for Theatre Research. Thus far my discussion of embodied research in the university has been fairly general; now I will attempt to propose some concrete ways forward. In doing so, I will pause only briefly to consider the structure and content of PaR PhDs, before moving on to ask how more advanced (and potentially larger-scale) projects of embodied research could be framed in a university context.

If embodied research takes place in relation to existing fields of technique, then doctoral programs culminating in such research must begin by requiring the demonstration of competency in the relevant fields.

Professional artistic work may or may not suffice in this regard, depending on the nature of the research project. Interdisciplinary projects, for example, may require a candidate who is proficient in one discipline to achieve at least basic competency in another. Having done this, the researcher's task would then be to develop substantially new technique, either within a given field or at the intersection of two or more fields. The format of the resulting thesis or dissertation—written prose, audiovisual recordings, websites, etc.—would be determined by the need for documentation of this new technique. As such, it would be assessed neither by the standards of traditional scholarly outputs (which must take the form of written texts) nor within the paradigm of the performing arts (which demand public performances), but according to the criterion of knowledge production. The key to a successful project would be to frame it narrowly enough to be able to make an original contribution to an existing field of knowledge. This suggests a very different emphasis from the "open" interdisciplinarity that has been associated with PaR—one more similar, in fact, to the traditional narrowly focused design of a PhD thesis in other fields.[7] If defined in clear enough terms, such projects could make a substantial contribution to research culture in the performing arts—as well, perhaps, as physical culture and everyday life. However, the best way to conceptualize doctoral work in fields of embodied knowledge is to think of it in relation to more advanced research. In the space that remains, I want to mention two specific kinds of useful research projects in embodied technique. These could be concrete opportunities for doctoral theses, but also for more advanced projects.

The first type of project involves the production of scholarly editions of existing materials, rendering them accessible and standardizing their citation in the same way as editions of old and rare manuscripts. This is a crucial task in establishing a new field and would be very appropriate for researchers who wish to engage with the historical depth of the archive. The films of Krishnamacharya, Stanislavski, and Grotowski mentioned above would be fine starting points for building the archive of embodied technique. Leading the way in this direction, Paul Allain has recently produced a DVD of Grotowski and Cieslak's *The Constant Prince* (Grotowski 2005), with better quality video and English subtitles to allow more viewers to access the textual dimension of the performance. At present, there is nothing like a scholarly edition of Grotowski's films that can be reliably cited and cross-referenced. Such an archive would not only provide a firmer basis for the analysis of Grotowski's work, but could also be the basis for new research projects in related areas of technique. Bypassing the debate over what is or is not "Grotowskian" (see Chapter 3), the establishment of such an archive could help move the field of Grotowski studies towards more nuanced comparative analysis and begin to establish a more coherent framework with which to describe the contributions to knowledge that Grotowski made—as well as how they relate to those of Thomas Richards, Rena Mirecka, Włodzimierz Staniewski, the Performance Group, Judson Dance Theatre, and others. Of course, the Grotowski archive can only ever be fragmentary, because most of the work he led was not documented. Nevertheless, a scholarly edition of existing audiovisual materials could significantly alter the way Grotowski's work is understood in the present day.

Several recent publications from Routledge Press have experimented with the inclusion of multimedia documents as part of book publications. Włodzimierz Staniewski and Alison Hodge's *Hidden Territories: The Theatre of Gardzienice* (2004) includes a CD-ROM with a range of audiovideo materials: not just performance excerpts, but also documentary footage from Gardzienice's expeditions in the 1970s, as well as more recent demonstrations of training and rehearsal technique. In a recent article, I set out to analyze this particular multimedia document from a specifically epistemological perspective, treating it as an example of substantive research output from a sustained and innovative project in embodied technique (Spatz 2013). The DVD-ROM packaged with Phillip Zarrilli's *Psychophysical Acting* is an even more extensive multimedia resource, "featuring exercises, production documentation, interviews, and reflection" (Zarrilli 2009). Both discs were created by Peter Hulton. Other Routledge books offer "companion websites" with multimedia resources (Zarrilli *et al.* 2010; Graham and Hoggett 2009), while CDs and DVDs like MICHA (2007), Forsythe (2012), and Hodge (2013) should be considered analogous to monographs and cited as documents of embodied technique and research. At the same time, the technology of CDs and DVDs already seems outdated in comparison with the potential of much larger (and usually faster) online databases.[8]

Scholarly multimedia editions documenting Suzuki Training or Viewpoints could go a long way in framing and articulating the epistemic content of such practices, as well perhaps as helping us to move beyond the limiting notions of "styles" or "schools" of acting and towards a recognition of acting technique as a complex field of knowledge. In addition, we might want to revisit the countless works of ethnographic documentation that stand as testaments to the knowledge of embodied technique that structures dance, song, and ritual worldwide. While I would not wish to collapse the distinction between theatre and ritual— insofar as it may be culturally and historically grounded—there is every reason to examine theatre and dance performance documentation alongside documents of "folk" and "ritual" practice, as we lay groundwork for embodied technique as a scholarly field. Alan Lomax's work on "cantometrics" and "choreometrics" is a valuable precursor to this project, though unfortunately limited by its structuralist assumptions (Lomax 1968). In any case, the development of multimedia archives along these lines should allow us to ask, and begin to answer, the kinds of questions that have been at the heart of this book: What are the similarities and differences, at the level of technique, between Grotowski's work with Cieslak and the current work of Thomas Richards; between the Haitian *yanvalou* as practiced by the Workcenter and in Haiti; between Zarrilli's "bodymind" training and that of Suzuki or Barba; between these pedagogies of "actor training" and the work of the Michael Chekhov Association and other such professional and pedagogical networks; between Viewpoints training at SITI Company in New York City and at Naropa University in Boulder, Colorado; between athletic and somatic schools of postural yoga; or between physical training for performance and for martial arts? In short: *What can a body do?*

The publication of scholarly editions of existing multimedia documents could set the stage for the framing and realization of new embodied research projects. This is the second of my proposed routes forward in the implementation of embodied research within academia. If they are to attain scholarly rigor, such projects must be framed by an epistemic context that is both synchronic and diachronic. This context can surely include the vast archive of writing, but if the work itself unfolds through embodied practice, rather than through spectatorship and conversation, then it is likely that a multimedia document contextualized with respect to a multimedia archive will be more relevant. Nelson's idea of a "practice review"—alongside or in place of a literature review—is exactly what is needed to establish the epistemic frame of such projects (2013: 34–35). Although Nelson rejects a "more traditional model of research"—"progressive" and "incremental"—in which "the aim is to add another small stone to the cairn built up over the years," he acknowledges: "Other practitioners will undoubtedly be working in territory similar" to that of the researcher (99). It is therefore "perfectly possible, and indeed necessary, in PaR to sketch the intellectual and practical context in which your work will be undertaken." I find it curious that Nelson's idea of the practice review emphasizes synchronic over diachronic contexts; I can think of no reason why this should be so. Instead, I would advocate for practice reviews in embodied research to engage as fully as possible with the diachronic and synchronic archives of the relevant fields. This would require a review of related technique as it has been discovered and practiced in other contexts, with as great a geographical and historical scope as possible. Generally speaking—and as in other fields—the greater the synchronic and dia-chronic scope of the practices reviewed, the more likely the research is to make a genuinely new contribution to knowledge.

Many questions attend the notion of a "multimedia document" of new embodied technique. How should it be formatted in order to most effectively convey the epistemic content of the documented practice? How should such documents locate themselves with respect to the archive of existing works? How can they cite previously published multimedia documents—and make themselves available, in turn, for citation? How might the digital grammar of slow motion, montage, split-screen, and multiangle recording contribute to our understanding of the epistemic structure of embodied technique?[9] Some artists and practitioners may object that the approach outlined here does not recognize the basis of their work in direct presence and nontransmissible encounter. This is certainly Kris Salata's take on the Workcenter's practice; and as Kershaw notes, "there was always a powerful undertow running through the community of researchers in the UK and elsewhere that was extremely wary of *any* kind of documentation" (in Smith and Dean 2009: 120). Indeed, the embodied researcher I envision is not freed from the academic requirement to produce a stable, circulating docu-ment, but is simply enabled to work in a different medium. For some, the need to produce a stable document of any kind may pose an unac-ceptable burden. To reiterate, then: I am not suggesting that embodied research be moved entirely into the academy. This is not possible and would be unfortunate. I am simply pointing out that embodied research has always needed, and will always need, some kind of sponsorship—whether it be royal, public, or commercial. Unlike the Indian state that supported Krishnamacharya, the Soviet regimes that supported Sta-nislavski and Grotowski, the capitalist marketplace that currently supports yoga and martial arts worldwide, or the medical industry that has begun to support some kinds of somatic bodywork, the university—ideally—values knowledge for its depth rather than its use value. It prioritizes the discovery of what is genuinely unknown over the mass production of what works. By engaging with academia and confronting its particular demands, researchers in embodied technique might find a new independence from the social institutions that have housed their work in the past, as well as a new way of understanding and articulating what it is they do.

The fourth division

Personally, I do not find it stifling or limiting to conceive of the (embo-died) researcher as one who organizes embodied practice around the goal of producing (multimedia) documents. I am eager to imagine how one might plan a complex, multiyear project of workshops, classes, training sessions, rehearsals, informal showings, and performances, if all of this were framed from the beginning as a multimedia book project. The final research outcome of such a project could perhaps take a form like that of Zarrilli's *Psychophysical Acting*—a book with DVD—or its next generation online equivalent. However, in this case, the goal of producing a stable archival document would be an organizing principle from the start—as in any other academic discipline. Rather than stifling creativity, I wonder what new possibilities and freedoms for the practitioner could be opened up by framing ongoing embodied practice as research in this sense. I certainly do not think that artists and practitioners should look to academia merely with a strategic eye on funding and material support. Instead, the entry of embodied research into academia should be seen as replacing one set of demands and constraints with another. Such an embodied researcher would be freed of the requirement to produce public spectacles, as theatre artists must do, or marketable classes, as yoga teachers must do. In place of these demands, academia would substitute its own: to produce a stable and citable document, in whatever format, that contributes new knowledge to the existing archive of a field. This epistemic requirement is distinct from those posed by the demands of artistic production and capitalist pedagogy, although it is not necessarily more or less difficult to meet. Most likely, some practitioners will recognize in themselves the call to be researchers in this sense—in addition to or instead of artists and teachers—while others will find this challenge unrewarding.

It may even be possible to call for an academic "division" of embodied research that would extend beyond the performing arts to include all areas of embodied practice—all the *techne* or technique(s) of embodiment. Such a division would require its own disciplinary formations and methodologies, allowing it to produce multimedia monographs and other documents of embodied research. It would draw upon, but also push back against, the commercial infrastructure of embodied practice as developed by privately run yoga, martial arts, acting, and dance studios and their associated national and international professional associations. While according long overdue respect to the embodied knowledge that structures such practices, the epistemology of embodied research would require more synchronic and diachronic rigor and transparency in their naming and assessment. As a top-level domain within the epistemological map of the university, the "fourth division" of embodied technique—alongside the sciences, social sciences, and humanities—might finally allow for the kind of substantive interdisciplinary and transdisciplinary interactions between performing, healing, martial, and ritual arts that performance studies theorizes and makes thinkable but cannot practically accomplish.

To increase the epistemic—and perhaps also demographic—diversity of academia is a stated goal for Practice as Research (Nelson 2013: 114). However, it appears that PaR, at least as it has developed in the UK, has mostly paved the way for conceptual and experimental performing artists to enter academia. The notion of embodied research proposed here would open the door to a much wider and more radically diverse range of practitioners. It is fairly easy to see how these ideas could be extended beyond performing arts to the domain of physical culture. Collaborative endeavors between universities and the many independent organizations that already offer teacher training and credentials in yoga, martial arts, and somatic bodywork could foster the growth of a more historically aware and epistemologically rigorous—but no less thoroughly embodied or well-trained—research culture in these areas. Set apart from the marketplace, where "schools" of practice compete through the cultivation of public images, such an epistemically oriented context could create a space in which comparative analysis and embodied expertise would hold more sway. It is more difficult to apply the ideas offered here to research in everyday life, not because this is any less structured by technique, but because the ethics of experimentation become delicate and risky when the researcher's own identity is at stake. What kind of research in gender technique could legitimately take place within a university context? Certainly, such research could not follow the model of scientific or sociological research, with a disinterested researcher experimenting with or upon the gender of hapless subjects. Rather, we might ask how communities that are already developing alternative gender technique could be supported by academia in exchange for their epistemic service to the public.

At a time when some are questioning the need for education and research in long-established areas of academia, like philosophy and theatre, it might be worth risking boldness by not only defending these venerable disciplines, but also calling for an expansion of our epistemological commitment to include other vitally important and historically neglected areas of transmissible knowledge. Beyond the politics of this or the next election cycle, research and education will have a tremendous influence upon the kind of world we live in. Alongside countless informal pedagogies, the availability and contents of formal education, from kindergarten through graduate school, profoundly affects the organization of society. In this sense, as I have suggested, knowledge is politics in the long term. There is no doubt that universities can be aligned with the most repressive regimes of power. Today, the "global university" may share with neoliberalism the fantasy of a complete "freedom from responsibility," as Tom Looser warns (2012: 99). One cannot then accept the value of the university uncritically. On the other hand, as Looser makes clear, the most dangerous university is one behind which there is no fundamentally epistemic project (105). Our historical moment is not one in which we can afford to abandon the legacy of the university. For that reason, I have moved in this chapter from a broad vision of how and why embodied research might find a home for itself within academia—and how such support would differ from the state and market support that enabled the projects described in previous chapters—towards concrete proposals for implementing embodied research in the university. It may be hard to imagine this kind of research finding institutional support in the present cultural climate, but the living heritage of embodied knowledge—and our future as embodied creatures—demands nothing less.

Notes

1 These articles and columns have names like: "The Neoliberal Plan for Higher Education" (Cersonsky 2012); "Learning as Freedom" (Roth 2012); "How to Defend Universities" (Seabright 2012); "What is College For?" (Gutting 2011); "Our Universities: Why Are They Failing?" (Grafton 2011); "Public Education for the Public Good" (Newfield 2011); and "A Faustian Bargain" (Petsko 2010)—to name just a few. The most chilling description of the current crisis is provided by Howard Hotson, who suggests that it is merely part of a larger historical narrative in which the private corporation—designed by Europe in the early modern period to extract profit from global empire—is now "returning home to colonize us" (2012). Hotson's lecture is worth listening to in full, to understand the extent to which business priorities have already arrived at the "heart of the system," at least in the UK. For an illustration of how the landscape of higher education is changing in the US, see Rosenthal and Schnee's critique of the development process for a new community college in the City University of New York (2013).
2 For the early integration of actor training into academia, see McTeague 1993. For related tensions in university dance departments, see the introduction to Foster 2009. Grotowski points to the missed opportunity for extended laboratory work in US universities in one of his last texts (1995: 117–18). Richard Schechner makes the same observation even more pointedly: "[W]hat kind of experimental or laboratory work is actually being done at universities? The facilities are there, the money though not unlimited is certainly there, but mostly, in the USA at least, professors see their role as teachers of theatre history or trainers of persons for places in today's theatre. Very little is being done to advance the kind of experimental laboratory work comparable either to what goes on in the sciences or what was done by Stanislavski,

Meyerhold or Grotowski. The universities host or control enormous material and human resources. Why have we not critically examined their work and the possibilities, or failures, of the universities as sites of theatre laboratories?" (in Schino 2009: 202).

3 Grotowski's Objective Drama program at the University of California is an exception that proves the rule: a rare and short-lived moment in which academia explicitly supported pure "blue skies" research in embodied technique.

4 Current opinion on the validity and long-term significance of PaR differs radically between regions. Writing in a UK context, John Freeman worries that his "half-cautions" and partial critiques of PaR amount to "swimming against an overwhelmingly strong tide" of its acceptance and celebration (2010: 283). Yet I found myself swimming against the opposite tide—an intense, institutionalized skepticism towards PaR—in the US, when I first began to formulate this book project as a doctoral thesis at the CUNY Graduate Center.

5 One exception is Arthur J. Sabatini, who writes of the need to "re-examine and historicize research by artists outside of academia and relate or adapt it to existing discourses and approaches to research ... in the university" (in Riley and Hunter 2009: 118). It may be that, as a result of their different developmental histories, perspectives on PaR from the United States and Canada will pay greater attention to the need for historical contextualization, as seems to be the case for some articles in a recent special issue of *Theatre Topics* (Peck 2013).

6 There is an unfortunate typographical error in Nelson's printed diagram, but it seems clear that the circle on the bottom right should be labeled "know-that" (2013: 37). For more on this typology of knowledge, see my note 9 on post-Rylean philosophical debates in Chapter 1.

7 In the US, the MFA degree exists as a terminal qualification in performing arts. The key difference between an MFA and a PhD (or DFA) in embodied research, as I see it, is that the latter would not aim to create a single, complex, artistically successful event, as in the conventional MFA thesis production. Rather, a doctoral project in the performing arts should entail the thorough and systematic exploration of a clearly framed area of technique, culminating in the documentation of new technique. This would most likely take proportionally longer to accomplish than an MFA—again, more like a doctoral dissertation than a masters thesis.

8 I will just mention a few points on the vast and unmapped landscape of online video databases, arranged roughly in order from the vast and uncurated to the bespoke: *YouTube* <youtube.com>; *Vimeo* <vimeo.com>; *Digital Theatre Plus* <www.digitaltheatreplus.com>; *AusStage* <www.ausstage.edu.au>; University of Bristol Theatre Collection <www.bris.ac.uk/theatrecollection>; *Faculti* <facultimedia.com>; *Ethnographic Video for Instruction and Analysis* <eviada.org>; *YogaGlo* <www.yogaglo.com>; *Performance Parkour* <www.2pknetwork.com>; *Studio West* <www.studiowest.org>; *Odin Teatret Archives* <www.odinteatretarchives.com>; *Journal for Artistic Research* <jar-online.net>; *Routledge Performance Archive* <www.routledgeperformancearchive.com>; *Video Journal of Performance* <videojournalperformance.com>; *CTR Interventions* <www.contemporarytheatrereview.org/interventions>. We have scarcely begun to imagine the kinds of mappings needed to navigate this complex archive and render its knowledge content accessible to scholars and practitioners in diverse fields.

9 Video artist Bill Viola's radically slowed-down recordings of basic interactions are not usually thought of in terms of acting and performance technique. However, in *The Quintet of the Astonished* (1998), Viola worked with actors rather than untrained individuals. Although he was "less interested in a dramatic portrayal of the emotions per se than in the transitions from one emotion to the next," Viola nevertheless "gave his actors two sets of instructions: they could either 'work from the outside in,' as in the technique analyzed by movement theorist Paul Ekman, 'or from the inside out,' as in Method acting" (Noland 2009: 67–69). The resulting video may therefore be worth considering as documentation of embodied technique. What details of acting technique become visible when 1 minute of practice is expanded to 16 minutes of video footage?

BIBLIOGRAPHY

Abhyasa Yoga Center (2013) Abhyasa Yoga Center website. <www.abhyasayoga center.com>, accessed 9/7/13.

Adams, Rachel, and David Savran, eds. (2002) *The Masculinity Studies Reader*. Oxford: Blackwell Publishers.

Addison, Heather (2003) *Hollywood and the Rise of Physical Culture*. New York: Routledge.

Ahmed, Sara (2006) *Queer Phenomenology: Orientations, Objects, Others*. Durham, NC: Duke University Press.

Albright, Ann Cooper (2011) "Situated Dancing: Notes from Three Decades in Contact with Phenomenology." *Dance Research Journal* 43.2: 7–18.

Alcoff, Linda (1988) "Cultural Feminism versus Post-structuralism: The Identity Crisis in Feminist Theory." *Signs* 13.3: 405–36.

Alcoff, Linda, and Elizabeth Potter (1993) *Feminist Epistemologies*. New York: Routledge.

Allain, Paul, ed. (2009) *Grotowski's Empty Room*. New York: Seagull Books.

Allegranti, Beatrice (2011) *Embodied Performances: Sexuality, Gender, Bodies*. New York: Palgrave Macmillan.

Allegue, Ludivine, Simon Jones, Baz Kershaw, and Angela Piccini, eds. (2009) *Practice-as-Research in Performance and Screen*. New York: Palgrave Macmillan.

Allen, Louisa, ed. (2011) *Young People and Sexuality Education: Rethinking Key Debates*. New York: Palgrave Macmillan.

Alter, Joseph (2007) "Yoga and Physical Education: Swami Kuvalayananda's Nationalist Project." *Asian Medicine* 3: 20–36.

Anderson, Patrick (2010) *So Much Wasted: Hunger, Performance, and the Morbidity of Resistance*. Durham, NC: Duke University Press.

Aristotle (1999) *Nicomachean Ethics*. Translated by Terence Irwin. Indianapolis: Hackett Publishing Company.

Armstrong, Sara K. (2012) Review of Richard Tinning's *Pedagogy and Human Movement: Theory, Practice, Research*. *Theatre Topics* 22.1: 104–5.

Arnold, John H., and Sean Brady (2011) *What Is Masculinity? Historical Dynamics from Antiquity to the Contemporary World*. New York: Palgrave Macmillan.

Asad, Talal (2011) "Thinking about the Secular Body, Pain, and Liberal Politics." *Cultural Anthropology* 26.4: 657–75.

Ashtanga Yoga Shala (2013) Ashtanga Yoga Shala website. <www.aysnyc.org>, accessed 4/7/13.

Auslander, Philip (1999) *Liveness: Performance in a Mediatized Culture.* New York: Routledge.

Bailey, Marlon M. (2011) "Gender/Racial Realness: Theorizing the Gender System in Ballroom Culture." *Feminist Studies* 37.2: 365–86.

——(2013) *Butch Queens Up in Pumps: Gender, Performance, and Ballroom Culture in Detroit.* Ann Arbor: University of Michigan Press.

——(2014) "Engendering Space: Ballroom Culture and the Spatial Practice of Possibility in Detroit." *Gender, Place & Culture: A Journal of Feminist Geography* 21.4: 489–507.

Baldwin, James (1972) *No Name in the Street.* New York: Vintage.

Bales, Melanie, and Rebecca Nettl-Fiol, eds. (2008) *The Body Eclectic: Evolving Practices in Dance Training.* Chicago: University of Illinois Press.

Banks, Daniel (2013) "The Welcome Table: Casting for an Integrated Society." *Theatre Topics* 23.1: 1–18.

Barba, Eugenio (1972) "Words or Presence." *TDR* 16.1: 47–54.

——(1988) "Eugenio Barba to Phillip Zarrilli: About the Visible and the Invisible in the Theatre and about ISTA in Particular." *TDR* 32.3: 7–14.

——(1995) *The Paper Canoe: A Guide to Theatre Anthropology.* New York: Routledge.

Barba, Eugenio, and Nicola Savarese (1991) *A Dictionary of Theatre Anthropology: The Secret Art of the Performer.* New York: Routledge.

Barker, Meg, and Darren Langdridge (2010) *Understanding Non-Monogamies.* New York: Routledge.

Barker, Sarah A. (2002) "The Alexander Technique: An Acting Approach." *Theatre Topics* 12.1: 35–48.

Barnett, Ronald, ed. (2012) *The Future University.* New York: Routledge.

——(2013) *Imagining the University.* New York: Routledge.

Barrett, Estelle, and Barbara Bolt, eds. (2007) *Practice as Research: Context, Method, Knowledge.* New York: I. B. Tauris.

Barrett, William (1978) *The Illusion of Technique.* New York: Anchor Books.

Barthes, Roland (1989) *Sade, Fourier, Loyola.* Berkeley: University of California Press.

Bartow, Arthur, ed. (2006) *Training of the American Actor.* New York: Theatre Communications Group.

Bauer, J. Edgar (2012) "Darwin, Marañón, Hirschfeld: Sexology and the Reassessment of Evolution Theory as a Non-Essentialist Naturalism." In *(Dis)Entangling Darwin: Cross-disciplinary Reflections on the Man and His Legacy,* ed. Sara Graça da Silva, Fátima Vieira, and Jorge Bastos da Silva, 85–102. Newcastle: Cambridge Scholars Publishing.

Bauer, Robin (2007) "Playgrounds and New Territories: The Potential of BDSM Practices to Queer Genders." In *Safe, Sane, and Consensual: Contemporary*

Perspectives on Sadomasochism, ed. Darren Langdridge and Meg Barker. New York: Palgrave Macmillan.

——(2008) "Transgressive and Transformative Gendered Sexual Practices and White Privileges: The Case of the Dyke/Trans BDSM Communities." *WSQ* 36.3–4: 233–53.

Baumrin, Seth (2009) "Ketmanship in Opole: Jerzy Grotowski and the Price of Artistic Freedom." *TDR* 53.4: 49–77.

BBC (2014) "India court recognises transgender people as third gender." *BBC*, April 15. <www.bbc.co.uk/news/world-asia-india-27031180>, accessed 6/11/14.

Beauvoir, Simone de (1953) *The Second Sex*. London: Jonathan Cape.

Beck, Sara (2012) "Uniting body and mind, with a bit of a stretch." *New York Times*, March 1.

Bell, Catherine, ed. (2007) *Teaching Ritual*. Oxford: Oxford University Press.

——(2009) *Ritual: Perspectives and Dimensions*. Oxford: Oxford University Press. Orig. publ. 1997.

Bell, David (2006) *Science, Technology and Culture*. New York: Open University Press.

Bengson, John, and Marc A. Moffett, eds. (2011) *Knowing How: Essays on Knowledge, Mind, and Action*. New York: Oxford University Press.

Benjamin, Walter (1999) "The Work of Art in the Age of Mechanical Reproduction." In *Illuminations*. London: Random House. Orig. publ. 1936.

Bharucha, Rustom (1993) "Goodbye Grotowski." In *Theatre and the World: Performance and the Politics of Culture*, 43–54. London: Routledge.

Bhaskar, Roy, Cheryl Frank, Karl Georg Høyer, Petter Næss, and Jenneth Parker (2010) *Interdisciplinarity and Climate Change: Transforming Knowledge and Practice for Our Global Future*. New York: Routledge.

Biagini, Mario (2008) "Meeting at La Sapienza." *TDR* 52.2: 150–77.

Biggs, Michael, and Henrik Karlsson, eds. (2011) *The Routledge Companion to Research in the Arts*. New York: Routledge.

Bikram Yoga (2012) Bikram Yoga website. <bikramyoga.com>, accessed 12/10/12.

Black, Daniel (2014) "Where Bodies End and Artefacts Begin: Tools, Machines and Interfaces." *Body & Society* 20.1: 31–60.

Blair, Rhonda (1992) "Liberating the Young Actor: Feminist Pedagogy and Performance." *Theatre Topics* 2: 13–23.

——(2008) *The Actor, Image, and Action: Acting and Cognitive Neuroscience*. New York: Routledge.

Blau, Herbert (1983) "Universals of Performance: Or, Amortizing Play." *SubStance* 37/38: 140–61.

Böhler, Arno, Krassimira Kruschkova, and Susanne Valerie (2014) *Wissen wir, was ein Körper vermag? Rhizomatische Körper in Religion, Kunst, Philosophie*. Bielefeld: Transcript Verlag.

Boisvert, Raymond D. (2008) "The Will to Power Versus the Will to Prayer: William Barrett's *The Illusion of Technique* Thirty Years Later." *Journal of Speculative Philosophy* 22.1: 24–32.

Bokwa Fitness (2012) Bokwa Fitness website. <bokwafitness.com>, accessed 12/10/12.

Bornstein, Kate (1994) *Gender Outlaw: On Men, Women, and the Rest of Us.* New York: Routledge.

Bornstein, Kate, and S. Bear Bergman (2010) *Gender Outlaws: The Next Generation.* Berkeley: Seal Press.

Boston, Jane, and Rena Cook, eds. (2009) *Breath in Action: The Art of Breath in Vocal and Holistic Practice.* London and Philadelphia: Jessica Kingsley Publishers.

Bourdieu, Pierre (1990) *The Logic of Practice.* Oxford: Blackwell Publishers. Orig. publ. 1980.

——(2001) *Masculine Domination.* Stanford: Stanford University Press. Orig. publ. 1998.

Bourdieu, Pierre, and Loïc J. D. Wacquant (1992) *An Invitation to Reflexive Sociology.* Chicago: University of Chicago Press.

Broad, William (2012) *The Science of Yoga: The Risks and the Rewards.* New York: Simon & Schuster.

Broadhurst, Susan, and Josephine Machon (2012) *Identity, Performance and Technology: Practices of Empowerment, Embodiment and Technicity.* New York: Palgrave Macmillan.

Brook, Peter (1968) *The Empty Space.* New York: Macmillan Publishing.

——(2009) *With Grotowski: Theatre Is Just a Form.* Edited by Georges Banu and Grzegorz Ziolkowski with Paul Allain. Wrocław: The Grotowski Institute.

Brown, Bryan (2013) "Tracing the Laboratory Line: The Phenomenon of the Theatre Laboratory and Its Manifestations in Russia." PhD diss., University of Leeds.

Brown, Wendy (2013) "Reclaiming Democracy: An Interview with Wendy Brown on Occupy, Sovereignty, and Secularism." *Critical Legal Thinking* blog, January 30. <criticallegalthinking.com/2013/01/30/reclaiming-democracy-an-interview-with-wendy-brown-on-occupy-sovereignty-and-secularism>, accessed 9/24/13.

Brownmiller, Susan (1975) *Against Our Will: Men, Women, and Rape.* New York: Simon & Schuster.

Burrows, Jonathan (2010) *A Choreographer's Handbook.* New York: Routledge.

Burt, Ramsay (2006) *Judson Dance Theater: Performative Traces.* New York: Routledge.

Butler, Judith (1988) "Performative Acts and Gender Constitution: An Essay in Phenomenology and Feminist Theory." *Theatre Journal* 40.4: 519–31.

——(1989) "Foucault and the Paradox of Bodily Inscriptions." *Journal of Philosophy* 86.11: 601–7.

——(1990) *Gender Trouble.* New York: Routledge.

——(1993a) *Bodies That Matter: On the Discursive Limits of "Sex."* New York: Routledge.

——(1993b) "Critically Queer." *Gay and Lesbian Quarterly* 1: 17–32.

——(2004) *Undoing Gender.* New York: Routledge.

Campo, Giuliano, and Zygmunt Molik (2010) *Zygmunt Molik's Voice and Body Work: The Legacy of Jerzy Grotowski*. New York: Routledge.

Canguilhem, Georges (2008) "Health: Crude Concept and Philosophical Question." *Public Culture* 20.3: 467–77.

Canning, Charlotte (2013) "Editorial: Performance and the Everyday." *Theatre Research International* 38.3: 179–80.

Carlson, Marvin (2011) "Inheriting the Wind: A Personal View of the Current Crisis in Theatre Higher Education in New York." *Theatre Survey* 52.1: 117–23.

Carnicke, Sharon Marie (1998) *Stanislavsky in Focus*. New York: Routledge.

Case, Sue-Ellen (2008 [1988]) *Feminism and Theatre*. New York: Palgrave Macmillan.

Casey, Edward S. (1987) *Remembering: A Phenomenological Study*. Indianapolis: Indiana University Press.

CBC (2014) "Della Wolf is B.C.'s 1st child with 3 parents on birth certificate." *CBC News*, British Columbia, February 6. <www.cbc.ca/news/canada/british-columbia/della-wolf-is-b-c-s-1st-child-with-3-parents-on-birth-certificate-1.252 6584>, accessed 6/11/14.

Center for Performance Research, NYC (2012) Center for Performance Research, NYC, website. <cprnyc.org>, accessed 12/11/12.

Centre for Performance Research, Wales (2012) Centre for Performance Research, Wales, website. <www.thecpr.org.uk>, accessed 12/11/12.

Cerankowski, Karli June, and Megan Milks (2014) *Asexualities: Feminist and Queer Perspectives*. New York: Routledge.

Cersonsky, James (2012) "The neoliberal plan for higher education." *In These Times*, September 26.

Certeau, Michel de (1984) *The Practice of Everyday Life*. Berkeley, CA: University of California Press. Orig. publ. 1980.

Certeau, Michel de, Luce Giard, and Pierre Mayol (1998) *The Practice of Everyday Life, Volume Two: Living and Cooking*. Minneapolis: University of Minnesota Press.

Cetina, Karin Knorr [Karin D. Knorr] (1979) "Tinkering toward Success: Prelude to a Theory of Scientific Practice." *Theory and Society* 8.3: 347–76.

——[Karin D. Knorr-Cetina] (1981) *The Manufacture of Knowledge: An Essay on the Constructivist and Contextual Nature of Science*. New York: Pergamon Press.

——(1992) "The Couch, the Cathedral, and the Laboratory: On the Relationship between Experiment and Laboratory in Science." In *Science as Practice and Culture*, ed. Andrew Pickering, 113–38. Chicago: University of Chicago Press.

——(1999) *Epistemic Cultures: How the Sciences Make Knowledge*. Cambridge: Harvard University Press.

——(2007) "Culture in Global Knowledge Societies: Knowledge Cultures and Epistemic Cultures." *Interdisciplinary Science Reviews* 32.4: 361–75.

Connerton, Paul (1989) *How Societies Remember*. New York: Cambridge University Press.

Coole, Diana, and Samantha Frost (2010) *New Materialisms: Ontology, Agency, and Politics*. Durham, NC: Duke University Press.

Coulter, H. David (2001) *Anatomy of Hatha Yoga: A Manual for Students, Teachers, and Practitioners*. Honesdale, PA: Body and Breath.

Crease, Robert P., and John Lutterbie (2006) "Technique." In *Staging Philosophy: Intersections of Theatre, Performance, and Philosophy*, ed. David Krasner and David Z. Saltz, 160–79. Ann Arbor: University of Michigan Press.

Crossley, Nick (2004) "Ritual, Body Technique, and (Inter)subjectivity." In *Thinking through Rituals*, ed. Kevin Schilbrack, 31–51. New York: Routledge.

——(2006) *Reflexive Embodiment in Contemporary Society*. New York: Open University Press.

——(2007) "Researching Embodiment by Way of 'Body Techniques.'" *Sociological Review* 55.s1: 80–94.

Csapo, Eric, and William J. Slater (1995) *The Context of Ancient Drama*. Ann Arbor: University of Michigan Press.

Csordas, Thomas (2004) "Health and the Holy in the Afro-Brazilian Candomblé." In *Cultural Bodies*, ed. Helen Thomas and Jamilah Ahmed, 241–59. Oxford: Blackwell Press.

Daily Mail Reporter (2011) "Are these the most PC parents in the world? The couple raising a 'genderless baby' … to protect his (or her) right to choice." *Daily Mail*, May 24. <www.dailymail.co.uk/news/article-1389593/Kathy-Witterick-David-Stocker-raising-genderless-baby.html>, accessed 12/06/12.

Damasio, Antonio (1994) *Descartes' Error: Emotion, Reason, and the Human Brain*. New York: Penguin Putnam.

Daniel, Yvonne (2005) *Dancing Wisdom: Embodied Knowledge in Haitian Vodou, Cuban Yoruba, and Bahian Candomblé*. Chicago: University of Illinois Press.

De Landa, Manuel (1991) *War in the Age of Intelligent Machines*. New York: Zone Books.

De Michelis, Elizabeth (1995) "Some Comments on the Contemporary Practice of Yoga in the UK, with Particular Reference to British *Hatha Yoga* Schools." *Journal of Contemporary Religion* 10.3: 243–55.

——(2005) *History of Modern Yoga: Patanjali and Western Esotericism*. London and New York: Continuum Books.

DeFrantz, Thomas F. (2004) *Dancing Revelations: Alvin Ailey's Embodiment of African American Culture*. Oxford: Oxford University Press.

Deleuze, Gilles (1990) *Expressionism in Philosophy: Spinoza*. New York: Zone Books.

Deleuze, Gilles, and Félix Guattari (1987) *A Thousand Plateaus*. Minneapolis: University of Minnesota Press.

Depraz, Natalie, Francisco J. Varela, and Pierre Vermersch (2003) *On Becoming Aware: A Pragmatics of Experiencing*. Philadelphia: John Benjamins Publishing.

Desikachar, Kausthub (2005) *The Yoga of the Yogi: The Legacy of T. Krishnamacharya*. New York: North Point Press.

Dolan, Jill (2001) *Geographies of Learning: Theory and Practice, Activism and Performance*. Middletown, CT: Wesleyan University Press.

——(2005) *Utopia in Performance: Finding Hope at the Theater*. Ann Arbor: University of Michigan Press.

Dunne, Joseph (1992) *Back to the Rough Ground: Practical Judgment and the Lure of Technique*. Notre Dame, IN: University of Notre Dame Press.

Dworkin, Andrea (1987) *Intercourse*. New York: Basic Books.

East Yoga (2013) *East Yoga: A Vinyasa Yoga Studio*. Website. <eastyoga.com>, accessed 4/7/13.

Eddy, Martha (2009) "A Brief History of Somatic Practices and Dance: Historical Development of the Field of Somatic Education and Its Relationship to Dance." *Journal of Dance & Somatic Practices* 1: 5–27.

Elliot, Patricia (2010) *Debates in Transgender, Queer, and Feminist Theory: Contested Sites*. Burlington, VT: Ashgate.

Evans, John, Brian Davies, and Jan Wright, eds. (2004) *Body Knowledge and Control: Studies in the Sociology of Education and Physical Culture*. New York: Routledge.

Evans, Mark (2008) *Movement Training for the Modern Actor*. New York: Routledge.

Evans, Mark, and Simon Murray (2012) "Editorial." *Theatre, Dance, and Performer Training* 3.2: 141–44.

Farrer, D. S., and John Whalen-Bridge, eds. (2011) *Martial Arts as Embodied Knowledge: Asian Traditions in a Transnational World*. Albany: State University of New York Press.

Fausto-Sterling, Anne (1993) "The five sexes: Why male and female are not enough." *The Sciences*, March/April, 20–24.

——(2000) *Sexing the Body*. New York: Basic Books.

Feinberg, Leslie (1998) *Trans Liberation: Beyond Pink or Blue*. Boston: Beacon Press.

Fischer-Lichte, Erika (2008) *The Transformative Power of Performance*. New York: Routledge.

Fitzmaurice Voicework (2014) *Fitzmaurice Voicework*. Website. <fitzmauricevoice.com>, accessed 5/28/14.

Fleishman, Mark (2012) "The Difference of Performance as Research." *Theatre Research International* 37.1: 28–37.

Forsythe, William (2012) *Improvisation Technologies: A Tool for the Analytical Dance Eye*. Berlin: Hatje Cantz Verlag.

Foster, Susan Leigh (1986) *Reading Dancing: Bodies and Subjects in Contemporary American Dance*. Berkeley: University of California Press.

——, ed. (1995) *Choreographing History*. Bloomington: Indiana University Press.

——, ed. (2009) *Worlding Dance*. New York: Palgrave Macmillan.

Foucault, Michel (1988) "Technologies of the Self." In *Technologies of the Self: A Seminar with Michel Foucault*, ed. Luther H. Martin, Huck Gutman, and Patrick H. Hutton, 16–49. Amherst: University of Massachusetts Press.

——(1995) *Discipline and Punish: The Birth of the Prison*. New York: Vintage Press. Orig. publ. 1975.

Frank, Adam D. (2006) *Taijiquan and the Search for the Little Old Chinese Man: Understanding Identity through Martial Arts*. New York: Palgrave Macmillan.

Frank, David John, and Jay Gabler (2006) *Reconstructing the University: Worldwide Shifts in Academia in the 20th Century.* Stanford: Stanford University Press.

Frankiel, Tamar (2001) "Prospects in Ritual Studies." *Religion* 31: 75–87.

Freeman, John (2010) *Blood, Sweat & Theory: Research through Practice in Performance.* Faringdon, Oxon: Libri Publishing.

Galison, Peter, and David J. Stump (1996) *The Disunity of Science: Boundaries, Contexts, and Power.* Stanford: Stanford University Press.

Gardiner, Judith Kegan, ed. (2002) *Masculinity Studies and Feminist Theory.* New York: Columbia University Press.

Gehm, Sabine, Pirkko Huseman, and Katharina von Wilcke, eds. (2007) *Knowledge in Motion: Perspectives of Artistic and Scientific Research in Dance.* New Brunswick and London: Transaction Publishers.

George, Laura (2007) "'The *Technique* of Ordinary Poetry': Coleridgean Notes toward a Genealogy of *Technique.*" *European Romantic Review* 18.2: 195–203.

Germon, Jennifer (2009) *Gender: A Genealogy of an Idea.* New York: Palgrave Macmillan.

Gibson, James J. (1986) *The Ecological Approach to Visual Perception.* Hillsdale, NJ: Lawrence Erlbaum Associates.

Glassner, Barry (1989) "Fitness and the Postmodern Self." *Journal of Health and Social Behavior* 30.2: 180–91.

Gleick, James (1987) *Chaos: Making a New Science.* New York: Penguin Books.

Goffman, Erving (1977) "The Arrangement between the Sexes." *Theory and Society* 4.3: 301–31.

Golding, Sue (1997) *The Eight Technologies of Otherness.* New York: Routledge.

Goldman, Alvin I. (2010) "Why Social Epistemology Is *Real* Epistemology." In *Social Epistemology,* ed. Adrian Haddock, Alan Millar, and Duncan Pritchard, 1–28. Oxford: Oxford University Press.

Gonzalez-Arnal, Stella, Gill Jagger, and Kathleen Lennon (2012) *Embodied Selves.* New York: Palgrave Macmillan.

Goodall, Jane (2008) *Stage Presence.* London and New York: Routledge.

Gordon, Mel (2010) *Stanislavsky in America: An Actor's Workbook.* New York: Routledge.

Gough, Richard, and Simon Shepherd, eds. (2009) *Performance Research: On Training* 14.2.

Grafton, Anthony (2011) "Our universities: Why are they failing?" *New York Review of Books,* November 24.

Graham, Scott, and Steven Hoggett (2009) *The Frantic Assembly Book of Devising Theatre.* New York: Routledge.

Grant, Susan (2013) *Physical Culture and Sport in Soviet Society: Propaganda, Acculturation, and Transformation in the 1920s and 1930s.* New York: Routledge.

Green, Thomas A., and Joseph R. Svinth, eds. (2003) *Martial Arts in the Modern World.* Westport, CT: Praeger Publishers, Greenwood Publishing Group.

Gregg, Melissa, and Gregory J. Seigworth (2010) *The Affect Theory Reader.* Durham, NC: Duke University Press.

Gronow, Jukka (2009) "Fads, Fashions, and 'Real' Innovations: Novelties and Social Change." In *Time, Consumption and Everyday Life: Practice, Materiality and Culture*, ed. Elizabeth Shove, Frank Trentmann, and Richard Wilk, 129–42. New York: Berg Publishers.

Grosz, Elizabeth (1994) *Volatile Bodies: Towards a Corporeal Feminism.* Bloomington: Indiana University Press.

Grotowski, Jerzy (1968) *Towards a Poor Theatre.* Denmark: Odin Teatret.

——(1990) Untitled text, transcribed by Bruno Chojak from a video recording of a meeting with Anatoly Vassiliev's company in Pontedera, Italy.

——(1995) "From the Theatre Company to Art as Vehicle." In *At Work With Grotowski on Physical Actions*, by Thomas Richards, 115–35. New York: Routledge.

——(2005) *Il Principe Constante di Jerzy Grotowski: Ricostruzione* ["The Constant Prince" of Jerzy Grotowski: Reconstruction]. Introduced by Paul Allain, edited by Ferruccio Marotti, 48 min. Rome: Centro Teatro Ateneo and Università di Roma "La Sapienza."

——(2008) "Reply to Stanislavski." Translated by Kris Salata. *TDR* 52.2: 31–39.

Grotowski Institute (2012) Grotowski Institute website. <www.grotowski-institute.art.pl>, accessed 12/11/12.

Gutting, Gary (2011) "What is college for?" *New York Times*, December 14.

Hadot, Pierre (1995) *Philosophy as a Way of Life: Spiritual Exercises from Socrates to Foucault.* Malden, MA: Wiley-Blackwell Press.

Halberstam, Judith (1998a) *Female Masculinities.* Durham, NC: Duke University Press.

——(1998b) "Transgender Butch: Butch/FTM Border Wars and the Masculine Continuum." *GLQ* 4.2: 287–310.

Hamera, Judith (2007) *Dancing Communities: Performance, Difference and Connection in the Global City.* New York: Palgrave Macmillan.

Haney, David P. (1999) "Aesthetics and Ethics in Gadamer, Levinas, and Romanticism: Problems of Phronesis and Techne." *PMLA* 114.1: 32–45.

Haraway, Donna (1988) "Situated Knowledges: The Science Question in Feminism and the Privilege of Partial Perspective." *Feminist Studies* 14.3: 575–99.

——(2004) *The Haraway Reader.* New York: Routledge.

Harding, James Martin, and Cindy Rosenthal, eds. (2011) *The Rise of Performance Studies: Rethinking Richard Schechner's Broad Spectrum.* New York: Palgrave Macmillan.

Hargreaves, Jennifer, and Patricia Vertinsky, eds. (2007) *Physical Culture, Power, and the Body.* New York: Routledge.

Harker, Richard, and Stephen A. May (1993) "Code and Habitus: Comparing the Accounts of Bernstein and Bourdieu." *British Journal of Sociology of Education* 14.2: 169–78.

Harvey, David (2000) *Spaces of Hope.* Edinburgh: Edinburgh University Press.

Haver, William (1997) "Queer Research; or, How to Practice Invention to the Brink of Intelligibility." In *The Eight Technologies of Otherness*, ed. Sue Golding, 277–92. New York: Routledge.

Heagberg, Kathryn (2013) "Yogaglo patent issued: What's happening, and what it means for you." *Yoga International*, December 10. <yogainternational.com/article/view/yogaglo-patent-issued>, accessed 6/13/14.

Heidegger, Martin (1977) *The Question Concerning Technology and Other Essays*. Translated by William Lovitt. New York: Harper & Row.

——(1982) *The Basic Problems of Phenomenology*. Translated by Albert Hofstadter. Bloomington: Indiana University Press.

Herdt, Gilbert, ed. (1993) *Third Sex, Third Gender: Beyond Sexual Dimorphism in Culture and History*. New York: Zone Books.

Hirschkind, Charles (2011) "Is There a Secular Body?" *Cultural Anthropology* 26.4: 633–47.

Hobsbawm, Eric, and Terence Ranger, eds. (1983) *The Invention of Tradition*. Cambridge: Cambridge University Press.

Hodge, Alison (2013) *Core Training*. DVD. New York: Routledge.

——, ed. (2010) *Actor Training for the Relational Actor*. New York: Routledge.

Hodgkin, R. A. (1990) "Techne, Technology and Inventiveness." *Oxford Review of Education* 16.2: 207–17.

Hotson, Howard (2012) "Big Business at the Heart of the System: Understanding the Global University Crisis." Speech presented to the Society for Research into Higher Education. <http://www.srhe.ac.uk/conference2012/media/HowardHotson-SRHE-2012.mp3>.

Hsieh, Yu-Chieh (2012) "Shaping Young People's Gender and Sexual Identities: Can Teaching Practices Produce Diverse Subjects?" In *Educational Diversity: The Subject of Difference and Different Subjects*, ed. Yvette Taylor, 75–96. New York: Palgrave Macmillan.

Huberdeau, Rémy (2012) *Transforming FAMILY*. 10 min. <vimeo.com/44619131> and <www.lgbtqparentingconnection.ca/socialchange/Transforming FamiliesFilm.cfm>, accessed 6/11/14.

Hulton, Peter (2009) Review of Matthew Reason's *Documentation, Disappearance and the Representation of Live Performance*. *Studies in Theatre & Performance* 29.3: 340–42.

——, ed. (2012) *Arts Archives*, University of Exeter. <arts-archives.org>, accessed 12/20/12.

Huxley, Michael (2011) "F. Matthias Alexander and Mabel Elsworth Todd: Proximities, practices and the psycho-physical." *Journal of Dance & Somatic Practices* 3.1–2: 25–42.

Identity Project (2014) Identity Project webpage. <www.identityprojectsf.com>, accessed 6/11/14.

Ingold, Tim (2007) *Lines: A Brief History*. New York: Routledge.

——(2011) *Being Alive: Essays on Movement, Knowledge and Description*. New York: Routledge.

International Centre for Theatre Research (2012) *Théâtre des Bouffes du Nord*. Website. <www.bouffesdunord.com>, accessed 12/11/12.

Isasi-Díaz, María, and Eduardo Mendieta, eds. (2012) *Decolonizing Epistemologies: Latino/a Theology and Philosophy*. New York: Fordham University Press.

Iyengar, B. K. S. (1966) *Light on Yoga*. New York: Schocken Books.

Jagger, Gill (2012) "Embodied Subjectivity, Power and Resistance: Bourdieu and Butler on the Problem of Determinism." In *Embodied Selves*, ed. Stella Gonzalez-Arnal, Gill Jagger, and Kathleen Lennon, 209–29. New York: Palgrave Macmillan.

Joas, Hans (1996) *The Creativity of Action*. Chicago: University of Chicago Press.

Johnson, Don Hanlon (1995) *Bone, Breath, and Gestures: Practices of Embodiment*. Berkeley, CA: North Atlantic Books.

Johnson, Mark (2007) *The Meaning of the Body: Aesthetics of Human Understanding*. Chicago: University of Chicago Press.

Kapchan, Deborah (2003) "Performance." In *Eight Words for the Study of Expressive Culture*, ed. Burt Feintuch, 121–45. Chicago: University of Illinois Press.

Kaplan, E. Ann, and George Levine, eds. (1997) *The Politics of Research*. New Brunswick: Rutgers University Press.

Kapsali, Maria (2010) "'I Don't Attack It, but It's Not for Actors': The Use of Yoga by Jerzy Grotowski." *Theatre, Dance and Performance Training* 1.2: 185–98.

Kemp, Ric (2012) *Embodied Acting: What Neuroscience Tells Us about Performing*. New York: Routledge.

Kershaw, Baz (2007) *Theatre Ecology: Environments and Performance Events*. Cambridge: Cambridge University Press.

Kershaw, Baz, and Helen Nicholson (2011) *Research Methods in Theatre and Performance*. Edinburgh: Edinburgh University Press.

Kessler, Suzanne J., and Wendy McKenna (1978) *Gender: An Ethnomethodological Approach*. Chicago: University of Chicago Press.

Kolankiewicz, Leszek (2012) "Grotowski in a Maze of Haitian Narration." *TDR* 56.3: 131–40.

Krasner, David, ed. (2000) *Method Acting Reconsidered: Theory, Practice, Future*. New York: St. Martin's Press.

Krishnamacharya, Sri Tirumalai (1934) *Yoga Makaranda*. Madurai: C. M. V. Press. <www.scribd.com/doc/55460748/Yoga-Makaranda>, accessed 4/7/13.

Krüger, Hans-Peter (2010) "Persons and Their Bodies: The *Körper / Leib* Distinction and Helmuth Plessner's Theories of Ex-centric Positionality and *Homo absconditus*." *Journal of Speculative Philosophy* 24.3: 256–74.

Lacquer, Thomas (1990) *Making Sex: Body and Gender from the Greeks to Freud*. Cambridge: Harvard University Press.

Lakoff, George, and Mark Johnson (1999) *Philosophy in the Flesh: The Embodied Mind and Its Challenge to Western Thought*. New York: Basic Books.

Lamont, Michèle (2009) *How Professors Think: Inside the Curious World of Academic Judgment*. Cambridge: Harvard University Press.

Lande, Brian (2007) "Breathing Like a Soldier: Culture Incarnate." *Sociological Review* 55.s1: 95–108.

Lane, Riki (2009) "Trans as Bodily Becoming: Rethinking the Biological as Diversity, Not Dichotomy." *Hypatia* 24.3: 136–57.

Laster, Dominika (2010) "Grotowski's Bridge Made of Memory: Embodied Memory, Witnessing and Transmission in the Grotowski Work." PhD diss., New York University.

Latour, Bruno (1983) "Give Me a Laboratory and I Will Raise the World." In *Science Observed: Perspectives on the Social Study of Science*, ed. Karin Knorr-Cetina and Michael Mulkay, 141–70. London: Sage Publications.

Lea, Jennifer (2009) "Liberation or Limitation? Understanding Iyengar Yoga as a Practice of the Self." *Body & Society* 15: 71–92.

Leggett, Trevor (1987) *Zen and the Ways*. Tokyo: Charles E. Tuttle Company.

Leonard, Tom (2008) "Pregnant man Thomas Beatie gives birth to baby girl." *Telegraph*, July 3. <www.telegraph.co.uk/news/worldnews/northamerica/usa/22426 66/Pregnant-man-Thomas-Beatie-gives-birth-to-baby-girl.html>, accessed 9/24/13.

Leys, Ruth (2011) "The Turn to Affect: A Critique." *Critical Inquiry* 37.3: 434–72.

Lex, Barbara W. (1979) "The Neurobiology of Ritual Trance." In *The Spectrum of Ritual: A Biogenetic Structural Analysis*, ed. E. G. d'Aquili, C. D. Laughlin, and J. McManus, 117–51. New York: Columbia University Press.

Lima, Cecília de (2013) "Trans-meaning: Dance as an Embodied Technology of Perception." *Journal of Dance & Somatic Practices* 5.1: 17–30.

Lomax, Alan (1968) *Folk Song Style and Culture*. Washington, DC: American Association for the Advancement of Science.

Looser, Tom (2012) "The Global University, Area Studies, and the World Citizen: Neoliberal Geography's Redistribution of the 'World'." *Cultural Anthropology* 27.1: 97–117.

Löwenstein, David (2012) "Why Know-How and Propositional Knowledge Are Mutually Irreducible." Conference paper, Gesellschaft für Analytische Philosophie. <duepublico.uni-duisburg-essen.de/servlets/DocumentServlet?id = 31200>, accessed 9/23/13.

Lutterbie, John (2011) *Toward a General Theory of Acting: Cognitive Science and Performance*. New York: Palgrave Macmillan.

Lyttle, Bethany (2009) "Physical culture: Bonding with their downward-facing humans." *New York Times*, April 9. <www.nytimes.com/2009/04/09/fashion/ 09fitness.html>, accessed 6/11/14.

MacKinnon, Catharine A. (2006) *Are Women Human? and Other International Dialogues*. Cambridge: Harvard University Press.

Maehle, Gregor (2006) *Ashtanga Yoga: Practice & Philosophy*. Novato, CA: New World Library.

Magnat, Virginie (2013) *Grotowski, Women, and Contemporary Performance: Meetings with Remarkable Women*. New York: Routledge.

Mahmood, Saba (2005) *Politics of Piety: The Islamic Revival and the Feminist Subject*. Princeton: Princeton University Press.

Mahmoud, Jasmine (2014) "'What a Body Can Do': A Praxis Session by Ben Spatz, Zihan Loo, Christine Germain, Donia Mounsef, Ira Murfin, Justin Zullo and Krista DeNio." *Performance Research* 19.3: 150–51.

Malague, Rosemary (2012) *An Actress Prepares: Women and "the Method."* New York: Routledge.

Marcus, Sharon (1992) "Fighting Bodies, Fighting Words: A Theory and Politics of Rape Prevention." In *Feminists Theorize the Political*, ed. Judith Butler and Joan W. Scott, 385–403. New York: Routledge.

Margolis, Ellen, and Lissa Tyler Renaud, eds. (2010) *The Politics of American Actor Training*. New York: Routledge.

Markula, Pirkko (2008) "Affect[ing] Bodies: Performative Pedagogy of Pilates." *International Review of Qualitative Research* 1.3: 381–408.

Martin, Randy (1998) *Critical Moves: Dance Studies in Theory and Politics*. Durham, NC: Duke University Press.

Matthews, John (2011) *Training for Performance: A Meta-Disciplinary Account*. London: Methuen.

Mauss, Marcel (1973) "Techniques of the Body." Translated by Ben Brewster. *Economy and Society* 2.1: 70–88.

——(2006) *Techniques, Technology and Civilisation*. Edited by Nathan Schlanger. New York: Durkheim Press.

McAllister-Viel, Tara (2007) "Speaking with an International Voice?" *Contemporary Theatre Review* 17.1: 97–106.

McCarthy, E. Doyle (1996) *Knowledge as Culture: The New Sociology of Knowledge*. New York: Routledge.

McConachie, Bruce, and F. Elizabeth Hart (2006) *Performance and Cognition: Theatre Studies and the Cognitive Turn*. New York: Routledge.

McConnell, Dana (2013) "The Fulcrum: An Interrogation of Power." Conference paper, Association for Theatre in Higher Education, Orlando, FL.

McGushin, Edward F. (2007) *Foucault's Askēsis: An Introduction to the Philosophical Life*. Evanston: Northwestern University Press.

McKenzie, Jon (1998) "Genre Trouble: (The) Butler Did It." In *The Ends of Performance*, ed. Peggy Phelan and Jill Lane, 217–35. New York: New York University Press.

——(2001) *Perform or Else: From Discipline to Performance*. New York: Routledge.

McNiff, Shaun (1998) *Art-Based Research*. London: Jessica Kingsley Publishers.

McTeague, James H. (1993) *Before Stanislavsky: American Professional Acting Schools and Acting Theory 1875–1925*. Metuchen, NJ: Scarecrow Press.

Mellon School of Theater and Performance Research at Harvard University (2014) "Theatre among the Other Arts," 6–17 June 2011. Mellon School of Theater and Performance Research, Harvard University, website. <thschool.fas.harvard.edu>, accessed 6/4/14.

Mellor, Philip A., and Chris Shilling (2010) "Body Pedagogics and the Religious Habitus: A New Direction for the Sociological Study of Religion." *Religion* 40.1: 27–38.

Melrose, Susan (2003) "Who Knows—and Who Cares (about Performance Mastery)?" Symposium on Virtuosity and Performance Mastery, 31 May–1 June. <www.sfmelrose.org.uk/e-pai-2003-04/performancemastery>.

——(2006) "Who Knows—*and Who Cares*—about Performance Mastery (?)" In *A Performance Cosmology: Testimony from the Future, Evidence of the Past*, ed. Judie Christie, Richard Gough, and Daniel Watt, 132–39. New York: Routledge.

Melrose, Susan, and Stefanie Sachsenmaier (2013) "Just in Time: 'Momentary' Events in the Making of Rosemary Butcher's Signature Practices." In Conference Program, Performance Studies International 19, Stanford University.

Merleau-Ponty, Maurice (2002) *Phenomenology of Perception*. New York: Routledge. Orig. publ. 1945.

MICHA (2007) *Master Classes in the Michael Chekhov Technique*. Michael Chekhov Association, DVD. New York: Routledge. <www.michaelchekhov.org/store/stream-master-classes>, accessed 6/12/14.

Mieszkowski, Katharine (2009) "The baby's a ... we're not telling!" *Salon*, June 30. <www.salon.com/2009/06/30/sweden_2>, accessed 12/06/12.

Mohan, A. G. (2010) *Krishnamacharya: His Life and Teachings*. Boston: Shambhala Press.

Mohler, Courtney Elkin (2013) "Lynn Riggs and the Double-Edged Sword of 'Race' Specific Casting." Conference paper, Association for Theatre in Higher Education, Orlando, FL.

Moran, Joe (2002) *Interdisciplinarity*. New York: Routledge.

Movement Research (2012) Movement Research website. <movementresearch.org>, accessed 12/11/12.

Mroz, Daniel (2008) "Technique in Exile: The Changing Perception of *Taijiquan*: From Ming Dynasty Military Exercise to Twentieth-Century Actor Training Protocol." *Studies in Theatre and Performance* 28.2: 127–45.

——(2011) *The Dancing Word: An Embodied Approach to the Preparation of Performers and the Composition of Performances*. New York: Rodopi Press.

Mumford, Lewis (1952) *Art and Technics*. New York and London: Columbia University Press.

Muñoz, José Esteban (2009) *Cruising Utopia: The Then and There of Queer Futurity*. New York: New York University Press.

Murphy, Jarrett (2006) "The gentle combat of Mapes Avenue." *Village Voice*, May 9.

Namaste, Vivian (2005) *Sex Change, Social Change*. Toronto: Women's Press.

Nascimento, Cláudia Tatinge (2009) *Crossing Cultural Borders through the Actor's Work: Foreign Bodies of Knowledge*. New York: Routledge.

Nellhaus, Tobin (2010) *Theatre, Communication, Critical Realism*. New York: Palgrave Macmillan.

Nelson, Robin (2013) *Practice as Research in the Arts: Principles, Protocols, Pedagogies, Resistances*. New York: Palgrave Macmillan.

Newcombe, Suzanne (2007) "Stretching for Health and Well-Being: Yoga and Women in Britain, 1960–80." *Asian Medicine* 3: 37–63.

Newfield, Christopher (2008) *Unmaking the Public University: The Forty Year Assault on the Middle Class*. Cambridge: Harvard University Press.

——(2011) "Public education for the public good." *Chronicle of Higher Education*, August 28.

Ngũgĩ wa Thiong'o (1997) "Enactments of Power: The Politics of Performance Space." *TDR* 41.3: 11–30.

Nia Now (2012) *Nia Now*. Website. <www.nianow.com/practice>, accessed 12/10/12.

Nicholson, Linda (1994) "Interpreting Gender." *Signs* 20.1: 79–105.

Noë, Alva (2012) *Varieties of Presence*. Cambridge: Harvard University Press.

Noland, Carrie (2009) *Agency and Embodiment: Performing Gestures / Producing Culture*. Cambridge: Harvard University Press.

Noland, Carrie, and Sally Ann Ness, eds. (2008) *Migrations of Gesture*. Minneapolis: University of Minnesota Press.

O'Shea, Janet (2006) "Dancing through History and Ethnography: Indian Classical Dance and the Performance of the Past." In *Dancing from Past to Present: Nation, Culture, Identities*, ed. Theresa Jill Buckland, 123–52. Madison: University of Wisconsin Press.

PARIP (Practice as Research in Performance) (2012) *Practice as Research in Performance: 2001–2006*. Website. <www.bristol.ac.uk/parip>, accessed 12/13/12.

Parker, Andrew, and Eve Kosofsky Sedgwick (1995) *Performativity and Performance*. New York: Routledge.

Parker, Jenneth (2001) "Social Movements and Science: The Question of Plural Knowledge Systems." In *After Postmodernism: An Introduction to Critical Realism*, ed. José López and Garry Potter, 252–59. New York: Athlone Press.

Parker-Starbuck, Jennifer (2011) *Cyborg Theatre: Corporeal/Technological Intersections in Multimedia Performance*. New York: Palgrave Macmillan.

Parry, Richard (2007) "*Episteme* and *Techne*." In *Stanford Encyclopedia of Philosophy*. <plato.stanford.edu/entries/episteme-techne>, accessed 8/13/13.

Peck, James, ed. (2013) *Theatre Topics* 23.2.

Performance Philosophy (2014) *Performance Philosophy: A Research Network for the Field of Performance Philosophy*. Website.<performancephilosophy. ning.com>, accessed 6/4/14.

Petsko, Gregory A. (2010) "A Faustian Bargain: Open Letter to George M. Philip, President of the State University of New York." *Genome Biology* 11.138.

Phelan, Peggy (1993) *Unmarked: The Politics of Performance*. New York: Routledge.

Pickering, Andrew (1995) *The Mangle of Practice: Time, Agency, and Science*. Chicago: University of Chicago Press.

Pitches, Jonathan (2006) *Science and the Stanislavsky Tradition of Acting*. New York: Routledge.

——(2007) "Roots or Routes;:The Technical Traditions of Contemporary Physical Theatre." In *Physical Theatres: A Critical Reader*, ed. John Keefe and Simon Murray, 47–54. New York: Routledge.

Polanyi, Michael (2009) *The Tacit Dimension*. Chicago: University of Chicago Press. Orig. publ. 1966.

Potter, Nicole, ed. (2002) *Movement for Actors*. New York: Allworth Press.

Pradier, Jean-Marie (1990) "Towards a Biological Theory of the Body in Performance." *New Theatre Quarterly* 6.21: 86–98.

Pred, Allan (1981) "Social Reproduction and the Time-Geography of Everyday Life." *Geografiska Annaler: Series B, Human Geography* 63.1: 5–22.

Prior, Ross (2012) *Teaching Actors: Knowledge Transfer in Actor Training.* Chicago: Intellect.

Rabinow, Paul, and Nikolas Rose (2006) "Biopower Today." *BioSocieties* 1: 195–217.

Rancière, Jacques (1991) *The Ignorant Schoolmaster: Five Lessons in Intellectual Emancipation.* Stanford: Stanford University Press.

——(2004) *The Politics of Aesthetics: The Distribution of the Sensible.* New York: Continuum.

Rappaport, Roy (1999) *Ritual and Religion in the Making of Humanity.* New York: Cambridge University Press.

Rawlins, F. I. G. (1950) "Episteme and Techne." *Philosophy and Phenomenological Research* 10.3: 389–97.

Raymond, Janice G. (1979) *The Transsexual Empire: The Making of the She-male.* Boston: Beacon Press.

Read, Alan (1993) *Theatre and Everyday Life: An Ethics of Performance.* New York: Routledge.

Rich, Emma, Rachel Holroyd, and John Evans (2004) "'Hungry to Be Noticed': Young Women, Anorexia and Schooling." In *Body Knowledge and Control: Studies in the Sociology of Physical Education and Health*, ed. John Evans, Brian Davis, and Jan Wright, 173–90. New York: Routledge.

Richards, Thomas (1995) *At Work with Grotowski on Physical Actions.* New York: Routledge.

——(2008) *Heart of Practice.* New York: Routledge.

Riley, Shannon Rose, and Lynette Hunter, eds. (2009) *Mapping Landscapes for Performance as Research: Scholarly Acts and Creative Cartographies.* New York: Palgrave Macmillan.

Roach, Joseph (1993) *The Player's Passion: Studies in the Science of Acting.* Ann Arbor: University of Michigan Press.

——(2011) "A New Poetics: Performance Studies and the Research University." Lecture at the Mellon School of Theater and Performance Research at Harvard University. <thschool.fas.harvard.edu/icb/icb.do?keyword=k76089&pageid= icb.page386654>, accessed 9/22/13.

Robb, Alice (2013) "Ballet is in crisis because it's turning into a sport." *New Republic*, October 14. <www.newrepublic.com/article/115169/ballet-competitions-turn-art-sport>, accessed 10/19/13.

Roberts, John (2006) *Philosophizing the Everyday: Revolutionary Praxis and the Fate of Cultural Theory.* London and Ann Arbor: Pluto Press.

Roms, Heike (2012) "The Practice Turn: Performance and the British Academy." In *Contesting Performance: Global Sites of Research*, ed. Jon McKenzie, Heike Roms, and C. J. W.-L. Wee, 51–70. New York: Palgrave Macmillan.

Rosenthal, Bill, and Emily Schnee (2013) "The New Community College at CUNY and the Common Good." *Thought & Action* 29: 87–100.

Roth, Michael S. (2012) "Learning as freedom." *New York Times*, September 5.

Rothblum, Esther (2011) "Fat Studies." In *The Oxford Handbook of the Social Science of Obesity*, ed. J. Cawley, 173–83. New York: Oxford University Press.

Rothblum, Esther, Sondra Solovay, and Marilyn Wann, eds. (2009) *The Fat Studies Reader*. New York: New York University Press.

Rothfield, Philipa (2009) "Between the Foot and the Floor, Dancing with Nietzsche and Klossoswki." In *Somatechnics: Queering the Technologisation of Bodies*, ed. Nikki Sullivan and Samantha Murray, 207–24. Farnham, Surrey: Ashgate Publishing.

Roubal, Petr (2003) "Politics of Gymnastics: Mass Gymnastic Displays under Communism in Central and Eastern Europe." *Body & Society* 9.2: 1–25.

Rowe, Sharon Māhealani (2008) "We Dance for Knowledge." *Dance Research Journal* 40.1: 31–44.

RT (2013) "Germany to become first European state to allow 'third gender' birth certificates." *RT*, <rt.com/news/third-gender-birth-germany-592/>, accessed 9/24/13.

Rubin, Gayle (1975) "The Traffic in Women." In *Toward an Anthropology of Women*, ed. Rayna Reiter, 157–210. New York: Monthly Review Press.

Rubin, Henry (2003) *Self-Made Men: Identity and Embodiment among Transsexual Men*. Nashville: Vanderbilt University Press.

Ruddick, Sara (1995) *Maternal Thinking: Towards a Politics of Peace*. Boston: Beacon Press.

Ruiz, Fernando Pagés (2001) "Krishnamacharya's Legacy." *Yoga Journal*. <www.yogajournal.com/wisdom/465>, accessed 12/10/12.

Ryle, Gilbert (2000) *The Concept of Mind*. New York: Penguin Books. Orig. publ. 1949.

Salah, Trish (2007) "Undoing Trans Studies." *Topia* 17: 150–55.

Salamon, Gayle (2010) *Assuming a Body: Transgender and Rhetorics of Materality*. New York: Columbia University Press.

Salata, Kris (2007) "Directing the Unwritten: The Legacy of Jerzy Grotowski." PhD diss., Stanford University.

——(2008) "Toward the Non-(Re)presentational Actor: From Grotowski to Richards." *TDR* 52.2: 107–25.

——(2012) *The Unwritten Grotowski: Theory and Practice of the Encounter*. New York: Routledge.

Sandahl, Carrie, and Philip Auslander, eds. (2005) *Bodies in Commotion: Disability and Performance*. Ann Arbor: University of Michigan Press.

Sanford, Matthew (2006) *Waking: A Memoir of Trauma and Transcendence*. New York: Rodale.

——(2013) *Matthew Sanford: Transformative, Interactive, Pratical*. Website. <www.matthewsanford.com>, accessed 9/7/13.

Schatz, Howard, and Beverly Ornstein (2002) *Athlete*. New York: HarperCollins.

Schatzki, Theodore R. (1996) *Social Practices: A Wittgensteinian Approach to Human Activity and the Social*. Cambridge: Cambridge University Press.

Schatzki, Theodore R., Karin Knorr Cetina, and Eike von Savigny, eds. (2001) *The Practice Turn in Contemporary Theory*. New York: Routledge.

Schechner, Richard (1985) *Between Theatre and Anthropology*. Philadelphia: University of Pennsylvania Press.

——(2001) "Rasaesthetics." *TDR* 45.3: 27–50.

——(2008) "Comment: Grotowski and the Grotowskian." *TDR* 52.2: 7–13.

Schechner, Richard, and Lisa Wolford (1997) *The Grotowski Sourcebook*. New York: Routledge.

Schieffelin, Edward L. (1998) "Problematizing Performance." In *Ritual, Performance, Media*, ed. Felicia Hughes-Freeland, 194–207. New York: Routledge.

Schino, Mirella (2009) *Alchemists of the Stage: Theatre Laboratories in Europe*. New York: Icarus Publishing Enterprise and Routledge.

Schlanger, Nathan (1998) "The Study of Techniques as an Ideological Challenge: Technology, Nation, and Humanity in the Work of Marcel Mauss." In *Marcel Mauss: A Centenary Tribute*, ed. Wendy James and N. J. Allen, 192–212. New York: Berghahn Books.

Seabright, Paul (2012) "How to defend universities." *Times Literary Supplement*, March 7.

Sedgwick, Eve Kosofsky (1985) *Between Men: English Literature and Male Homosocial Desire*. New York: Columbia University Press.

——(1990) *Epistemology of the Closet*. Berkeley: University of California Press.

——(1994) *Tendencies*. New York: Routledge.

——(1995) "'Gosh, Boy George, You Must Be Awfully Secure in Your Masculinity!'" In *Constructing Masculinity*, ed. Maurice Berger, Brian Wallis, and Simon Watson, 11–20. New York: Routledge.

Sennett, Richard (2009) *The Craftsman*. New York: Penguin Books.

Sheets-Johnstone, Maxine (2009) *The Corporeal Turn: An Interdisciplinary Reader*. Charlottesville, VA: Imprint Academic.

Shepherd, Simon (2006) *Theatre, Body and Pleasure*. New York: Routledge.

——(2009) "The Institution of Training." *Performance Research* 14(2): 5–15.

Sherbourne Health Centre (2013) *Check It Out Guys*. Website. <www.check-itoutguys.ca>.

Shilling, Chris (2003) *The Body and Social Theory*. London: Sage Publications.

——, ed. (2007) *Embodying Sociology: Retrospect, Progress and Prospects*. Sociological Review Monographs. Oxford: Blackwell. Also available as *Sociological Review* 55.s1.

Shklovsky, Victor (1965) "Art as Technique." In *Russian Formalist Criticism: Four Essays*. Translated by Lee T. Lemon and Marion J. Reis, 3–24. Lincoln: University of Nebraska.

Shove, Elizabeth, Mika Pantzar, and Matt Watson (2012) *The Dynamics of Social Practice: Everyday Life and How It Changes*. London: Sage Publications.

Shove, Elizabeth, and Nicola Spurling, eds. (2013) *Sustainable Practices: Social Theory and Climate Change*. New York: Routledge.

Shove, Elizabeth, Frank Trentmann, and Richard Wilk, eds. (2009) *Time, Consumption and Everyday Life: Practice, Materiality and Culture*. New York: Berg Publishers.

Shumway, David R., and Ellen Messer-Davidow (1991) "Disciplinarity: An Introduction." *Poetics Today* 12.2: 201–25.

Shusterman, Richard (1999) *Bourdieu: A Critical Reader*. Oxford: Blackwell Publishers.

Siebers, Toby (2008) *Disability Theory*. Ann Arbor: University of Michigan Press.

Simonton, Dean Keith (1979) "Multiple Discovery and Invention: Zeitgeist, Genius, or Chance?" *Journal of Personality and Social Psychology* 37.9: 1603–16.

Singleton, Mark (2010) *Yoga Body: The Origins of Modern Posture Practice*. Oxford: Oxford University Press.

Singleton, Mark, and Jean Byrne, eds. (2008) *Yoga in the Modern World: Contemporary Perspectives*. New York: Routledge.

Sjoman, N. E. (1996) *The Yoga Tradition of the Mysore Palace*. New Delhi: Abhinav Publications.

Sloterdijk, Peter (2013) *You Must Change Your Life*. Malden, MA: Polity Press.

Slowiak, James, and Jairo Cuesta (2007) *Jerzy Grotowski*. New York: Routledge.

Smith, Benjamin Richard (2007) "Body, Mind and Spirit? Towards an Analysis of the Practice of Yoga." *Body & Society* 13.2: 25–46.

Smith, Hazel, and Roger T. Dean (2009) *Practice-led Research, Research-led Practice in the Creative Arts*. Edinburgh: Edinburgh University Press.

Smith, Linda Tuhiwai (1999) *Decolonizing Methodologies: Research and Indigenous Peoples*. New York: Zed Books.

Spatz, Ben (2008) "To Open a Person: Song and Encounter at Gardzienice and the Workcenter." *Theatre Topics* 18.2: 205–22.

——(2009) "A Series of Openings: The Year of Grotowski in New York City." *Slavic and Eastern European Performance* 29.3: 18–25.

——(2013) "Citing Musicality: Performance Knowledge in the Gardzienice Archive." *Studies in Musical Theatre* 7.2: 221–35.

Spottiswoode, Jocelyn (2013) "Transgender man gives birth in Germany." *Telegraph*, September 11. <www.telegraph.co.uk/news/worldnews/europe/germany/103018 62/Transgender-man-gives-birth-in-Germany.html>, accessed 9/24/13.

Staniewski, Włodzimierz, and Alison Hodge (2004) *Hidden Territories: The Theatre of Gardzienice*. With CD-ROM by Peter Hulton, Arts Archives. New York: Routledge.

Stanislavski, Konstantin (2008) *An Actor's Work: A Student's Diary*. Translated by Jean Benedetti. New York: Routledge. Orig. publ. 1936.

Stanley, Jason (2011) *Know How*. New York: Oxford University Press.

Stoltenberg, John (1989) *Refusing to Be a Man*. Portland: Breitenbush Books.

Strathern, Andrew, and Pamela J. Stewart (1998) "Embodiment and Communication: Two Frames for the Analysis of Ritual." *Social Anthropology* 6.2: 237–51.

Stryker, Susan, Paisley Currah, and Lisa Jean Moore (2008) "Introduction: Trans-, Trans, or Transgender?" *WSQ* 36.3–4: 11–22.

Stryker, Susan, and Nikki Sullivan (2009) "King's Member, Queen's Body: Transsexual Surgery, Self-Demand Amputation and the Somatechnics of Sovereign Power." In *Somatechnics: Queering the Technologisation of Bodies*, ed. Nikki Sullivan and Samantha Murray, 49–63. Farnham, Surrey: Ashgate Publishing.

Stryker, Susan, and Stephen Whittle, eds. (2006) *The Transgender Studies Reader.* New York: Routledge.

Sudnow, David (2001) *Ways of the Hand: Organization of Improvised Conduct.* Cambridge: MIT Press.

Sullivan, Graeme (2010) *Art Practice as Research: Inquiry in the Visual Arts.* Thousand Oaks, CA: Sage Publications.

Sullivan, Nikki, and Samantha Murray (2009) *Somatechnics: Queering the Technologisation of Bodies.* Farnham, Surrey: Ashgate Publishing.

Sutton, David (2014) "Cooking Is Good to Think." *Body & Society* 20.1: 133–48.

Swan, Liz Stillwaggon (2011) *Yoga: Philosophy for Everyone: Bending Mind and Body.* Hoboken, NJ: Wiley-Blackwell Press.

Syman, Stefanie (2010) *The Subtle Body: The Story of Yoga in America.* New York: Farrar, Straus and Giroux.

Tagliabue, John (2012) "Swedish school's big lesson begins with dropping personal pronouns." *New York Times*, November 13. <www.nytimes.com/2012/11/14/world/europe/swedish-school-de-emphasizes-gender-lines.html>, accessed 12/06/12.

Taylor, Astra (2008) *Examined Life.* Film. New York: Zeitgeist Films.

Taylor, Diana (2003) *The Archive and the Repertoire.* Durham, NC: Duke University Press.

Taylor, Paul (2013) *Race: A Philosophical Introduction.* Malden, MA: Polity Press.

Thomas, Helen (2003) *The Body, Dance and Cultural Theory.* New York: Palgrave Macmillan.

Thrift, Nigel (2008) *Non-Representational Theory: Space, Politics, Affect.* New York: Routledge.

Tinning, Richard (2010) *Pedagogy and Human Movement: Theory, Practice, Research.* New York: Routledge.

Toporkov, Vasily (2004) *Stanislavski in Rehearsal.* New York: Routledge.

Travis, John (2009) "Is the (blue) sky falling in the UK?" American Association for the Advancement of Science, February 12. <news.sciencemag.org/2009/02/blue-sky-falling-u.k >, accessed 6/12/14.

Turner, Bryan S. (2005) "Introduction—Bodily Performance: On Aura and Reproducibility." *Body & Society* 11.4: 1–17.

Urban Research Theater (2014) *Urban Research Theater: Projects by Ben Spatz.* Website. <www.urbanresearchtheater.com>, accessed 5/14/14.

Valentine, David (2007) *Imagining Transgender: An Ethnography of a Category.* Durham, NC: Duke University Press.

Vaneigem, Raoul (2001) *The Revolution of Everyday Life.* London: Rebel Press. Orig. publ. 1967.

Varela, Francisco J. (1999) *Ethical Know-How: Action, Wisdom, and Cognition.* Stanford: Stanford University Press.

Varela, Francisco J., Evan Thompson, and Eleanor Rosch (1991) *The Embodied Mind: Cognitive Science and Human Experience.* Cambridge: MIT Press.

Wallis, Mick (2005) "Thinking through *Techne*." *Performance Research* 10.4: 1–8.

Warner, Michael, ed. (1993) *Fear of a Queer Planet: Queer Politics and Social Theory*. Minneapolis: University of Minnesota Press.

Watson, Ian, ed. (2001) *Performer Training: Developments across Cultures*. Amsterdam: Harwood Academic Publishers.

——, ed. (2002) *Negotiating Cultures: Eugenio Barba and the Intercultural Debate*. New York: Manchester University Press.

——(2013) "The Odin Actor: Embodied Technology, Memory, and the Corporeal Archive." *Theatre, Dance and Performance Training* 4.3: 399–411.

Wax, Emily (2010) "'Yoga wars' spoil spirit of ancient practice, Indian agency says." *Washington Post*, August 23. <http://www.washingtonpost.com/wp-dyn/content/article/2010/08/22/AR2010082203071.html>.

Weiss, Gail, and Honi Fern Haber, eds. (1999) *Perspectives on Embodiment: The Intersections of Nature and Culture*. New York: Routledge.

Weiss, Margot (2011) *Techniques of Pleasure: BDSM and the Circuits of Sexuality*. Durham, NC: Duke University Press.

Welton, Donn, ed. (1998) *Body and Flesh: A Philosophical Reader*. Malden, MA: Blackwell Publishers.

Wheelahan, Leesa (2010) *Why Knowledge Matters in Curriculum: A Social Realist Argument*. New York: Routledge.

White, R. Andrew (2006) "Stanislavsky and Ramacharaka: The Influence of Yoga and Turn-of-the-Century Occultism on the System." *Theatre Survey* 41.7: 73–92.

Wikipedia (2014) "Gender-Specific and Gender-Neutral Pronouns." *Wikipedia*. <en.wikipedia.org/wiki/Gender-specific_and_gender-neutral_pronouns>, accessed 6/11/14.

Wilcox, Hui Niu (2009) "Embodied Ways of Knowing, Pedagogies, and Social Justice: Inclusive Science and Beyond." *NWSA Journal* 21.2: 104–20.

Wilson, August (1998) "The Ground on Which I Stand," *Callaloo* 20.3: 493–503.

Wolford, Lisa (1996) *Grotowski's Objective Drama Research*. Jackson: University Press of Mississippi.

Wray, K. Brad (2011) *Kuhn's Evolutionary Social Epistemology*. New York: Cambridge University Press.

Wylam, Lisa Wolford (2008) "Living Tradition: Continuity of Research at the Workcenter of Jerzy Grotowski and Thomas Richards." *TDR* 52.2: 126–49.

Wyman-McGinty, Wendy (1998) "The Body in Analysis: Authentic Movement and Witnessing in Analytic Practice." *Journal of Analytical Psychology* 43: 239–60.

Young, Harvey (2010) *Embodying Black Experience: Stillness, Critical Memory, and the Black Body*. Ann Arbor: University of Michigan Press.

Zarrilli, Phillip B. (1995) *Acting (Re)Considered*. New York: Routledge.

——(2009) *Psychophysical Acting: An Intercultural Approach after Stanislavski*. With DVD-ROM by Peter Hulton, Arts Archives. New York: Routledge.

Zarrilli, Phillip B., Jerri Daboo, and Rebecca Loukes (2013) *Acting: Psychophysical Phenomenon and Process*. New York: Palgrave Macmillan.

Zarrilli, Phillip B., Bruce McConachie, Gary Jay Williams, and Carol Fisher
Sorgenfrei (2010) *Theatre Histories: An Introduction.* New York: Routledge.
Zarrilli, Phillip B., and Bella Merlin (2007) *Contemporary Theatre Review* 17.1:
1–116.
Zumba Fitness (2012) Zumba Fitness website. <zumba.com>, accessed 12/10/12.

INDEX

academia *see* universities
actor training 131–32, 148–51, 250n2;
   intersections with cultural identity
   160–62; intersections with physical
   culture 154–57; limitations of
   117–22, 167–68n18; politics of 7,
   162–63; sexism and other
   prejudices in 151, 158–60
Actors Studio 165
affect theory *see* critical affect theory
affordances *see* Gibson, James
agency: and knowledge 30; and
   nature 35, 179; in learning gender
   199–200; material and human 76;
   old account of 156–57; sedimenting
   50–56
Ahmed, Sara 13, 21n4, 45–46, 162
Alexander Technique 97–101, 107–8,
   154–56; *see also* somatics
American Idol 4; *see also So You
   Think You Can Dance*
American Society for Theatre
   Research 20, 243
Aristotle 27–28, 120
artistic research *see Journal of
   Artistic Research*; practice as
   research
arts: as craft 231; definition of 9;
   etymology 29, 231; limitations of
   arts discourse 230–34; range of 9,
   231; *see also* public sphere
Arts Archives 242
asana 76–80, 86, 98, 141
asexuality 208
Ashtanga Yoga *see* yoga

Authentic Movement 100
automaticity 52–53, 152, 175

Barba, Eugenio 29, 112, 116–17,
   151–52, 165n2, 168n20
Barnett, Ronald 216, 218–21
Bausch, Pina 232
BDSM 208–9, 214n15
Benjamin, Walter 29
Bikram Yoga *see* yoga
biopolitics 83, 109n1; *see also*
   Foucault, Michel
body type 106, 110n8, 166–67n14;
   and see healthism
bodymind *see* psychophysical
bodywork *see* somatics
Bourdieu, Pierre 51–53, 69n10,
   174–75, 223–24, 237
branching pathways *see* fractal
   geometry
breathing technique 72, 76–80, 90, 99,
   100, 108–9, 212n4
Brook, Peter 14, 58, 121–22
Brown, Wendy 35
Buddhism 47, 72, 109
Butler, Judith: and agency 8, 51–52;
   and *catachresis* 176; and gender
   performativity 18, 70n16, 159,
   170–73, 181–82, 187, 197–209; and
   new gender politics 179, 209

capitalism 12–13, 167n16, 176,
   218–21, 247–48; capitalist market
   48, 80–86, 105–8, 148–49, 167n17,
   218–21, 247–50

275

INDEX

Massumi, Brian 4, 15
materialism *see* realism
Matthews, John 10, 52–53, 119–21
Mauss, Marcel 29–33, 42–43, 55, 61,
    68n6, 73, 104
McConachie, Bruce 24, 67n1
McKenzie, Jon 53, 57–58, 109n2
Melrose, Susan 58, 235
Merleau-Ponty, Maurice 12, 35,
    110n5
Mirecka, Rena 6, 21n6, 136, 245
Monk, Meredith 146
motherhood *see* kinship
Movement Research 121–22, 224
Mumford, Lewis 29
Muñoz, José Esteban 19
Mysore: region 76–80, 142, 224; style
    of teaching 89–91
mysticism 115, 133–35, 143–47,
    166n10; *see also* religion;
    spirituality

Newfield, Christopher 220–21, 250n1
new materialism *see* realism
Nicolaigarden 205
Noë, Alva 22, 42–43, 45, 50

Olympics 40, 84, 99–100, 110n8
ontology *see* realism
organicity: and disability 102; in
    Grotowski 131, 138–41, 146,
    166n7; in Mauss 30–31, 42–43; in
    Stanislavski 127–31, 166n7

PARIP 226
Paris is Burning see house/ball scene
particle zoo *see* lexicons
pedagogy *see* training
peer review 235–41
performance philosophy 14–15, 21n5
performance as research *see* practice
    as research
Performance Studies International
    2–3
performativity 9–10, 51–57, 70n16,
    159, 172–73, 198
performing arts *see* arts
PhD *see* doctoral degrees
Phelan, Peggy 58–59, 230; *see also*
    ephemerality

phenomenology 12, 21n4, 45–46, 96–97
philosophy, performance
    see performance philosophy
physical culture: and actor training
    154–57; and physical education
    104–9; definition of 74–75;
    see also training
physical education *see* physical
    culture
physical training *see* training,
    physical
Pickering, Andrew 44–46, 61–62,
    67n1, 76, 129, 177, 180, 191, 206
Pilates, Joseph 84
Polanyi, Michael 24
polyamory 208
power-knowledge *see* knowledge and
    power
practice: and the practical 223–24; as
    research 225–50; of everyday life
    68n7, 172; review 229, 246–47;
    theory 38–48, 68n7; *see also*
    technique
pranayama 76; *see* breathing technique
presence 34, 45, 113–17, 153, 242,
    247; *see also* ephemerality;
    liveness; Noë, Alva
pronouns 205, 210–11, 214n16
psychophysical 130, 155–57,
    167–68n18
public sphere: and actor training
    17, 117; and politics of embodied
    practice 7, 9, 146, 160–65, 232,
    244, 248–49; and (psychoanalytic)
    fatherhood 195; and the university
    218; in the work of Stanislavski
    and Grotowski 124–27, 135–38

queer: identity 200–201, 203–4;
    research 203; theory 19–20,
    180–82, 194, 198, 209; training
    163, 203; *see also* sexual identity

racial identity *see* ethnic identity
Rancière, Jacques 9, 144, 199, 220
rape 192–94
realism (aesthetic) 122, 132, 139,
    165–66n4
realism (philosophical): and
    embodiment 67n1, 133, 179–80,